To Hans Dieter Betz,
With much gratitude
for your guidance.
Chris

PAULINE CHRISTIANITY

SUPPLEMENTS TO
NOVUM TESTAMENTUM

EDITORIAL BOARD

C.K. BARRETT, Durham - P. BORGEN, Trondheim
J.K. ELLIOTT, Leeds - H.J. DE JONGE, Leiden
A.J. MALHERBE, New Haven
M.J.J. MENKEN, Utrecht - J. SMIT SIBINGA, Amsterdam

Executive Editors
M.M. MITCHELL, Chicago & D.P. MOESSNER, Dubuque

VOLUME CIV

PAULINE CHRISTIANITY

Luke-Acts and the Legacy of Paul

BY

CHRISTOPHER MOUNT

BRILL
LEIDEN · BOSTON · KÖLN
2002

This book is printed on acid-free paper.

Die Deutsche Bibliothek – CIP-Einheitsaufnahme

Mount, Christopher
Luke-acts and the legacy of Paul
Boston ; Köln : Brill, 2002
  (Supplements to Novum testamentum ; Vol. 104)
  ISBN 90–04–12472–1

Library of Congress Cataloging-in-Publication Data

Library of Congress Cataloging-in-Publication Data is also available

ISSN   0167-9732
ISBN   90 04 12472 1

© Copyright 2002 by Koninklijke Brill NV, Leiden, The Netherlands

All rights reserved. No part of this publication may be reproduced, translated, stored in a retrieval system, or transmitted in any form or by any means, electronic, mechanical, photocopying, recording or otherwise, without prior written permission from the publisher.

Authorization to photocopy items for internal or personal use is granted by Brill provided that the appropriate fees are paid directly to The Copyright Clearance Center, 222 Rosewood Drive, Suite 910 Danvers MA 01923, USA.
Fees are subject to change.

PRINTED IN THE NETHERLANDS

TABLE OF CONTENTS

Acknowledgements		vii
Abbreviations		ix
I.	The Acts of the Apostles and Pauline Christianity	1
II.	The Acts of the Apostles in Early Christianity	11
	Irenaeus	12
	Traditions of Authorship and Titles	29
	Acts and the Apocryphal Acts in the Second Century	44
III.	Lk-Acts, Its Audience, and the History of Christianity	59
	The Prefaces of Lk-Acts	60
	Paul's Farewell Speech and the Literary Paulinism of Lk-Acts	83
	Jesus' apocalyptic discourse and the coming of the kingdom	85
	Jesus' farewell and the coming of the kingdom	88
	Paul's farewell and the coming of the kingdom	94
IV.	The Paul of Acts and Pauline Communities in Early Christianity	105
	Ephesus	111
	Paul's Farewell	128
	Corinth	131
	Thessalonica and Beroea	140
	Philippi	142
	Paul's Mission with Barnabas	149
	Rome	152
V.	Lk-Acts and the Construction of Christian Origins in the Second Century	163
Bibliography		181
Index of Ancient Literature		197

ACKNOWLEDGEMENTS

This volume is a revised version of my dissertation accepted by the University of Chicago. I am grateful to the Editorial Board of *Supplements to Novum Testamentum* for accepting this study for publication. Any work such as this takes place in a web of social relationships that shape the thinking of the author. I owe special thanks to my teachers, Hans Dieter Betz, Adela Yarbro Collins, and Arthur Droge. Their perceptive criticisms, careful scholarship, and support made this volume possible. I also wish to extend thanks to D. Dale Walker and Matt Jackson-McCabe, colleagues with whom I have engaged in many a profitable conversation about Christian origins. The University of Iowa School of Religion generously supplied the resources for Travis Voth to help proofread the manuscript and compile the index. I am grateful for his assistance.

LIST OF ABBREVIATIONS

AB	Anchor Bible
ABD	*Anchor Bible Dictionary*
ANRW	*Aufstieg und Niedergang der römischen Welt*
BBET	Beiträge zur biblischen Exegese und Theologie
BDAG	W. Bauer, F. W. Danker, W. F. Arndt, and F. W. Gingrich, *Greek-English Lexicon of the New Testament*, 3rd edition
BETL	Bibliotheca Ephemeridum theologicarum Lovaniensium
BHT	Beiträge zur historischen Theologie
BWANT	Beiträge zur Wissenschaft vom Alten und Neuen Testament
CBQMS	Catholic Biblical Quarterly—Monograph Series
EKKNT	Evangelisch-katholischer Kommentar zum Neuen Testament
ErFor	Erträge der Forschung
FRLANT	Forschungen zur Religion und Literatur des Alten und Neuen Testaments
GNT	Grundrisse zum Neuen Testament
GTA	Göttinger theologische Arbeiten
HTKNT	Herders theologischer Kommentar zum Neuen Testament
HUT	Hermeneutische Untersuchungen zur Theologie
JSNTSup	Journal for the Study of the New Testament—Monograph Series
LCL	Loeb Classical Library
LSJ	Liddell-Scott-Jones, *Greek-English Lexicon*
PWSup	Supplement to Pauly-Wissowa, *Real-Encyclopädie der classischen Altertumswisssenschaft*
SANT	Studien zum Alten und Neuen Testament
SBL	Society of Biblical Literature
SBLDS	SBL Dissertation Series
SBLMS	SBL Monograph Series
SBLSBS	SBL Sources for Biblical Study
SBT	Studies in Biblical Theology

SNTSMS	Society for New Testament Studies Monograph Series
TDNT	G. Kittel and G. Friedrich, eds., *Theological Dictionary of the New Testament*
WUNT	Wissenschaftliche Untersuchungen zum Neuen Testament

Concerning references to the four canonical gospels

In general, the abbreviations Mt, Mk, Lk, and Jn are used when referring to the texts that have come to be included as gospels in the New Testament canon. Matthew, Mark, Luke and John are used when referring to a specific theory of authorship associated with these texts. The major exception to this practice is in the title of this monograph, in which Luke-Acts is used instead of Lk-Acts, in deference to the standard practice of referring to this text. Also, 'Gospel' is capitalized when it refers to the Christian story about Jesus as it came to be understood by ecclesiastical writers after the first century, particularly in relation to texts about Jesus associated with the apostles; otherwise, 'gospel' is not capitalized.

Concerning references to secondary literature

All references are given in the form author (last name only, in most cases), title (sometimes shortened), page numbers. The full bibliographical information can be found in the bibliography at the end.

CHAPTER I

THE ACTS OF THE APOSTLES AND PAULINE CHRISTIANITY

In 1845 F. C. Baur outlined the *Tendenz* of the Acts of the Apostles in relation to his understanding of the influence of Paul's legacy on the development of early Christianity.[1]

> [The sacrifice of historical truth to bias in the portrayal of Paul in the Acts of the Apostles] took place at a time when, in consequence of all those efforts of his Judaeo-Christian opponents, of which his own Epistles show us the by no means trivial beginnings,[2] Paulinism [German: *Paulinismus*] was so far overcome that it could only maintain itself in the way of concession, by modifying the hardness and directness of its opposition to the law and Judaism; when it was reduced to come to an understanding with the powerful Jewish-Christian party by which it was opposed, so as to harmonise conflicting views and interests, and form a unity on a new basis.[3]

In his reconstruction of the place of the Acts of the Apostles in early Christianity, Baur correlated the Acts of the Apostles with the Pauline letters in terms of the category of 'Paulinism.' For Baur, this 'Paulinism' stood in opposition to Jewish Christianity and was the historical manifestation of the decisive role played by Paul in the origin of Christianity.

---

[1] On *Tendenz*-criticism in relation to the Acts of the Apostles, see Haenchen, *The Acts of the Apostles*, pp. 15–24; for Baur's general place in the history of scholarship, see Kümmel, *The New Testament: The History of the Investigation of Its Problems*, pp. 126–43; Baird, *History of New Testament Research. Volume One: From Deism to Tübingen*, pp. 258–94. On Baur's place in the history of scholarship on Acts, see Gasque, *A History of the Interpretation of the Acts of the Apostles*, pp. 21–106.

[2] See Baur, *Paul, the Apostle of Jesus Christ. His life and work, his epistles, and his doctrine. A contribution to a critical history of primitive Christianity* (translated from the second German edition; translation revised by A. Menzies), vol. 1, p. v, with reference to his article 'Die Christuspartei in der korinthischen Gemeinde, der Gegensatz des petrinischen und paulinischen Christentums in der ältesten Kirche, der Apostel Petrus in Rom.' On the importance of Baur's formulations of party conflict in this article, see Kümmel, *The New Testament: The History of the Investigation of Its Problems*, pp. 129–32.

[3] Baur, *Paul, the Apostle of Jesus Christ*, 1.12. The text of this and the following quotation from Baur's work remained unchanged between the first edition published by Baur (1845) and the second edition published after Baur's death by Eduard Zeller (1866).

That Christianity, in the universal historical importance which it achieved, was the work of the Apostle Paul is undeniably a matter of historical fact; but in what manner he brought this about, how we are to conceive of his relations with the elder Apostles, whether it was in harmony with them or in contradiction and opposition to them, that he carried out these principles and opinions which he was the first to enunciate, this still requires a more thorough and searching inquiry.[4]

The portrayal of Paul in the Acts of the Apostles marks the endpoint of the decisive struggle between the historical Paul and his Jewish-Christian opponents.

Baur's specific understanding of the relationship between party conflict and literature in early Christianity has been subjected to extensive criticism and revision.[5] Nevertheless, the idea of 'Pauline Christianity' has become ubiquitous in New Testament scholarship to describe early Christian communities or movements associated with Paul and his legacy, and the portrayal of Paul in the Acts of the Apostles is regularly connected to such communities or movements.[6] This Pauline Christianity associated with Paul's legacy has been delineated literarily (in relation, for example, to the corpus of Pauline letters),[7] theologically (in relation, for example, to attitudes toward the Law and Judaism;[8] compare the anti-Paulinism of the Pseudo-Clementine literature[9]), socially (in relation, for example, to the persona of Paul as the basis for a community's self-identity),[10] and/or historically (in terms, for example, of the evolution of certain churches whose foundations are attributed to Paul).[11] This importance of Paul and his legacy for mapping the contours of early Christianity, an importance suggested by the shape of the

---

[4] Baur, *Paul, the Apostle of Jesus Christ*, 1.3–4.

[5] See, e.g., Haenchen, *The Acts of the Apostles*, pp. 17–24.

[6] See, e.g., Lüdemann, *Early Christianity according to the Traditions in Acts*, p. 8; Koester, *Introduction to the New Testament*, p. 321; Jervell, *The Theology of the Acts of the Apostles*, pp. 123–27.

[7] The problem of the relation of the narrative of Acts to the Pauline letters has been a recurring theme. See, e.g., Harnack, *The Date of the Acts and of the Synoptic Gospels*, pp. 100–103; Knox, 'Acts and the Pauline Letter Corpus,' pp. 279–87; Conzelmann, 'Luke's Place in the Development of Early Christianity,' esp. pp. 302–9.

[8] Baur's definition is theological.

[9] Cf. Strecker, *Das Judenchristentum in den Pseudoklementinen*, pp. 187–96.

[10] Blasi, *Making Charisma: The Social Construction of Paul's Public Image*, esp. pp. 87–88 on Acts in relation to Pauline Christianity; cf. MacDonald, *The Legend and the Apostle*, pp. 17–53, 97–103.

[11] Haenchen, *The Acts of the Apostles*, p. 86; Lüdemann, *Early Christianity according to the Traditions in Acts*, p. 8; Jervell, *The Unknown Paul*, p. 68; see chapter 4 below.

New Testament canon, consistently establishes the interpretive context for the portrayal of Paul in Acts.

For Baur and those who have followed him in his identification of Paulinism or Pauline Christianity as a movement in early Christianity, Pauline Christianity is both an assessment of the historical Paul in terms of his place in the origin and development of Christianity inferred from the collection of Pauline letters in the New Testament, as well as a label for a movement or movements defined by Paul's legacy, for which the portrayal of Paul in Acts is taken to be evidence. The Paul of the New Testament has thus come to define a category by which early Christian communities and literature can be mapped in relation to other forms of early Christianity.[12] In this mapping of the contours of early Christianity, the term 'Paulinism' or 'Pauline Christianity' admits of a certain equivocation between the description of a phenomenon associated with early Christian groups on the one hand, and on the other hand that understanding of Christianity held by Paul himself as an individual. In attempts to describe Paul and his legacy, the portrayal of Paul in Acts has been taken both as evidence for the historical Paul and as evidence for later forms of Pauline Christianity. The often suggested possibility that the author was himself a companion of Paul aggravates the potential confusion inherent in the term 'Paulinism' or 'Pauline Christianity' as applied to the portrayal of Paul in Acts: in what sense is the portrayal of Paul in Acts determined by a direct relationship to Paul (the supposed 'we' of the author in the second half of Acts, for example)[13] or by an indirect, evolutionary connection to Paul in terms of some form of 'Pauline Christianity' to which the author belongs? In either case, the Acts of the Apostles is generally taken to be an important text for understanding the influence of Paul on the development of early Christianity.

---

[12] For Baur, the history of early Christianity is determined by the dynamic interaction of competing systems of thought, and 'Paulinism' is that system of ideas characteristic of the thought of Paul and his legacy. On Baur's formulation of Paul's place in the development of early Christianity, see Regner, *"Paulus und Jesus" im 19. Jahrhundert*, pp. 53–71. In what follows, 'Pauline Christianity' will be used as a more general term for not only the theological, but also the literary and social dimensions of the influence of Paul and his legacy on the formation and development of early Christian communities.

[13] Jervell (*The Theology of the Acts of the Apostles*, pp. 1–10) belongs to a long line of scholars who have argued that the author was a companion of Paul. For example, Harnack (*The Acts of the Apostles*, p. 162) resolved the question of sources for the second half of Acts by arguing that the author wrote as an eyewitness. See chapter 4 below.

For example, Vielhauer intends by the 'Paulinism' of Acts to raise the question of the author's direct relationship to those theological ideas held by Paul himself;[14] Baur's summary of the *Tendenz* of the Acts of the Apostles in terms of 'Paulinism' intends a description of a certain faction in early Christianity determined by Paul's theological legacy. Nevertheless, both construe the relationship between the Paul of the New Testament letters and the Paul of Acts in terms of evolutionary development from the historical Paul to the place of Paul's legacy in the emergence of catholic ('mainstream') Christianity in the second century.[15] For both, the Acts of the Apostles and its portrayal of Paul mark a decisive stage in the development of Paul's legacy (that is, the Paul of the Pauline letters) as it is incorporated into the catholic church (whose understanding of Paul is supposedly reflected by the portrayal of Paul in Acts);[16] for both, the Pauline letters and the Acts of the Apostles—that is, the Paul of the New Testament—determine the development of 'mainstream' Christianity.[17] In fact, since F. C. Baur's thesis of a second-century attempt by the author of Acts to integrate Pauline and Jewish-Christian factions in the early church, the portrayal of Paul in Acts may fairly be characterized as 'the' problem

---

[14] 'On the "Paulinism" of Acts,' p. 33.

[15] Vielhauer closes his investigation of the Paulinism of the author of Acts (that is, of the author's connection to the theology of Paul himself) with an assessment of the author's place in early Christianity (p. 49): "With the presuppositions of his historiography he no longer stands within earliest Christianity, but in the nascent early catholic church. His concept of history and his view of earliest Christianity are the same as theirs; whether he gave these views to them or received from them is a question whose answer could be attempted only on the broad basis of a New Testament and patristic investigation." Prior to such an investigation, however, the question of whether, in fact, the author stands in the nascent early catholic church with the presuppositions of his historiography needs to be clarified. That this is the case is not obvious, for there is no other early Christian text that adopts the standards for historical investigation suggested by Lk 1:1–4.

[16] Conzelmann ('Luke's Place in the Development of Early Christianity,' p. 304), on the other hand, denies that Luke is early Catholic, but still locates him within the Pauline tradition (p. 308).

[17] Overbeck ('Zur Einleitung in die Apostelgeschichte,' pp. xxxi-xxxii) rejected Baur's idea that Acts reflects a synthesis of Pauline and Jewish Christianity in the second century. Nevertheless, he identified Acts as representative of catholic Christianity in the second century. Although Jervell *(The Theology of the Acts of the Apostles*, pp. 123–27; *The Unknown Paul*, pp. 1–51) replaces any notion of development or historical distance between the Paul of the Pauline letters and the Paul of Acts in early Christianity with a harmonized reading of the Paul of Acts and the Paul of the letters, his specific reconstruction of early Christianity preserves the importance of the narrative of Acts for understanding 'mainstream' Christianity.

for integrating Paul, his letters, and 'his' churches into a history of early Christianity.[18] How the irenic portrayal of Paul's relationship to other early Christians in the Acts of the Apostles relates to the more problematic relationship of Paul to other Christians suggested by his own letters remains a crux for defining Paul's place in the history of early Christianity.[19]

Although Baur separated Acts from the Pauline letters as a reliable source for the historical Paul, he maintained the connection in terms of the evolutionary development of Paul's theological ideas.[20] Baur thus

---

[18] The portrayal of Paul in Acts may not be 'the' problem of Lk-Acts (Haenchen, *The Acts of the Apostles*, p. 121). Nevertheless, interpreting the narrative picture of Paul has been a recurring problem in understanding Acts. The 19th century debate whether the author would not (*Tendenz* criticism) or could not (source criticism) write an accurate history of the early church was closely connected to the author's portrayal of Paul. The search for an answer to the problem of sources for Acts invariably involves the problem of the author's personal relationship to Paul, and attempts to reconcile the Paul of Acts with the Paul of the epistles continue to the present. The shift in the second half of the 20th century to an understanding of Acts in terms of the author as theologian rather than as historian (the work of Dibelius, Haenchen, and Conzelmann stands out in this transition) has repeatedly raised the question of the author's relation to the theology of Paul. For example, Vielhauer ('On the "Paulinism" of Acts,' esp. pp. 48–49) explicitly dealt with the problem of Luke's theological Paulinism. (See comments above.) The recent interest in sociological interpretations of the New Testament has produced several studies focusing on the social realities of the author's community. Not surprisingly, the portrayal of Paul has been subjected to sociological analysis and correlated with sociologically defined communities. See, e.g., Blasi, *Making Charisma: The Social Construction of Paul's Public Image*, pp. 117–41; the persuasiveness of his sociological analysis, of course, depends on the historical plausibility of his reconstruction of various forms of Pauline Christianity (on Acts, see pp. 39–88).

[19] Even the problem of developing a chronology of Paul's letters and sorting out his relation with the churches he claims to have founded depends heavily on the narrative of Acts. The importance of the story about Paul before Gallio in Acts is perhaps the most obvious example (see, e.g., Becker, *Paul: Apostle to the Gentiles*, esp. p. 16; see chapter 4 below), but no less significant is the use of Acts to explain Paul's movements before and after the so-called Jerusalem council. On Acts as a historical source for early Christianity, see Hengel, *Acts and the History of Earliest Christianity*, esp. pp. 71–126.

[20] The assumption by Baur shared by many subsequent New Testament scholars that the Pauline letters serve as a reliable basis for reconstructing the 'historical' Paul tends to minimize the fact that the collection of Pauline letters in the New Testament is itself already a particular construction of Paulinism. The collection of Pauline letters in the New Testament is not an unfiltered source for reconstructing the historical Paul that can easily be separated from later tendential definitions of Christian origins. See chapter 5 below for the place of Paul in the construction of Christian origins in the second century.

On the other hand, Baur recognized that the issue of the reliability of the narrative of the Acts of the Apostles for reconstructing the life and work of Paul was not just a matter of sources available to the author about Paul (adequate or otherwise; on the

anticipated the notion of 'trajectories' that has come to prominence in New Testament scholarship, and in effect Baur defined a Pauline trajectory through early Christianity. He did not use the language of trajectory[21] or social science[22] that has become popular and has shifted attention away from theological to social constructs of Christianity. Nevertheless, Baur correlated Acts with the needs of an early Christian faction. For Baur, the Acts of the Apostles defined a specific community conflict in early Christianity. Reconstructing the interpretive context for Acts was for Baur a question of defining the place on a trajectory occupied by the text. Baur's postulation, however, of a continuing opposition between Jewish and Pauline Christianity into the second century was not generally well received (even by some of his followers),[23] and his general theory of early Christian development based on conflict and synthesis came under attack. The possibilities implicit in Baur's use of early Christian literature to describe competing factions were put on a new footing by Walter Bauer. Walter Bauer's study of orthodoxy and heresy in early Christianity laid the groundwork for what has become a detailed reconstruction of Christianity in terms of competing movements.[24] Bauer's study established the basis for a reconceptualization of early Christianity along lines similar to those charted by F. C. Baur, though with the potential for more diversity built in. Based on the assumption that texts mirror distinct factions or communities in early

investigation of the sources of Acts prior to Baur, see Haenchen, *The Acts of the Apostles*, pp. 24–26) but also of the intentionality of the author. In this, Baur anticipated the interests of redaction criticism. Baur's conclusion, however, that historical truth lies on one side only has not generally been accepted as the narrative of Acts has been mined for reliable Pauline traditions that can be distinguished from the compositional intentions of the author and used to reconstruct the historical Paul. Even as a clear notion of the importance of the author's intentionality has been recovered in redaction criticism, this intentionality has continued to be pursued in terms of an assumed relation to Pauline traditions or sources as the basis for the author's portrayal of Paul. The connection between Acts and Paulinism established by Baur remains. See chapter 4 below on Pauline sources for the narrative of Acts.

[21] On 'trajectories' see especially Robinson and Koester, *Trajectories through Early Christianity*, pp. 1–19; in relation to the Acts of the Apostles, cf. Koester, *Introduction to the New Testament*, p. 321 (see note 25 below).

[22] For example, Blasi, *Making Charisma: The Social Construction of Paul's Public Image*, pp. 87–88, 117–41.

[23] See Haenchen, *The Acts of the Apostles*, pp. 17–24; cf. Jervell, *The Unknown Paul*, p.13.

[24] Bauer (*Orthodoxy and Heresy in Earliest Christianity*) challenged the notion that 'orthodoxy' was the original form of Christianity in all geographical areas of early Christianity. On the reception of his work, see the appendix to the English translation, pp. 286–316.

Christianity, the use of early Christian literature to reconstruct 'trajectories' and communities evolving over time has become common.[25] The evolution of Pauline Christianity has come to have much more complexity than that proposed by Baur, now traced not only through Acts, but also through non-canonical texts such as the *Acts of Paul*.[26]

As a result, Baur's somewhat simplistic notion of Pauline and Petrine (Jewish) Christianity has been replaced by a plurality of early Christian communities now defined not only theologically but also socially. Nevertheless, the category of Pauline Christianity still occupies an important place in scholarship on Acts. The portrayal of Paul in Acts has never been separated from Pauline Christianity as a presupposed phenomenon in early Christianity so that in the history of scholarship on the Acts of the Apostles, various understandings of Pauline Christianity have consistently influenced the reconstruction of historical, social, and literary contexts for the interpretation of this text in general and the Paul of Acts in particular. There are, however, reasons to question the adequacy of the category 'Pauline Christianity' as it has been used for understanding the place of Acts in early Christianity. The starting point for constructing the category of Pauline Christianity to describe historical development in early Christianity continues to be the shape of the New Testament canon. The importance of the Pauline letters alongside the narrative of Acts for understanding early Christianity is, however, a late second-century construction of Christian origins intended to establish a normative interpretation of apostolic tradition against perceived heresy.[27] In contrast to the importance Acts has played since the end of the second century as a description of 'mainstream' ('catholic,' 'normative,' or whatever adjective one chooses to establish a center and periphery) Christianity, in fact the reception of Acts prior to the end of the second century suggests that the text of Acts was not particularly important in the life of early Christian communities, Pauline or otherwise. Instead, the Acts of the Apostles gained attention only toward the end of the second century in the context of intellectual attempts to define true versus heretical forms of Christianity. In this context, the otherwise unknown author of Lk-Acts was connected to

---

[25] Koester, *Introduction to the New Testament*, p. 321: "Luke must have belonged to the circle of churches that claimed Peter and Paul as their authorities."

[26] See, e.g., Blasi, *Making Charisma: The Social Construction of Paul's Public Image*, pp. 109–111; cf. MacDonald, *The Legend and the Apostle*, pp. 17–53, 97–103.

[27] See chapter 2 below.

Paul. The Pauline legacy of what has come to be the New Testament as a collection including four Gospels, the Acts of the Apostles, and the Pauline letters is a late second-century construction. The evidence for this conclusion will be presented in chapter two below and summarized in chapter five.

The author's portrayal of Paul in the narrative of Acts is in fact closely tied to his intention to narrate a reliable account of the origin of Christianity. The mission of Paul serves to define the unity of Christianity. This legacy of Paul as it is presented in the narrative of Acts, however, is a literary construct overlaid by the author on sources that to a large extent are not in themselves determined by Paul's legacy. For the author, Paul's role in the spread of Christianity from Jerusalem to Rome is not an apology for Paul (for an audience concerned with inner-Christian polemics or the delineation of heretical forms of Christianity in relation to Paul's legacy). Instead, the portrayal of Paul in Acts is a literary construct determined by the author's intention to demonstrate the coherence and reliability of Christian stories about the past in the context of Hellenistic culture. The evidence for these conclusions will be presented in chapters three and four below. In chapter three, the problem of the intended audience, genre, and purpose of the narrative of Acts will be addressed to demonstrate that the text of Acts was intended to establish an identity for Christians within Graeco-Roman culture. The basis for this identity is the author's literary pretension to have investigated the origins of Christianity in terms of the standards for historical truth of Hellenistic historiography. Understood in this way, the text of Acts and the portrayal of Paul in Acts do not presuppose specific ('Pauline') Christian communities as a social correlate, but instead the author constructs 'Pauline' Christianity to explain the origin of Christianity for a broadly defined audience. In chapter four, a detailed examination of the author's method in portraying Paul's mission in early Christianity will be undertaken to demonstrate that the Pauline communities portrayed in Acts are a narrative construct of the author, not the remains of Pauline traditions in early Christianity that presuppose Pauline communities. The Paul of Acts does not mirror social, theological, or literary forms of Pauline Christianity in early Christianity; nor is the portrayal of Paul in Acts dependent on an amorphous body of Pauline traditions available to the author from Pauline communities.

In short, the portrayal of Paul in the book of Acts does not presuppose some form of 'Pauline Christianity' as the term is commonly used in modern scholarship to describe early Christian traditions, movements, and communities connected to Paul; Paul's role in the origin of Christianity is a literary construct of the author that gained prominence only toward the end of the second century. Chapter five will address the implication of this conclusion for the study of Christian origins. The place of Acts alongside the Pauline letters in the Christian canon is the result of competing attempts in the second century to construct Christian origins; it is not indicative of some form of Pauline Christianity as descriptive of a movement or communities connected to Paul in early Christianity.

To establish these claims about the context in early Christianity for the portrayal of Paul in the narrative of Acts, three specific points need attention: (1) the reception of Acts in early Christianity (especially as this pertains to the correlation of Acts with early Christian communities and inner-Christian conflicts), (2) the social and literary context of the composition of Lk-Acts as this context relates to the author's intentions in his portrayal of Paul, and (3) the traditions redacted by the author to construct the narrative about Paul in Acts (that is, the question of the author's relation to Paul and the Pauline communities supposedly preserving his legacy). These points will be taken up in order in the following three chapters. Chapter two will address the first point—a point that relates to the question of how the second half of Lk-Acts came to be identified by the secondary title 'The Acts of the Apostles.' Chapters three and four will take up the second and third points in detail—both of which relate to the author's intentions for the text of Acts and the Paul of Acts.[28] In the last chapter, some concluding comments will be offered on the place of the portrayal of Paul in Acts in relation to various attempts to construct Christian origins in the second century that have shaped the Christian New Testament.

---

[28] In terms of literary theory, the implied author of a text can be distinguished from the actual author. The former is a literary construct suggested by the text, whereas the latter is an actual person who wrote (or dictated) the text. Since we probably do not have any reliable information about the actual author of Lk-Acts independent of the text (beyond, perhaps, a name), references in what follows to the author of Lk-Acts and his or her intentions are to the literarily implied author of the text (whose male identity is created by the participle in Lk 1:3). The theoretical distinction between the implied author and actual author of Lk-Acts provides a critical perspective on the process by which a biography of the implied author of Lk-Acts was constructed in the second century and information from this biography was used to interpret the text. See chapter 2 below.

CHAPTER 2

THE ACTS OF THE APOSTLES IN EARLY CHRISTIANITY

The idea that early Christian texts can be correlated with specific Christian communities is popular in New Testament studies.¹ Yet, in the case of the Acts of the Apostles, its original literary context (the subject of chapter 3 below) and its reception in early Christianity (the subject of this chapter) provide little support for such a correlation—whether such a community behind Acts is considered Pauline or not. The Gospel according to Luke and the Acts of the Apostles are first specifically identified as such by Irenaeus in his writing against heresies.² Prior to Irenaeus, the text known to him as the Gospel according to Luke is attested as part of Marcion's collection of scripture. Marcion probably used an edited form of the text of Lk for his lone gospel.³

---

¹ That specific Christian communities can be reconstructed from the texts of the four gospels is widely taken for granted. Much of the recent scholarship on the apocryphal acts has also been occupied with reconstructing the communities behind these texts. (See, e.g., MacDonald, *The Legend and the Apostle*, pp. 17–53.) On Acts, see e.g. Esler, *Community and Gospel in Luke-Acts*, esp. pp. 24–26; Talbert, *Literary Patterns, Theological Themes and the Genre of Luke-Acts*, p. 135; Jervell, *The Theology of the Acts of the Apostles*, p. 123. Sterling (*Historiography and Self-Definition*, p. 378) frames his inquiry into the genre and function of Acts in terms of such notions of communities: "How did Luke-Acts function among the mixed communities it addressed?" Sociological terminology influences many of the recent attempts to reconstruct early Christian communities behind the gospels, Acts, and apocryphal acts. Nevertheless, the idea that the text of Acts provides a window through which one can view the realities of early church communities is at least as old as F. C. Baur, whose interpretation of the *Tendenz* of Acts served as a basis for reconstructing factions in early Christianity. (See chapter 1 above.) For a somewhat general critique of the 'mirror reading' of Acts to produce a community, see Johnson, 'On Finding the Lukan Community,' pp. 87–100; see also Wisse, 'The Use of Early Christian Literature as Evidence for Inner Diversity and Conflict,' esp. p. 188. For a general critique of the idea that the audience of the four gospels can be defined as a specific local community or group of communities, see especially Bauckham, 'For Whom Were Gospels Written?' pp. 9–48.

² Irenaeus composed his work against the heretics sometime around 185 at Lyons, according to information supplied by Eusebius (*Hist. eccl.* 5.4–5).

³ On Marcion's choice of Lk, see Harnack, *Marcion: The Gospel of the Alien God*, p. 29; see also von Campenhausen, *The Formation of the Christian Bible*, pp. 147–63; for a different assessment of the relation of the text of Lk to Marcion's gospel, see Knox,

Justin probably knew the text of Lk as well.[4] On the other hand, the circulation of the text of Acts prior to Irenaeus is obscure. Irenaeus is the first writer explicitly to take up the text of Acts, dispelling the fog of possible allusions to and dependence on Acts that characterizes the earlier reception of the text.[5] Consequently, his comments concerning Lk and Acts are important for locating the reception of these texts in the social and literary context of early Christianity.

Irenaeus

In book 3 of *Adversus haereses*,[6] after having exposed in books one and two what he considers to be the perversity of the teachings of the heretics, Irenaeus begins his proofs against the heretics from scripture. These proofs are in defense of the life-giving Gospel.

> Call to mind, then, the things which I have stated in the two preceding books, and, taking these [proofs from scripture] in connection with them, you will have from me a very copious refutation of all the heretics; and faithfully and strenuously you will resist them in defense of the only true and life-giving faith, which the Church has received from the apostles and imparted to her children. For the Lord of all gave to his apostles the power of the Gospel, through whom also we have known the truth, that is, the doctrine of the Son of God; to whom also did the Lord declare: "The one who hears you hears me; and the one who despises you, despises me, and him who sent me."[7]

Marcion and the New Testament, pp. 77–113.

[4] O'Neill (*The Theology of Acts in Its Historical Setting*, pp. 29–44) has argued that Justin knew only a precursor to the text of Lk. O'Neill's thesis is too conjectural to gain unqualified support, but points out the difficulty of placing the text of Lk prior to Marcion. Papias, e.g., is silent about Lk. On the other hand, the longer ending to Mk, Mk 16:9–20, probably makes use of Lk 24.

[5] For lists of possible allusions to or dependencies on Acts, see e.g., Haenchen, *The Acts of the Apostles*, pp. 3–14; Conzelmann, *Acts of the Apostles*, pp. xxvi-xxxi. Prior to Irenaeus, what is convincing evidence for knowledge of Acts depends very much on the subjectivity of the interpreter. Note the exchange between Rordorf ('Paul's Conversion in the Canonical Acts and in the *Acts of Paul*,' pp. 137–44), Hills ('The *Acts of Paul* and the Legacy of the Lukan Acts,' pp. 145–58), Bauckham ('The *Acts of Paul*: Replacement of Acts or Sequel to Acts?' pp. 159–68), and Marguerat ('The *Acts of Paul* and the Canonical Acts: A Phenomenon of Rereading,' pp. 169–84). The reception of Acts prior to Irenaeus will be taken up in greater detail below.

[6] Eusebius (*Hist. eccl.* 5.7) cites the title of this work as ἐλέγχου καὶ ἀνατροπῆς τῆς ψευδωνύμου γνώσεως (*Refutation and Overthrow of Knowledge Falsely So-Called*; often referred to in English by the shortened title *Against Heresies*).

[7] *Adv. haer.*, preface to book 3. Translations adapted from the English translation printed in the *Ante-Nicene Fathers*, vol. 1. The text was originally written in Greek, but

Irenaeus makes explicit the specific content of this Gospel, this doctrine of the Son of God that he intends to defend with proofs from scripture against the corruptions of the heretics:

> These [apostolic witnesses] have all declared to us that there is one God, Creator of heaven and earth, announced by the law and the prophets; and one Christ, the Son of God. If any one does not agree to these truths, he despises the companions of the Lord; nay more, he despises Christ himself the Lord; yea, he despises the Father also, and stands self-condemned, resisting and opposing his own salvation, as is the case with all heretics.[8]

To defend this Gospel on the basis of scripture, Irenaeus is forced to address the problem of the boundaries of apostolic witness to the Gospel in scripture and tradition. Consequently, the first concern of Irenaeus in book 3 is to delineate a gospel canon[9] and a unified ecclesiastical tradition[10] as the standard for the apostolic proclamation of the Gospel by the true church. In effect, Irenaeus constructs an account of Christian origins as the historical correlate of his fourfold gospel canon. Apart from listing Mt, Mk, Lk, and Jn as the divinely ordained, fourfold canon witness to the Gospel,[11] Irenaeus provides no complete list of scripture.[12] Paul's proclamation of the Gospel in his letters belongs alongside this fourfold gospel collection,[13] but Irenaeus has no interest in prescribing the boundaries of the letter portion of scripture. Instead, his attention is devoted to the four written gospels. According to Irenaeus, his fourfold gospel canon mirrors "the tradition of the apostles manifested throughout the whole world"[14] that is preserved by the succession of presbyters in the churches.[15] Apostolic preaching of the

---

apart from fragments survives only in Latin translation. For a recent critical edition of the text, accompanied by a translation into French and retroversion into Greek, see Rousseau and Doutreleau, *Irénée de Lyon. Contre les hérésies* (Sources Chrétiennes).

[8] *Adv. haer.* 3.1.2. Cf. 3.11.7. Marcion's 'heresy' associated with his own construction of apostolic witness is thus already engaged at the beginning of book 3.

[9] *Adv. haer.* 3.1.1. For Irenaeus, each of the four written gospels gives one aspect of this Gospel. See, e.g., *Adv. haer.* 3.11.8.

[10] *Adv. haer.* 3.2–4.

[11] See *Adv. haer.* 3.1; cf. 3.11.8.

[12] On the development of lists of scripture, see Hahneman, *The Muratorian Fragment and the Development of the Canon*, pp. 83–131.

[13] For Irenaeus, the Gospel according to Luke preserves the Gospel as proclaimed by Paul (*Adv. haer.* 3.1.1), which is in complete harmony with the Gospel proclaimed by all the other apostles (*Adv. haer.* 3.14). On Luke the author of the Gospel according to Luke as a companion of Paul, see below under *Traditions of Authorship and Titles*.

[14] *Adv. haer.* 3.3.1.

[15] *Adv. haer.* 3.2.2; see also 3.3.

Gospel thus preserved in the Irenaean construction of a fourfold gospel canon and ecclesiastical tradition stands over against the corruptions of the Gospel spread by the heretics, who "consent neither to scripture nor to tradition."[16]

Texts known as gospels and collections of letters were important in the life of Christian communities at least as early as the middle of the second century.[17] Irenaeus's collection of gospels and letters presupposes the status already accorded to such texts in Christian communities[18], and his fourfold canon of gospels should not be abstracted from the needs created by the liturgical use of such texts.[19] Nevertheless, to the

---

[16] *Adv. haer.* 3.2.2. Irenaeus goes to great lengths to refute claims that the apostles as a group did not proclaim the true Gospel. He rejects any notion that the true Gospel is to be found by limiting or adding to the message of the apostles as a whole (whether this is the Ebionite rejection of Paul [*Adv. haer.* 3.15], the Marcionite rejection of all apostles but Paul [*Adv. haer.* 3.13] or the Valentinian *Gospel of Truth* [*Adv. haer.* 3.11.9]). On the preservation of this apostolic witness in texts, see especially *Adv. haer.* 3.11.7. Though Irenaeus claims to be able to refute the heretics from any single gospel in his fourfold canon, his arguments depend on abstracting a Gospel from the details of each of the four written gospels, none of which is complete in itself. See especially 3.11.8 and 3.11.9. Cf. 3.14.3.

[17] Justin comments on the use of gospel texts, which he calls memoirs of the apostles, in conjunction with the reading of Jewish scriptures in Christian gatherings. See *1 Apol.* 66.3; 67.3–4. Polycarp was an active collector of letters, both those of Paul and of Ignatius, for use in the church. (See Polycarp *Phil.* 13. He repeatedly refers to Paul by citing passages from the Pauline corpus, and encourages the reading of Paul's letters; see *Phil.* 3.2.) The comments in *1 Clem.* 44 (on Paul's correspondence to the Corinthians) and Ignatius (see, e.g., *Eph.* 12) suggest that some of Paul's letters were known and used in the life of local communities.

[18] See, e.g., *Adv. haer.* 3.11.7.

[19] For example, Justin's comments on the reading of the prophets (the Jewish scriptures) and the memoirs of the apostles in religious services (see note 17 above) suggest that some sort of decision on what was acceptable and not acceptable to use in such cases had been made, at least in principle.

The Muratorian canon list makes this liturgical dimension to the emergence of authoritative texts explicit. (This list is traditionally dated around 200 at Rome, although a later date and province in the east have been argued by Sundberg, 'Canon Muratori: A Fourth-Century List,' pp. 1–41; Hahneman, *The Muratorian Fragment and the Development of the Canon*, esp. pp. 215–18; cf. pp. 1–4.) Beginning at line 71 (cited according to Schneemelcher, *New Testament Apocrypha*, rev. ed. (1991), 1.36): "Also of the revelations we accept only those of John and Peter, which (latter) some of our people do not want read in the Church. But Hermas wrote the Shepherd quite lately in our time in the city of Rome, when on the throne of the church of the city of Rome the bishop Pius, his brother, was seated. And therefore it ought indeed to be read, but it cannot be read publicly in the Church to the other people either among the prophets, whose number is settled, or among the apostles to the end of time." The need to decide what texts were appropriate for public reading in the church generated such lists.

The problem of what texts were or were not to be read in public continued into the

extent that written gospels are important for his defense of Christianity against heresies, Irenaeus's fourfold gospel canon is an intellectual response to Marcion.[20] Just as Marcion used a single gospel to refute what he saw as perversions of the Christian Gospel, Irenaeus uses a precisely defined collection of gospel texts to refute heresy. For both Marcion and Irenaeus, a gospel canon correlated with a reconstruction of apostolic history became a weapon against heresy.[21] Irenaeus, however, did not interpret apostolic history in terms of the collection of Pauline letters. For Irenaeus, writing a generation after Marcion and his Bible, an important third member to the two basic parts of Christian scripture defined by Marcion has emerged as a weapon against heresy. What is particularly remarkable, indeed unprecedented, in Irenaeus's intellectual defense of his construction of a fourfold gospel canon and a normative ecclesiastical tradition as a weapon against heretics is the importance the Acts of the Apostles takes as a part of scripture.[22] The

---

fourth century. Eusebius's canon list in *Hist. eccl.* 3.25 involves texts approved for public reading in the church. In *Hist. eccl.* 2.23 he defends the epistles of James and Jude on the basis of their widespread use in churches, and in *Hist. eccl.* 2.15 Eusebius reports that Peter authorized the public reading of Mk. In *Hist. eccl.* 6.12 Eusebius quotes from a work of Serapion, bishop of Antioch around 190, in which Serapion seeks to exert his influence on the church at Rhosssus to prevent the reading of the Gospel of Peter (presumably in public), although he had earlier approved it.

[20] See von Campenhausen, *The Formation of the Christian Bible*, p. 203. Marcion established a single written text as an authoritative gospel on the basis of his construction of Christian origins based on his reading of a collection of Pauline letters. The close connection established by Marcion between apostolic history and an authoritative text about Jesus is presupposed by Irenaeus in his construction of a gospel canon and apostolic tradition. See chapter 5 below.

[21] The use of canon as a tool against heresy is evident in the Muratorian canon list and Eusebius (see note 19 above); both proscribe the use of certain texts. Even if the Muratorian canon should be dated in the fourth century rather than at the end of the second century, as Hahneman (*The Muratorian Fragment and the Development of the Canon*, esp. pp. 215–18) has argued, Marcion and Irenaeus are decisive for the emergence of the concept of a canon of gospel texts that admits of no additions or subtractions. Irenaeus excludes even the theoretical possibility of a change in his fourfold gospel canon (*Adv. haer.* 3.11.8; cf. 3.11.9). Hahneman (p. 93) has underestimated the importance of Marcion as a precursor to Irenaeus for the development of the idea of a Christian canon at the end of the second century.

[22] See *Adv. haer.* 3.13–15, especially 3.14.4–3.15.1, for the importance of the narrative of Acts as a weapon against heretics who accept the text of Lk. On the importance of the narrative of Acts for Irenaeus's genealogy of heresy, see, e.g., his description of Simon in the preface to *Adv. haer.* book 3. See also *Adv. haer.* 1.23, in which he uses the narrative of Acts to provide important information about a certain Simon at Rome (whom he calls the father of all heretics in the preface to book 3). Irenaeus connects the Simon of Acts with a report of the activities of a certain Simon the Magician in

text of Acts, previously obscure, neither gospel nor epistle,[23] becomes essential in his argument against the heretics. For Irenaeus, the Acts of the Apostles provides an account of Christian origins that establishes a scriptural basis for the unity of the apostolic proclamation of the Gospel preserved in his construction of a normative ecclesiastical tradition, a canon of written gospels, and a collection of Pauline letters.[24] The result is a unanimous voice of scripture and tradition refuting the perversions of the heretics. The relatively obscure text of Lk-Acts, identified by Irenaeus as the Gospel according to Luke and the Acts of the Apostles, became the focal point in intellectually defining Christian scripture and tradition in the dispute between Marcion and Irenaeus.

For Irenaeus, the narrative of the Acts of the Apostles establishes the historical foundation for his claim that the Gospel is properly attested by a collection of apostolic witnesses (against any claim that some or all of the apostles did not have true knowledge of the Gospel). The narrative of Acts, read by Irenaeus as an account of the origin of a unified apostolic tradition,[25] demonstrates that from the beginning all the apostles preached the same Gospel and thus supports Irenaeus's claim for the unity and perfection of his fourfold gospel canon alongside the gospel preached by Paul in his letters.[26] Irenaeus introduces his defense of the fourfold gospel canon in book 3 of *Adversus haereses* with an allusion to the narrative of the Acts of the Apostles.[27]

> We have learned from none others the plan of our salvation, than from those through whom the Gospel has come down to us, which they did at one time proclaim, and at a later period, by the will of God, handed down to us in the scriptures, to be the ground and pillar of our faith. For it is unlawful to assert that they preached before they possessed "perfect knowl-

---

Rome. He probably received this report from Justin (*1 Apol.* 1.26; Irenaeus elsewhere quotes from Justin; see *Adv. haer.* 4.6.2). Justin does not, however, make the connection to the narrative of Acts. The legend of Simon at Rome is developed in the *Acts of Peter* 4–32.

[23] See, e.g., Haenchen, *The Acts of the Apostles*, p. 9: "In Acts the Christian reader encountered a book unlike any he had previously known, and one which was neither necessary nor customarily used in preaching or instruction."

[24] This collection of Pauline letters includes the Pastorals, which were absent from Marcion's collection of Pauline letters. On the importance of the Pastorals for Irenaeus's understanding of the Acts of the Apostles, see below under *Traditions of Authorship and Titles*.

[25] This tradition is explicitly defined in *Adv. haer.* 3.2–4. See below under *Traditions of Authorship and Titles* for more discussion on the relation of Acts to this tradition.

[26] See, e.g., *Adv. haer.* 3.11.8–9. On Paul, his letters, and Acts, see especially 3.13.

[27] *Adv. haer.* 3.1.1.

edge," as some do even venture to say, boasting themselves as improvers of the apostles.

For after our Lord rose from the dead, and the apostles were invested with power from on high when the Holy Spirit came down upon them, they were filled with full assurance and had perfect knowledge: they departed to the ends of the earth, preaching the glad tidings of the good things sent from God to us and proclaiming the peace of heaven to men, who indeed do all equally and individually possess the Gospel of God.[28]

Matthew also issued a written Gospel among the Hebrews in their own dialect, while Peter and Paul were preaching at Rome and laying the foundations of the Church. After their departure, Mark, the disciple and interpreter of Peter, did also hand down to us in writing what had been preached by Peter. Luke also, the companion of Paul, recorded in a book the Gospel preached by him. Afterwards, John, the disciple of the Lord, who also had leaned upon his breast, did himself publish a Gospel during his residence at Ephesus in Asia.[29]

Irenaeus turns explicitly to the narrative of the Acts of the Apostles in *Adv. haer.* 3.12, after he has delineated the "first principles of the Gospel"[30] from these written gospels.

For Irenaeus, the scriptural witness of the narrative of the Acts of the Apostles to the unity of the apostles in the proclamation of the Gospel corresponds to the apostolic deposit of truth that forms the basis of a normative ecclesiastical tradition preserved in the churches.[31] The reliability of this tradition is guaranteed by the churches established by the apostles and maintained by a succession of apostolic bishops.

> It is within the power of all, therefore, in every Church, who may wish to see the truth, to contemplate clearly the tradition of the apostles manifested throughout the whole world; and we are in a position to reckon up those

---

[28] See Acts 1:8; Lk 24:49; also Lk 2:14. Irenaeus's allusion to the narratives of Lk and Acts at this point anticipates his explicit defense of the reliability of the Acts of the Apostles based on the reliability of the Gospel according to Luke. See discussion below in this section.

[29] Greek fragment preserved by Eusebius *Hist. eccl.* 5.8.2–4: Ὁ μὲν δὴ Ματθαῖος ἐν τοῖς Ἑβραίοις τῇ ἰδίᾳ αὐτῶν διαλέκτῳ καὶ γραφὴν ἐξήνεγκεν εὐαγγελίου, τοῦ Πέτρου καὶ τοῦ Παύλου ἐν Ῥώμῃ εὐαγγελιζομένων καὶ θεμελιούντων τὴν ἐκκλησίαν. Μετὰ δὲ τὴν τούτων ἔξοδον, Μάρκος, ὁ μαθητὴς καὶ ἑρμηνευτὴς Πέτρου, καὶ αὐτὸς τὰ ὑπὸ Πέτρου κηρυσσόμενα ἐγγράφως ἡμῖν παραδέδωκεν. Καὶ Λουκᾶς δέ, ὁ ἀκόλουθος Παύλου, τὸ ὑπ' ἐκείνου κηρυσσόμενον εὐαγγέλιον ἐν βίβλῳ κατέθετο. Ἔπειτα Ἰωάννης, ὁ μαθητὴς τοῦ Κυρίου, ὁ καὶ ἐπὶ τὸ στῆθος αὐτοῦ ἀναπεσών, καὶ αὐτὸς ἐξέδωκεν τὸ εὐαγγέλιον, ἐν Ἐφέσῳ τῆς Ἀσίας διατρίβων. See Rousseau and Doutreleau, *Irénée de Lyon. Contre les hérésies. Livre III*, 2.22–24.

[30] *Adv. haer.* 3.11.7.

[31] See, e.g., *Adv. haer.* 3.2.2; 3.4.1; 3.5.1. Compare *Adv. haer.* 3.11.9–3.14.3 (note especially 3.12.9) with 3.2.1–3.5.1.

who were by the apostles instituted bishops in the churches, and the succession of these men to our own times...[32]

In this apostolic succession of bishops in the church, Irenaeus aligns himself specifically with Rome. Among the churches in which the apostles instituted bishops, Rome is preeminent because it was founded and organized by Peter and Paul.[33] The importance of Peter and Paul for the status of the church at Rome is suggested by other early Christian authors and is closely related to the tradition of these apostles' martyrdom at Rome.[34] For Irenaeus, the supposed founding of the church at Rome by Peter and Paul demonstrates an original apostolic unity. Such an original unity provides a powerful slogan of polemics.[35] As early as Clement and Ignatius, the status accorded to the church at Rome by virtue of its association with both Peter and Paul (particularly as glorious martyrs) is the basis for appeals to unity in the context of disputes about leadership in local church communities.[36] Irenaeus explicitly cites the letter of Clement to the church at Corinth as an example of Rome's exercise of the authority of Peter and Paul.[37] Irenaeus has constructed a lineage of apostolic succession in the early church that defines apostolic authority (and thus what is for Irenaeus a standard for Christian doctrinal truth) in terms of the church at Rome founded by Peter and Paul.[38]

---

[32] *Adv. haer.* 3.3.1. See also 3.2.2.

[33] *Adv. haer.* 3.3–4; esp. 3.3.2. See also 3.1.1.

[34] See, e.g., *1 Clem.* 5; Ignatius *Rom.* 4. On the role of both Peter and Paul at Rome, see also the *Acts of Peter* 1–8.

[35] On the importance of Peter and Paul for the church at Rome, see Bauer, *Orthodoxy and Heresy in Earliest Christianity*, pp. 111–13. Although Bauer exaggerates the unity and intention with which the Roman church pursued its polemical tactics against heresy, the importance of the connection of Peter and Paul to the foundation of the church at Rome as a standard for ecclesiastical tradition should not be discounted.

[36] Clement, in his letter to the Corinthians concerning factionalism, appeals to the example of Peter and Paul, who are pillars of the Church and who both died in service to the gospel at Rome (*1 Clem.* 5; cf. 44). Ignatius (*Rom.* 9) entreats the church at Rome to remember the church in Syria in prayer since he himself will no longer be there as shepherd. This is probably an appeal to the authority, or at least the status, of the church in Rome against the threat of ecclesiastical disorder in Syria. See Bauer, *Orthodoxy and Heresy in Earliest Christianity*, pp. 108–29. This status is probably due to the special connection between the church at Rome and the apostles Peter and Paul. (See also Ignatius *Rom.* 4.)

[37] See *Adv. haer.* 3.3.2–3: "In the time of this Clement, no small dissension having occurred among the brethren at Corinth, the Church in Rome dispatched a most powerful letter to the Corinthians, exhorting them to peace, renewing their faith, and declaring the tradition which it had lately received from the apostles..."

[38] Irenaeus's attitude toward the church at Rome is evident in his letter to Victor

Irenaeus sees the role of Peter and Paul in the narrative of Acts through the lens of this construction of Christian tradition so that together the Acts of the Apostles and the tradition of the Church become an unshakable (for Irenaeus) bulwark against all heresies that corrupt the Gospel.[39] This alignment of Peter, Paul, and Rome, however, represents an attitude toward Peter and Paul that belongs to a different conceptual world than that of the narrative of Acts, despite the importance of the figures of Peter and Paul in Acts. In Acts, the characters of Peter and Paul define the emergence of Christianity as a historical movement from Jerusalem to Rome.[40] Each belongs to a certain stage in this movement. They are neither coequal founders of the church of Rome nor coequal martyrs at Rome,[41] nor is there in the narrative of Acts an alignment of Peter, Paul, and Rome as determinants of normative Christian doctrine and practice over against heresy in local church disputes.[42] Instead, they are characters unifying stages in the development of an empire-wide religious movement defined over against the religious and political realities of the Graeco-Roman world (including Judaism).[43] For all the importance of Acts for Irenaeus as a source of historical information about the early church, Acts does not share the perspective on the history of Christianity that has shaped Irenaeus's understanding of the origin of Christianity. Irenaeus's static construction of Christian origins in terms of the preservation by the apostles of the Gospel proclaimed by Jesus has little to do with the interests of

---

concerning the Paschal controversy (see Eusebius *Hist. eccl.* 5.23–24). Although he disagrees with Victor in his harsh handling of the Asian churches in the dispute over the observation of Easter, he acknowledges the importance of the leadership of the church at Rome in setting the standard for ecclesiastical doctrine and practice, and he appeals to the practice of earlier Roman bishops in their toleration of differences concerning this matter.

[39] The Simon of Acts 8 thus becomes the father of all heresies against the true gospel proclaimed by the apostles. See the preface to book 3 of *Adv. haer.* See note 22 above.

[40] The perspective of Acts on the relationship of Peter and Paul and the foundation of the church at Rome will be developed in chapters 3 and 4 below.

[41] Peter's death is not even alluded to in the narrative of Acts.

[42] In Paul's farewell to the leaders of the Christians in Ephesus in Acts 20:17–35, Paul alone represents the standard for the preaching of the gospel against which (future) distortions of the truth are to be measured. For the significance the author attaches to the death of Paul, see chapter 3 under *Paul's Farewell Speech and the Literary Paulinism of Lk-Acts.*

[43] This point will be taken up in detail in chapter 3. In Acts, Peter and Paul belong to different historical moments of the church—historical moments defined by the succession of the characters of John, Jesus, the Twelve, and Paul. In Acts, Paul in relation to Rome defines the Christian present.

the author of Lk-Acts in portraying the development from the Judaism of Jesus to the Christianity of Paul.[44] Instead, the narrative of Acts has been co-opted by Irenaeus for reasons other than a common conceptual matrix. Read in terms of Irenaeus's static construction of apostolic tradition aligned with Peter, Paul, and Rome, the narrative of Acts provides a useful scriptural refutation of both the assumptions behind Marcion's delineation of Christian history and scripture (which played the Gospel proclaimed by Paul off against the message proclaimed by the rest of the apostles) and the construction of ecclesiastical tradition by Valentinians and other heretics claiming apostolic authority.[45]

As part of the true Church, Irenaeus himself, bishop of Lyons, claims authority to delineate and interpret the scriptures against the heretics.[46] In this undertaking, the narrative of Acts emerges from complete obscurity to a position of importance as a resource in defending the Irenaean construction of Christian origins, now preserved in the Christian scriptures. For Irenaeus, the need to define a normative ecclesiastical tradition determines the interpretive matrix for Acts, in which context the text of Acts becomes relevant for the life of the church (as defined by Irenaeus) in its struggle against heresy. Ironically, the text of Acts, the second part of a work introduced explicitly with the intention of replacing other gospel accounts,[47] becomes the scriptural basis for defending a construction of Christianity based on a normative apostolic tradition correlated with a canon of four written gospels.[48]

---

[44] See chapter 3 under *Paul's Farewell Speech and the Literary Paulinism of Lk-Acts*.

[45] Not only is the narrative of Acts read as an account of the unchanging unity of the early Christian proclamation of the Gospel, Acts provides the basis for a genealogy of heresy. See note 22 above on Simon Magus.

[46] In *Adv. haer.* 3.3.3 and 3.3.4, Irenaeus establishes his connection with normative ecclesiastical tradition from the apostles preserved by the Church. In 3.3.3 the apostolic lineage of the church of Rome is set forth. In 3.3.4 Irenaeus aligns Polycarp, who himself was instructed and appointed bishop by the apostles, with Rome as a defender of apostolic truth: "[Polycarp] coming to Rome in the time of Anicetus caused many to turn away from the aforesaid heretics [that is, Valentinus and Marcion] to the Church of God, proclaiming that he had received this one and sole truth from the apostles..." Irenaeus claims a personal connection to Polycarp. See also Irenaeus's letter to Florinus, quoted by Eusebius in *Hist. eccl.* 5.20.4–8.

[47] Lk 1:1–4. See below under *Traditions of Authorship and Titles*. The author's intention to replace inadequate literary accounts of the Christian past has become in the social and literary context in which Irenaeus writes but one contribution to a larger construction of the Gospel. The narrative of Lk, in its reception in early Christianity, has been removed from its original literary context and has become a reservoir of gospel material about Jesus from which the one true Gospel can be known. See *Adv. haer.* 3.14.3.

[48] See *Adv. haer.* 3.5.1. Marcion and Irenaeus are the first Christian writers to cor-

The Irenaean claims about the Gospel according to Luke and the Acts of the Apostles presuppose different receptions for the narrative of Lk and that of Acts in early Christianity. For Irenaeus, it is self-evident that the Gospel according to Luke belongs to the fourfold gospel canon. The individual texts in his gospel canon apparently have enough general acceptance in the life of Christian communities as to be in no need of defense, at least for his intended audience.[49] Irenaeus defends the fourfold gospel canon against those who use a reduced or expanded norm for the Christian Gospel.[50] Irenaeus does not defend the authority of any particular gospel within this fourfold canon, but rather the fourfold canon itself—a closed collection of divinely ordained witnesses to the Gospel.[51] The text of Lk is, therefore, by the time of Irenaeus apparently established as an important text about Jesus in the life of at least some Christian communities.[52]

In contrast to his attitude toward the Gospel according to Luke, Irenaeus is compelled to defend the text of Acts. His comments in book 3 suggest that, whereas at least parts of the Gospel according to Luke

---

relate a gospel canon with a construction of Christian origins as a method of argument against heresy to define Christian truth. Marcion constructed Christian origins on the basis of the Pauline letters; Irenaeus on the basis of the Acts of the Apostles. 'Orthodoxy' is best understood not as a specific trajectory of doctrine or church order in the early church, but instead as a method of argumentation to establish a universal, unchanging deposit of truth preserved for the Church of the (polemicist's) present based on a construction of apostolic tradition. Eusebius pursued this method of argumentation in a comprehensive manner in his *Hist. eccl.* (though his conceptual framework and doctrinal system differed from that of Irenaeus; note, e.g., his negative comments about Irenaeus's millenarianism, *Hist. eccl.* 3.39.11–12).

[49] This audience is favorable to Irenaeus's perspective on early Christianity. See his preface to book 3 of *Adv. haer.*; see also the prefaces to books 1 and 2.

[50] See *Adv. haer.* 3.11.7–9. Irenaeus associates a limitation of this canon with heresy. Use of only one gospel is for him connected to distortions of the gospel (see especially *Adv. haer.* 3.11.7). The implication of Irenaeus's arguments is that the use of a plurality of gospel texts (that is, some combination of at least Mt, Mk, Lk, and Jn) is a common practice in the churches he would consider to be faithful to apostolic tradition. See note 16 above on Irenaeus's claims to be able to refute his opponents on the basis of whichever gospel text they accept (see 3.11.7). On the other hand, Irenaeus rejects any gospel texts beyond Mt, Mk, Lk, and Jn as having scriptural authority. Note, e.g., his comments on the so-called *Gospel of Truth*. See *Adv. haer.* 3.11.9.

[51] *Adv. haer.* 3.11.8. The speculative nature of this defense suggests that these arguments are intended for those who already are predisposed to accept a plurality of gospel texts. This speculative defense of the fourfold gospel canon in 3.11.8 should be read as the theological correlate of the historical tradition that Irenaeus reports in 3.1.1 concerning the circumstances of the composition of the four gospels.

[52] Some of these communities were Christian, some heretical, according to Irenaeus. See, e.g., *Adv. haer.* 3.11.7; 3.11.9; 3.14.4; 3.15.1.

are accepted as authoritative, the text identified by him as the Acts of the Apostles is relatively unused (or unknown) as an authoritative Christian text. The salient points of his defense of the authority of Acts are worth noting:

> Thus also does Luke, without respect of persons, deliver to us what he had learned from the apostles, as he has himself testified, saying, "Even as those who from the beginning were eyewitnesses and ministers of the word delivered to us."[53]
>
> Now if anyone set Luke aside, as one who did not know the truth [that is, as one who does not narrate the truth in the Acts of the Apostles], he will manifestly reject the Gospel of which he claims to be a disciple. For through him we have become acquainted with very many and important points of the Gospel; for instance, the generation of John...[there follows a long list of such items]. There are also many other particulars to be found mentioned by Luke alone, which are made use of by both Marcion and Valentinus....[54]
>
> It follows then, as of course, that these men must either receive the rest of his narrative, or else reject these parts also. For no persons of common sense can permit them to receive some things recounted by Luke as being true, and to set others aside, as if he had not known the truth. If they reject the whole: Marcion's followers will then possess no Gospel; for mutilating that according to Luke, as I have said already, they boast in having the Gospel. As for the followers of Valentinus, they must give up their utterly vain talk; for they have taken from [that according to Luke] many occasions for their own speculation, to put an evil interpretation upon what he has well said. If, on the other hand, they feel compelled to receive the remaining portions also, then by studying the perfect Gospel and the doctrine of the apostles [*perfecto euangelio et apostolorum doctrinae*], they will find it necessary to repent, that they may be saved from the danger.[55]
>
> But again, we state the same against those who do not recognize Paul as an apostle: that they should either reject the other words of the Gospel which we have come to know through Luke alone, and not make use of them; or else, if they do receive all these, they must necessarily admit also that testimony concerning Paul, when [Luke] tells us....[56]
>
> It may be, indeed, that it was with this view that God set forth very many Gospel truths, through Luke's instrumentality, which all should esteem it necessary to use in order that all persons, following his subsequent testimony which treats upon the acts and doctrine of the apostles [*actibus et doctrina apostolorum*], and holding the unadulterated rule of truth, may be saved.[57]

---

[53] *Adv. haer.* 3.14.2.
[54] *Adv. haer.* 3.14.3.
[55] *Adv. haer.* 3.14.4.
[56] *Adv. haer.* 3.15.1.
[57] *Adv. haer.* 3.15.1.

Unlike the individual gospels of his canon, to which the Gospel according to Luke belongs, Irenaeus does not claim Acts has any self-evident authority in any Christian community, especially those communities of his opponents.[58] Instead, the authority of Acts depends on the authority of the Gospel according to Luke (which is, apparently, widely recognized in some form or another among his opponents). The usefulness of Acts for Irenaeus's argument depends on the fact that his opponents are using at least parts of the Gospel according to Luke. Acts is the rest of the narrative of Luke and thus must be accepted along with the Gospel according to Luke. That Irenaeus does not deal with specific arguments against Acts suggests Irenaeus's opponents did not explicitly reject this text. Rather, the text was either unknown or unimportant to them.[59] Apparently, Irenaeus has pulled Acts off the shelf (so to speak), dusted it off, and put it to use to establish his construction of the standard for the Gospel—a unified constellation of apostolic witnesses in scripture and tradition.

Although Irenaeus reads the Gospel according to Luke and the Acts of the Apostles as narratives by the same author,[60] the connection between the narratives is determined by his canon of four gospels. For Irenaeus, the Gospel according to Luke and the Acts of the Apostles are quite distinct, the former supplying details of the Gospel, the latter of the doctrine of (all) the apostles (that is, that all the apostles, including Paul, agreed in preaching the same Gospel).

The obscurity from which Irenaeus rescued the text of Acts reflects the relative lack of importance of Acts in the life of the early Christian communities and prevents any firm conclusions about precursors to Irenaeus's use of Acts for this scholarly debate about canon.[61] The

---

[58] Contrast this with his claims about the gospels, *Adv. haer.* 3.11.7.

[59] Irenaeus states that the Valentinians allege that the risen Lord conversed with his disciples for a period of eighteen months, a length of time that contradicts the account in Acts 1 (*Adv. haer.* 1.3.2). That Marcion would have adopted the text of Lk and the Pauline letters without clearly commenting on Acts if the narrative of Acts was widely known seems quite unlikely. See note 64 below. See also below under *Traditions of Authorship and Titles*.

[60] Note the connection Irenaeus draws between Lk 1:2 and Paul's farewell address in *Adv. haer.* 3.14.2. See below under *Traditions of Authorship and Titles* for Irenaeus's understanding of Luke the companion of Paul as the author of the Gospel according to Luke and the Acts of the Apostles.

[61] On the place of the apocryphal acts in early Christianity in relation to narratives about Jesus, apostolic letters, and the narrative of Acts, see below under *Acts and the Apocryphal Acts in the Second Century*.

legend of the foundation of the church of Rome by Peter and Paul to which Irenaeus appeals as the standard for apostolic tradition is independent of the text of Acts. Acts almost certainly did not have much importance at Rome prior to Irenaeus.[62] Justin betrays no certain knowledge of the text.[63] Marcion, a careful critic of texts, apparently made no mention of a text potentially so damaging to his reconstruction of the history of Christianity.[64] The traditional association of Peter, Paul, and Rome—an association that for Irenaeus presents the empirical proof of the unity of the apostles in the proclamation of the Gospel—defines the conceptual matrix in which Irenaeus reads Acts,[65] not a trajectory in early Christianity by which Acts came to Irenaeus.

---

[62] To the extent that Bauer (*Orthodoxy and Heresy in Earliest Christianity*, p. 113, n. 2) is right that Rome (or better, certain factions at Rome) had an interest in extending Peter's influence at Paul's expense, Acts would hardly have been of importance to such a faction.

[63] Haenchen (*The Acts of the Apostles*, p. 8) has argued that Justin knew Acts on the basis of *1 Apol.* 50.12, but dependence on the end of Lk is sufficient to account for Justin's description. See, e.g., Strange, *The Problem of the Text of Acts*, p. 180. As Haenchen points out, δύναμιν ... λαβόντες in *1 Apol.* 50.12 does correspond to λήμψεσθε δύναμιν in Acts 1:8. However, δύναμιν is also used of the coming of the spirit in Lk 24:49, and the flow of *1 Apol.* 50:12 corresponds closely to the end of Luke without reference to the narrative of Acts. According to Justin:

... καὶ εἰς οὐρανὸν ἀνερχόμενον ἰδόντες καὶ πιστεύσαντες καὶ δύναμιν ἐκεῖθεν αὐτοῖς πεμφθεῖσαν παρ' αὐτοῦ λαβόντες καὶ εἰς πᾶν γένος ἀνθρώπων ἐλθόντες ...

The phrase ἐκεῖθεν αὐτοῖς πεμφθεῖσαν παρ' αὐτοῦ corresponds to ἀποστέλλω ... ἐφ' ὑμᾶς in Lk 24:49, and the sequence λαβόντες ... ἐλθόντες in Justin fulfills Jesus' final command to the apostles in Lk 24:49, ὑμεῖς δὲ καθίσατε ἐν τῇ πόλει ἕως οὗ ἐνδύσησθε ἐξ ὕψους δύναμιν. Finally, πιστεύσαντες in Justin is an interpretation of προσκυνήσαντες in Lk 24:52 as a response to the ascension.

See Conzelmann (*Acts of the Apostles*, pp. xxx-xxxi) for other possible reminiscences of Acts in Justin. Justin's knowledge of Acts cannot be ruled out, but if he was acquainted with the narrative of Acts, it does not seem to have been very important to him.

[64] If Acts had been important either in the intellectual or liturgical life of the churches at Rome or Asia Minor, Marcion could easily have edited it to make his point about the apostle Paul in relation to the other apostles. (Note, e.g., the rewriting of the history of Acts by Pseudo-Clementine *Recognitions* 1.27–71, on which see Jones, 'An Ancient Christian Rejoinder to Luke's Acts of the Apostles: Pseudo-Clementine *Recognitions* 1.27–71,' esp. pp. 239–44.) Instead, his reconstruction of apostolic history and apparent silence about Acts suggest the unimportance of Acts. Harnack's speculation (*Marcion. The Gospel of the Alien God*, p. 163, n. 86) that Marcion learned about the persecution of the apostles from the Acts of the Apostles is unnecessary. Lk 21:12–19, which according to Harnack (pp. 39, 42) was subjected to minor editing by Marcion and thus certainly did not escape his notice, makes explicit mention of the persecution of the apostles for proclaiming Jesus.

[65] Note that in *Adv. haer.* 3.1.1 (quoted above in part), Irenaeus conflates the beginning of Acts ("...[after] the apostles were invested with power from on high when the

Irenaeus does associate himself with Polycarp. Polycarp was a collector of letters, most notably those of Paul and Ignatius, in defense of ecclesiastical truth. Whether Polycarp's interest in such letters would have extended to Acts cannot be determined, though there is no compelling reason to suppose so.[66] Possible allusions to Acts by Polycarp are doubtful at best.[67]

Irenaeus cites Acts according to certain variants that have come to be identified as belonging to the so-called 'Western' text of Acts. Most notably, he knows the form of the apostolic decree that includes the golden rule.[68] However, the origin of the 'Western' text of Acts remains an unsolved problem.[69] The insertion of the negative form of the golden rule into the apostolic decree perhaps suggests an attempt to give the apostolic decree a continuing relevance for Christians everywhere,[70] but does not imply that a major revision of Acts existed prior to Irenaeus. Against the likelihood of such a revision, three points are worth noting. First, there has as yet been no persuasive demonstration of an inner coherence for a second-century revision of Acts as the basis for the 'Western' text of Acts.[71] Second, if such a revision had been carried

---

Holy Spirit came down...[they] departed to the ends of the earth...") with the tradition of Peter and Paul at Rome ("...Matthew also issued a written Gospel among the Hebrews in their own dialect, while Peter and Paul were preaching at Rome and laying the foundations of the Church...").

[66] In the early manuscript tradition, the text of Acts has no special association with the letters of Paul. The suggestion by Strange (*The Problem of the Text of Acts*, p. 179; see note 71 below on Strange's theory about the text of Acts) that the reading of the Gospel alongside the Apostle (that is, gospel texts and Pauline letters) would have provided a life-setting in early Christian communities for Acts is unlikely in view of its obscurity in the life of Christian communities. There is no compelling evidence to suggest that Acts, either in its composition or reception prior to Irenaeus, was closely connected with the Pauline letters. See chapter 4 below.

[67] Conzelmann (*Acts of the Apostles*, pp. xxvii-xxix) has compiled a list of these possible allusions. See also Haenchen, *The Acts of the Apostles*, pp. 3–14.

[68] See, e.g., *Adv. haer.* 3.12.14. For a discussion of the variants associated with the apostolic decree in Acts, see Strange, *The Problem of the Text of Acts*, pp. 87–106.

[69] Aland and Aland (*The Text of the New Testament*, 2nd ed., pp. 54–55) argue that there was no distinctive early 'Western' text and that the text of codex Bezae Cantabrigiensis could not have existed as early as the second century.

[70] Cf. Strange, *The Problem of the Text of Acts*, pp. 90, 104.

[71] For a recent discussion of the history of scholarship on the 'Western' text of Acts, see Strange, *The Problem of the Text of Acts*, pp. 1–34. The theory proposed by Strange himself, that the two forms of the text of Acts are due to revisions intended by the author, but not incorporated until the posthumous editing and publication of Acts later in the second century, is not convincing. To support his theory that Acts was edited and published later in the second century, he argues that Acts was not known

out before Irenaeus, one would expect a much wider dissemination of this form of the text of Acts. The obscurity of the reception of Acts prior to Irenaeus would suggest no one form of the text would have gained prominence before the end of the second century, making room for competing forms of the text. Third, the 'Western' text of Acts lacks any major additions to or expansions of the stories in Acts, particularly those about Peter and Paul (especially in terms of traditions about their martyrdom). This absence of substantive expansions of the text of Acts in its 'Western' version suggests that this form of the text does not have its origin in a major revision prior to its emergence as scripture in the writings of Irenaeus, before which time the text would likely have been dealt with in a much freer manner.[72] Instead, the variants characteristic

---

prior to Irenaeus because it had not been published. He asks the question (p. 179), "If Acts found a home in the 'Apostle'-section of the emerging canon in the third century, why did it not find it in the second century?" He continues with the claim that "the reading of the 'Apostle' alongside 'Gospel' from the earliest times would have provided a potential life-setting for the book in the church." A few pages later (p. 183), he attributes the publication of Acts to the threats to the church created by Marcion and Valentinus. His suggestions, though interesting, do not solve the problem of the reception of Acts in the second century. First, the circumstances associated with Marcion and Valentinus that Strange construes as a plausible explanation for the editing and publication of Acts posthumously just as easily answer his question about why Acts found a place in the emerging canon of the third century, but was relatively obscure prior to Irenaeus. Second, if the reading of the 'Apostle' alongside the 'Gospel' is a plausible life-setting for the book of Acts in the church prior to Marcion (in fact, the manuscript tradition for Acts does not indicate that the text of Acts was integrated into the Pauline letter collection; Acts was transmitted with the gospels or with the catholic letters; see notes 172 and 173 below), why was the text of Acts not published sooner? In other words, either Acts has a potential life-setting in the church from very early, in which case there is no reason to suppose it was published later in the second century; or, the relevance of Acts for the canon develops only late in the second century, in which case its previous obscurity is not evidence for it not having been published. The lack of knowledge of Acts prior to Irenaeus needs to be explained in terms of the character of the text, not a late publication of the text. Third, Strange nowhere demonstrates that the published text of Acts has any tendencies that would associate it with an editing after Marcion. Fourth, there is little evidence that Acts was of much importance in the liturgical life of the church even after Irenaeus, so its obscurity prior to Irenaeus is hardly surprising. (See note 171 below on the comments of Chrysostom and Augustine that suggest Acts was relatively unknown even in their day.) In short, Strange's explanation for the 'Western' text of Acts creates as many difficulties as it attempts to solve and does not explain the reception of Acts in the second century.

[72] Three texts produced in the second century perhaps indicate the type of freedom that might be expected in the use of Acts before it became scripture. The *Epistula Apostolorum*, the *Acts of Peter*, and the *Acts of Paul* were all written before or nearly contemporaneously with the work of Irenaeus, and dependencies on the narrative of Acts have been argued for all three. Yet all three substantively modify the narrative

of the 'Western' text of Acts suggest rather modest attempts to explain the standard text.[73] Some of these explanatory glosses may have had their origin with Irenaeus himself;[74] many likely arose subsequently, after the text became important for reconstructing a certain version of apostolic history as the basis for the emerging canon. There is no compelling reason to suppose Acts was widely known prior to Irenaeus based on the 'Western' text of Acts.

The close connection of the emergence of the text of Acts in early Christianity with the intellectual pursuits of Irenaeus in defense of Christian unity is perhaps evident in some of the correspondence between East and West at this time preserved by Eusebius. The account of the martyrs of Lyons and Vienne[75] refers to the martyrdom of Stephen in the narrative of Acts.[76] This text was sent from the churches of Vienne and Lyons to churches in the East while Irenaeus was bishop of Lyons. A little later, Polycrates, bishop of Ephesus, wrote to Victor at Rome concerning the Paschal controversy.[77] In this letter, he perhaps alludes to Acts 5:29.[78] Irenaeus intervened with Victor on behalf of the churches from the East in this controversy.[79]

The situation with respect to the text of Acts in early Christianity before and after Irenaeus could not stand in sharper contrast. Whereas Acts has little prominence prior to Irenaeus, shortly afterwards the Acts of the Apostles is widely cited, often alongside the fourfold collection of

---

framework of Acts. On the apocryphal acts, see below under *Acts and the Apocryphal Acts in the Second Century*. On the *Epistula Apostolorum*, see chapter 4 under *Rome*. The author of Pseudo-Clementine *Recognitions* 1.27–71, probably writing shortly after the time of Irenaeus, used the narrative of Acts as a source but wrote from quite a different perspective. See Jones, 'An Ancient Jewish Christian Rejoinder to Luke's Acts of the Apostles: Pseudo-Clementine *Recognitions* 1.27–71,' esp. p. 243. See note 204 below.

[73] See, e.g., the comments of Strange, *The Problem of the Text of Acts*, pp. 52–56, though the conclusions he draws from his observations are not persuasive; see note 71 above.

[74] The lack of widespread attestation of 'Western' variants for the text of Acts known by Irenaeus makes it impossible to retrace their origin to earlier revisions of Acts with any certainty.

[75] See Eusebius *Hist. eccl.* 5.1–2.

[76] *Hist. eccl.* 5.2.5.

[77] This letter is cited by Eusebius *Hist. eccl.* 5.24.

[78] See Eusebius *Hist. eccl.* 5.24.7.

[79] Theophilus of Antioch in *Ad Autolycum* 2.34 cites the negative form of the golden rule (which corresponds to the form of the Apostolic Decree in Acts 15:20 and 15:29 cited by Irenaeus; see note 68 above), though with no direct allusion to the narrative of Acts. Grant ('The Bible of Theophilus of Antioch,' p. 188) goes beyond the evidence when he concludes that the New Testament at Antioch in Theophilus's day included the Acts of the Apostles.

gospels.⁸⁰ The Muratorian canon, perhaps belonging to the end of the second century,⁸¹ takes for granted what Irenaeus defended: the Gospel according to Luke and the Acts of the Apostles belong in the canon. Likewise, the old gospel prologue to the Gospel according to Luke presupposes the gospel canon defined by Irenaeus.⁸² After citing some biographical information about the author Luke,⁸³ the old gospel prologue goes on to situate the Gospel according to Luke in relationship to Mt, Mk, Jn, and Acts. The prologue follows a geographical as well as a temporal ordering of the gospels, placing the Gospel according to Matthew in Judea, that according to Mark in Italy, and (subsequent to these two) that according to Luke in Achaea. Following the writing of his Gospel, the same Luke wrote the Acts of the Apostles. Later comes the Gospel of John, written by the apostle John after Revelation. The prologue includes an explanation of the differences between the beginning of the Gospel according to Luke and that of the other Gospels—Luke's intention is deduced from the preface, and the reason for his narrative beginning with the birth of John the Baptist is interpreted.⁸⁴ This old gospel prologue thus explains, with reference to Luke, what is taken for granted: the fourfold gospel canon alongside the Acts of the Apostles.

In short, there is little evidence prior to Irenaeus to suggest how he came to ascribe such importance to the Acts of the Apostles in his *Adversus haereses*. Shortly after his work, the Acts of the Apostles begins to

---

⁸⁰ Tertullian, e.g., accepts the Acts of the Apostles as scripture, in contrast to the *Acts of Paul*. See below under *Acts and the Apocryphal Acts in the Second Century*. Nevertheless, the Acts of the Apostles does not have the same prominence as the gospels and Pauline letters. Clement of Alexandria, e.g., quotes Acts only 10 times, according to von Campenhausen (*The Formation of the Christian Bible*, p. 295, n. 151).

⁸¹ See note 19 above on the attempt to redate this canon list to the fourth century.

⁸² For the text of this prologue, see Aland, *Synopsis Quattuor Evangeliorum*, p. 533. This prologue has been identified as belonging to a collection of so-called anti-Marcionite prologues, but is independent and not particularly anti-Marcionite. See Haenchen, *The Acts of the Apostles*, n. 1, pp. 10–12. Apart from the dubious connection to polemics against Marcion, there is little reason to date the prologue earlier than Irenaeus. Instead, since the prologue assumes what Irenaeus had to defend—the fourfold gospel canon alongside the Acts of the Apostles—it was probably not written before the end of the second century. It may, in fact, have been written much later. The prologue reflects a development of biographical information about Luke that was probably unknown to Irenaeus. See below under *Traditions of Authorship and Titles*. On the problem of the date of the prologue, see McDonald, 'Anti-Marcionite (Gospel) Prologues,' *ABD* 1.262–63.

⁸³ See below under *Traditions of Authorship and Titles*.

⁸⁴ δηλῶν διὰ τοῦ προοιμίου τοῦτο αὐτὸ ὅτι πρὸ αὐτοῦ ἄλλα ἐστὶ γεγραμμένα ... ὡς ἀναγκαιοτάτην οὖν οὖσαν ἐν ἀρχῇ παρειλήφαμεν τὴν τοῦ Ἰωάννου γέννησιν, ὅς ἐστιν ἀρχὴ τοῦ εὐαγγελίου ...

be cited as scripture and placed alongside the fourfold gospel collection defined by Irenaeus. Though the Acts of the Apostles still had no firm place in the life of Christian communities long after the writings of Irenaeus,[85] its importance as scripture in the intellectual defense of apostolic truth was assured. Irenaeus himself was probably the first to formulate the significance of Acts for this defense.[86]

Traditions of Authorship and Titles

Irenaeus's designation of Lk-Acts as the Gospel according to Luke and the Acts of the Apostles[87] does presuppose a certain history of reception in the life of early Christian communities. This reception, as suggested above, needs further consideration. The title 'Gospel according to Luke' (εὐαγγέλιον κατὰ Λουκᾶν, or the shortened form κατὰ Λουκᾶν) is secondary[88] and depends on the separation of the narrative of Acts from that of Lk.[89] The author of Lk-Acts characterized neither his own

---

[85] See below under *Acts and the Apocryphal Acts in the Second Century*.

[86] Harnack's perceptive comments on the place of Acts in the New Testament canon (*The Origin of the New Testament*, pp. 96–97) are worth quoting in part: "…there is very much in the development of things leading to the foundation of the New Testament that can and ought to be explained from the practice of public reading and other causes, without recourse to the hypothesis of conscious creation. Even the addition to the Gospels of Apostolic Epistles in some form or another is an arrangement that might easily have arisen quite independently and in essentially similar fashion in different Churches. But *the form in which the addition is made under the dominating influence of the Acts of the Apostles* could not have occurred automatically and at the same time in different Churches…*the placing of this book (the Acts) in the growing Canon shows evidence of reflection, of conscious purpose, of a strong hand acting with authority; and by such conscious action the Canon began to take form as Apostolic-Catholic*. It cannot have happened otherwise; for the sense of purpose expressed in the structure cannot have been unconscious." If Irenaeus was the individual behind this conscious purpose, his views would likely have been disseminated very rapidly due to his connections to churches at Rome and in the East.

[87] See, e.g., *Adv. haer.* 3.11.7–8 ([*euangelium*] *secundum Lucam*); 3.13.3 (*actus apostolorum*).

[88] Although Hengel ('The Titles of the Gospels and the Gospel of Mark,' pp. 64–84) overestimates the likelihood for the early use of such titles, he correctly points out that the longer form is not later than the shorter (p. 66). $\mathfrak{P}^{66}$ and $\mathfrak{P}^{75}$ both attest the longer title early in the third century. His argument that such titles go back into the first century, however, conflates the question of the use of εὐαγγέλιον as a title with the question of the origin of the traditions of authorship. Papias, e.g., relates the tradition of authorship associated with the texts of Mt and Mk, but he does not refer to the texts as gospels. Neither the author of Mt nor of Lk-Acts construes Mk as a gospel. (See note 90 below.)

[89] Acts 1:1–2 is a secondary preface suggesting the intended unity of the narrative of Lk-Acts. See chapter 3 under *The Prefaces of Lk-Acts*. On the relation of Lk 1:1–4 to the construction of the Pauline mission in Acts, see chapter 4 below.

work nor that of his predecessors as 'gospels.'⁹⁰ The designation of a written text as a gospel is not attested before Marcion and Justin⁹¹ and coincides with the emergence of such texts in the life of Christian communities as authoritative written records of the words of Jesus.⁹² In collections, such written records came to be designated as '[the Gospel] according to [...].'⁹³ Irenaeus, defending his canon of four gospels, provides the earliest evidence for the designation of Lk as the Gospel according to Luke.

The origin of the traditions of authorship, however, must be considered apart from their eventual use as titles in the form [εὐαγγέλιον] κατὰ [...]. The authorship ascriptions themselves probably antedate

---

⁹⁰ See Lk 1:1–4; Acts 1:1–2. In fact, the author avoids the noun εὐαγγέλιον entirely in Lk. The author of Lk-Acts does not construe the use of εὐαγγέλιον in Mk 1:1 as a designation of a literary genre. Instead, the author of Lk-Acts characterizes Mk in Lk 1:1 as a διήγησις 'concerning the events accomplished among us' (περὶ τῶν πεπληροφορημένων ἐν ἡμῖν πραγμάτων; cf. λόγος, Lk 1:2). The author of Lk-Acts is not writing a gospel, but a narrative about the proclamation of the word. The unwarranted conclusion that εὐαγγέλιον was an earlier literary form has suggested a distinction in genre between Lk and Acts that would not have occurred to the author of Lk-Acts. (See chapter 3 under *The Prefaces of Lk-Acts* on the genre of Lk-Acts.) The separation of the author's διήγησις into an εὐαγγέλιον and a πρᾶξεις is the result of the reception of these texts in the second century, not the intentions of the author. (Contrast Jervell, *The Theology of the Acts of the Apostles*, pp. 1, 116–17.)

⁹¹ See Koester, *Ancient Christian Gospels*, esp. p. 36. See also Gundry, 'ΕΥΑΓΓΕΛΙΟΝ: How Soon a Book?' pp. 321–25. Dormeyer ('Die Kompositionsmetapher "Evangelium Jesu Christi, des Sohnes Gottes" Mk 1.1. Ihre theologische und literarische Aufgabe in der Jesus-Biographie des Markus,' pp. 452–68) has argued for the literary character of εὐαγγέλιον in Mk 1:1, but Koester's response (*Ancient Christian Gospels*, p. 13, n. 4) is to the point: εὐαγγέλιον is a message in Mk 1:1, not a title. Cf. Lk 1:1–4, on which see previous note. Only as the authority of written texts began to exceed that of oral tradition was εὐαγγέλιον construed as a literary genre, and therefore title, of a narrative about Jesus.

⁹² Justin's description of the gospels as "memoirs of the apostles" (see *1 Apol.* 66.3; 67.3–4) suggests such a context, as does Marcion's designation of a written text as a gospel in his collection of Christian scripture. Irenaeus treats the words of Jesus as distinct from the written gospels, but always cites a written gospel. Thus, he preserves a distinction that was no longer meaningful but which was rooted in the transition from oral to written standards for the words of Jesus. See von Campenhausen, *The Formation of the Christian Bible*, pp. 191–92.

⁹³ Hengel's attempt ('The Titles of the Gospels and the Gospel of Mark,' esp. p. 65) to refute Harnack by demonstrating that such titles could have existed apart from the collection of such texts alongside one another is unconvincing. The designation κατὰ Λουκᾶν presupposes two developments: (1) the emergence of the idea that the Gospel is contained in a written narrative; (2) the collection of more than one such written narrative alongside one another. Such conditions probably did not exist prior to Marcion, and it is therefore not surprising that the first instances of such usage first occur shortly after Marcion in responses to his canon of one written gospel.

their use as titles (whether in conjunction with εὐαγγέλιον or otherwise), as the evidence from Papias indicates.[94] His comments suggest an attempt to connect books about Jesus (both his own and that of Mk and Mt, none of which he identifies as gospels) to authentic (oral) traditions about Jesus based on the preaching of the apostles.[95] Thus, Papias claims that the text of Mk preserved the preaching of Peter and the text of Mt derived from the work of the apostle Matthew.[96] He claims that his own work, by contrast, contains reliable oral traditions from the preaching of the other apostles. For Papias, the attributions of authorship for the texts of Mt and Mk explain the differences (and deficiencies) of the actual narratives of Mk and Mt in terms of the experiences of the authors in relation to the preaching of the Gospel.[97]

---

[94] See Eusebius *Hist. eccl.* 3.39.

[95] According to Eusebius, Papias in the preface to his five volume work on the interpretation of the sayings of Jesus claimed to have carefully gathered reliable oral traditions from the apostles about what Jesus taught, for he preferred the living voice of oral tradition to what could be learned from books. Hengel pays too little attention to this intermediate development of apostolic authority between anonymous text and apostolic gospel in his argument that all the authorship attributions are very early. Cf. Schneemelcher, *New Testament Apocrypha*, rev. ed. (1991), 1.79, n. 7. The apostolic traditions of authorship are important for Justin (indicated by his reference to memoirs of the apostles) and Irenaeus (see, e.g., *Adv. haer.* 3.1.1; 3.5.1), apart from their use as titles. Justin's designation of these texts as 'memoirs' emphasizes their historical reliability. This concern for authenticity is firmly embedded in the tradition cited by Irenaeus in *Adv. haer.* 3.1.1.

[96] Μάρκος μὲν ἑρμηνευτὴς Πέτρου γενόμενος, ὅσα ἐμνημόνευσεν, ἀκριβῶς ἔγραψεν, οὐ μέντοι τάξει, τὰ ὑπὸ τοῦ κυρίου ἢ λεχθέντα ἢ πραχθέντα. οὔτε γὰρ ἤκουσεν τοῦ κυρίου οὔτε παρηκολούθησεν αὐτῷ, ὕστερον δέ, ὡς ἔφην, Πέτρῳ· ὃς πρὸς τὰς χρείας ἐποιεῖτο τὰς διδασκαλίας, ἀλλ' οὐχ ὥσπερ σύνταξιν τῶν κυριακῶν ποιούμενος λογίων, ὥστε οὐδὲν ἥμαρτεν Μάρκος οὕτως ἔνια γράψας ὡς ἀπεμνημόνευσεν... [Mark, having become Peter's translator, wrote accurately, though not in order, the things either said or done by the Lord, as many things as he remembered. For he neither heard the Lord nor followed him, but later, as I said, followed Peter. Peter was accustomed to teach as the need arose {or: using chreiai}, but did not as it were produce an ordered arrangement of the sayings of the Lord, so that Mark in no way erred by so having written some as he remembered...] Ματθαῖος μὲν οὖν Ἑβραΐδι διαλέκτῳ τὰ λόγια συνετάξατο, ἡρμήνευσεν δ' αὐτὰ ὡς ἦν δυνατὸς ἕκαστος. [Matthew arranged the sayings in the Hebrew language {or: in the Hebrew manner of discourse}, and each translated them as he was able.] Text cited according to Eusebius, *The Ecclesiastical History* 3.39.15–16 (edition by Kirsopp Lake, LCL). Irenaeus, at least, interprets this information about Matthew as a reference to Matthew's proclamation of the Gospel among the Jewish people (Ὁ μὲν δὴ Ματθαῖος ἐν τοῖς Ἑβραίοις τῇ ἰδίᾳ αὐτῶν διαλέκτῳ καὶ γραφὴν ἐξήνεγκεν εὐαγγελίου [*Adv. haer.* 3.1.1; cited by Eusebius *Hist. eccl.* 5.8.2–4]).

[97] The lack of order in Mk is thus explained by Mark's dependence on the preaching of Peter. Papias's comments concerning the text of Mt are more problematic, but seem to indicate that the present text of Mt is judged difficult to interpret because of its

The actual authorship ascriptions and apostolic connections attributed by Papias to the texts of Mk and Mt obscure the original social and literary context in which these texts emerged.[98] The original anonymity of both Mk and Mt reflects the absorption of the author's voice into the worship and early preaching of the Christian communities that were based on the oral traditions about Jesus.[99] These texts were written within a context in which early Christian communities were attempting to interpret their traditions about Jesus vis-à-vis the Jewish scriptures' account of God's actions in history for God's people.[100] Such narratives were not intended for outsiders,[101] but for religious communities conscious of God's actions in the past and present for them. The traditions about Jesus thus committed to writing were not related by an authorial 'I' but an implicit 'we' of the early followers of Jesus who preserved traditions about Jesus.[102] Such written texts probably circulated under the authority of the oral tradition about Jesus, not the relationship of the author to the apostles.[103] The original anonymity of written texts about Jesus in the context of early Christian communities correlates

---

connection to Hebrew discourse (either in terms of language or manner of composition; Papias may intend an assessment of the Jewish perspective of Mt).

[98] Although the reliability of these ascriptions to Matthew and Mark continues to be defended (see, e.g., Gundry, *Mark*, pp. 1026-45; Luz [*Matthew 1-7*, pp. 94-95] acknowledges the difficulties in assessing the information reported by Papias, but does not accept its reliability), the problems have not been resolved. The reliability of Papias for historical information about the origin of these texts is no better than the oral sources on which he claims to be dependent—sources about which little is known (cf. Eusebius *Hist. eccl.* 3.39.15). In any case, Papias is not a careful sifter of traditions, but an indiscriminate collector of stories (see Eusebius *Hist. eccl.* 3.39.2-17). His interest in reporting the information about Mk and Mt is to situate his own work on the sayings of Jesus in relation to other texts known to him. The origin of the attributions to Matthew and Mark remains as obscure as the origin of these texts themselves in early Christianity.

[99] The author of neither Mt nor Mk identifies himself or herself in these texts. The document Q was probably written anonymously as well.

[100] See Mk 1:1-2; Mt 1:1; cf. Lk 1:1, in which πεπληροφορημένων perhaps suggests that the narratives of the many have their point of departure in the fulfillment of Jewish scripture (cf. Lk 24:44).

[101] Schüssler Fiorenza ('Miracles, Mission, and Apologetics: An Introduction,' pp. 1-26) emphasizes the "public-societal dimension of Christian literature." This dimension does not in itself resolve the question of the intended audience of early Christian literature in general or Lk-Acts in particular.

[102] See especially the 'we' in Jn 1:14; 3:11; 21:24. Note the authority of the ἐκκλησία as a gathering of the followers of Jesus to exercise the authority of Jesus in Mt 18:15-18 (cf. 16:18-19).

[103] Neither the author of Mk nor Mt claims apostolic authority for their text. In contrast, compare Lk 1:2 and the addition to Jn in 21:24.

well with the early Christian conceptual world determined by oral traditions about Jesus and the religious authority of the Septuagint—that is, a religious outlook on history rooted in the Jewish sense of community as the people of God.[104] The comments of Papias on the authorship of Mt and Mk shift the authority of the text from the community experiencing the Gospel of God's salvation to an apostle preaching the Gospel.

The social and literary context in which Lk-Acts was written presupposes this shift. The texts that Irenaeus knows as the Gospel according to Luke and the Acts of the Apostles were not written anonymously in the strict sense. The author speaks in his own voice in the prologue to the narrative (compare also Acts 1:1), addressing a literary patron.[105] Further, the author's literary intentions are determined by prior Christian written texts (Lk 1:1–4) over which he asserts his own interpretive authority (not the authority of a community) according to Hellenistic standards of knowledge about the past.[106] Lk-Acts does not emerge out of the anonymity of public worship of a Christian church community, but out of the intellectual inquiry of an individual, the authorial 'I,' into apostolic traditions.[107] In speaking with his own voice, the author shifts the literary context of his work from the anonymous interpretive voice of early Christian communities rooted in Judaism to the authoritative voice of an author writing a Hellenistic narrative that is specifically Christian. The author is self-consciously a Christian writer working within the context of Hellenistic literary culture. The traditions of Jesus are no longer conceived as part of an anonymous narrative whose authority belongs to the Christian community, but rather as pieces of the Christian past whose ordering into a narrative depends on the authority of an author writing according to the standards of truth for history in Hellenistic literary culture.[108]

---

[104] Hengel ('The Titles of the Gospels and the Gospel of Mark,' p. 73) acknowledges that Jewish texts tended to be written anonymously, but dismisses this much too easily as an explanation for the anonymity of Mt and Mk. The beginning of both Mt and Mk reflect a religious outlook determined by the Septuagint.

[105] Hengel ('The Titles of the Gospels and the Gospel of Mark,' p. 73) points out that literary productions in the Graeco-Roman world tended not to be written anonymously, in contrast to the practice in Judaism.

[106] See chapter 3 under *The Prefaces of Lk-Acts*.

[107] See especially Lk 1:2. Note also the inquiry of Papias into apostolic tradition as the basis for his own composition in five volumes of the *Sayings of the Lord Explained* (Eusebius *Hist. eccl.* 3.39.1–17).

[108] More precise points on the genre of Lk-Acts will be developed in chapter 3 below.

Although the author does not identify himself by name, he was certainly known to his patron, Theophilus, and those to whom he distributed a copy of his work.[109] The contrast in the prologue to Lk between the 'I' of the author and the 'many' of other attempts to write an account of the words and deeds of Jesus (see Acts 1:1) indicates that the author had no intention of remaining anonymous. In fact, his primary narrative source may have already been attributed to Mark.[110] If so, the text of Lk would have been from the beginning identified with its author by his original audience, especially in relation to the text of Mk. Furthermore, the text of Lk was most likely passed on in relation to other texts that were already identified by author so that the name of the actual author of Lk-Acts would have been readily preserved in the transmission of Lk. The tradition of authorship connected with Lk-Acts cannot be easily dismissed as inauthentic.[111]

The attribution of Lukan authorship to the text of Lk does not presuppose its circulation with the text of Acts. The oft-repeated claim

---

[109] See comments by von Campenhausen, *The Formation of the Christian Bible*, p.126, n. 92; Dibelius, *Studies in the Acts of the Apostles*, p. 104.

[110] The date for the composition of Lk-Acts, which has been argued to be as early as 60 or as late as the middle of the second century, cannot be resolved with certainty. The author's conceptual similarities with Papias (in terms of the investigation of apostolic traditions) and self-conscious orientation toward Hellenistic culture, however, suggest a date in the second century. Since a date after 110 for Lk-Acts is plausible, there is no reason to suppose the author received the text of Mk anonymously. (In contrast to Lk-Acts, Mt preserves the sense of authorial anonymity of Mk and may have been written earlier than Lk and received Mk unattributed to an author. Papias comments on both Mt and Mk, but does not mention Lk.) There is, perhaps, an implicit criticism of the author of Mk in the portrayal of John Mark in Acts 13:13; 15:36–40. His unreliability leads to his separation from the Pauline mission, with the result that Mark disappears with Barnabas from the narrative of Acts and is certainly not a witness of the arrival of the gospel in Rome with Paul. (Contrast Col 4:10.) On the portrayal of John Mark in Lk-Acts, see Black, 'The Presentation of John Mark in the Acts of the Apostles,' pp. 235–54; also *Mark: Images of an Apostolic Interpreter*, pp. 25–44.

[111] The preservation of authentic traditions of authorship for texts from antiquity without an explicit naming of the author in the text itself is hardly noteworthy. Furthermore, Marcion's unascribed edited version of Lk does not prove that the text came to him without an attribution of authorship any more than the failure to identify the πολλοί in Lk 1:1 indicates these texts were unattributed. Since Marcion adopted only one written gospel, neither he nor his followers had any need of a designation presupposing a collection of gospels. Moreover, to the extent that this edited version of Lk was taken by Marcion to preserve the true content of the Gospel of Jesus, Marcion himself is the author of the text as it stands in his collection of Christian scriptures in relation to the Pauline letters. Noteworthy in this regard is that Marcion's gospel lacked the first two chapters of the text of Lk and thus the prologue in which the author identifies himself in relation to the apostles and other texts about Jesus.

that the tradition of Lukan authorship depends on an inference from the collection of Pauline letters in relation to the 'we' of the narrative of Acts is unnecessary.[112] Instead, it is more likely that the Pauline letters were mined for information about an otherwise unknown Luke after the connection between the Gospel of Luke and the Acts of the Apostles had been made. We can see this process in Irenaeus himself.

Irenaeus probably had no traditional information about the Luke who wrote Lk-Acts. Instead, Irenaeus himself supplies the key biographical information about the author. According to Irenaeus, this Luke is one and the same with the Luke mentioned in the Pauline letter corpus: "Luke also, the companion of Paul, recorded in a book the Gospel preached by him."[113] Irenaeus knows little more than this about him, and he makes this statement in the context of his defense of the apostolic origin of the four gospels in his fourfold canon.

In what Irenaeus presents in *Adv. haer.* 3.1.1 as known to all about the composition of the four canonical gospels, Irenaeus is not simply repeating information from his sources, but is constructing a new set of historical relationships. For example, Irenaeus is dependent on Papias for most of his information about Mt and Mk. However, Irenaeus interprets the information from Papias in light of his fourfold gospel canon and the importance of the church at Rome. He describes Mt and Mk as written gospels. Further, he interprets Papias's comment concerning the composition of Mt in the 'Hebrew dialect' as a reference to Matthew's mission 'among the Hebrews,'[114] a mission which he correlates with the preaching of Peter *and Paul* in Rome.[115] Thus, Papias's bare literary descriptions of the texts of Mt and Mk have become for Irenaeus part of the coordinated spread of the Gospel of God throughout the world based on the preaching of the apostles. The connection of Paul to the preaching of Peter at Rome allows Irenaeus to connect the composition of Lk to that of Mk at Rome, one gospel based on the preaching of Peter and one gospel based on the preaching of Paul.[116] Without

---

[112] See especially Col 4:14; 2 Tim 4:11; Phlm 23; Acts 16:10–17; 20:5–21:18; 27:1–28:16.

[113] *Adv. haer.* 3.1.1. See note 29 above for the Greek text of this passage. See also 3.14.1–3.15.1.

[114] Papias: Ματθαῖος μὲν οὖν Ἑβραΐδι διαλέκτῳ τὰ λόγια συνετάξατο; Irenaeus: Ὁ μὲν δὴ Ματθαῖος ἐν τοῖς Ἑβραίοις τῇ ἰδίᾳ αὐτῶν διαλέκτῳ καὶ γραφὴν ἐξήνεγκεν εὐαγγελίου.

[115] Ὁ μὲν δὴ Ματθαῖος ἐν τοῖς Ἑβραίοις τῇ ἰδίᾳ αὐτῶν διαλέκτῳ καὶ γραφὴν ἐξήνεγκεν εὐαγγελίου, τοῦ Πέτρου καὶ τοῦ Παύλου ἐν Ῥώμῃ εὐαγγελιζομένων καὶ θεμελιούντων τὴν ἐκκλησίαν.

[116] There is no need to suggest, as does Haenchen (*The Acts of the Apostles*, p. 9), that this assertion by Irenaeus that the Gospel according to Luke is based on the preaching

reporting anything more about the composition of Lk, Irenaeus goes on to report that afterward John the disciple of the Lord published a gospel during his residence at Ephesus in Asia. This statement about Jn appears to be a conflation of two traditions known to Irenaeus, that of the apostle John's authorship of Jn and that of John's stay in Ephesus.[117] There is no evidence that prior to Irenaeus these two bits of tradition about John were connected, and even after Irenaeus there is concerning Jn, relative to the traditions reported by Irenaeus about the other gospels, quite a bit of variance. The overall goal of Irenaeus's interpretive reporting of this information about Mt, Mk, Lk, and Jn is to connect them together into a unified proclamation of the Gospel by the apostles. The temporal indicators, which Irenaeus supplies, give a sense of historical coherence to the production of these four gospels.

What, then, can be said about his claims concerning the author of Lk? Of the four gospels, Irenaeus presents the fewest details about the circumstances of the composition of Lk, and what he does relate about the author Luke is nothing more than what Irenaeus elsewhere deduces from the narrative of Acts and the corpus of Pauline letters.

> But that this Luke was inseparable from Paul, and his fellow-laborer in the Gospel, he himself clearly evinces, not as a matter of boasting, but as bound to do so by the truth itself. For he says ... "we came to Troas" ... "we endeavored to go into Macedonia"... "we spoke to the women who had assembled" ... "we sailed from Philippi after the days of unleavened bread, and came to Troas, where we stayed seven days"...[118]

Irenaeus goes on with evidence from the Pauline letters concerning this Luke:

> As Luke was present at all these occurrences, he carefully noted them down in writing, so that he cannot be convicted of falsehood or boastfulness, because all these [particulars] proved both that he was senior to all those who now teach otherwise, and that he was not ignorant of the truth. That he was not merely a follower, but also a fellow-laborer of the apostles, but especially Paul, Paul has himself declared also in the Epistles, saying:

---

of the gospel by Paul is derived from passages in the Pauline letters in which Paul speaks of "his gospel." The inference that Lk contains the preaching of the gospel by Paul requires only the identification of the author of Lk as Luke the companion of Paul. Irenaeus is making inferences based on supposed historical circumstances; he is not attempting to expand the content of Paul's gospel as presupposed in his letters.

[117] For a detailed discussion of the issues associated with the authorship of the fourth gospel, see Barrett, *The Gospel According to St. John*, pp. 100–134; Hengel, *The Johannine Question*, pp. 2–5, 74–108; idem, *Die johanneische Frage*, pp. 13–25, 204–74.

[118] *Adv. haer.* 3.14.1.

"Demas has forsaken me, ... and is departed to Thessalonica; Crescens to Galatia, Titus to Dalmatia. Only Luke is with me." From this he shows that he was always attached to and inseparable from him. And again he says, in the Epistle to the Colossians: "Luke, the beloved physician, greets you." But surely if Luke, who always preached in company with Paul, and is called by him "the beloved," and with him performed the work of an evangelist, and was entrusted to hand down to us a Gospel, learned nothing different from him, as has been pointed out from his words, how can these men, who were never attached to Paul, boast that they have learned hidden and unspeakable mysteries?

This defense of Luke as a reliable witness to the message proclaimed by Paul takes place in the context of Irenaeus's use of the narrative of Acts to refute those who allege that Paul alone knew the truth of the Gospel. This defense of Luke is but a continuation of his argument for the unity of apostolic proclamation of the Gospel reliably preserved in the fourfold gospel canon begun in *Adv. haer.* 3.1.1. Yet, whereas Irenaeus relates incidental details from tradition about Mt, Mk, and Jn in 3.1.1, he conveys nothing about Lk other than that which is directly related to his own apologetic interests and which can be deduced from the texts he construes as scripture. Irenaeus's claims about the author of Lk, that (1) he was a companion of Paul and (2) he recorded the Gospel preached by Paul, appear to be biographical details Irenaeus has supplied for an otherwise unknown Luke. Irenaeus has identified this Luke on the basis of the Acts of the Apostles read alongside his collection of gospels and Pauline letters (including the Pastorals). Remarkably, Irenaeus reports nothing about Luke that cannot be deduced from *his* canon based on the assumption that Luke the author of Lk-Acts is the same Luke who was the companion of Paul mentioned in the Pauline letters.[119] Irenaeus's assertions about the author of Lk and Acts are pointedly

---

[119] After Irenaeus, the biography of this Luke is filled out. The old gospel prologue to the Gospel according to Luke (see note 82 above) adds specific biographical details about this Luke, including his place of origin (Antioch), his manner of life (unmarried and without child), age at death, and place of burial. Eusebius (*Hist. eccl.* 3.4.6) reports the tradition that Luke was from Antioch, but not the other biographical details contained in the old gospel prologue. There is no reason to suppose that any of this information is reliable. His place of origin may be an inference from the importance of Antioch in the narrative of Acts, his manner of life an inference from expectations for a follower of Paul, and the details associated with his death intended simply to fill out his biography—though the connection of his place of death and the writing of his gospel to Greece may be inferences from the prominence Macedonia and Achaea have in the narrative of Acts and in the Pauline letters. Rather than reliable information, the old gospel prologue represents an expansion of the information supplied by Irenaeus about

intended to refute the claims of the heretics, but depend primarily on the narrative of Acts and the deutero-Pauline text of 2 Timothy, both of which were unknown or unused by his opponents. The connection between the author of Lk-Acts and Luke the companion of Paul seems to have arisen in the context of Irenaeus's attempt to create a unified apostolic tradition of the proclamation of the Gospel over against heresy in the early church.[120] In fact, Irenaeus readily introduces similar connections elsewhere to strengthen his construction of a normative ecclesiastical tradition over against heresy.[121]

The supposition that Irenaeus himself is responsible for conflating Luke the otherwise unknown author of Lk-Acts and Luke the companion of Paul is strengthened by two further considerations. First, in *Adv. haer.* 3.15.1, Irenaeus turns from those who elevate Paul to those who reject Paul.

> But again, we allege the same against those who do not recognize Paul as an apostle: that they should either reject the other words of the Gospel which we have come to know through Luke alone, and not make use of them...

The implication of this statement is that there are Christians who make use of the Gospel according to Luke, though they reject the apostle Paul. This would seem to presuppose that such Christians do not associate the text of Lk with Paul and thus must not be aware that the author was supposedly a companion of Paul and recorded Paul's gospel. Irenaeus himself describes Luke at one point in very general

---

Luke probably based largely on further inferences from Acts and the Pauline letters. The modern discussion of 'Luke the physician' is but a continuation of the process begun by Irenaeus.

[120] The general tendency among the church fathers to conflate separate individuals with common names is evident, e.g., in the identification of Clement the companion of Paul (Phil 4:3) with Clement of Rome who wrote the letter to the Corinthians. That these are one and the same person is reported by Eusebius (*Hist. eccl.* 3.15), who probably depends on Origen (*Commentary on John* 6:36) for this information. See Williamson, *Eusebius. The History of the Church*, p. 124, n. 4. Origen also equates the Hermas of Rom. 16:14 with the Hermas of the *Shepherd of Hermas*. See his *Commentary on Romans* 10:31. See Hahneman, *The Muratorian Fragment and the Development of the Canon*, p. 47.

[121] See, e.g., his connection of Papias to Polycarp and to the apostle John (*Adv. haer.* 5.33.4, cited in Eusebius *Hist. eccl.* 3.39.1; see Barrett, *The Gospel According to St. John*, p. 105). See also his connection of the Simon of Acts 8 with the tradition of a Simon at Rome in a report he received from Justin (compare *Adv. haer.* 1.23 with *1 Apol.* 1.26; see note 22 above). See also Haenchen (*The Acts of the Apostles*, p. 536, n. 5) on the identity of Sosthenes in Acts 18 and 1 Corinthians 1 for the problem of making false connections based on a similarity of names. On the problem of identifying Sosthenes in Acts 18, see chapter 4 below on *Corinth*.

terms merely as a follower of the apostles,[122] a description that probably derives from Lk 1:1–4[123] and does not depend on the narrative of Acts.

Second, there is no reason to suppose that Marcion chose to edit Lk because the author was supposedly connected to Paul.[124] In terms of the four gospels of Irenaeus's canon, only Lk does not have almost insurmountable difficulties associated with its adoption. The close connection in widely known traditions of Mt, Mk, and Jn to apostles whom Marcion rejected likely removed them from any possible consideration. On the other hand, the paucity of tradition associated with the author of Lk would have made the text of Lk a good candidate for Marcion's literary ax.[125] By excising the prologue, Lk 1:1–4,[126] Marcion removed the gospel from any connection to the apostles (Lk 1:2) who had falsified the gospel and was left with a narrative that probably had no traditional connection to any single apostle prior to Irenaeus's response to Marcion's canon.[127]

Notwithstanding Irenaeus's suggestions to the contrary, the ascription of Lk-Acts to a certain Luke in early Christianity does not resolve the question of the historical reliability of the narrative or its portrait of Paul.[128] Not only does Irenaeus's identification of the author of Lk-Acts as a companion of Paul go beyond what can legitimately be inferred

---

[122] *Adv. haer.* 3.10.1; note 3.14.1: "*That [Luke] was not merely a follower, but also a fellow laborer of the apostles*, but especially of Paul, Paul has himself declared also in the Epistles…" (italics added). Cf. the old gospel prologue to Luke (see Aland, *Synopsis Quattuor Evangeliorum*, p. 533) and Eusebius *Hist. eccl.* 3.4.6.

[123] See, e.g., Haenchen, *The Acts of the Apostles*, pp. 9–12.

[124] Against Hengel, 'The Titles of the Gospels and the Gospel of Mark,' p. 69. Harnack (*Marcion: The Gospel of the Alien God*, pp. 28–29) does not attribute Marcion's selection of Lk to the author's connection to Paul, but rather to the unacceptablility of his other choices.

[125] That Marcion's options were limited to these four gospels is probably an anachronistic assumption, though the emergence of the fourfold canon in response to Marcion would suggest that these four were indeed gaining prominence in the middle of the second century. Other texts identified as gospels in the second century had apostolic associations that would have diminished their appeal to Marcion: for example, the Gospel of Thomas and the Gospel of Peter.

[126] Marcion apparently rejected the entire first two chapters of Lk. The narratives of the birth of John and Jesus, heavily influenced by what Marcion could only see as Jewish corruptions of the Gospel, would have been unacceptable to him.

[127] There is no reason to suppose that Justin connected Lk to Paul. The claims by the author in Lk 1:1–4 would have been sufficient to establish the text as legitimately belonging with other texts classed as 'memoirs of the apostles.' Both Irenaeus and much later Eusebius describe Luke as a follower of the apostles in general, an inference derived from Lk 1:1–4. (See *Adv. haer.* 3.10.1; *Hist. eccl.* 3.4.6.)

[128] This question will be taken up in detail in the next two chapters.

from the text of Acts,[129] the author makes no claims in Lk 1:1–4 to be any closer to the events he narrates in Lk-Acts than is his patron Theophilus.[130] Since there is no evidence that prior to Irenaeus the authorship ascription of Lk-Acts was accompanied by any traditions of the author's association with particular apostles, especially Paul, there is no reason (apart from Irenaeus's apologetic interests) to conclude that the Luke of Philemon and the deutero-Pauline tradition was the author of Lk-Acts. Nevertheless, for Irenaeus the supposed connection between the otherwise unknown author of Lk-Acts and the Luke who accompanied Paul is crucial for his defense of the Gospel proclaimed by all the apostles. Irenaeus's Luke unites the fourfold gospel canon and the Pauline letters in the Irenaean collection of scriptural witnesses to the Gospel. In Irenaeus's defense of the teaching of the one, true, universal church, Lk-Acts has become 'Pauline.'[131]

Irenaeus's title for the second volume of Lk-Acts attributed to this 'Pauline' Luke is secondary[132] and depends on two developments: (1) a differentiation between the narrative of Lk and the narrative of Acts in terms of content based on the emergence of texts about Jesus as gospels in Christian communities as a distinct Christian genre (that is, εὐαγγέλιον and πράξεις as distinct types of narratives); and (2) a reading of the narrative of Acts in the matrix of a construction of apostolic unity in the preaching of the Gospel (that is, the qualification of πράξεις with τῶν ἀποστόλων).

In antiquity, πράξεις was often used to describe the content of writings containing accounts of the deeds of noteworthy individuals.[133] For example, Diodorus describes the content of his first book as πράξεις τῶν

---

[129] On the author's knowledge about Paul, see chapter 4 below.

[130] See chapter 3 under *Paul's Farewell Speech and the Literary Paulinism of Lk-Acts* on the author's understanding of the handing over of tradition from the servants of the word to the present, the 'us' of Lk 1:2. The author's incorporation of the 'we' in Acts conveys the impression of an eyewitness account, but there is no need to suppose that this eyewitness is the author rather than a reliable, but unnamed, source. The improbability that an eyewitness composed the portrayal of Paul in the narrative of Acts has been pointed out repeatedly. See chapter 4 below, especially on *Philippi*.

[131] Writing shortly after Irenaeus, Clement of Alexander knows Luke wrote the Acts of the Apostles (*Stromata* 5.82.4) and goes so far as to say that Luke translated Hebrews into Greek for Paul (see Eusebius *Hist. eccl.* 6.14; Haenchen, *The Acts of the Apostles*, p. 12).

[132] Cf. Hengel (*Acts and the History of Earliest Christianity*, p. 36): "The title by which we know Acts ... does not do justice to its content and is therefore probably secondary ...."

[133] See BDAG, s.v. πρᾶξις; Maurer, πρᾶξις, *TDNT* 6.644; Wikenhauser, *New Testament Introduction*, pp. 324–25; idem, *Die Apostelgeschichte und ihr Geschichtswert*, pp. 94–104.

βασιλέων.¹³⁴ Josephus takes note of those who have recounted the deeds of Pompey (οἱ τὰς κατὰ Πομπήιον πράξεις ἀναγράψαντες).¹³⁵ The phrase (αἱ) πράξεις αὐτοῦ is used several times in the Greek translation of 2 Chronicles to describe the content of writings about certain individuals.¹³⁶ As a description of content, it could also be used as a title,¹³⁷ but does not reflect a distinct genre in antiquity in relation to, for example, history or biography. History was generally conceived to be about the important deeds of individuals,¹³⁸ and historical events could be ordered around a central historical figure.¹³⁹ Callisthenes, Alexander's court historian, apparently wrote a Πράξεις Ἀλεξάνδρου; Sosylus wrote of the exploits of Hannibal in Πράξεις Ἀννίβα.¹⁴⁰ As a term referring to the exploits of great individuals, however, it could be used to describe the content of works that were not histories in a generic sense. For example, Lucian compares the task of writing a βίος setting down the schemes of Alexander the false prophet with the task of writing down τὰς πράξεις of Alexander the son of Philip. One individual was, according to Lucian, as disreputable as the other was honorable in his deeds.¹⁴¹ The subject of *Pseudo-Callisthenes* (also known as *The Alexander Romance*) is the deeds (πράξεις) of Alexander, and the various titles for the work include βίος Ἀλεξάνδρου τοῦ Μακεδόνος or βίος Ἀλεξάνδρου τοῦ Μακεδόνος καὶ πράξεις.¹⁴² In early Christianity, πράξεις was a description of content that served as a title for narratives about the deeds of the apostles.¹⁴³ While Irenaeus can use *actus apostolorum* (πράξεις τῶν ἀποστόλων)

---

¹³⁴ Diodorus Siculus 3.1.1.

¹³⁵ *Antiquities* 14.68.

¹³⁶ 2 Chron 12:15; 13:22; 28:26 (LXX). The content of these writings is described in terms of both the words and deeds of the individual in question.

¹³⁷ On the use of a description of content as a title, see Hengel, 'The Titles of the Gospels and the Gospel of Mark,' p. 74.

¹³⁸ See Fornara, *The Nature of History in Ancient Greece and Rome*, pp. 91–98; cf. p. 63.

¹³⁹ Dihle, *A History of Greek Literature from Homer to the Hellenistic Period*, p. 221; cf. p. 290.

¹⁴⁰ See Wikenhauser, *New Testament Introduction*, p. 325; idem, *Die Apostelgeschichte und ihr Geschichtswert*, pp. 98–100.

¹⁴¹ τοσοῦτος εἰς κακίαν οὗτος, ὅσος εἰς ἀρετὴν ἐκεῖνος. See *Alexander the False Prophet* 1.

¹⁴² See von Lauenstein, *Der griechische Alexanderroman. Rezension Γ. Buch I*, pp. 2–3; see also Stoneman, *The Greek Alexander Romance*, pp. 17–32. Wikenhauser (*Die Apostelgeschichte und ihr Geschichtswert*, p. 103) draws an unwarranted distinction between what he calls *Praxeisliteratur* and biography, a distinction that confuses what was a description of content that could be applied to various types of works for a distinct literary genre in antiquity.

¹⁴³ The use of πράξεις as a description of content and thus as a title for narratives about the apostles is not a technical generic description in early Christianity and does not in itself resolve the question of the relation of Acts to the apocryphal acts nor

as a title for Acts,[144] elsewhere he describes the content of Acts as *de actibus et doctrina apostolorum* (περὶ τῶν τε πράξεων καὶ τῆς διδαχῆς τῶν ἀποστόλων).[145] Tertullian's description of the *Acts of Paul* as *Acta Pauli, quae perperam scripta sunt*[146] suggests that the title is an inaccurate description of the content: the *Acts of Paul* does not set forth what Paul did.[147]

The problem with Irenaeus's designation of the second half of the narrative of Lk-Acts as a πράξεις is not that this designation in itself is misleading as a description of the content of Acts, but that it is used contrastively with εὐαγγέλιον as a description of Lk and thus misconstrues the relationship of Acts to Lk. According to the author of Lk-Acts, he is writing a διήγησις (Lk 1:1), the first part of which he describes as an account περὶ πάντων ὧν ἤρξατο ὁ Ἰησοῦς ποιεῖν τε καὶ διδάσκειν (Acts 1:1). This is the verbal equivalent of Irenaeus's description of Acts as *de actibus et doctrina apostolorom* (περὶ τῶν τε πράξεων καὶ τῆς διδαχῆς τῶν ἀποστόλων). In other words, for the author of Lk-Acts, the content of the first volume of his work (Lk) is not characterized as an εὐαγγέλιον [Ἰησοῦ][148] but as a πράξεις Ἰησοῦ.[149]

Whereas πράξεις Ἰησοῦ would be a legitimate description of the content of the first volume of Lk-Acts, πράξεις τῶν ἀποστόλων is not an accurate description of the intention of the author for the second volume of Lk-Acts. In contrast to the implications of τῶν ἀποστόλων, Paul (the major character in the second half of the book) as portrayed in the narrative of Acts is not an apostle according to the requirements laid out in Acts 1:21–25.[150] Paul's status as an apostle is of very little

---

the question of the literary influences on the genre of these works (in terms of novel, biography, or history). On the relation of Acts to the apocryphal acts, see below under *Acts and the Apocryphal Acts in the Second Century*.

[144] *Adv. haer.* 3.13.3.

[145] *Adv. haer.* 3.15.1. See Rousseau and Doutreleau, *Irénée de Lyon. Contre les hérésies. Livre III*, 2.278–79.

[146] Evans, *Tertullian's Homily on Baptism*, p. 37: "Acts of Paul, which are falsely so named." Tertullian goes on to ask, "How could we believe that Paul should give a female power to teach and to baptize, when he did not allow a woman even to learn by her own right?"

[147] See below under *Acts and the Apocryphal Acts in the Second Century*.

[148] See Mk 1:1. See also note 90 above.

[149] Similarly, such a designation would be an accurate description of the content of Mk as well. On the close connection of the apocryphal acts to narratives about Jesus, see below under *Acts and the Apocryphal Acts in the Second Century*. The terms εὐαγγέλιον and πράξεις do not help sort out the literary relation between Lk-Acts, other narratives about Jesus, and other narratives about apostles in early Christianity.

[150] See chapter 4 under *Paul's Mission with Barnabas* on the incidental designation of

interest to the author of Lk-Acts. A number of other non-apostolic figures play an important role in the narrative: for example, Stephen, Philip, and James. Moreover, the narrative of Acts recounts neither the death of Peter nor the death of Paul, both 'acts' of great importance in other second-century accounts of the apostles.[151] The title 'Acts of the Apostles' completely obscures the author's intentions in the text. There is no need to look anywhere else than to the ecclesiastical interests of Irenaeus for this title, a title that served his apologetics against heresy and perfectly balanced his understanding of the fourfold gospel canon and the doctrine of the apostles (who all proclaimed the same Gospel). In the context of these ecclesiastical interests, the need to label this singular text as τῶν ἀποστόλων first arose in early Christianity.[152]

In short, the designation of Lk-Acts as the Gospel according to Luke and the Acts of the Apostles presupposes a reinterpretation of the narrative unity of Lk-Acts based on the different routes Lk and Acts took into the Irenaean canon, a canon in which they were reintegrated not as a single narrative but as two distinct narratives. In its reception, Lk did not replace but instead became part of a collection of similar texts, a collection treated as a reservoir of information about Jesus defining the Gospel for Christian communities. In this context, even the narrative integrity of Lk was compromised as it became a source for stories and sayings about Jesus to be pieced together with sayings and stories of Jesus from other gospels.[153] In Irenaeus's canon of four gospels, the individuality of the interpretive story of Lk-Acts and the authorial 'I' were submerged into a general conception of the Gospel as preserved in writings connected to apostles, in which context Lk became the Gospel according to Luke—a Luke identified by Irenaeus as the companion of Paul.

Paul as an apostle in Acts 14:4, 14.

[151] See below under *Acts and the Apocryphal Acts in the Second Century*.

[152] On the connection of the Acts of the Apostles to the apocryphal acts, see below. The Acts of the Apostles shares in common with the earliest apocryphal acts the title πράξεις, but differs from them in the general reference to the apostles rather than to the πράξεις of a specific apostle. If the title of the Acts of the Apostles had been created in analogy to the earliest apocryphal acts, 'Acts of Peter and Paul' would seem a more probable choice. Instead, the general reference to 'apostles' suggests the apologetic context in which this otherwise obscure text came to be used.

[153] Cf. Papias, who conceives of Mk as a somewhat disorganized collection of material about Jesus based on Peter's preaching and in need of supplementation with sayings of Jesus collected from other apostles.

This 'Pauline' Luke and the second half of Lk-Acts became important in disputes about heresy among Christian intellectuals at the end of the second century. In this context, the title 'Acts of the Apostles' becomes intelligible. Removed from the narrative unity of Lk-Acts and correlated with the fourfold canon of written gospels construed as collections of stories bearing witness to the Gospel, Acts was read as an account of (all) the apostles (including Paul) preaching the Gospel. The Acts of the Apostles so-called belongs to a very specific context in early Christianity: an intellectual response to heretical interpretations of the Gospel based on heretical constructions of (apostolic) Christian origins. The social setting of this dispute about true and heretical forms of Christianity, a dispute in which Irenaeus's 'Pauline' Luke and 'Acts of the Apostles' emerged, does not lie in specific Christian communities, but rather among competing Christian intellectuals. The title 'Acts of the Apostles' presupposes no correlation with the life of local Christian communities, Pauline or otherwise.

Acts and the Apocryphal Acts in the Second Century

This specifically defined context in which the Acts of the Apostles was read at the end of the second century, however, has been consistently obscured by the canonical status the text of Acts achieved after Irenaeus. The effect this status has had on understandings of the place of Acts in early Christianity is most clearly seen in the way comparisons have been carried out between the Acts of the Apostles and a group of texts sharing similar titles to that of the Acts of the Apostles, but eventually excluded from the canon: the so-called apocryphal acts, narratives about the adventures of apostles. Of particular interest in comparison to the Acts of the Apostles are the *Acts of Peter* and the *Acts of Paul*, two of the earliest of the apocryphal acts (probably written in the second half of the second century) and corresponding to Acts in the prominence of Peter and Paul, respectively. In the various efforts by scholars to reconstruct the center and periphery of Christianity in the second century, the Acts of the Apostles has regularly occupied a position in the center and the so-called apocryphal acts have been placed on the periphery. The language often used in comparing these texts is indicative of their relative positions: early/late, canonical/apocryphal, historical/novelistic and legendary, serious/popular, theological/entertaining, original/supplemental, orthodox/heretical. Such language of comparison has given the Acts of the Apostles a place of unwarranted prominence and importance in the life of early Christian communities in comparison to the apocryphal acts. Even when Acts has been considered late and unreliable, its stories about the apostles have been central in the reconstruction of early Christianity: F. C. Baur associated Acts with a grand synthesis in the second century of competing early Christian factions (defined as Petrine and Pauline!). Although the relative obscurity of Acts in the second century has often been noted, the text has generally been viewed as belonging to the center of Christianity, whereas the apocryphal acts have tended to be viewed as secondary developments of πράξεις literature in one way or another dependent on canonical Acts.[154] The principal points of this literary and social/historical comparison and reconstruction of the respective places of canonical Acts and the apocryphal acts in second-century Christianity need to be reconsidered.

Tertullian is the first church father to comment on an 'apocryphal' act. Writing concerning baptism, he warns against following Thecla's example in the *Acts of Paul*.[155]

> But if certain Acts of Paul, which are falsely so named, claim the example of Thecla for allowing women to teach and to baptize, let men know that in Asia the presbyter who compiled that document, thinking to add of his own to Paul's reputation, was found out, and though he professed he had done it for love of Paul, was deposed from his position. How could we believe that Paul should give a female power to teach and to baptize, when he did not allow a woman even to learn by her own right? *Let them keep silence*, he says, *and ask their husbands at home*.[156]

Tertullian thus levels two criticisms against the *Acts of Paul*. First, Tertullian claims that the author of the *Acts of Paul* was subjected to ecclesiastical censure somewhere in Asia for passing off false stories about Paul. Second, Tertullian argues that the example of Thecla contradicts Paul's own teaching in 1 Cor 14:34–35. In contrast to these two criticisms of the *Acts of Paul*, Tertullian in the same treatise appeals to the narrative of Acts as a reliable account of the actions of the apostles and their

---

[154] Cf. note 176 below.
[155] *De baptismo* 17. Whether Tertullian has the entire work or only the section of the *Acts of Paul* concerning Paul and Thecla (which by the fourth century was circulating independently of the *Acts of Paul*; see MacDonald, 'Apocryphal and Canonical Narratives about Paul,' p. 57) cannot be established with certainty. His comments concerning the motives of the author of the work suggest he is referring to a larger text than just the section of the *Acts of Paul* concerning Thecla.
[156] Translation by Evans, *Tertullian's Homily on Baptism*, p. 37.

followers.[157] His criticisms of the *Acts of Paul* appear at first to be historical arguments against the reliability of the *Acts of Paul*. In fact, however, they are tendentious arguments for a particular reading of the historical Paul.

What Tertullian reports as a judicial verdict in some otherwise unidentified church against the (unnamed) author of the *Acts of Paul* cannot be taken at face value. The *Acts of Paul* was widely known in the early church. Eusebius, writing in the first quarter of the 4th century, reports that most are familiar with the *Acts of Paul*, though he himself does not rank it with those writings "which according to the Church are true, genuine, and recognized."[158] Nevertheless, the *Acts of Paul* is, according to Eusebius, to be distinguished from the writings published by the heretics (including the *Acts of Peter*, *Acts of John*, *Acts of Andrew*, and acts of other apostles).[159] Eusebius gives no indication that he knows the report of ecclesiastical condemnation against the *Acts of Paul* passed on by Tertullian (nor does anyone else in early Christianity).[160] Further, there is no tradition of authorship associated with the *Acts of Paul* in the early church. The text appears to have been composed anonymously. That Tertullian somehow has reliable information about the author, information that no one else seems to have, is therefore doubtful. At best Tertullian is passing on a confused report of an ecclesiastical response to the introduction or use of the *Acts of Paul* in some local

---

[157] See, e.g., *De baptismo* 18.

[158] See *Hist. eccl.* 3.25. The translation is by Williamson.

[159] On the *Acts of Peter*, see *Hist. eccl.* 3.3. Eusebius's categories for writings in 3.25 are somewhat confusing. He appears to present four categories: recognized, disputed, spurious, and heretical. However, his categories 'disputed' and 'spurious' actually overlap and in fact reflect Eusebius's own judgment on writings that are disputed. Those disputed works that Eusebius rejects, he classes as spurious. Thus, Eusebius offers three categories, recognized, disputed, and heretical, but offers his own opinion on those books considered disputed, classing as spurious the ones he rejects. The *Acts of Paul* is for Eusebius spurious. The epistles of James, Jude, 2 Peter, and 2 and 3 John are disputed. In short, Eusebius's canon list indicates that the *Acts of Paul* is familiar to most, though not accepted by all as canonical. The list of holy scripture in the 6th century codex Claromontanus (a list probably going back to the third or fourth century) includes the *Acts of Paul*.

[160] Tertullian wrote in Latin from North Africa. There is no reason to suppose that Eusebius would have had access to Tertullian's report when he composed his history of the church. On the other hand, that Tertullian had information about the censure of the *Acts of Paul* from the Greek East that Eusebius failed to uncover seems unlikely. Eusebius apparently went to great lengths to report any information about ecclesiastical use and censure of early Christian texts. If he had been aware that an ecclesiastical verdict had been rendered against the *Acts of Paul*, he would have reported it.

church community. Perhaps some presbyter in Asia was censured for using the *Acts of Paul* alongside other writings of Paul as scripture.[161]

In fact, Tertullian seems to be given to exaggeration of ecclesiastical verdicts against texts he dislikes. Speaking against the *Shepherd of Hermas*, he comments in one place that the book has been rejected by every church synod.[162] There is no corroborating evidence for this statement in other early Christian writers, and Tertullian himself appears to have been more receptive of the book in his earlier writings.[163] His harsh criticism of the *Shepherd of Hermas* in *De pudicitia* appears to be a rhetorical ploy to controvert the widespread popularity of the book.[164] Likewise, his report of an ecclesiastical judgment against the author of the *Acts of Paul* appears to be, at the very least, rhetorically exaggerated.

Tertullian's comments on the author of the *Acts of Paul* are noteworthy for the positive portrayal of the author's motive ("for love of Paul") and social status in the church (presbyter). Connecting the text to such an author is hardly a resounding condemnation (the author is not even called a heretic, a popular epithet hurled against the authors of unacceptable texts).[165] Instead, Tertullian's characterization of the author suggests a rather positive reception of the *Acts of Paul*, if not by Tertullian, then by others on whom Tertullian is dependent for this information. Indeed, that Tertullian even bothers to refute a hypothetical use of the *Acts of Paul* to support women carrying out baptism suggests the popularity of the text.[166] Tertullian's readiness to pass on this

---

[161] For other disputes about what should and should not be read in church meetings, see the ecclesiastical verdict rendered against the use of the Gospel of Peter reported by Eusebius (*Hist. eccl.* 6.12.2). Note also the comment in the Muratorian canon that the *Shepherd of Hermas* is useful for private reading, but is not to be read in church.

[162] *De pudicitia* 10; see Hahneman, *The Muratorian Fragment and the Development of the Canon*, p. 62.

[163] See *De oratione* 16; Hahneman, *The Muratorian Fragment and the Development of the Canon*, pp. 61–62.

[164] On the reception of the *Shepherd of Hermas* in the early church, see Hahneman, *The Muratorian Fragment and the Development of the Canon*, pp. 61–71.

[165] See, e.g., Eusebius *Hist. eccl.* 3.25 on the texts produced by 'heretics.'

[166] MacDonald (*The Legend and the Apostle*, pp. 17–53) has argued that Tertullian's statement is evidence for a group of women who are using the story to legitimate ministries of women that subvert male ecclesiastical authority (see, e.g., p. 19). That Tertullian knew such a group of women is doubtful. Tertullian's treatise *De baptismo* begins as a polemic against a woman who rejects baptism. (Paragraph 1: "And in fact a certain female viper from the Cainite sect, who recently spent some time here, carried off a good number with her exceptionally pestilential doctrine, making a particular point of demolishing baptism." Translation by Evans, *Tertullian's Homily on Baptism*.) In paragraph 17, he alludes to the teaching of this woman in a hypothetical, rhetorical

dubious report of ecclesiastical censure of the supposed author of the *Acts of Paul* is due to his argument against the *Acts of Paul* on grounds of the proper (for him) role of women in the church.

The actions of Thecla are completely unacceptable to Tertullian, and Tertullian cites Paul himself to refute the example of Thecla. His appeal to 1 Cor 14:34–35 appears to establish a comparison between the historical Paul and an unreliable story about Paul and Thecla preserved in the *Acts of Paul*. Instead, his choice of 1 Cor 14:34–35 (rather than a text like Gal 3:26–28) reflects a reading of Paul through the lens of an ecclesiastical tradition that suppressed the role of women in Paul's actual theology and ministry.[167] This tradition readily accepted the Paul of the Pastoral Epistles and the Acts of the Apostles, while rejecting the Paul of the *Acts of Paul*, not because the former corresponded better to the 'historical' Paul of the letters, but because the former supported an acceptable image of Paul for defining ecclesiastical ('apostolic') tradition.[168] Whereas for Tertullian the Acts of the Apostles has a venerable connection to the Gospel according to Luke and presents a reliable account of the actions of the apostles, the *Acts of Paul* can be questioned

---

exaggeration of the opposite extreme to which some other woman might go to corrupt baptism ("But the impudence of that woman who assumed the right to teach is evidently not going to arrogate to her the right to baptize as well—unless perhaps some new serpent appears, like that original one [*nisi si quae nova bestia venerit similis pristinae*], so that as that woman abolished baptism, some other should of her own authority confer it.") The immediately following, crucial sentence makes no reference to a group of women: "But if certain Acts of Paul, which are falsely so named, claim [*quod si quae Acta Pauli ... defendunt*—on Acta Pauli as the subject of the clause, see Evans, *Tertullian's Homily on Baptism*, p. 100] the example of Thecla for allowing women to teach and to baptize, let men know that in Asia the presbyter who compiled that document..." Tertullian is refuting a hypothetical possibility, not an actuality, and no individual or community (whether associated with women or otherwise) known to Tertullian can be reconstructed from Tertullian's comment.

[167] The addition of the Pastoral letters to the Pauline corpus reflects this perspective. 1 Cor 14:34–35 has itself come under criticism as non-Pauline (see, e.g., Conzelmann, *1 Corinthians*, p. 246). See MacDonald (*The Legend and the Apostle*, pp. 54–77) for a possible relation of the Pastoral letters to the stories in the *Acts of Paul* concerning the role of women in the church.

[168] Problems with the narrative of the Acts of the Apostles were, therefore, resolved in other ways. Immediately after rejecting the example of Thecla in the *Acts of Paul*, Tertullian turns to the example of Philip and Paul as presented in the Acts of the Apostles. The baptisms administered by Philip (Acts 8:38) and to Paul (Acts 9:18) present difficulties for Tertullian's concern not to administer baptism too hastily. The Acts of the Apostles, however, firmly belongs to Tertullian's canon of scripture, and so he explains in terms of the peculiar historical circumstances why the example of Philip and Paul cannot be followed in all cases concerning baptism.

both in terms of its authorship and content.¹⁶⁹ Ultimately, this verdict against the *Acts of Paul* prevailed, despite evidence for a widespread popularity of the text. Ironically, in contrast to the widespread familiarity with the *Acts of Paul* suggested by Eusebius,¹⁷⁰ about eighty years after Eusebius wrote, Chrysostom produced a series of Homilies on Acts to counter a widespread ignorance of this book, some not even being aware of its existence (despite its firm place in the canon)!¹⁷¹

In the early manuscript tradition, Acts is often transmitted alone. When grouped with other texts, sometimes it is placed with the gospels,¹⁷² at other times with the Catholic Epistles.¹⁷³ This suggests that even after Eusebius Acts did not acquire a fixed position in the public life of the church.¹⁷⁴ That Acts came to be included in canon lists,

---

¹⁶⁹ Tertullian's interest in the authorship of the *Acts of Paul* corresponds with Irenaeus's emphasis on the historical trustworthiness of the Acts of the Apostles based on its authorship by Luke the companion of Paul and author of the Gospel according to Luke. For Irenaeus and those sharing his ecclesiastical interests, the Acts of the Apostles preserves an eyewitness account of early Christianity. Despite Irenaeus's insistence to the contrary, the Paul of Acts and the Paul of the Pauline letter collection do not easily 'fit' together. The problematic connection between these two images of Paul has repeatedly been obscured, from Irenaeus to the present, by the 'we' sections of Acts taken to be the author's eyewitness participation in the Pauline mission. See, e.g., *Adv. haer.* 3.14.1. (The author's relation to traditions about Paul will be taken up in chapter 4 below.) In at least one instance, the author of the *Acts of Paul* reveals more knowledge about the historical Paul than does the author of Lk-Acts. In contrast to the author of the *Acts of Paul*, who portrays Paul as actually writing a letter to the church at Corinth in imitation of the Pauline letters, the author of Lk-Acts displays little interest in any of the Pauline letters, much less a corpus of Pauline letters. τὰ πολλὰ γράμματα with reference to Paul in Acts 26:24 means 'higher learning' (cf. BDAG, s.v. γράμμα), attributed by Festus to Paul in the context of his defense before Agrippa. Note that in Acts 28:21 γράμματα means 'letters,' but refers only to letters from Judea. (The possibility that Paul wrote a letter to the Roman church prior to his arrival seems to be excluded by the narrative of his reception at Rome [28:15–31].) Though the author makes clear he is writing in the literary tradition of the Septuagint and other narratives about Jesus, he makes no attempt to write in the literary tradition of the Pauline corpus. Whether the author of Lk-Acts knew that Paul wrote letters cannot be determined, but the Paul of Acts is not a letter-writer. On the author's possible use of the Pauline letters as a source, see chapter 4 below.

¹⁷⁰ *Hist. eccl.* 3.25.

¹⁷¹ See *Homilies on Acts*, Homily 1. This ignorance may be a rhetorical exaggeration, but cf. Augustine, *Homilies on John*, Tractate vi.18, who also comments on the obscurity of the Acts of the Apostles.

¹⁷² E.g., 𝔓⁴⁵—3rd century.

¹⁷³ E.g., 𝔓⁷⁴—7th century. This grouping of Acts with the Catholic Epistles arose in the 4th century according to Aland and Aland, *The Text of the New Testament*, 2nd ed., p. 50.

¹⁷⁴ In the canon list preserved in the 6th century codex Claromontanus, Acts is listed

despite its relative unimportance in the life of early Christian communities, is a relic of its usefulness for imposing a certain interpretation upon scripture and ecclesiastical tradition. Canon lists are a means by which the ecclesiastical hierarchy introduced into the church a standard of center and periphery by which ecclesiastical truth could be measured. Such lists in early Christianity influenced which texts survived (that is, were copied in a culture where the vast majority of people did not have the ability to read and write). Although the Acts of the Apostles suddenly gained its authoritative status in the writings of Irenaeus at about the same time that the *Acts of Paul* and the *Acts of Peter* emerged,[175] about 150 years later Acts was firmly established in the canon list of Eusebius, whereas the *Acts of Paul* was considered spurious, and the *Acts of Peter* was placed among those books altogether wicked. The judgment of time has agreed with Eusebius: Acts has survived intact, the *Acts of Peter* and the *Acts of Paul* only in fragments. This result, however, is far from being a reflection of the relative prominence of Acts in relation to the *Acts of Peter* and the *Acts of Paul* in early Christianity: it derives from Irenaeus's use of canonical Acts to construct a unified apostolic history as the basis for his canon of four gospels and collection of Pauline letters.

The problem of comparing and locating Acts and the apocryphal acts in relation to one another and the larger context of early Christianity is tied to the characters in these texts. Tertullian rejected the *Acts of Paul* as the misguided portrayal of Paul by a devoted Paulinist. Irenaeus used the Paul of the Acts of the Apostles (and the 'Pauline' Luke) to construct a unified tradition of the apostolic proclamation of the Gospel defining the one true church, in which church the (one) Gospel proclaimed by all the apostles is preserved. In modern scholarship, F. C. Baur used Acts to reconstruct a synthesis of Pauline and Petrine forms of Christianity in the second century. Yet the actual difficulties of connecting the characters of Acts and the apocryphal acts to groups and trajectories of early forms of Christianity (whether under-

---

at the end.

[175] The *Acts of Peter* is attested by its use by the author of the *Acts of Paul*; see Schneemelcher, *New Testament Apocrypha*, rev. ed. [1991], 2.275. On the chronological priority of the *Acts of Peter* to the *Acts of Paul*, see Stoops, 'The *Acts of Peter* in Intertextual Context,' pp. 57–86. For a defense of the chronological priority of the *Acts of Paul*, see MacDonald, 'Which Came First? Intertextual Relationships Among the Apocryphal Acts of the Apostles,' pp. 11–42; cf. Pervo, 'Egging on the Chickens: A Cowardly Response to Dennis MacDonald and Then Some,' pp. 43–56.

stood in terms of true and heretical forms of Christianity or Pauline and Petrine factions) are formidable.

The literary relationship of the Acts of the Apostles to the apocryphal acts, suggested by their titles, is manifestly problematic.[176] Not only does the narrative of Acts not supply the framework for either the *Acts of Peter* or the *Acts of Paul*,[177] quite possibly the text of Acts emerged as the 'Acts of the Apostles' after the composition of the *Acts of Peter* and the *Acts of Paul*. Attempts to specify the literary relationship of the apocryphal acts to the Acts of the Apostles have tended to assume an importance for the latter work in the middle of the second century that cannot be established.[178] Literarily, the Acts of the Apostles differs from

---

[176] On πράξεις as a title for early Christian texts, see above under *Traditions of Authorship and Titles*. The repeated assertion that the latter assume knowledge of the former is, at least without substantial qualification, unwarranted. Conzelmann (*Acts of the Apostles*, p. xxxi), e.g., simply asserts without qualification that the *Acts of Peter* assumes the existence of Acts. On the complex relation between canonical Acts and the *Acts of Peter*, see Thomas, 'Canon and Antitype: The Relationship Between the *Acts of Peter* and the New Testament,' pp. 185–206. Pervo ('A Hard Act to Follow: The *Acts of Paul* and the Canonical Acts,' pp. 3–32) explains the literary relation between Acts and the *Acts of Paul* in terms of an attempt by the latter to correct and perhaps supplant the former. Contrast Bauckham ('The *Acts of Paul* as a Sequel to Acts,' pp. 105–152), who argues that the *Acts of Paul* narrates events that took place after the end of Acts. Although Pervo takes a position opposite to that of Bauckham, both assume the narrative of Acts would have warranted such attention in the second century. Although points of contact between the canonical Acts on the one hand and the *Acts of Paul* and the *Acts of Peter* on the other have been argued (see, e.g., the exchange between Rordorf, 'Paul's Conversion in the Canonical Acts and in the *Acts of Paul*,' pp. 137–44; Hills, 'The *Acts of Paul* and the Legacy of the Lukan Acts,' pp. 145–58; Bauckham, 'The *Acts of Paul*: Replacement of Acts or Sequel to Acts?' pp. 159–68; and Marguerat, 'The *Acts of Paul* and the Canonical Acts: A Phenomenon of Rereading,' pp. 169–84), no entirely satisfactory explanation of the similarities and differences has yet been argued. Moreover, even if the author of, for example, the *Acts of Paul* was familiar with the narrative of Acts, there does not seem to be anything in the surviving fragments of the *Acts of Paul* that suggests the author presumed such familiarity on the part of the audience for the work.

[177] For example, the elaborate framework of Paul's trial that brings him to Rome as a prisoner is absent in the *Acts of Paul*. In the *Acts of Paul*, Paul comes to Rome as a free man, not a prisoner. On the difficulty of reconstructing the narrative of the *Acts of Paul*, see Schneemelcher, *New Testament Apocrypha*, rev. ed. (1991), 2.218–33.

[178] Tertullian's comments suggest that the *Acts of Paul* was written to increase Paul's reputation for love of Paul. Even if Tertullian is an unreliable source for information about the literary and psychological motives of the author, the *Acts of Paul* does in fact presuppose a collection of Pauline letters. The so-called Third Letter to the Corinthians is part of the *Acts of Paul*. That the *Acts of Paul* was put together and circulated in the context of writings going under Paul's name is therefore plausible. That the Acts of the Apostles belonged to these 'Pauline' writings is much less likely. But cf. the observations of Bauckham, 'The *Acts of Paul*: Replacement of Acts or Sequel to Acts?' pp. 165–66, on

the *Acts of Peter* and the *Acts of Paul* in being a narrative not constructed around the life of any one character. In both the *Acts of Peter* and the *Acts of Paul*, a single apostle appears to move through the narrative from beginning to end, and secondary characters are subordinated to the character of the primary apostle.[179] Both of these apocryphal acts end with the apostle's martyrdom. In the Acts of the Apostles, on the other hand, the life of no single character defines the boundaries of the narrative. The characters of Peter and Paul each have a particular role to play in the development of Christianity. There is no narration of the death of either of these two main characters (though Paul's death is foreshadowed). The development of the narrative is not determined by the life (or death) of an apostle, but by the author's interest in the spread of Christianity from Jerusalem to Rome.[180]

Instead, the *Acts of Peter* and the *Acts of Paul* (and the other apocryphal acts to a lesser or greater extent) resemble what came to be identified in the second century as gospel texts about Jesus, particularly those dependent on the literary form of Mk,[181] more than they resemble Acts with respect to narrative structure and religious motive.[182] The apocryphal acts and such gospel literature are accounts of a divine man[183] who travels about, does miracles, preaches and teaches,[184] gathers followers, and

---

the relation of the *Acts of Paul* to the Lukan Acts, 2 Timothy, Titus, 1 Corinthians, and 2 Corinthians.

[179] For example, whatever the importance Thecla had in the source material used by the author of the *Acts of Paul*, the character of Thecla has been subordinated to the character of Paul in the *Acts of Paul* as a whole. Note also Tertullian's assessment of the author's motivation: "for love of Paul." Paul's role in the *Acts of Peter* is probably a later addition influenced by the Acts of the Apostles. See Thomas, 'Canon and Antitype: The Relationship Between the *Acts of Peter* and the New Testament,' p. 195.

[180] These points will be developed in chapters 3 and 4. To be sure, Paul's mission defines the endpoint of the narrative recounting the emergence of Christianity. Nevertheless, Paul is but one character in the historical movement that leads from Jerusalem to Rome.

[181] Such gospel literature dependent on the literary form of Mk was well established in the life of Christian communities in the second half of the second century.

[182] See Bovon, 'The Synoptic Gospels and the Noncanonical Acts of the Apostles,' pp. 19–36. MacDonald ('Apocryphal and Canonical Narratives about Paul,' p. 60) concurs with Bovon, but tries to force Acts into this gospel pattern as well, following the lead of Wrege, *Die Gestalt des Evangeliums: Aufbau und Struktur der Synoptiker sowie der Apostelgeschichte*, pp. 151–60.

[183] On the influence of concepts of a divine man on the gospel narratives, see Betz, 'Jesus as Divine Man,' in *Synoptische Studien*, pp. 18–34. See also Smith, 'Good News Is No News: Aretalogy and Gospel' in *Map is not Territory*, pp. 190–207.

[184] Note especially Paul's beatitudes in the *Acts of Paul* 3.5–6 in comparison with those of Jesus in Mt 5:3–11 and Lk 6:20–22.

as a result of conflict with the civil authorities (conflict created by the defining character of the divine man) is put to death, but subsequently appears to (or promises to appear to) certain individuals. Within this common narrative framework, the hopes and the aspirations of Christians are preserved in the forms of legends and principles of conduct associated with a semi-divine character who becomes the paradigm for Christian existence.[185] The apocryphal acts thus appear to be a secondary development in Christianity of ('gospel') narratives of divine men. In the apocryphal acts, Jesus assumes his position in the divine realm, and the apostles become the emissaries of the divine realm on earth. The apocryphal acts thus supplement narrative accounts about Jesus (not the narrative of the Acts of the Apostles) as ways of imagining Christian existence. In the life and death of the apostle (as of Jesus), the reality of Christian existence is mediated to the reader.[186]

In the apocryphal acts, the leading apostles are almost interchangeable in terms of the plot dynamics (though certainly localized geographically in terms of traditions about the area of their activities) and are immediately present to the reader as the model of Christian existence.[187] These characters act in ways that are determined by the literary expectations of the genre in relation to ideals of asceticism (particularly renunciation of sexual love) in early Christianity. The similar-

---

[185] The renunciation of this world, which in the case of the apocryphal acts takes the specific form of renouncing sexual love, leads to a devotion to the leading character of the narrative, whether Jesus in the gospels or the apostle in the apocryphal acts. Compare, e.g., Jesus' requirements of discipleship (e.g., Mt 10:37–39) with Thecla's devotion to Paul in the *Acts of Paul* 3.7–40. This devotion to the leading character of the narrative mediates the disciple's relationship to God.

[186] See especially Peter's discourse on his death in the *Acts of Peter* 37–39. Stowers ('Comment: What Does *Unpauline* Mean?' in *Paul and the Legacies of Paul*, pp. 75–76) observes that the synoptic gospels differ from the apocryphal acts in that the former grow out of *chreiai* and *gnomai* so that plot is minimal and sequential development is static. In the latter, he argues, plot is fundamental. His analysis, however, underestimates the importance of the plot element introduced by the passion narrative for understanding the literary form of the synoptic gospels. The source material available to the authors of the synoptic gospels was different from that available to the authors of the apocryphal acts, but this does not mean that the gospels as literary wholes are 'quite different' from the apocryphal acts. No amount of elaboration of the *chreiai* and *gnomai* under the influence of epideictic rhetoric explains the form of the gospels. Bultmann's assessment that the gospels are distinctive creations of early Christianity still merits attention. (See chapter 3 under *The Prefaces of Lk-Acts* on the genre of Lk-Acts.)

[187] This is also the case for the Jesus of Mt, Mk, and Jn. On the other hand, in Lk-Acts the characters (including Jesus) serve a larger vision of historical movement and are strikingly 'historicized' (that is, distanced from the reader—see chapter 3 under *Paul's Farewell Speech and the Literary Paulinism of Lk-Acts*).

ities of these narratives centered on different apostles suggest that the apostles do not define competing social matrices and trajectories definable as, for example, 'Pauline Christianity' or 'Petrine Christianity.'[188] Instead, the apostles in the genre seem to reflect almost interchangeably a certain commonality in the ideological construction of life shared by early Christians.[189]

One feature of the apocryphal acts as a group that sets them apart from the canonical gospels as a group (and Acts) is the theme of the renunciation of sexual love by those who accept the teaching of the apostle. In the case of Thecla in the *Acts of Paul*, Paul (who represents Jesus)[190] becomes the object of her devotion in a way that leads her into a life of sexual abstinence. In the *Acts of Peter*, the renunciation of sexual love by certain women devoted to Peter creates the conflict that ultimately leads to the execution of the apostle at the hands of the state.[191] This theme can be correlated with the widespread appeal of the ideal of asceticism in second century Christianity.[192] The apocryphal acts themselves, in their very similarity to one another at the level of

---

[188] The complex similarities and differences among the Pauline and deutero-Pauline letters, the apocryphal acts, the canonical gospel literature, and Lk-Acts suggest the unlikelihood of a simple correlation of the character of Paul in these texts to communities and trajectories in first- and second-century Christianity adequately labeled 'Pauline.' See chapter 5 below.

[189] See Cameron, *Christianity and the Rhetoric of Empire*, pp. 113–16.

[190] See, e.g., the confusion Thecla experiences between the identity of Paul and that of Jesus (*Acts of Paul* 3.21).

[191] *Acts of Peter* 34–41; differently, though, in the *Acts of Paul* 11. The execution of Christians by the state probably informs an interest in the deaths of the apostles. Compare, e.g., the executions of Ignatius, Polycarp, and Justin, as well as the account of the martyrs at Lyons and Vienne (Eusebius *Hist. eccl.* 5.1); on the execution of Christians, see Pliny *Letters* 10.96.3 and Tacitus *Annals* 15.44.

[192] Noted even by pagans—see Galen's comments on the asceticism of a group of Christians (the fragment from Galen's lost summary of Plato's *Republic* is preserved only in an Arabic quotation; see Walzer, *Galen on Jews and Christians*, p. 15):

'Most people are unable to follow any demonstrative argument consecutively; hence they need parables, and benefit from them'—and he (Galen) understands by parables tales of rewards and punishments in a future life—'just as now we see the people called Christians drawing their faith from parables [and miracles], and yet sometimes acting in the same way [as those who philosophize]. For their contempt of death [and of its sequel] is patent to us everyday, and likewise their restraint in cohabitation. For they include not only men but also women who refrain from cohabiting all through their lives; and they also number individuals who, in self-discipline and self-control in matters of food and drink, and in their keen pursuit of justice, have attained a pitch not inferior to that of genuine philosophers.'

On Galen and the Christians, see also Wilken, *The Christians as the Romans Saw Them*,

narrative plot yet divergence at the level of theological viewpoint,[193] suggest the widespread popularity of this ideal in various theological traditions. Whereas the synoptic material emerged in conflict with Jewish religious and political structures, the legendary material in the apocryphal acts conveys the ideal of sexual abstinence as a response to the Graeco-Roman world.[194] Attempts to locate the apocryphal acts (or the legends behind the apocryphal acts) in marginal social groups are quite misleading.[195] In the late second century, it is the lives of the apostles in the apocryphal acts, not the Acts of the Apostles, that reflect the ideals of many early Christian communities.

Although the narrative framework of Lk-Acts initially depends on Mk,[196] this framework is rapidly left behind in Acts as the narrative of the expansion of the proclamation of the word (Lk 1:2) exceeds the boundaries of the life of any individual so that Christianity is viewed as a historical movement determined by a sequence of characters. The 'acts' of both Peter and Paul are dropped as soon as their role in the historical movement of which they are a part is complete.[197] There is

---

pp. 68–93.

Cf. Justin *2 Apol.* 2, whose description of the experiences of a woman who converted should be compared to the portrayal of such women in the apocryphal acts. One appeal of Marcionite Christianity as a social phenomenon in early Christianity was probably its strong stand on sexual renunciation, which resonated throughout early Christian traditions. This ideal can be traced to the earliest layers of Christianity (see, e.g., 1 Cor 7:1). Of course, to claim that this ideal was widespread in early Christianity does not mean that its actual practice need be as widespread.

[193] Eusebius (*Hist. eccl.* 3.25, cf. 3.3) classified the *Acts of Paul* only as spurious, the *Acts of Peter* as heretical.

[194] The resulting tensions with Graeco-Roman society can perhaps be seen in Justin's account (*2 Apol.* 2) of the woman who became estranged from her husband upon becoming a Christian. See note 192 above. See also Brown, *Body and Society*, p. 157.

[195] See above, e.g., on Tertullian's comments on the author of the *Acts of Paul* in *De baptismo* 17. Note the tension between his characterization of the text as at least potentially heretical in the hands of uncontrolled women yet supposedly written by a presbyter of the (true) church.

[196] Lk 1:1 is at least a reference to Mk, and the whole structure of Lk is very similar to Mk.

[197] That the absence of an account of Paul's death is repeatedly posed as a problem suggests that the role of Paul in Acts is being fundamentally misconstrued. MacDonald ('Apocryphal and Canonical Narratives about Paul,' pp. 63–68), e.g., argues that the expectations set up by the genre of Acts require an account of the death of Paul, but an actual narrative of his death has been suppressed for political reasons. The author of Lk-Acts certainly has an interest in shifting the blame for Paul's death from the Romans to the Jews (note especially Acts 21:13), but MacDonald's way of posing the problem ignores the importance of Peter in the narrative of Acts and thus the function of Peter and Paul in the narrative.

an almost complete lack of ethical/moral teaching in Acts;[198] instead, speeches focus on historical movement: most tellingly, Paul's farewell speech interprets the transition from the past to the Christian present,[199] but has very little specific ethical or theological exhortation.[200] The result is a vision of historical movement encompassing the Jewish and Graeco-Roman world in God's plan for Christianity.[201] By not ending with Paul's death, the narrative of Lk-Acts affirms life in this world, with all its history, culture, and religion.[202] In contrast, the apocryphal acts celebrate the death of the apostle and renunciation of this world.[203] The historical vision in Lk-Acts probably lacked any firm point of contact with early Christian communities prior to the attempt by Irenaeus to define a standard for Christian truth over against heresy, in which attempt the preaching of the Gospel by all the apostles, but especially Peter and Paul at Rome, became the measure for order in a hierarchically defined Christendom *in this world*.

In terms of early Christian narrative literature, the narrative structure of Lk-Acts is actually an anomaly, whereas the apocryphal acts appear to arise from the same literary impulses that gave rise to the gospels: the portrayal of Christianity in terms of the life (or acts) of a divine man. Whereas (Lk-)Acts stands almost alone,[204] the *Acts of Peter*

---

[198] Contrast Paul's beatitudes in *Acts of Paul* 3.5–6.

[199] See chapter 3 under *Paul's Farewell Speech and the Literary Paulinism of Lk-Acts*.

[200] Contrast Peter's final words in the *Acts of Peter* 36–39.

[201] For example, politically, Paul is portrayed as a Roman citizen well treated by Romans (see Lentz, *Luke's Portrait of Paul*, e.g. pp. 3–4, on the portrayal of Paul's social status). Paul in his appeal to Caesar acknowledges the political authority of Rome over Christians. In contrast to the interest in the death of the apostles evident throughout the second century, the author of Lk-Acts downplays the implied death of Paul at Rome and attributes this death to the obstinate rejection of the gospel by the Jews (note Acts 21:13). See MacDonald, 'Apocryphal and Canonical Narratives about Paul,' pp. 64–68, though he misconstrues the significance of the author's portrayal of the implied death of Paul for the genre of Acts; see also note 197 above.

[202] For the author of Lk-Acts, Christianity is not only the fulfillment of Jewish history, culture, and religion, but also the fulfillment of pagan history, culture, and religion. See, e.g., Acts 17:22–31; Vielhauer, 'On the "Paulinism" of Acts,' p. 37.

[203] See Perkins, 'This World or Another? The Intertextuality of the Greek Romances, the Apocryphal Acts and Apuleius' *Metamorphoses*,' p. 253.

[204] Jones ('An Ancient Jewish Christian Rejoinder to Luke's Acts of the Apostles: Pseudo-Clementine *Recognitions* 1.27–71,' esp. pp. 239–44; *An Ancient Jewish Christian Source on the History of Christianity*, esp. pp. 157–68) has persuasively argued that the source behind Pseudo-Clementine *Recognitions* 1.27–71 is an account of the origin of Christianity influenced by but critical of the narrative of the Acts of the Apostles and the role ascribed to Paul in it. If the author of the source behind *Recognitions* 1.27–71 was a Jewish Christian writing about 200 C.E., this competing account of the origin

and the *Acts of Paul* were still literarily influencing the construction of lives of the apostles into the 6th century, and the genre seems to have resonated with the life of early Christians everywhere.[205]

That Acts, an obscure text until the late second century, belongs in a trajectory that defines a prominent ecclesiastical tradition in the second century before Irenaeus is unlikely. The canonical status of Acts is the result of a late second-century apologetic for a certain form of Christianity. This apologetic has obscured the place of Acts and its image of Paul in early Christianity prior to Irenaeus. For Irenaeus, the fourfold gospel canon, the account of the apostles (including Paul) in Acts, and the Pauline letters established the grounds for his claim that the true church was built on the foundation of the proclamation of the Gospel by all the apostles, a Gospel received by them from Jesus and handed on from them to their successors in the church (among whom Irenaeus counts himself). In a modern version of this 'history,' the Paul of Acts and of the Pauline letters has been correlated with a social and/or literary phenomenon in early Christianity identified as 'Pauline' and given prominence in reconstructing Paul's role in the literary, theological, or social history of early Christianity. Although the specific historical claims made by Irenaeus at the end of the second century supporting his correlation of the Paul of the letters and the Paul of Acts (based on the 'Pauline' author, Luke the companion of Paul) have been widely challenged in modern scholarship, as has his genealogy of the apostolic proclamation of the Gospel, the influence of the canon remains. The canon continues to bias reconstructions of the place in early Christianity of the portrayal of Paul in Acts while obscuring the extent to which Lk-Acts and the Paul of Acts do not easily fit into the usually smooth syntheses of early Christian developments often offered as the background for this text.[206] The

---

of Christianity is not only a critical commentary on the Acts of the Apostles, but an implicit rejoinder to Irenaeus's use of the Acts of the Apostles to defend Paul against those Jewish Christians who do not recognize Paul as an apostle. See *Adv. haer.* 3.15.1.

[205] The list of such works connected to the character of Paul includes the *Acts of Andrew and Paul*, *Acts of Peter and Paul*, and *Acts of Xanthippe and Polyxena*. See MacDonald, 'Apocryphal and Canonical Narratives about Paul,' p. 57.

[206] See, e.g., the determined effort to locate Acts vis-à-vis the Pauline corpus in terms of the author's knowledge of them (e.g., Knox, 'Acts and the Pauline Letter Corpus,' pp. 282–86) or lack of knowledge of them (e.g., Harnack, *The Date of the Acts and of the Synoptic Gospels*, pp. 100–103). It is generally thought to be inconceivable that an author writing a history of the spread of the gospel in which Paul plays a central role could be ignorant of the Pauline letters (unless writing quite soon after the death of Paul).

social and literary forces shaping the reception of the so-called Acts of the Apostles into the canon need to be separated from the social and literary context informing the composition of Lk-Acts and its portrayal of Paul. The following two chapters are an attempt to rethink the place in early Christianity to which Lk-Acts and its portrayal of Paul belong.

This belief, however, already assumes the centrality to Paul's legacy as defined by the emerging canon—a late second century construct. See chapter 4 below.

CHAPTER 3

LK-ACTS, ITS AUDIENCE, AND THE HISTORY OF CHRISTIANITY

Once the 'Pauline' Luke and the 'Acts of the Apostles' constructed at the end of the second century are set aside, are there compelling reasons to think that the original composition of Lk-Acts was determined by some form of 'Pauline Christianity'? An answer to this question involves paying attention to the text and its portrayal of Paul in relation to its intended audience and in relation to its sources, particularly about Paul. The relation of Lk-Acts and its portrayal of Paul to its intended audience is the subject of this chapter; the relation of the author to sources possibly determined by some form of 'Pauline Christianity' is the subject of the next chapter.

The author of Lk-Acts has produced a singular narrative among early Christian texts: he has reconceptualized the life of Jesus as a part of a larger narrative of the spread of Christianity (Acts 1:1).[1] This extended account of the history of early Christianity is necessary for an ordered account[2] of "the events that have been accomplished among us" (Lk 1:1).[3] For the author's primary narrative source Mk,[4] as well as for the other narratives about Jesus dependent on the form of Mk,[5] Christian identity and the development of the church are sufficiently determined by an account of the life of Jesus.[6] Unlike the immediacy of

---

[1] τὸν μὲν πρῶτον λόγον ἐποιησάμην περὶ πάντων, ὦ Θεόφιλε, ὧν ἤρξατο ὁ Ἰησοῦς ποιεῖν τε καὶ διδάσκειν...

[2] καθεξῆς, Lk 1:3. See also παρηκολουθηκότι ἄνωθεν, Lk 1:3. On the meaning of the terms of the prologue to Lk-Acts, see below under *The Prefaces of Lk-Acts*.

[3] τῶν πεπληροφορημένων ἐν ἡμῖν πραγμάτων. Cf. λόγων ('stories,' 'accounts'), Lk 1:4.

[4] See Lk 1:1—ἐπειδήπερ πολλοὶ ἐπεχείρησαν ἀνατάξασθαι διήγησιν.

[5] Including Mt and perhaps Jn.

[6] See, e.g., Mk 1:1; Mt 28:16–20 (cf. Mt 16:18; 18:15–20); Jn 20:19–23 (cf. Jn 3:11). See also chapter 2 under *Acts and the Apocryphal Acts in the Second Century*. Barrett (*Luke the Historian in Recent Study*, p. 60) comments concerning Lk-Acts: "Luke had to write this book in such a way as to show that the story of the Church was not an independent or spontaneous movement, but the outcome of the life of Jesus." Not only do the narratives of Mt, Mk, and Jn all achieve this without the need for a successive narrative of the church, but no other 'gospel' (Q, Thomas, etc.) felt the need to narrate a development of the church to supplement the message of Jesus.

the life of Jesus for the church in such narratives,[7] the author of Lk-Acts speaks in his own voice as part of a present in which the life of Jesus is clearly perceived as belonging to a past different from the present and mediated by a tradition in need of investigation.[8] The author connects the life of Jesus to his audience in three places: introducing his work as author in the prefaces to the two volumes, Lk 1:1–4 and Acts 1:1–2, and expanding the horizon of his narrative to include the readers' present through the literary device of the farewell address delivered by the character Paul in Acts 20:17–38. In these passages, the author draws his audience into the narrative (Lk 1:1–4) and correlates the life of Jesus (Acts 1:1) with the ministry of Paul, whose farewell address (Acts 20:17–38) joins the Christian present to the Jewish past of Jesus, the apostles, and Paul. The author portrays Paul as God's chosen instrument (Acts 9:15) in the movement of the word (Lk 1:2) from Jerusalem to Rome, from the past of Jesus to the present of the Christian. Christian origins, according to the author of Lk-Acts, are determined by a history that extends from the life of Jesus to the ministry of Paul. The prefaces to Lk-Acts and Paul's farewell speech are identifiable forms important for understanding the social and literary context of Lk-Acts, and in particular the link between this context and the author's portrayal of Paul.[9]

The Prefaces of Lk-Acts

Despite what came to be the canonical separation of Lk-Acts, the connection of the narrative of Lk with the narrative of Acts, established by Acts 1:1–2, has been recognized since Irenaeus. There is, however, no consensus on the interpretive implications of this connection. Specifically, the problem of genre, the question of how Lk-Acts ought to be read (the answer to which often leads to explicit conclusions about the social context of this reading), needs to be clarified to understand the

---

[7] See also the preface to the Gospel of Thomas.
[8] See Lk 1:1–4; Acts 1:1–2. On the author's understanding of the life of Jesus as something that belongs to the past, see Conzelmann, *The Theology of St. Luke*, e.g., p. 186.
[9] Suggestive for the importance of this link between the author's prefaces and the portrayal of Paul in Lk-Acts is the reappearance of the first person pronoun in connection with Paul's travels in the latter part of Acts. On the problem of the appearance of the first person plural pronoun in the latter part of Acts, Conzelmann's conclusions (*Acts of the Apostles*, p. xl) are worth noting: "The only certainty is that by using 'we' the author attempts to convey the impression of an eyewitness account." See Lk 1:2. On the problem of the 'we' narrator of Acts, see chapter 4 under *Philippi*.

social and literary context for the portrayal of Paul in Lk-Acts.[10] For example, Charles Talbert identifies Lk-Acts as a biography plus succession narrative in the pattern exemplified in the accounts of the lives of certain philosophers in Diogenes Laertius. For Talbert, the Jesus of Lk-Acts is portrayed as the founder of Christianity followed by successors proclaiming the true doctrine of the founder to legitimate a local religious community. David Aune, on the other hand, reads Lk-Acts as a general history so that the narrative becomes an account of the emergence of Christianity as a "national consciousness" over against Judaism.[11]

The problem of the genre of Lk-Acts involves at least two related issues: (1) the general relation of this text to other Graeco-Roman, Jewish, and Christian writings;[12] (2) the specific relation of Acts to Lk (a problem aggravated by the legacy of the canon). Since Lk 1:1–4 is a general preface and Acts 1:1–2 is a secondary preface introducing the second book of a larger whole,[13] Lk-Acts should be taken as a single work.[14] The differences between Lk and Acts are to be attributed to the differences of source material constraining the narrative. This con-

---

[10] Genre as an explicit interpretive tool for understanding Acts has received a great deal of attention in relation to recent emphases on social-literary approaches in New Testament studies. See, e.g., Talbert, *Literary Patterns, Theological Themes and the Genre of Luke Acts*, p. 135; idem, *What is a Gospel?* pp. 134–35. See also Sterling, *Historiography and Self-Definition*, pp. 1–19; cf. p. 378. In contrast, Conzelmann (*Acts of the Apostles*, pp. xl–xli) minimizes the helpfulness of genre comparisons in favor of emphasizing the theological shaping of the text by the author. He makes no attempt to correlate Lk and Acts in terms of genre.

[11] *The New Testament in Its Literary Environment*, pp. 140–41.

[12] These categories are obviously not mutually exclusive; they belong to the language of New Testament studies and like all such generalizations have strengths and weaknesses.

[13] τὸν μὲν πρῶτον λόγον ἐποιησάμην (Acts 1:1) should be translated 'I wrote the first volume.' λόγος can be used of one part of a narrative work (LSJ, s.v.; cf. BDAG, s.v.); see διήγησις, Lk 1:1. πρῶτος can be used for πρότερος; see BDAG, s.v. πρῶτος. Cf. Josephus *Against Apion* 2.1: διὰ μὲν οὖν τοῦ προτέρου βιβλίου—'in the first volume.' On the prefaces to Lk-Acts, see Cadbury, *The Making of Luke-Acts*, pp. 198–99. See also Sterling, *Historiography and Self-Definition*, p. 131. Haenchen (*The Acts of the Apostles*, p. 136, n. 3) argues that Lk 1:1–4 applies only to the third gospel.

[14] The relation between the farewell addresses of Jesus and Paul further establishes the narrative unity of Lk-Acts. See below under *Paul's Farewell Speech and the Literary Paulinism of Lk-Acts*. The narrative of Acts was not an afterthought. The narrative of Lk, ending as it does with the disciples waiting in Jerusalem for the divine spirit, does not achieve the author's stated goal in Lk 1:1–4, as the author's preface in Acts 1:1–2 indicates. The narrative of Lk is a beginning (τὸν πρῶτον λόγον περὶ πάντων ὧν ἤρξατο ὁ Ἰησοῦς ποιεῖν τε καὶ διδάσκειν) to which Acts is the necessary end.

clusion, as well as its implications for how the narrative form of Lk-Acts ought to be read, has repeatedly been obscured by a comparative method characterized by a narrow selection and definition of comparative similarities and differences.

Bultmann's judgments on the gospels have determined much of the current debate about the genre of the gospels. According to Bultmann, the gospels are not biographies,[15] but unique creations of Christianity growing out of the immanent forces of development in the oral tradition about Jesus in relation to the Christ-myth and Christ-cult of Hellenistic Christianity.[16] His characterization of the gospels is informed by previous work on the distinction between *Hochliteratur* and *Kleinliteratur*,[17] a distinction that introduces an explicit link between community and text: *Kleinliteratur* emerges spontaneously from the community. The Christian kerygma, as the essential and definitive presupposition of the gospels (the proclamation of the man who lived in the flesh as Lord), gives rise to a uniquely Christian form of literature (over against Graeco-Roman and Jewish forms of literature, with which broad genre comparisons are unhelpful).[18] Thus, Bultmann links gospel as message and gospel as written text. He comments, "*[T]he Gospels are expanded cult legends*,"[19] and goes on to say:

> Mark was the creator of this sort of Gospel; the Christ myth gives his book, the book of secret epiphanies, not indeed a biographical unity, but an unity based upon the myth of the kerygma.... Matthew and Luke strengthened the mythical side of the gospel at points by many miracle stories and by their infancy narratives and Easter stories. But generally speaking they have not really developed the Mark type any further, but have simply made use of an historical tradition not accessible to Mark but available to them. There

---

[15] Contrast, e.g., Votaw ('The Gospels and Contemporary Biographies in the Greco-Roman World,' p. 10), who in 1915 suggested that the gospels were biographies and that the "nearest parallels" to the gospels among Greek biographical writings were accounts of the lives of Epictetus, Apollonius, and Socrates. Unfortunately, he did not clarify what "nearest parallels" might mean. How near is near? How should 'nearness' be established? This methodological imprecision has characterized much of the comparison of the gospels to Graeco-Roman literature.

[16] See Bultmann, *History of the Synoptic Tradition*, second edition (1968), pp. 368–74. Although Bultmann insisted on the uniqueness of the gospels as literary wholes, he did a great deal of comparison of the literary units that make up the gospels with corresponding genres in Greek and Jewish literature.

[17] Cf. comments by Cadbury, *The Making of Luke-Acts*, p. 131. On the history of this scholarship, see Dormeyer, *Evangelium als literarische und theologische Gattung*, pp. 48–107.

[18] See Bultmann's comments (*History of the Synoptic Tradition*, second edition [1968], p. 372) in response to previous attempts at comparison, including those of Votaw.

[19] *History of the Synoptic Tradition*, second edition (1968), p. 371 (italics his).

was no real development of the type of Gospel created by Mark before John, and there of course the myth has completely violated the historical tradition.

Whether or not Mark is sufficiently explained by Bultmann's hypothesis, his comparison of Lk with Mk, Mt, and Jn (assessing "real development") has left Acts out of account. In what sense Lk-Acts really remains a 'gospel' of the type created by Mark is open to question. Lk-Acts cannot be explained with reference only to the Christ-myth and Christ-cult of Hellenistic Christianity. The author of Lk-Acts has in fact rejected an understanding of the origin of Christianity based on the so-called expanded cult legend of Mk.[20]

Many have accepted Bultmann's conclusions.[21] Others, however, have rejected his assertion of generic identity among Mk, Mt, Lk, and Jn and generic difference between these gospels and Graeco-Roman literature. There has been a proliferation of other configurations of similarities and differences. The work of Charles Talbert on the gospels, particularly Lk-Acts, is a good example of the attempt to reintegrate the gospels into the Graeco-Roman cultural milieu.[22] He concludes that Mk and Lk-Acts belong to separate categories of Graeco-Roman biography, thus reversing Bultmann's construction of similarity and difference.[23] Specifically, Lk-Acts belongs to a type of biography best exemplified by Diogenes Laertius. According to Talbert, the a+b+c pattern of founder, successors, and summary of teaching has become in Lk-Acts a+b with c, the doctrinal summary, incorporated in the speeches in Acts.[24] This conclusion is surprising given the lack of doctrinal teaching in Acts.[25] He achieves this result using a method of comparison that

---

[20] See discussion below in this section.
[21] See the restatement of this position by Schneemelcher, *New Testament Apocrypha*, rev. ed. (1991), 1.77–87.
[22] See *What Is a Gospel?*, e.g., p. 15. He attempts explicitly to refute Bultmann's hypotheses.
[23] *What Is a Gospel?*, pp. 134–35. Cf. Burridge, *What Are the Gospels?*, p. 240.
[24] *Literary Patterns, Theological Themes and the Genre of Luke-Acts*, p. 131.
[25] Note, e.g., the lack of any precise doctrinal content for the threat from false teachers warned against in Paul's farewell address in Acts 20:28–31 (see below under *Paul's Farewell Speech and the Literary Paulinism of Lk-Acts*). The speeches in Acts 2:14–36; 7:2–53; 13:16–41; and 15:13–21 all present a theory of (salvation) history, but not the content of Christian doctrine as one would expect if such speeches were epitomes of the teaching of a philosophical school. Cf. MacDonald's attempt ('Apocryphal and Canonical Narratives about Paul,' pp. 63–68) to explain the absence of a martyrdom at the ending of Acts so that Acts can be linked in terms of genre to the gospels and apocryphal acts. The willingness to force the narrative of Acts into molds that it does

selectively defines certain similarities (with some biographies in Diogenes Laertius over against similarities with Mk) and suppresses differences (for example, concerning the speeches in Acts): his similarities are "remarkable"; any differences are "not decisive."[26]

Although Talbert's conclusions have not been widely accepted, this methodological procedure has been repeated to establish virtually every genre identification proposed for the gospels in general and Lk-Acts in particular offered in response to Bultmann. The conclusions of, for example, Aune (Lk-Acts as general history),[27] Richard Pervo (Acts, as distinct from Lk, as a novel),[28] Gregory Sterling (Lk-Acts as apologetic history),[29] and Dennis MacDonald (for whom the gospel is the most important literary model for Acts)[30] all suffer the same methodological problems as exemplified by Talbert. The proposed comparisons (genre identifications) rhetorically and methodologically define certain similarities over against differences in an arbitrary manner to establish *the* genre of Lk-Acts.[31]

---

not fit is an indication of the problems underlying the way comparisons have been carried out.

[26] *Literary Patterns, Theological Themes and the Genre of Luke-Acts*, pp. 132–33.

[27] Using the same method, Aune (e.g., in *The New Testament and Its Literary Environment*, pp. 140–41) has come to opposite conclusions from Talbert. Rather than merging Acts into Lk, Aune merges Lk into Acts and posits a sharp generic distinction between Lk-Acts and the other canonical gospels. Although Lk-Acts certainly has similarities with Hellenistic historiography (note the point above on the speeches in Acts; see discussion below in this section), Aune can point to no other text in his category of universal history that shares more features in common with Lk-Acts than Lk-Acts shares with Mk. In what sense, then, is Lk-Acts more like universal history than it is like Mk (which Aune classifies as a biography)?

[28] Pervo, *Profit with Delight: The Literary Genre of the Acts of the Apostles*, e.g., pp. 136–38; idem, 'Must Luke and Acts Belong to the Same Genre?' pp. 309–16. Cf. Conzelmann (*Acts of the Apostles*, pp. xl–xli), who distinguishes Lk and Acts, but identifies Acts as a historical monograph.

[29] *Historiography and Self-Definition*, p. 374; cf. p. 19.

[30] 'Apocryphal and Canonical Narratives about Paul,' p. 59; cf. pp. 63–68. MacDonald has in a sense returned to Bultmann's point of departure, that (Lk-)Acts is in fact distinctly Christian literature. The rhetoric of decisive similarities and marginal differences remains, but Talbert's comparison with Graeco-Roman literature has been replaced by MacDonald's comparison with Christian literature. A sense of lack of progress in attempts to identify the genre of Lk-Acts is hard to avoid.

[31] Alexander (*The Preface to Luke's Gospel*, p. 167) concludes concerning the prefaces of Lk-Acts, "... Luke's preface-style seems to be more closely related to that of the 'scientific tradition' than it is to that of Hellenistic Jewish literature or to any other Greek literary tradition." Alexander rejects any attempt to read Lk-Acts as "Greek history" in favor of reading it in light of the scientific tradition (pp. 200–212), despite the fact that the content of Lk-Acts hardly resembles the mathematical or medical

In any comparison, differences as well as similarities are important. The arbitrary selection and definition of certain specific similarities over against specific differences, with the resulting suppression of other possible generic configurations of similarities and differences, arise from an inadequate approach to comparison. Any comparison requires three terms.[32] Logically, the statement 'x resembles y' is incomplete without the addition of terms to make relative similarities and differences observable: 'x resembles y more than z with respect to v' or 'x resembles y more than w resembles z with respect to v.' 'Resembles' should be always qualified by 'more than' and 'with respect to.' In other words, comparison is always partial, relative, and determined by the interests of the observer. For example, Bultmann's partial comparisons of Mk, Mt, Lk, and Jn determined by his interests in the synoptic tradition are illuminating relative to his interests, but provide only a partial account of the narrative form of Lk-Acts. Talbert minimizes whether Lk-Acts may resemble Mk more than Lk-Acts resembles certain biographical forms in Diogenes Laertius with respect to certain characteristics, as well as whether Lk-Acts resembles Hellenistic historiography more than Lk-Acts resembles such biographies with respect to, for example, the speeches. Aune fails to take into account the resemblance between Lk-Acts and the other canonical gospels (which he considers biographies) with respect to narrative structure and content (obscuring the rather difficult problem of really demonstrating that any Graeco-Roman gen-

---

treatises which begin with such prefaces (p. 202). In her search for the genre of Lk-Acts, Alexander minimizes the conceptual and linguistic parallels between Lk 1:1–4 and Hellenistic historiography (especially Josephus), while emphasizing the general lack of dedications in Greek historiography. Furthermore, Alexander (following Overbeck, see p. 14) overstates the detachability of the preface from the content of Lk-Acts, a detachability supposedly characteristic of prefaces in the scientific tradition but not of prefaces to history. (On the close connection of the prefaces to Lk-Acts and the portrayal of Paul in Acts, see below under *Paul's Farewell Speech and the Literary Paulinism of Lk-Acts*; see also note 43 below.) Alexander has confused the question of whether Lk-Acts *is* Greek historiography (it is not in a strict sense; see below) with the question of whether the author appeals to the conventions of Hellenistic historiography to give an account of the origin of Christianity (he does; see below in this section). Lk-Acts is no more a scientific treatise than it is a Greek history. Alexander's narrowly conceived comparison of similarities and differences, however, leads her to assert that Lk-Acts is the former and not the latter. Even if the presence of the dedication is due to the influence of the scientific tradition (it need not be; see note 69 below), this does not warrant ignoring the influence of standards of Hellenistic historiography on the author's conception of his task.

[32] See Smith, *Drudgery Divine. On the Comparison of Early Christianities and the Religions of Late Antiquity*, p. 51.

eral history looks very much like Lk-Acts at all). Pervo minimizes (1) the narrative connection of Acts with Lk, (2) links with Hellenistic historiography (for example, the speeches in Acts), and (3) differences between Acts and ancient novels (for example, in terms of the relation of characters to the plot).[33] In each case, the value of the insights gained by these comparisons is overshadowed by the claim to have discovered the definitive genre for drawing a literary map with which to locate and interpret Lk-Acts.[34] The resulting suggestions for understanding the specific literary and social context in which Lk-Acts and the Paul of Acts emerged are not compelling.[35]

---

[33] On similarities with ancient novels, see also Edwards, 'Acts of the Apostles and Chariton's *Chaereas and Callirhoe*: A Literary and Sociohistorical Study,' pp. 1–14. The differences between Hellenistic historiography and novels cannot be construed primarily in terms of fictional narrative. The difference is not whether the narrative is fictional, but on the constraints controlling the narrative (e.g., relationship to sources or traditions; see Lk 1:1–4). The anti-historical tendency characteristic of Greek thought tended to push historiography toward rhetoric and narrative fiction. See Aristotle's distinction between poetry and history (*Poetics* 9; discussed in this section below). See also Collingwood, *The Idea of History*, pp. 17–31.

[34] The underlying problem is the attempt to establish discrete genre categories based on a monothetic approach to classification. A polythetic mode of classification is required for any phenomena not capable of differentiation on the basis of a specific characteristic or specifically definable set of characteristics (in terms of genre, such characteristics as form, content, and function are often thought to establish discrete genre categories). On these modes of classification, see Smith, 'Fences and Neighbors: Some Contours of Early Judaism,' pp. 1–5. The classification of texts (i.e., genre groupings) arises from a clustering of shared characteristics. Some texts may share a large number of characteristics, others may not (so-called mixed genres, e.g.). If such a polythetic mode of classification were undertaken, it seems probable that Mk and Lk-Acts would, e.g., share a cluster of characteristics that would create meaningful (generic) differences vis-à-vis other ancient texts. Because genre has been treated as a set of discrete categories (of, e.g., biography, history, fictional narrative, gospel) into which Lk-Acts must be placed, Talbert's rhetoric, and that of those who have responded to him, has been shaped by the language of 'decisive' similarities and 'unimportant' differences, a language that allows the interpreter to discard as inconsequential whatever does not fit the particular genre favored by the investigator. Because genre has been so closely tied to the conception of discrete categories such as history, biography, novel, or gospel in the investigation of early Christian narrative texts, perhaps intertextuality offers a more useful model for understanding the relation of Lk-Acts to other texts. Cf. the comments of Valantasis ('The Nuptial Chamber Revisited: The *Acts of Thomas* and Cultural Intertextuality,' pp. 261–63) on the use of a broad model of intertextuality to understand the apocryphal acts.

[35] Although Burridge (*What Are the Gospels?*, pp. 24–25) appeals to literary theories to untangle the problem of the genre of the gospels, he does not address the more fundamental problems associated with establishing comparisons and contrasts. The problem with genre studies applied to Lk-Acts is not that they are not 'correct' in relation to some true notion of genre, but that they have not done what has

Although the debate about the genre of Lk-Acts has been characterized by an unsuccessful attempt to discover a definitive point of similarity or difference to determine comparison, this search for *the* genre of Lk-Acts has illuminated the complexity of the literary relations of Lk-Acts, a complexity that scholars have relentlessly minimized.[36] The various comparisons (with historiography, biography, novel, gospel traditions)[37] suggest oral and literary traditions within which the author was writing and placing his work,[38] traditions that are important indications of the social and literary (and thus interpretive) matrix within which Lk-Acts belongs. None, though, exhaustively defines the literary relations of Lk-Acts, and some are more useful than others for understanding the author's portrayal of Paul in the second half of the narrative of Acts. In what follows, a search for the definitive genre of Lk-Acts will not be pursued. Instead, those comparisons with Graeco-Roman and Jewish literature have been chosen that are most useful for a nar-

---

been claimed for them. Burridge (p. 218) concludes concerning the synoptic gospels: "Thus, there is a high degree of correlation between the generic features of Graeco-Roman βίοι and those of the synoptic gospels; in fact, they exhibit more of the features than are shown by works at the edges of the genre.... This is surely a sufficient number of shared features for the genre of the synoptic gospels to be clear..." Since he only carried out a detailed comparison with what he defines as Graeco-Roman βίοι, it is not clear how he can conclude that he has discovered a sufficient number of shared features to determine the genre of the synoptic gospels. In any case, his analysis of Lk has minimized Acts (see p. 256). Moreover, although in his examples of βίοι he makes a point of noting that the subject's name comes at the very start or immediately after the prologue (see, e.g., p. 162), he fails to explain why Jesus' name does not appear in the narrative of Lk until after Herod, Zechariah, Elizabeth, John, and Mary have been introduced. He has paid insufficient attention to differences that might call into question his definitive genre identification of Lk.

[36] See Schneemelcher (*New Testament Apocrypha*, rev. ed. [1991], 1.77–87) who rejects this debate as sterile and returns to Bultmann's solution without considering the nature of the problem. One likely reason for the minimizing of this complexity is the desire to discover *the* genre that explains the genesis of the narrative of Lk-Acts and thus its interpretation.

[37] One literary comparison, however, is noteworthy for its absence: no one has proposed a generic influence from the literary tradition of the Pauline letters, a striking absence given the author's willingness to incorporate many literary influences and all the more evident in comparison with the *Acts of Paul*. Although the author at times writes in a style reminiscent of the Septuagint, incorporates the narrative of Mk, adopts the convention of speeches in Hellenistic historiography, he does not have Paul write letters nor does he imitate the style of Pauline letters.

[38] Sterling (*Historiography and Self-Definition*, pp. 1–19) has suggested this approach to genre, but ends up arguing that one specific literary tradition (apologetic historiography; cf. p. 374) best explains the narrative of Lk-Acts.

rowly defined purpose: to explain why the author constructed Paul's role in early Christianity the way he did for his audience.

The assertion is often made against Bultmann and those who have followed him in his identification of the gospels as *sui generis* that a text, if it were indeed *sui generis*, would be uninterpretable.[39] Genre as a relation to other texts (e.g., in terms of conventions) is taken to be the key to the meaning of a specific text since it is thought that genre determines meaning.[40] This maxim is repeated often enough that it requires some attention.[41] That Bultmann's gospels, if indeed *sui generis*, would be uninterpretable is doubtful. Bultmann himself describes the proper context for their interpretation: the immanent forces of development in the tradition in relation to the Christ-myth and Christ-cult of Hellenistic Christianity. A community participating in such a cult could probably understand the gospels so-defined without ever having read (or listened to) any generically similar Graeco-Roman or Jewish text. Genre (in terms of the broad categories of biography, history, and novel, for example) as a key to the interpretation of the gospels has been exaggerated. Genre conventions and interpretation are ultimately tied to a social context of reading, and meaning is socially construed. It is only when texts are isolated from their proper social context of meaning that they become opaque. Bultmann is right to imply the sufficiency of an interpretive community for the meaningfulness of a text produced within that community.[42] Genre expectations (and more broadly, expec-

---

[39] For example, Burridge, *What Are the Gospels?*, p. 255.

[40] See, e.g., Burridge, *What Are the Gospels?*, pp. 52–54. When this principle is used in conjunction with an arbitrary method of comparison to establish literary conventions, an almost endless generation of interpretations becomes possible.

[41] The theoretical roots for this claim (at least as it is often made in New Testament studies) lie in the work of Hirsch (*Validity in Interpretation*). Even if Hirsch's analysis of the determinacy of meaning linked to genre is accepted (and this is by no means a given in literary criticism), he makes a crucial distinction between broad genres (that is, what the genre categories of biography, history, novel would be as applied to ancient texts) and intrinsic (text-specific) genres (pp. 86–111). Only the latter are determinative of meaning. This distinction ought to raise doubts that Burridge (*What Are the Gospels?*, pp. 240, 255–59) has uncovered the key to the understanding of the gospels when he concludes that the gospels are biographies (a broad genre)—a conclusion that is taken to be important for their relation to the historical Jesus (pp. 257–58).

[42] Although genre is part of a social context of meaning, the latter cannot be reduced to the former. Genre formalizes certain conventions of written communication and as such can guide the production and interpretation of written texts. The prerequisite for written communication to take place, however, is a social context guiding the production and interpretation of written texts, not preexistent genre categories. The texts of Mt, Mk, Lk-Acts, and Jn are difficult for modern scholars to interpret because

tations created by intertextuality) are always correlated with social communities of readers, that is, social contexts of meaning. What follows is an attempt to elucidate the literary and social context of meaning for the portrayal of Paul in Lk-Acts suggested by the prefaces to Lk-Acts.

The prefaces to Lk-Acts establish links to a complex web of literary traditions that define the nature of the participation in Hellenistic literary culture implied for the audience of Lk-Acts.[43] Lk-Acts is concerned with events (πραγμάτων, Lk 1:1),[44] specifically their historical accuracy and order.[45] These events are qualified in four important ways:[46] (1) The criterion of their selection is πεπληροφορημένων—those events capable of being designated as 'accomplished,' that is, 'fulfilled.'[47] The author

---

the original social context of their production and reading has been lost. Recourse to the broad genres of history, biography, or novel is a poor substitute for this original social context.

[43] The literary influences suggested by the prefaces do not exhaust the literary influences on Lk-Acts. Undoubtedly the expectations of popular storytelling have influenced the episodes in Acts. See, e.g., Pervo, *Profit with Delight*, pp. 12–85. Nevertheless, the prefaces of Lk-Acts establish the author's rhetorical stance toward the narrative as a whole, to which the individual characters and episodes are subordinated. This rhetorical stance is an intentional literary artifice (for the bulk of the narrative that follows, the author simply adopts the third-person, omniscient narrator of Mk) that helps determine the author's intentions for the narrative as a whole. Of course, it would be a mistake to simply read off the author's intentions from the prefaces alone, apart from an analysis of the content of Lk-Acts. The prefaces composed by ancient authors were not necessarily in themselves determinative or exhaustive guides to the intentions for their texts as a whole. See Burridge, *What Are the Gospels?*, pp. 55–69. Furthermore, authors do not always live up to the goals stated in the outset of their work. (For example, Josephus's stated intentions to refute those who claim that the Jews are a people of recent origin in his preface to *Against Apion* is at best only a partial guide to his actual apologetic interests as revealed by the actual content of *Against Apion*; see Droge, 'Josephus Between Greeks and Barbarians,' esp. pp. 116, 140. Lk 1:1–4 is not a description of the process of research and composition carried out in the rewriting of Mk.) As a result, the following discussion of the author's intentions as stated in the prefaces to Lk-Acts should not be read in isolation from the discussion of the actual content of the author's portrayal of Paul that will be taken up below under *Paul's Farewell Speech and the Literary Paulinism of Lk-Acts*, as well as in chapter 4.

[44] See also Acts 1:1—περὶ πάντων . . . ὧν ἤρξατο ὁ Ἰησοῦς ποιεῖν τε καὶ διδάσκειν ('concerning all that Jesus began to do and teach').

[45] For ἀκριβῶς, see Josephus *Jewish War* 1.2: τὸ δ' ἀκριβὲς τῆς ἱστορίας. See also Lucian, *How to Write History*, esp. 47, 51. For καθεξῆς, cf. ἑξῆς in Thucydides *The Peloponnesian War* 5.26.

[46] The prologue of Lk-Acts has been notoriously difficult to interpret. See, e.g., the large number of works cited in the bibliography on Lk 1:1–4 in Bovon, *Das Evangelium nach Lukas*, 1.29–30.

[47] 'Assured' is less likely. See Lk 24:44 and Acts 28:25–28. See also Sterling, *Historiography and Self-Definition*, pp. 333–35. The author of Lk-Acts repeatedly emphasizes the

thus assumes a theory of history that determines important events worthy of being investigated, ordered, and written.[48] Events currently circulating as 'accounts' or 'stories' (λόγων, Lk 1:4)[49] belong to a larger whole, the connection to which will produce certainty of knowledge concerning the particulars.[50] (2) These events have taken place 'among us.' In other words, the author of Lk-Acts is writing about events that have taken place in the recent past.[51] (3) These events are vouchsafed by eyewitnesses.[52] (4) The (unsatisfactory) attempts of others to write narratives (Lk 1:1) are contrasted with the careful investigation (παρηκολουθηκότι) of the events in question on the basis of which an ordered, accurate account can be written.[53] These four methodological issues are precisely the concerns found in Greek traditions of historiography begun by Thucydides that find their closest parallels in Josephus's prologue to his *Jewish War*.[54] The author of Lk-Acts thus places his work

---

'necessity' of events happening. See, e.g., Acts 2:23.

[48] Cf., e.g., the elaborate discussion by Josephus in the prologue of the *Jewish War* to establish the greatness of the war he is about to recount. Cf. also the prologue of Polybius (*Histories* 1.1.1–1.2.8; 1.4) and Thucydides (*The Peloponnesian War* 1.1). In the understanding of history presupposed by Lk 1:1, the events that are the subject of the author's narrative are important because of their significance in the divine plan for history. See discussion below in this section; see also below under *Paul's Farewell Speech and the Literary Paulinism of Lk-Acts*.

[49] The immediate context of Lk 1:1–4 indicates the meaning 'stories' (in the sense of accounts of incidents and events; cf. πράγματα, 1:1; on κατηχήθης, see BDAG, s.v. κατηχέω [meaning 1 is more likely than meaning 2a]) rather than 'teachings.' These λόγοι as stories or accounts are, of course, closely connected to the λόγος as the proclamation of the gospel (Lk 1:2; cf. Acts 18:25; 21:21, 24). The author claims to be ordering (καθεξῆς γράψαι) these stories into a narrative of events. The author thus invokes a semantic domain that identifies his task in relation to events preserved in partial accounts (λόγοι), to be distinguished from myths (μῦθοι), in need of organization into a regular history (ἱστορία). For the contrastive semantic domain of the word λόγος, see LSJ, s.v.

[50] Cf. Polybius's emphasis on understanding the particulars in light of the whole to perceive historical truth, rather than isolating the particulars in special histories (*Histories* 1.4.6–11).

[51] Cf. Josephus *Jewish War* 1.13–18.

[52] Note the appearance of the first person personal pronoun in the latter part of Acts. (On the 'we' narrator in Acts, see chapter 4 under *Philippi*.) See also Josephus *Jewish War* 1.18; *Against Apion* 1.55.

[53] Cf. Josephus *Jewish War* 1.1–3; *Against Apion* 1.46; 1.53–56; Lucian *How to Write History* 47. See Sterling, *Historiography and Self-Definition*, p. 344.

[54] Sterling (*Historiography and Self-Definition*, pp. 365–69, 374) links Lk-Acts to Josephus's *Antiquities* in terms of apologetic historiography, despite the fact that the criteria by which Josephus distinguishes the *Antiquities* from the *Jewish War* (see, e.g., *Jewish War* 1.17–18) indicate that Lk-Acts appeals to the historiographical methodology that

in a definite literary tradition⁵⁵—the writing of history about recent events marked out as important by a definite historiographical criterion of selection, attested by eyewitnesses,⁵⁶ and carefully investigated by the historian.⁵⁷

The social and literary context for the writing of such history extended from the past into the future so that such works were written in conversation with a literary past, present, and future. Concerning this literary past, the historian self-consciously continued the work of predecessors and debated the merits of previous efforts. For example, Josephus sees himself as continuing the work of past (biblical) historians,⁵⁸ as does the author of Lk-Acts.⁵⁹ Concerning the present, the

---

informs the *Jewish War*, not the *Antiquities*. According to Josephus, his ἀρχαιολογία is concerned with the origin and antiquity of the Jewish race (*Against Apion* 1.1) based on the investigation of reliable documents from the past (*Against Apion* 1.53–54; cf. *Jewish War* 1.17–18). On the other hand, his account of the Jewish war is about recent events (*Jewish War* 1.18; cf. 1.1; 1.13–16) about which he is qualified to give a reliable account over against unreliable narratives about the war (*Jewish War* 1.1–3). The expectation for such a reliable account of recent events is that either the author participated in the events about which he writes or at the very least made careful inquiry about events from those who were actually present (*Against Apion* 1.44–56). Josephus expected his account of the Jewish war to take its place alongside the reliable accounts of the earlier history of the Jews (*Jewish War* 1.17–18). Although the author of Lk-Acts intends to investigate the origin of Christianity, he does not do so as one translating the sacred works of his people (as Josephus describes his method of writing the *Antiquities* in *Against Apion* 1.54) to recount their antiquity, but as one investigating the recent history of God's actions to save God's people. As such, his account is intended to take its place alongside similar reliable accounts of the distant past and to replace unreliable accounts of the recent past. See discussion below in this section. For the author of Lk-Acts, his history of Christianity does not require an account of the origin of an ancient γένος (an account already supplied by the Septuagint), but instead a narrative of the actions of individuals in the recent past.

⁵⁵ See Sterling (*Historiography and Self-Definition*, pp. 1–19, esp. p. 15) for a discussion of genre in terms of literary traditions.

⁵⁶ The appearance of the first person pronoun (as an eyewitness) in the latter part of Acts thus links the narration of the ministry of Paul to the author's method as stated in Lk 1:1–4. Nevertheless, this first person narrator in the second half of Acts associated with Paul should not be confused with the author. In Lk 1:1–4, the author associates himself and Theophilus with the ἡμῖν of 1:2, to whom the tradition has been mediated by those who directly participated in the events (πράγματα, cf. 1:1) in question. The 'we' narrator of Acts, along with Paul, belongs to the time of those designated in 1:2 as οἱ ἀπ' ἀρχῆς αὐτόπται καὶ ὑπηρέται γενόμενοι τοῦ λόγου.

⁵⁷ The literary use of speeches in Acts also connects Lk-Acts to this historiographical tradition.

⁵⁸ *Jewish War* 1.14–18.

⁵⁹ Note the archaizing style that begins with Lk 1:5 under the influence of the Septuagint.

historian competed with contemporary historians or pretenders for the attention of an educated audience.[60] Concerning the future, historians offered their work as a deposit of historical truth for subsequent generations.[61] In other words, a narrowly defined community did not determine the audience for which a historian wrote.[62] Furthermore, such authors wrote to individuals in the present and future who might learn and act upon the lessons contained in the truthful recording of history.[63] Historians of important events of their time failed just to the extent that they lost sight of this audience that transcended temporal and geographical barriers for whom they were recording the truth[64] and instead wrote for the sake of personal gain in the present.[65] In short, such narratives presupposed an author and audience participating in a search

---

[60] Note, e.g., Josephus *Jewish War* 1.1–4; *Antiquities* 1.4; *Against Apion* 1.1; Polybius *Histories* 1.4.3; also Lk 1:1, where the author of Lk-Acts situates his work over against other narratives about Jesus. This orientation toward previous narratives about Jesus is implicit in Acts 1:1, as well, and explains the difference in narrative style between Lk and Acts. In Acts, the author is going beyond the efforts of his predecessors.

[61] See Josephus *Jewish War* 1.15; Josephus characterizes ancient historians in *Jewish War* 1.14–18 as having left reliable deposits of historical truth for the present. See also Thucydides 1.22, where he characterizes his history as a possession for all time. See also Lucian *How to Write History* 62. Cf. Acts 20:29–32, in which the author embraces all future readers in the historical certainty (truth) of the past.

[62] See Barton ('Can We Identify the Gospel Audiences?' pp. 186–88) for some recent critiques of the idea of a 'Lukan community'; see also Bauckham, 'For Whom Were Gospels Written?' pp. 9–48.

[63] See Lucian *How to Write History* 42; Thucydides 1.22. See also Lk 1:1–4; Acts 26:25–29.

[64] See Josephus *Jewish War* 1.30; also *Antiquities* 1.4. Lucian (*How to Write History* 51), commenting on the qualities of a good historian, states (*Luciani opera*, vol. 3, ed. M. D. Macleod): Μάλιστα δὲ κατόπτρῳ ἐοικυῖαν παρασχέσθω τὴν γνώμην ἀθόλῳ καὶ στιλπνῷ καὶ ἀκριβεῖ τὸ κέντρον καὶ ὁποίας ἂν δέξηται τὰς μορφὰς τῶν ἔργων ταῦτα καὶ δεικνύτω αὐτά, διάστροφον δὲ ἢ παράχρουν ἢ ἑτερόσχημον μηδέν. οὐ γὰρ ὥσπερ τοῖς ῥήτορσι γράφουσιν, ἀλλὰ τὰ μὲν λεχθησόμενα ἔστιν καὶ εἰρήσεται· πέπρακται γὰρ ἤδη· δεῖ δὲ τάξαι καὶ εἰπεῖν αὐτά. [Above all, let {the historian} furnish a mind like a mirror: clear, glistening, accurately focused. Whatever the appearances of the actions he receives, let him also display them without distortion, discoloration, or misrepresentation. For what is to be said {by the historian} is not as some write for orators, but is so in reality and will speak for itself, for it has happened already. It only needs to be put in order and recounted.]

[65] Josephus *Antiquities* 1.2. Note Josephus's personal defense in his *Life* (336–67) against Justus. Both Thucydides (1.22) and Josephus (*Against Apion* 1.53) deny that they are writing a 'prize essay' for the present. Lucian (*How to Write History* 7–13) attacks those who turn history into (self-serving) panegyric. The historian's commitment to the truth prohibits any turning from the truth to serve party interests. See, e.g., Josephus *Jewish War* 1.1–6; note also Josephus's attacks on those who praise the Romans at the expense of the Jews (*Jewish War* 1.16; 1.30).

for historical truth in a literary culture[66] that transcended the boundaries of any specific community localized in space and time.[67]

Lk-Acts stands out among early Christian narrative texts in that it has a formal preface, including a dedication.[68] The dedication to Theophilus probably indicates that the work was either produced specifically for or at the request of Theophilus, or that the work was being presented in a public literary context under the patronage of Theophilus.[69] This formal preface with dedication suggests Lk-Acts was intended for circulation in a reading public familiar with Hellenistic literary culture.[70] With this dedication, the author reorients his account of the 'events accomplished among us' from an immediate experience of Jesus through the voice of a Christian community[71] to the intellectual task,

---

[66] It would be wrong to construe this literary culture too narrowly since Lucian's comments on how to write history suggest that individuals of very modest abilities readily undertook the task of composing historical narratives. Although Lucian's comments are exaggerated for rhetorical effect (e.g., *How to Write History* 2), there should be nothing surprising about an early Christian author, obviously relatively well educated, claiming to adopt the standards of Hellenistic historiography for investigating the history of Christianity.

[67] Of course, such narratives were read in a public context. See, e.g., Lucian *How to Write History* 5. Not surprisingly, therefore, such narratives would include material intended to entertain and hold the attention of such an audience. The author of Lk-Acts certainly expected his work to be read in public Christian gatherings. Nevertheless, these specific audiences did not define the conceptual scope of such narratives.

[68] To Theophilus (Lk 1:3; Acts 1:1).

[69] For the literary implications of the dedication, see Cadbury, *The Making of Luke-Acts*, p. 204; von Campenhausen, *The Formation of the Christian Bible*, p. 128, esp. n. 101. See also Alexander, *The Preface to Luke's Gospel*, pp. 187–212. Alexander has attempted to orient the preface of Lk-Acts toward the tradition of scientific writings in antiquity, which were characterized by dedications in their prefaces. The importance of literary patronage and the use of dedications, however, cannot be restricted to the scientific tradition and thus the dedication to Theophilus in Lk 1:3 and Acts 1:1 cannot bear the weight Alexander places upon it to demonstrate that Lk-Acts belongs in the tradition of scientific writings in antiquity. See discussion above in this section concerning comparative methodologies for establishing the genre of Lk-Acts.

[70] The literary qualities of Lk-Acts in comparison to other early Christian texts have been widely noted. These literary qualities presuppose a level of education for the author and the audience implied by the prefaces that in all probability exceeded the level of literacy of most early Christians. (On ancient literacy among Greeks and Romans, see Harris, *Ancient Literacy*, esp. pp. 327–37.) The prologue to Lk-Acts suggests an orientation toward a well-educated Christian audience that extended beyond the social realities of any particular Christian community. Not surprisingly, Acts (crucial for the author's reconceptualization of the 'events accomplished among us') was not important in the life of early Christian communities and emerged in the second century only in a highly educated social matrix. See chapter 2 under *Irenaeus*.

[71] See chapter 2 under *Traditions of Authorship and Titles*. For the author, such an

signified by the dialogue between author and reader (patron),[72] of being a Christian in the Graeco-Roman world.[73]

The dialogue between author and reader in the preface to Lk-Acts suggests a social and literary context very similar to the one presupposed by the writings of Josephus.[74] In the formal preface to the *Jewish War*, Josephus speaks to his reader in the first person and undertakes, under the patronage of Roman emperors,[75] to recount for an educated audience[76] the events of the Jewish rebellion against Rome in such a way that he and the Jewish nation are exonerated and all the blame is placed at the feet of certain zealots.[77] In the *Antiquities*, Josephus writes explicitly for a patron and portrays the religious history of his people for an educated Hellenistic audience.[78] He characterizes his patron Epaphroditus as one devoted to learning and having a particular interest in history. In none of his extant works is there any evidence that he writes as a representative of a specific Jewish community seeking a self-understanding in the aftermath of the Roman defeat of the

---

inadequate perspective on the λόγος (Lk 1:2) is part of his implied criticism of his sources, the 'many' of Lk 1:1. Mk 1:1–2 is for the author neither an adequate expression of the beginning or the scope of the gospel of Jesus Christ. The author corrects this limited perspective by making the life of Jesus the first part of a historical development that goes beyond the confines of Palestine.

[72] The dialogue between author and patron may be a literary fiction (note, e.g., *Letter of Aristeas* 1–8), but the literary effectiveness of the fiction would depend on the reality of author-patron relations. The author of Lk-Acts is claiming to write in the context implied by such a relation.

[73] Note, e.g., the comments in Lk 2:1–2 and 3:1 that correlate the 'events accomplished among us' with important events and leaders of the Roman world. Dibelius (*Studies in the Acts of the Apostles*, p. 88), however, draws the unnecessary conclusion from the prologue of Lk-Acts that Lk-Acts was intended to address a non-Christian audience; on the Christian audience of Lk-Acts, see below in this section.

[74] There are a large number of similarities between Lk-Acts and the writings of Josephus. See, e.g., Mason, *Josephus and the New Testament*, pp. 185–225. See also discussion above in this section concerning the conventions of historiography. Sterling (*Historiography and Self-Definition*, pp. 365–69; cf. p. 374) has attempted to argue for the generic similarity between Lk-Acts and Josephus's *Antiquities*, but has not developed the social implications of this comparison to Josephus for understanding the social context of Lk-Acts.

[75] See his claims in the *Life* 361–67.

[76] See, e.g., the exaggerated claims he makes for the importance of the Jewish war in his prologue and his concern for style indicated at the end of Book 6.

[77] His self-defense in the *Life* (see esp. 336–67) suggests that he was accused of having taken certain liberties with the portrayal of his own role and that of the 'zealots' in his *Jewish War*.

[78] See *Antiquities* 1.8–9; cf. *Against Apion* 1.1; 2.1, 296; *Life* 430.

Jewish rebellion.⁷⁹ Josephus writes as an individual to other educated individuals and intends his works to be taken seriously in the context of Hellenistic literature.⁸⁰ His two smaller works, the *Life* and *Against Apion*, are responses to personal attacks on the accuracy of his prior literary efforts, the *Jewish War* and the *Antiquities*, respectively, in the context of this literary culture.⁸¹

The circumstances of the composition of the *Life of Apollonius* by Philostratus provide another useful comparison to Lk-Acts in this literary culture. Philostratus wrote under the literary patronage of the empress Julia Domna, the wife of Septimius Severus. The work is not actually dedicated to her, perhaps because she died before its publication. She drew Philostratus's attention to the memoirs (ὑπομνήματα) of Damis, a companion of Apollonius, and asked Philostratus to recast and edit them, paying attention to style and diction.⁸² Further, Philostratus indicates an interest in writing an accurate account of what Apollonius said and did to replace ignorance and misunderstanding⁸³

---

⁷⁹ The difficulty of specifying a narrowly defined community for whom Josephus is the mouthpiece should caution against too quickly identifying the author of Lk-Acts, who shares many similarities with Josephus, with a specific Christian community. Contrast Talbert (*Literary Patterns, Theological Themes and the Genre of Luke-Acts*, p. 135): "Both Luke's choice of genre type for his message to the church and his development of the type chosen were rooted in the *Sitz im Leben* of his community. The Lucan community was one that was troubled by a clash of views..." Sterling (*Historiography and Self-Definition*, p. 378) fails to clarify the relation of Lk-Acts to early Christian communities when he asks: "How did Luke-Acts function among the mixed communities it addressed?" Simply pluralizing 'community' to 'communities' does not help answer the question of the function of Lk-Acts.

⁸⁰ His audience is defined by participation in this literary culture, not by political or ethnic identity (whether Jewish, Greek, or Roman).

⁸¹ His defense of his *Jewish War* in his *Life* is also a defense of his own actions in the war in response to the attacks of a certain Justus, a more nationalistic author of a history of the Jewish war. See *Life* 336–67. Josephus's apology in *Against Apion* is probably also tied to his attempt to represent himself in the context of this literary culture in relation to his own past. On Josephus's representation of Judaism in *Against Apion*, see Droge, 'Josephus between Greeks and Barbarians,' esp. pp. 140–41.

⁸² 1.3. Compare Philostratus's description of this source with Justin's description of the gospels as ἀπομνημονεύματα (*1 Apol.* 67.3–4; cf. 66.3). The question of the actual relation of Philostratus to his alleged source material is still unresolved. To what extent Theophilus was responsible for supplying the author of Lk-Acts with the material that served as the basis for his narrative (perhaps Mk and Q, see Lk 1:1; perhaps the 'we' source for the narrative of Acts; but apparently not Pauline letters, see chapter 4 below) cannot be determined. Nevertheless, the author of Lk-Acts undertook the revision of stories about Jesus and the apostles with an evident interest in style and diction.

⁸³ 1.2.

expressed in inadequate or hostile sources.[84] Finally, under the literary patronage of Julia Domna, Philostratus writes to an unspecified general audience characterized as those who love learning.[85] For this audience, Philostratus writes an account of the life of a religious figure. The author of Lk-Acts writes to establish intellectual certainty about Christian stories construed as a sequence of historical events, not organized in terms of an individual's life. Nevertheless, the interest in religious figures from the East among certain segments of the Roman aristocracy, evidenced by Julia Domna's interest in Apollonius, perhaps suggests a context for the religious interests of Theophilus as a literary patron of Christianity.[86] There is no reason to suppose Lk-Acts was written at Rome or for a patron at Rome. Nevertheless, to the extent that Theophilus had the resources to indulge in literary patronage, he probably enjoyed at least a certain local status and stood between Graeco-Roman society and Christian faith. Under the patronage of such an individual, the author of Lk-Acts intends to write a narrative explaining the origin of Christianity, not for a Christian community to legitimate that particular Christian community, but to define a Christian identity for individuals in the Graeco-Roman world in the context of Hellenistic literary culture.[87]

The author of Lk-Acts claims to have adopted the standards for truth from the tradition of Hellenistic historiography, but he certainly did not intend to write a *history* in the strict sense of the content such a generic label would imply within Hellenistic literary culture. Nor is it likely that he intended to gain an audience for his work from within Hellenistic literary culture in general. No one else in antiquity formulated the object of inquiry into the past by the historian

---

[84] 1.3. Cf. Lk 1:1.

[85] 1.3. The author of Lk-Acts writes specifically for a literary patron and generally for Christians who, according to Lk 1:1–4, might be characterized as those interested in a learned inquiry into the past.

[86] Phil 4:22, e.g., suggests that Christianity penetrated into the households of members of the Roman aristocracy at a very early date. Judaism as well won the favor of members of the Roman aristocracy. Josephus (*Life* 3) claims to have gained the favor of Poppaea at Rome, who interceded with Nero on behalf of certain Jewish priests and from whom Josephus himself received gifts before returning to Judea.

[87] The dialogue between Paul and Agrippa (Acts 26:25–29) should be compared with the author's dialogue with Theophilus (Lk 1:1–4; Acts 1:1). The narrative of Lk-Acts is a learned inquiry into the past for a well-educated audience to explain what it is to be a Christian in terms of where Christianity came from.

as τὰ πεπληροφορημένα ἐν ἡμῖν πράγματα.[88] The author of Lk-Acts makes no effort to defend his failure to conform to the expectations for the subject matter of a historical narrative.[89] No pagan participant in Hellenistic literary culture would be inclined to accept that supposed happenings concerning the preaching of the word (Lk 1:2) constitute a worthy object of inquiry for the writing of a *history* of recent events.[90] Instead, the author's starting point and theory of history place him in a specific relationship to the literary tradition of biblical history.[91] Such history is an account of God's dealings with God's people mediated through the actions of divinely selected individuals.[92] Lk-Acts narrates the historical fulfillment of the sacred writings of the Jews.[93] The use of πεπληροφορημένων in Lk 1:1 anticipates the transition from 1:4 to 1:5.[94] The narrative style that begins in Lk 1:5 connects Lk-Acts to the

---

[88] Alexander (*The Preface to Luke's Gospel*, esp. p. 112) has argued against previous interpreters of Acts that πράγματα "is not characteristically used of the stuff of history." Nevertheless, see Josephus's prologue to *The Jewish War*. In his opening sentence, the πράγματα of the Jewish war against the Romans is introduced as the object of Josephus's interest. To refer to events of the past that are the object of the historian's interest, Josephus also uses πράξεις and τὰ γεγονότα (*Against Apion* 1.53–55). (On the use of πράξεις as a title, see chapter 2 under *Traditions of Authorship and Titles*.) In any case, the content of Lk-Acts as this is designated by πράγματα in Lk 1:1 is certainly not the content of other histories of events in antiquity. To say this, however, is to suggest the question of *how* the author came to formulate the object of his inquiry in such a manner. On this question, see discussion below in this section.

[89] Contrast Josephus (*Jewish War* 1.16), who defends his work against individuals who might object to his subject matter.

[90] On the subject matter for history, see Fornara, *The Nature of History in Ancient Greece and Rome*, pp. 91–98; cf. p. 63. The origins of religions could be the object of inquiry into the past, but Lk 1:1–4 orients the reader to events of the recent past, not to the history of a religious institution. On Cancik's proposal for Lk-Acts as a history of an institution ('The History of Culture, Religion, and Institutions in Ancient Historiography: Philological Observations Concerning Luke's Institutional History,' pp. 673–95), see Reasoner, 'The Theme of Acts: Institutional History or Divine Necessity in History,' pp. 635–59.

[91] For the author of Lk-Acts, the preaching of the word (Lk 1:2) is an announcement of a βασιλεία. This kingdom is the divine necessity in history (see Reasoner, 'The Theme of Acts: Institutional History or Divine Necessity in History,' pp. 635–59) that marks out important events (and persons) worthy of attention and investigation.

[92] Just as the biblical characters of, e.g., Abraham, Moses, Samuel, David, Elisha, and Elijah determine ancient history, so the author's portrayal of John, Jesus, Peter, and Paul determines the recent history of God's people. On the influence of the Septuagint for the author's understanding of history, see Sterling, *Historiography and Self-Definition*, pp. 352–63.

[93] Lk 24:44–49; cf. Acts 26:6, 27. Josephus characterizes the sacred writings of the Jews (*Against Apion* 1.53) as historical accounts in *Jewish War* 1.17–18.

[94] The stylistic transition from 1:4 to 1:5 is for the author's understanding of history

historiographical tradition of the Septuagint in several ways.⁹⁵ (1) The language and style is influenced by the Septuagint.⁹⁶ (2) The subject matter is God's intervention for the salvation of God's people through the birth of noteworthy individuals.⁹⁷ (3) The account is organized as a succession of divinely appointed heroes to carry forward these divine purposes. (4) Divine intervention as a legitimate causative explanation is taken for granted. (5) This divine intervention is often manifested in terms of the activity of the spirit of God.

The absence of any reasoned argument for such a theoretical departure from accepted canons of selection for historical events within the context of Graeco-Roman literary culture indicates an intended audience for Lk-Acts already inclined to accept 'fulfilled' events concerning the preaching of the word as worthy of historical inquiry. As a result, rather than defending his narrative in the context of other Graeco-Roman histories,⁹⁸ the author justifies his narrative over against previous Christian narratives.

Specifically, in Lk 1:1–4 the author further defines the literary context of his work vis-à-vis previous narratives judged to be deficient. The efforts of the many in Lk 1:1, πολλοὶ ἐπεχείρησαν, are contrasted with the work of the author in verse 3, ἔδοξε κἀμοὶ ... γράψαι.⁹⁹ The author

---

the type of smooth transition from preface to subject matter expected for a historian. See Lucian *How to Write History* 55 (*Luciani opera*, vol. 3, ed. M. D. Macleod): μετὰ δὲ τὸ προοίμιον, ἀνάλογον τοῖς πράγμασιν ἢ μηκυνόμενον ἢ βραχυνόμενον, εὐαφὴς καὶ εὐάγωγος ἔστω ἡ ἐπὶ διήγησιν μετάβασις. [After the preface, extended or shortened in proportion to the subject matter, let the transition to the narrative be unforced and smooth.] See also 44.

⁹⁵ Both Josephus (*Jewish War* 1.18) and the author of Lk-Acts conceptualize the beginning of their narratives in terms of where biblical history leaves off. Whereas Josephus gives a summary of events preceding his lifetime necessary for understanding the context of the Jewish war, the author of Lk-Acts conceptualizes biblical history as having ended with an unfulfilled expectation of salvation to be realized in the message proclaimed by John and Jesus. See Lk 2:25–38; cf. Lk 1:16–17, 32. See also Lk 16:16: ὁ νόμος καὶ οἱ προφῆται μέχρι Ἰωάννου.

⁹⁶ See, e.g., Fitzmyer, *The Gospel according to Luke (I-IX)*, pp. 113–27.

⁹⁷ In the narrative of Lk-Acts, the life of Jesus, though of central importance for the author's understanding of recent events, does not in itself mark the end of the διήγησιν περὶ τῶν πεπληροφορημένων ἐν ἡμῖν πραγμάτων. The life of Jesus has become but one part (a decisive part, to be sure) in the history of actions carried out by important individuals for the salvation of God's people. See discussion below under *Paul's Farewell Speech and the Literary Paulinism of Lk-Acts*.

⁹⁸ Note the extensive apology by Josephus in his prologue to the *Jewish War* to gain a hearing for his history.

⁹⁹ Alexander (*The Preface to Luke's Gospel*, p. 115) attempts to circumvent the negative connotations of ἐπεχείρησαν in the context of Lk 1:1–4 by arguing that the author

has thus placed his work not only in the literary tradition of Graeco-Roman and Jewish historiography, but also in the context of previous Christian texts.[100] In other words, Lk-Acts is self-consciously Christian literature, intended for an audience familiar with or at least aware of previous Christian texts and traditions while at the same time aware of Hellenistic standards of truth for historiography and Jewish assumptions about history expressed in the Septuagint. Whereas the public reading in Christian communities of texts about Jesus probably took place in terms of parts, not wholes,[101] the author of Lk-Acts expects

---

places himself alongside (rather than against) these πολλοί by invoking a common tradition (Lk 1:2) and a common purpose (καί, Lk 1:3). Such an interpretation, however, misses the criticism of the πολλοί implied by the adverbial qualifications to the author's decision to write supplied by παρηκολουθηκότι ἄνωθεν πᾶσιν ἀκριβῶς καθεξῆς in Lk 1:3. Furthermore, Lk 1:4 implies that certainty is not possible in relation to the attempts of the author's literary predecessors. There is thus no need to explain away the negative import of ἐπεχείρησαν, Alexander's defense of the canonical gospels notwithstanding ("If there is a failure, it could just as well be a failure to complete the task undertaken: how many would-be evangelists simply failed to achieve the success of Mark, Matthew and Luke in reducing the multiplex and varied Gospel tradition into a coherent written narrative? It is certainly not necessary to assume that those who did complete it are included in Luke's mild and ambiguous depreciation..." [pp. 115–16.])

[100] In the case of Mk, probably one of the sources for the author of Lk-Acts, Mk 1:1 sets up expectations arguably compatible with Bultmann's understanding of the kerygma (the proclamation of the man who lived in the flesh as Lord) as the presupposition for the narrative as a Christian text. On the other hand, Cancik ('Die Gattung Evangelium. Markus im Rahmen der antiken Historiographie,' pp. 94–98) has argued that the reader's generic expectations would depend on whether he or she were reading from a Graeco-Roman or Jewish point of view. From the former point of view, a reader would identify Mk as a life (*bios*) of a divine man; from the latter perspective, as a book of a prophet. For such readers, however, Mk 1:2 immediately undermines such genre expectations by establishing an intertextual link to the Septuagint: Jesus is the son of God in relation to Septuagintal prophecy. This connection between Jesus and the biblical past introduces an idea of history from a Christian perspective, an idea that suggests that Mk itself (at least as the text seems to have been read by the author of Lk-Acts) as a whole is something more than a *bios* or book of a prophet. (On Mk as a gospel, see chapter 2 under *Traditions of Authorship and Titles*.) See Adela Yarbro Collins, *Is Mark's Gospel a Life of Jesus? The Question of Genre*, pp. 44–45, 63; idem, *The Beginning of the Gospel*, pp. 27, 36–37. The author of Lk-Acts makes explicit the idea of history implicit in Mk 1:1–2.

[101] This type of reading is suggested by the practice of Jewish synagogues (as portrayed in Lk 4 and Acts 13) and later (liturgical?) divisions introduced into the texts. See especially Justin, who associates the reading of the memoirs of the apostles with the reading of the prophets, followed by an exhortation from the leader (*1 Apol.* 66.3; 67.3–4—cf. Lk 4:16–28; Acts 13:13–42). Papias suggests that Mk consists of *chreiai* that lack an overall order. See also *Acts of Peter* 20 (cited according to Schneemelcher, *New Testament Apocrypha*, rev. ed. [1991], 2.301–2): "And Peter went into the dining-room and saw that the gospel was being read. So he rolled up (the book) and said, 'You men who

his audience to assess the accuracy and order of his own narrative in relation to previous accounts (Lk 1:1–4). This expectation suggests that Lk-Acts was written for an educated Christian audience whose interest in the preaching of the λόγος (Lk 1:2) went beyond the needs of a local Christian community. Lk-Acts was not intended to be simply one more parochial Christian narrative for a local community.[102] To the extent that the author claims to have adopted Greek standards for reliable historiography, the intended audience is characterized not by participation in a local Christian community, but by participation as Christians in Hellenistic (literary) culture.[103] By claiming the standards of truth for writing history in the context of Hellenistic literary culture, the author excludes any interpretation of his work that reduces his effort to inner-Christian polemics or local community self-definition. He claims to be not first of all a theologian or polemicist for a local community, but a Christian participating as an educated individual[104] in Hellenistic culture.[105] The author of Lk-Acts bequeaths to educated Christian readers not a theological or polemical self-definition of a community vis-à-vis other Christian communities or Hellenistic culture but a positive place for Christianity in the Graeco-Roman world.[106] Such an understanding

---

believe and hope in Christ, you must know how the holy scripture of our Lord should be declared.... And now I will explain to you what has just been read to you....'" An explanation of the account of the transfiguration follows.

[102] Note Acts 26:26: οὐ γὰρ ἐστιν ἐν γωνίᾳ πεπραγμένον τοῦτο ('for this was not done in a corner'); note also the synchronism with Roman history at Lk 2:1–2; 3:1; Acts 11:28. Mk lacks these connections with the larger Graeco-Roman context.

[103] Harris (*Ancient Literacy*, p. 126) comments on literacy in the Hellenistic period: "[T]he production of works of scholarly learning was quite extensive, and must have been intended exclusively for the use of the individual reader—in fact exclusivity, the creation of a private, or nearly private, mental world, was presumably a large part of the aim of such authors." Just to the extent that the author of Lk-Acts orients his work towards this intellectual tradition, he addresses his audience as individuals belonging to the kingdom of God, not a specific community of Christians.

[104] 'I,' Lk 1:3.

[105] The author's distancing of Christianity from characteristically Jewish concerns (table fellowship, circumcision, temple, national restoration) would resonate with this Hellenistic culture. See Josephus, who, in his writings intended for a Graeco-Roman audience, downplays Jewish nationalism (Josephus aligns himself with Vespasian!), minimizes Jewish particularism (Josephus welcomes uncircumcised Gentiles into Jewish company [*Life* 113]), and portrays Jewish groups as philosophical schools (Josephus claims he is a Pharisee and describes this way of life as a school resembling the Stoics [*Life* 10–12; cf. *Jewish War* 2.119; *Antiquities* 18.11–25]).

[106] Cf. note 87 above on Paul's dialogue with Agrippa in Acts 26:25–29. Cf. also Paul's Areopagus speech, on which Vielhauer ('On the "Paulinism" of Acts,' p. 37) comments: "When the Areopagus speaker refers to the unity of the human race in its

of Christianity is, according to the author, just what is lacking in other texts about Jesus.

In short, the author of Lk-Acts has reconceptualized previous narratives about Jesus in terms of Hellenistic and Jewish historiography, but has defined 'historical' events in relation to the Septuagint perceived as fulfilled in the Christian gospel.[107] The author has thus asserted that certainty or truth about Christian λόγοι (Lk 1:4) is derived from the arrangement of these particulars into a reliable history of the recent past—a history determined by the author's understanding of the Septuagint and claiming the standards for truth of Hellenistic historiography. The author is thus concerned to demonstrate that the stories about the recent past of Christians can be investigated, determined to be historically accurate, and presented in an ordered account to provide a basis for certainty about the place of Christians in the historical unfolding of God's purposes within Graeco-Roman society between Jerusalem and Rome.[108]

Greek thought and Greek attempts to write history were plagued by the problem of the relation between general truths and specific historical facts. Aristotle, *Poetics* 9, expresses the dilemma for the Greek historian well:[109]

> It is also evident from what has been said that it is not the poet's function to relate actual events, but the *kinds* of things that might occur and are possible in terms of probability or necessity. The difference between the historian and the poet is not that between using verse or prose; Herodotus' work could be versified and would be just as much a kind of history in verse as in prose. No, the difference is this: that the one relates actual events, the other the kinds of things that might occur. Consequently, poetry is more

---

natural kinship to God and to its natural knowledge of God, and when he refers to the altar inscription and to the statements of pagan poets to make this point, he thereby lays claim to pagan history, culture, and religion as the prehistory of Christianity." In contrast, note that for Irenaeus the Acts of the Apostles is read as defining the history of true Christianity over against Christian heresies. In the canonization of the 'Acts of the Apostles,' the reference point for the text of Acts shifted from an outward orientation toward the Graeco-Roman world to an inward orientation toward ecclesiastical doctrine.

[107] See Lk 24:44–47.

[108] Compare Lk 1:5 with Acts 28:30–31. Not until the second volume of Lk-Acts does the intentionality of the author's voice in Lk 1:1–4 concerning Christian λόγοι really become clear as one problem after another is sorted out in the events following the death of Jesus. See, e.g., Acts 1:15–26; 6:1–6; 11:1–18; 15:1–35, 36–41; 21:18–26. See also note 43 above.

[109] Translation by Stephen Halliwell (*Aristotle. Poetics* [LCL, 1995]).

philosophical[110] and more elevated[111] than history, since poetry relates more of the universal,[112] while history relates particulars.

To compensate for that limitation, Greek historiography tended toward atemporal representations of the past to elicit general truths for the present.[113] This anti-historical tendency in Greek thought continually drew historical narrative toward rhetoric and narrative fiction. Thus, the construction of a narrative in Hellenistic historiography arose from a complex interplay of rhetoric, fictional narrative, and particular facts of the past. This complex interplay is grossly simplified in the dichotomy between fiction and history often applied to Lk-Acts.[114] Lk-Acts, to the extent it is influenced by the standards for truth of Hellenistic historiography, likely combines historical traditions, narrative fiction, and rhetoric in a way that will emerge only from a careful reading of the text.[115]

Nevertheless, in the author's conception of the plan of God, he partially resolves the problem of the relationship of general truths to specific historical facts—that is, of the difference between the past and the present. Because the author of Lk-Acts locates the specific historical events of his narrative in the purpose of God,[116] the author's historical

---

[110] φιλοσοφώτερον.

[111] σπουδαιότερον.

[112] Aristotle defines that which is universal as what a certain type of person will do or say either probably or necessarily.

[113] On the anti-historical tendency in Greek thought, see Collingwood, *The Idea of History*, pp. 20–31; see esp. his comments on Thucydides, pp. 30–31.

[114] Concerning the writing of history in antiquity, Fornara (*The Nature of History in Ancient Greece and Rome*, pp. 134–35) comments: "The need for imaginative recreation and inferential elaboration from the facts was the necessary consequence of the demands placed on all subsequent historians by Herodotus when he decided, following Homer, to present events with verisimilitude. Everything from needful circumstantial detail to the virtual reproduction of the thoughts of leading figures was injected into the historical narrative, often on mere grounds of probability."

[115] Thus, a complex interplay of fact, fiction, and rhetoric is to be expected in the portrayal of Paul. See below; see also chapter 4.

[116] See, e.g., Acts 20:27. In Lk-Acts, this divine plan is expressed in at least five ways: (1) prophetic oracles from the past (the sacred scriptures: Lk 24:44–47; Acts 2:22–36); (2) divine appointment of individuals (John, Jesus, the Twelve, Paul); (3) divine control of events (the death of Jesus: Acts 2:23–24; the rejection of unbelieving Jews and the acceptance of believing Gentiles: Acts 13:47–48; see also Acts 28:23–28; note that the author repeatedly emphasizes the necessity of events taking place; e.g., Lk 24:44); (4) divine visions and oracles which guide events (Lk 1:11–38; Acts 1:26; 9:1–19; 10:1–48; 11:27–30; 13:1–3; 16:9–10; 18:9–10; 21:10–14; 22:17–21; 27:23–25); and (5) the relationship between God and humanity established in the foundation of the world (Acts 7:48–50; 14:15–17; 17:24–31; cf. Lk 3:23–38). See also Reasoner, 'The Theme of Acts: Institutional

narrative unfolds not in an accidental but in a determined way, and therefore particular events in the past determine general truths for the present. Specifically, the death and resurrection of Jesus, though particular events of the past, were ordained by God[117] and are the basis for the preaching of repentance to all nations.[118] The historical particularity of the resurrection of Jesus becomes proof for a general message of repentance and escape from coming judgment.[119] As the purpose of God unfolds through the divine appointment of individuals for the proclamation of the word of God[120] (specifically John,[121] Jesus,[122] the Twelve,[123] and Paul[124]), the author of Lk-Acts preserves a sense of difference between the past and present while at the same time integrating the events of the past into a universal, general message of salvation.[125] Consequently, the author claims that his narrative of events from the recent past can produce certainty about religious truths.[126] In Paul's farewell discourse, this certainty is mediated to the Christian present from the past in which Jesus, the apostles, and Paul proclaim the kingdom of God based on Jesus' death and resurrection.

Paul's Farewell Speech and the Literary Paulinism of Lk-Acts

In Acts 20:32 Paul, having announced that the Ephesian elders will never again see him,[127] commends them to God and to the word of God's grace.[128] This 'word of God's grace,' which constitutes Christians as the people of God, is nothing less than the 'gospel of the grace of God,'[129] the 'preaching of the kingdom,'[130] the 'whole counsel of God,'[131]—indeed, the preaching of 'repentance toward God and faith

---

History or Divine Necessity in History?' pp. 635–59.
[117] See Lk 24:46; Acts 2:23–24.
[118] See Lk 24:44–48. Cf. Acts 17:31.
[119] See Acts 17:31; 20:21; 24:24–25.
[120] See Lk 1:2; cf. Acts 28:30–31.
[121] See, e.g., Lk 1:5–25. Concerning his preaching, see Lk 3:2, 15–18.
[122] See, e.g., Lk 1:26–38; 2:25–38.
[123] See, e.g., Acts 1:15–26.
[124] See, e.g., Acts 9:15.
[125] See, e.g., Lk 16:16. See also Conzelmann, *The Theology of St. Luke*, p. 185–87.
[126] That is, certainty about the relationship of the λόγος (Lk 1:2) to the λόγοι (Lk 1:4).
[127] Acts 20:25: καὶ νῦν ἰδοὺ ἐγὼ οἶδα ὅτι οὐκέτι ὄψεσθε τὸ πρόσωπόν μου ὑμεῖς πάντες.
[128] καὶ τὰ νῦν παρατίθεμαι ὑμᾶς τῷ θεῷ καὶ τῷ λόγῳ τῆς χάριτος αὐτοῦ.
[129] Acts 20:24: τὸ εὐαγγέλιον τῆς χάριτος τοῦ θεοῦ.
[130] Acts 20:25: κηρύσσων τὴν βασιλείαν.
[131] Acts 20:27: πᾶσαν τὴν βουλὴν τοῦ θεοῦ.

in our Lord Jesus,'[132] which Paul has gone about proclaiming both in public and in private among the Ephesians. In both form and content,[133] Paul's farewell speech in Acts 20:17–35 links the past to the readers' present by entrusting to the leaders of local Christian communities[134] this word of God's grace.[135] With Paul's farewell address, the foundational proclamation of the word of God,[136] in which Paul participates as God's chosen instrument to proclaim the gospel (Acts 9:15), has been testified to in its fullness.[137] The history of this proclamation[138] is now a certain foundation[139] for Christians as the people of God in the Graeco-Roman world.[140]

Paul's speech in Acts 20:17–35 differs from the final words of Jesus in that the latter are addressed to the apostles, the 'eyewitnesses and servants of the word' (Lk 1:2) who belong to a distinct period in the history of Christianity. What Jesus did and taught (Acts 1:1) has thus been historically distanced from the author's and readers' present (Lk 1:3).[141] This sense of historical distance is particularly evident in the

---

[132] Acts 20:21: τὴν εἰς θεὸν μετάνοιαν καὶ πίστιν εἰς τὸν κύριον ἡμῶν Ἰησοῦν.

[133] See Katter ('Luke 22:14–38: A Farewell Address,' pp. 44–135) for a survey of the form and function of a farewell discourse.

[134] Acts 20:28; cf. 20:17. There is no concept of apostolic succession here. In Acts, the office of apostleship has a narrowly defined historical function (Acts 1:21–22). Paul himself is not really considered an apostle in Acts (on Acts 14:4, 14, see chapter 4 under *Paul's Mission with Barnabas*), and the office certainly cannot be correlated with the needs of specific local communities. Note, for example, how the apostles are separated from the daily functioning of the Jerusalem community in Acts 6:1–5 so that they can focus on the ministry of the word, that is, the preaching of the gospel. The leaders of local churches in Acts function to keep the community true to the faith, that is, to the message of the word of God's grace proclaimed by the apostles and Paul. Cf. Acts 14:21–23.

[135] Typical of farewell speeches is the handing on from past to present of a deposit of truth (including warnings and exhortations) necessary to preserve the well being of the community after the departure (often in death) of the character. See Katter, 'Luke 22:14–38: A Farewell Address,' p. 125.

[136] See Lk 1:2; Acts 1:8, in which witnessing to Jesus is speaking the things about the kingdom of God, Acts 1:3 (cf. 28:30–31).

[137] See, e.g., Acts 20:20–21, 27; cf. 19:10.

[138] περὶ τῶν πεπληροφορημένων ἐν ἡμῖν πραγμάτων (Lk 1:1).

[139] Cf. τὴν ἀσφάλειαν, Lk 1:4.

[140] The author of Lk-Acts has little interest in the church viewed internally (Stephen, appointed to deal with needs of the community in Acts 6, is of importance in the narrative for his speech in Acts 7 before the Sanhedrin; the disputes in Acts 15 are important because their resolution affects the spread of the word). Instead, the author views the church in relation to the preaching of the word of God from Jerusalem to Rome that constitutes Christians as heirs of the kingdom of God.

[141] Conzelmann's *The Theology of St. Luke* (see, e.g., pp. 184, 211) remains an important

author's redaction of Mk to produce Jesus' farewell address in Lk 22:14–38[142] and apocalyptic discourse in Lk 21. In both cases, Jesus' final words have been historically differentiated from the present of the audience of Lk-Acts.[143]

Jesus' apocalyptic discourse and the coming of the kingdom

The apocalyptic discourse in Mk 13 characterizes the readers' present as a time of imminent expectation of the end associated with the destruction of Jerusalem. Jesus' address to the disciples is explicitly directed to the reader (Mk 13:14, 37). On the other hand, the author of Lk-Acts has disassociated the destruction of Jerusalem from the end of the age and in so doing has redirected the imminent expectation in Mk of the Parousia to an ongoing Christian mission in the Graeco-Roman world. The following points are relevant.

The events of Mk 13:9–13 are historically differentiated from the time of the present in Lk 21:12–19. These events, no longer part of the 'birth pangs' leading to the Parousia (Mk 13:8, a phrase omitted in Lk), instead lead to the destruction of Jerusalem (Lk 21:20–24), an event disassociated in Lk from the Parousia. Lk 21:12 introduces a temporal indicator (πρὸ δὲ τούτων πάντων: 'before all these things') absent in Mk, while Mk 13:10 (καὶ εἰς πάντα τὰ ἔθνη πρῶτον δεῖ κηρυχθῆναι

---

discussion of the author's sense of the past to which Jesus belongs. Conzelmann, however, focuses on Jesus, not Paul, and undervalues the significance of the narrative of Acts for understanding the author's redaction of earlier narratives and sources about Jesus. The author is less interested in portraying Jesus as the center of history than in explaining the development of Christianity out of Judaism in terms of the announcement of the kingdom of God as the Christian proclamation of the gospel in the Graeco-Roman world. Lk 16:16 divides history into two epochs, the time of the law and the prophets, followed by the time of the preaching of the kingdom of God. The time of the preaching of the kingdom of God is roughly divided into three periods: the time of Jesus, the time of the Twelve and Paul, and the time of the present. Jesus' proclamation of the kingdom belongs to that period of the second epoch in which the kingdom is offered to Israel; Paul's farewell address to the Ephesian elders establishes Christians as the people of God and heirs of the kingdom of God. The Twelve and Paul belong to a period in the history of the proclamation of the kingdom in which the message is gradually shifted away from Jewish nationalistic expectations, expectations that come to an end with the destruction of Jerusalem by Rome (Lk 21:20–24).

[142] On Lk 22:14–38 as a farewell address, see Katter, 'Luke 22:14–38: A Farewell Address,' pp. 128–35.

[143] The proper relation between Jesus and Christians that the author establishes in his redaction of the final words of Jesus in Mk is one aspect of his criticism of the way his sources have portrayed the life of Jesus in relation to 'the events accomplished among us' (Lk 1:1).

τὸ εὐαγγέλιον: 'and it is necessary that the gospel be proclaimed to all nations first') is omitted. Thus, Lk 21:12–19 places the events of Mk 13:9–13 in the readers' past but the apostles' future—that is, the time of Acts. For the author of Lk-Acts, this time is characterized by an increasingly obdurate rejection of the message of salvation by the Jews, to whom the message belongs first of all.[144] The description in Lk 21:12–19, especially verses 12–15, anticipates the narrative of Acts, corresponding to the experiences of Peter, John, his brother James, Stephen, and Paul at the hands of the Jews.[145] In Acts, Jewish resistance to the proclamation of the kingdom of God reaches its climax at Rome, where Paul announces a definitive rejection of Jewish national privilege in receiving the message of God's salvation, and salvation is sent to the Gentiles as those who will receive the message of God's kingdom.[146] The destruction of Jerusalem by Rome (Lk 21:20) is taken to be God's judgment upon the Jewish nation for its continued rejection of the message of salvation[147] and confirms Paul's rejection of Jewish national privilege in Acts 28:25–28.

Lk 21:20–24 describes the destruction of Jerusalem, an event that also belongs to the readers' past.[148] This event is determinative of the readers' present in that it marks the beginning of the 'times of the Gentiles' (not, as in Mk 13:24, the imminent Parousia). The destruction of Jerusalem is the political correlate of Christian integration into the Roman Empire as Paul turns decisively from the unbelieving Jews to the Gentiles at Rome (Acts 28:23–31). Although there is strictly speaking no connotation of mission in the phrase καιροὶ ἐθνῶν ('times

---

[144] See Acts 3:25–26. The initially favorable response to Peter's proclamation of the gospel in Acts 2 and 3 is replaced by the hostility of the Jews to Paul's proclamation of the gospel. See especially Acts 28:23–31, at Rome. This hostility of the Jews to the proclamation of the gospel has its basis in their rejection and crucifixion of Jesus. See, e.g., Acts 2:23 and Lk 19:41–48.

[145] Note especially how Peter (e.g., Acts 4:7–22), Stephen (Acts 6:8–10), and Paul (e.g., Acts 9:22) cannot be refuted in their orations (cf. Lk 21:15). Paul stands before King Agrippa because of the hostility of the Jews (Acts 26:2). See also the persecutions Paul himself heaped upon the church (summarized in Acts 26:9–11).

[146] See especially Acts 28:28, 31.

[147] See Lk 19:41–48; 21:20. The author's attitude toward the temple (admiration for which prompts Jesus' discourse in Lk 21:5–36) is evident in Stephen's speech, especially Acts 7:48–53.

[148] The destruction of the temple is presupposed by Stephen's speech in Acts. Cf. Lk 19:41–48, in which the announcement of the destruction of Jerusalem and the cleansing of the temple are placed alongside one another and are probably intended to be mutually interpretive.

of the Gentiles') in Lk 21:24, the renunciation of Jewish privilege in favor of the Gentiles by Paul at Rome, the center of political power, suggests an association of the 'trampling' of Jerusalem by Gentiles as a political event with the Gentile mission as a divine imperative defining the nature of the kingdom of God. By the end of the narrative of Acts, Christian identity has been decisively separated from Jewish national hopes and integrated into the political realities of the Roman world.[149]

The readers' present exists between Lk 21:24 and 21:25, for 21:25–28 describes the events to take place after the times of the Gentiles (21:24), events that belong to the readers' future. Lk 21:29–36 is addressed to the immediate audience of Jesus (the 'you' of Lk 21:12–20, that is, the immediate disciples) in view of the impending destruction of Jerusalem, but also to the reader in view of the suddenness with which the future (Lk 21:25–28) can become the present for those who are unprepared. The warning is a general ethical imperative in view of the coming judgment of the world.[150] The imminent expectation of the end in Mk has been muted in Lk-Acts as the realization of the kingdom of God has been reconceptualized.[151] The readers' present Christian identity, existing between Lk 21:24 (the destruction of Jerusalem) and Lk 21:25 (the Parousia) is determined by two historical developments according to Lk-Acts: (1) the enthronement in heaven of the resurrected Jesus as the Davidic king as promised in the Jewish scriptures,[152] and (2) the announcement of his rule to Jews and Gentiles by the apostles and Paul that constitutes the heirs of the kingdom, the people of God, in non-Jewish, Gentile terms through the preaching of Peter and Paul.[153]

---

[149] See chapter 4 under *Rome*.

[150] Cf. Acts 17:31. The final judgment has been disassociated from Jewish national expectations and the destruction of the temple.

[151] The so-called problem of the delay of the Parousia has played an important role in interpretations of Lk-Acts. See, e.g., Conzelmann's *The Theology of St. Luke*, pp. 135–36. The problem for the author of Lk-Acts is to orient Christians away from apocalyptic expectations associated with the Jewish nation (expressed in Mk in terms of linking the Parousia to the destruction of the temple) toward an identity as participants in the (ongoing) Graeco-Roman world. For the author of Mk, the present is a time of fear (Mk 16:8) as God's judgment of Jerusalem is worked out. For the author of Lk-Acts, the present is a time of optimistic expansion of the gospel in the Graeco-Roman world (Acts 28:30–31).

[152] Acts 2:22–36; cf. 3:17–26; 15:13–18.

[153] Acts 10:1–11:18; 20:32; cf. 14:22; also 13:46–48; 18:6; 28:23–31.

Jesus' farewell and the coming of the kingdom

Jesus' farewell address to the apostles, Lk 22:14–38, establishes historical continuity between Jesus and the Twelve (and thus between the end of Lk and the beginning of Acts) in terms of the coming of the kingdom. In Lk 22:29, Jesus confers the kingdom upon the apostles. This kingdom is expressed in terms associated with Jewish hopes of national restoration: the twelve tribes of Israel (22:30), the new covenant (22:20), and fulfillment of the Jewish Passover.[154] These Jewish hopes of national restoration shape the apostles' question in Acts 1:6: 'Lord, are you at this time restoring the kingdom to Israel?'[155] The risen Jesus, having already spent forty days teaching the apostles about the kingdom of God,[156] does not directly answer the apostles' question in Acts 1:6, but rather redirects the apostles' attention from the end of history[157] (understood by the apostles in terms of Jewish restoration) to the proclamation in Jesus' name of repentance for forgiveness to all the nations.[158] The answer to the apostles' question is to be found in the proclamation of salvation in Jesus.[159] This proclamation begins with Peter in Jerusalem to Jews in terms of their status as the people of God and the apostles' hope for a Jewish kingdom, but ends with Paul at Rome and a decisive rejection of Jewish privilege as the people of God and as the collective recipients of the message of the kingdom of God.[160] No Jewish national overtones to the kingdom of God remain in Paul's summary of his proclamation of the kingdom of God in his farewell speech. The message of the kingdom is characterized as repentance and faith in Jesus.[161] The apostles' question in Acts 1:6, with its national-political

---

[154] Cf. Lk 1:33, in which Jesus' kingdom is described in terms of ruling over the house of Jacob. See also Acts 26:6–7.

[155] Compare Peter's words in Acts 3:12–26, especially verses 19–26, with Paul's in Acts 26:6–8.

[156] Acts 1:3; see Lk 24:44–49.

[157] See Acts 1:11.

[158] Acts 1:8; cf. Lk 24:47. Conzelmann's suggestion (*The Theology of St. Luke*, p. 136) that the beginning of Acts formulates a solution to the delay of the Parousia lacks precision. The beginning of Acts separates the Parousia from Jewish expectations of the kingdom.

[159] In Acts 1:11, the promise of Jesus' return is affirmed (cf. Acts 17:31), but the apostles' expectations are redirected to matters at hand.

[160] See especially Acts 2:39; 3:19–26; 28:23–31. πρῶτον in Acts 3:26 anticipates the author's conception of the historical development of Christianity out of Judaism.

[161] Acts 20:21, 25; cf. Acts 28:31. Cf. also Acts 17:31, in which the resurrection of Jesus is understood in a Graeco-Roman context as the deification of a dead man. His resurrection does not signal the end of the age from an apocalyptic Jewish perspective. (On

Jewish overtones to the kingdom, does not express the author's understanding of the kingdom, but belongs to the author's historical differentiation between the Christian present and the Jewish past of Jesus, the Twelve, and Paul. This historical differentiation is marked by his understanding of the developments that lead to the constitution of the heirs of the kingdom in non-Jewish terms in the movement of the message of salvation from Jews to Gentiles.

The author portrays the apostles as not understanding the full developmental dimensions of this message (a misunderstanding evident in their question in Acts 1:6). Peter himself is at first unwilling to take the message to the Gentiles.[162] Jewish believers in Jerusalem repeatedly call into question the Gentile mission,[163] a dispute requiring a major council to resolve the relation between believing Jews and Gentiles. Only in Paul's call and mission is the full scope of the proclamation of the kingdom of God manifested.[164] In this proclamation of the word by Paul (Lk 1:2) lies the origin of Christianity as a distinct reality over against Judaism as the people of God.[165]

The apostles' question in Acts 1:6 not only misunderstands the scope of the message of salvation, but also the mode in which the kingdom is to be manifested. For the author, the kingdom of God foretold by the Law and the Prophets and proclaimed since John the Baptist[166] is not predicated on the national restoration of Israel, but instead on the reception of the spirit of God based on the preaching of faith in Jesus. The author's understanding of the reception of the spirit as the *sine qua non* of participation in the kingdom does not imply a completely realized eschatology, but instead establishes the nature of

---

this apocalyptic perspective, see Mt 27:52–53.) Note that Paul's proclamation of the gospel in the second half of Acts generalizes imagery associated in the first half of Acts with the apocalyptic restoration of Israel. Compare, e.g., Acts 2:38–40 and 3:19–21 with 13:38–39.

[162] Acts 10:9–29; 11:1–18, esp. verse 17.

[163] Acts 11:2–3; 15:1–5.

[164] See especially Acts 9:15; Acts 20:25–27.

[165] The designation 'Christian' is first used in the context of Paul's preaching. See Acts 11:25–26. In this new manifestation of the people of God, both Jews and Gentiles now share in the message of salvation. The rejection of Jewish national privilege in Lk-Acts should not be misconstrued as a rejection of individual Jews. Although the author of Lk-Acts recognizes the term 'Christian,' he probably prefers the idea of 'believer' (see, e.g., Acts 4:32; 26:27–28) or 'disciple' (Acts 14:22, e.g.) as a self-designation. Consequently, the terms 'Jew' and 'Christian' are not mutually exclusive. Paul, e.g., is both a Jew and a Christian (Acts 26:6, 28–29).

[166] Cf. Lk 16:16; 24:44–47.

the continuity between the present partial manifestation of the kingdom and the future complete manifestation of the kingdom at the Parousia. Specifically, reception of the spirit determines the people of God who share in the promises of the kingdom.[167] The spirit poured out on the day of Pentecost fulfills the prophecy of Joel concerning the restoration of the people of God in the last days.[168] This spirit is the correlate of the fulfillment of the restoration of the Davidic king, for Jesus has been enthroned in heaven, where he sits on the Davidic throne (Acts 2:30–36).[169] This spirit is experienced by Christians as the people of God and is closely tied to the ritual of baptism.[170]

The people of God as the true heirs of the kingdom are also defined by Christian ritual meals. In the author's portrayal of Jesus' final meal with the apostles, the celebration of the redemption of God's people marked by the Jewish Passover is replaced by the remembrance[171] of

---

[167] Note that the apostles' question about the realization of the kingdom in Acts 1:6 is bracketed by Jesus' teaching about the kingdom of God in terms of the reception of the spirit and the mission of the apostles (Acts 1:3–5, 7–8); the coming of the spirit and the mission of the apostles will constitute the heirs of the kingdom in a way unexpected by the apostles in Acts 1:6.

[168] Acts 2:16–21. The author of Lk-Acts omits from the citation of Joel 2:28–32 the reference to deliverance on Mount Zion and in Jerusalem, universalizing its prophetic reference.

[169] Cf. Acts 15:16–18, which characterizes the present time as one in which the Davidic throne has been reestablished and the day of salvation has begun. Although Acts 3:17–26 portrays the present period as one of waiting for Jesus to restore all things, this does not suggest that the author expects the Davidic throne to be established at some time in the future on earth. The restoration of all things in Acts 3:17–26 is couched in the language of Jewish expectations, but elsewhere the author presents this end in simple terms of judgment (Acts 17:31). Jesus' enthronement is anticipated by the angel's announcement at the conception of Jesus (Lk 1:32; cf. 2:25–38) and the announcement of the coming of the kingdom by John the Baptist (Lk 3:15–17; Acts 1:5; cf. Lk 16:16).

[170] On the connection of the spirit to baptism, see John's preaching, Lk 3:15–17; Acts 1:5; Peter's preaching, Acts 2:38; 10:47; Paul's preaching, Acts 19:1–7. Conzelmann's suggestion that the author appeals to the phenomenon of the spirit to solve the problem of the delay of the Parousia (*The Theology of St. Luke*, p. 136) is perhaps misleading. For the author of Lk-Acts, the reception of the spirit solves the problem of Gentile participation in the message of salvation. The reception of the spirit is decisive in the admission of Gentiles to the community of the people of God. See especially Acts 10:1–11:18. The author is not so much concerned with the delay of the Parousia in itself, but rather with the separation of the Parousia from events associated with the Jewish nation.

[171] The phrase τοῦτο ποιεῖτε εἰς τὴν ἐμὴν ἀνάμνησιν (Lk 22:19, absent in Mk 14:22) makes explicit the aspect of remembrance that connects the Passover and the ritual meal shared by the followers of Jesus.

Jesus' redemptive death for his followers.[172] The author's redaction of his sources to compose Jesus' farewell identifies those who participate in this ritual meal as heirs of the kingdom of God.[173]

The author of Lk-Acts explicitly connects this final celebration of the Passover between Jesus and the apostles with Jesus' death: πρὸ τοῦ με παθεῖν (Lk 22:15). Jesus has earnestly desired to celebrate this Passover with his apostles because this Passover marks a decisive transition signaled by his upcoming death. This transition is nothing less than the coming fulfillment of the kingdom of God: Jesus will not himself eat of the Passover until it is fulfilled in the kingdom of God (22:16). With this solemn introduction to the meal, Jesus blesses the cup and passes it to his disciples. They are to partake, but he does not.[174] From now on, Jesus will not drink from the fruit of the vine until the kingdom of God comes (22:18).

This saying of Jesus in Lk 22:18 corresponds to Mk 14:25. Mk 14:25 concludes the celebration of the Passover with a solemn pronouncement that Jesus will no longer (οὐκέτι) drink wine until he drinks it anew in the kingdom of God. In the introduction to the ritual meal in Lk 22:14–18, the author has transposed the saying of Jesus in Mk 14:25 from the end to the beginning of the meal, deleted the temporal qualifier οὐκετι, and omitted the Markan introduction to the meal καὶ ἐσθιόντων αὐτῶν. In Lk, Jesus does not actually eat the final Passover meal with the disciples. Instead, he presides over what is characterized not only as a Jewish Passover meal but also as a symposium.[175] In the

---

[172] Compare Lk 22:19–20 with Acts 20:28. Although the author of Lk-Acts pays little attention to the redemptive significance of the death and resurrection of Jesus (instead treating the resurrection as a sign from God—see Acts 2:32, 36; 17:31; cf. 2:22), both Jesus' farewell and Paul's farewell identify the blood of Jesus as constituting the church. On the difficulties of the text and translation of Acts 20:28, see Walton, *Leadership and Lifestyle*, pp. 94–98.

[173] See Katter ('Luke 22:14–38: A Farewell Address,' p. 145) for a good analysis of the author's composition of Jesus' farewell address.

[174] διαμερίσατε εἰς ἑαυτούς (22:17) is explained in 22:18: λέγω γὰρ ὑμῖν. The cup is for the apostles, not for Jesus. Contrary to the popular designation of this meal as the last supper (see, e.g., Katter, 'Luke 22:14–38: A Farewell Address,' p. 146, who characterizes this meal as Jesus' last with his disciples), this is not the last time Jesus eats with the apostles. See Acts 10:41, discussed below. Lk 22:18 marks the time of Jesus' upcoming suffering (22:15) as decisive for the manifestation of the kingdom of God.

[175] Commentators disagree whether Jesus only abstains from the ritual symbols or from the whole meal (see Katter, 'Luke 22:14–38: A Farewell Address,' pp. 146, 251). Lk 22:18 suggests that beginning with the cup Jesus passes to his disciples in 22:17, Jesus no longer eats and drinks with the apostles. Since, however, the author only presents a sequence of cup, bread, cup for the Passover meal, there is the possibility that the

course of this meal, Jesus explains the connection between his impending suffering (πρὸ τοῦ με παθεῖν, 22:15), the Passover (reconstituted in terms of the ritual meal observed by Jesus' followers; 22:16–20), and the coming of the kingdom (ἕως ὅτου πληρωθῇ ἐν τῇ βασιλείᾳ τοῦ θεοῦ, 22:16; ἕως οὗ ἡ βασιλεία τοῦ θεοῦ ἔλθῃ, 22:17).

This ritual meal (22:19–20) is to be a remembrance of Jesus' body and blood given for the salvation of his followers.[176] This suffering of Jesus establishes the new covenant (ἡ καινὴ διαθήκη) in his blood.[177] Participation in this remembrance of the suffering of Jesus is participation in the new covenant. In 22:28–30, Jesus again reflects on his upcoming suffering, now characterized as πειρασμοί. He covenants[178] to his disciples a kingdom in which they will eat and drink at his table.[179] The author of Lk-Acts intends this ritual meal to be understood as table fellowship with Jesus in the kingdom of God.[180]

The Emmaus story, Lk 24:13–35, is closely connected to Jesus' institution of this ritual meal in his farewell to the disciples. According to the story, the presence of the resurrected Jesus is recognized in the sharing of a meal.[181] In this meal, Jesus' disciples (symbolized by Cleopas and his companion in the story) experience the presence of Jesus and the salvation he has accomplished for them.[182] This salvation, however,

---

author intends the cup in 22:17 to be the third cup of the meal, and thus Jesus may have participated in earlier parts of the meal. However, to read the sequence in Lk 22:17–20 against reconstructions of the sequence of what actually happened at a Passover meal (see, e.g., Fitzmyer, *The Gospel According to Luke (X-XXIV)*, p. 1390) assumes the author is attempting to give a complete description of the meal and overlooks that 22:17 serves as the beginning of the meal. This beginning characterizes the meal not only as a Jewish Passover but also as a Greek symposium. See Katter, 'Luke 22:14–38: A Farewell Address,' pp. 132–35.

[176] For the author of Lk-Acts, this ritual meal is probably to be understood as Christian table fellowship. See, e.g., Acts 2:42.

[177] See especially Jer 31:31–34, in which the old covenant established when God brought Israel out of Egypt (a deliverance marked by the Passover) is contrasted with a new covenant, characterized among other aspects by a forgiveness of sins.

[178] διατίθεμαι is the verbal correlate of διαθήκη.

[179] The author of Lk-Acts makes clear that the kingdom of God will be manifested in an unexpected way. On the general coming of the kingdom, see Lk 17:21. In Lk 22:30, the traditional saying of Jesus about the twelve apostles sitting on thrones and ruling Israel (from Q, see Mt 19:28) has been reinterpreted as serving, not lordship (Lk 22:24–27).

[180] On this messianic banquet, see Lk 13:28–30.

[181] On this meal, see Betz, 'The Origin and Nature of Christian Faith according to the Emmaus Legend (Luke 24:13–32),' pp. 32–46, esp. p. 37.

[182] Betz, 'The Origin and Nature of Christian Faith according to the Emmaus Legend (Luke 24:13–32),' p. 42: "According to the Emmaus legend ... the Lord's Supper

comes in an unexpected form. Whereas Cleopas and his companion had hoped that Jesus of Nazareth was going to deliver Israel,[183] they are now confronted by two unexpected events: Jesus' death (Lk 24:20) and a report that now, three days later, Jesus is alive (Lk 24:22–23). Jesus corrects their lack of understanding of these events in two ways. First, he explains that according to the scriptures the death of the Christ was necessary for him to enter into glory (Lk 24:25–27).[184] 'His glory' (Lk 24:26) can be nothing less than the beginning of his messianic rule.[185] Second, Jesus as the one alive from the dead and the salvation thereby accomplished for his people are experienced in the present in the act of table fellowship, over which the resurrected Jesus presides. In table fellowship, his followers know him (Lk 24:31, 35) as their savior alive from the dead. This is the beginning of the table fellowship in the kingdom Jesus promised in his farewell (Lk 22:30). Jesus thus turns the expectations of the two disciples on the road to Emmaus away from hopes of a national restoration of Israel to the salvation experienced by the followers of Jesus constituted as the people of God in their common meal, at which meal Jesus in his messianic glory is perceived by faith.[186]

In the encounter with Cleopas and his companion on the road to Emmaus, Jesus does not actually share in the meal.[187] As he initiates the meal, he is taken from their presence.[188] In the Emmaus story, Jesus presides over a meal that symbolizes the present experience of Christians: knowing Jesus as savior in his absence.[189] In the sharing of table fellowship, Christians both experience the kingdom and anticipate its consummation at Jesus' Parousia.[190] However, the Twelve experience the promise of table fellowship with Jesus in the kingdom (Lk 22:30) in a very direct manner. Although Acts 1:4 is ambiguous,[191] Acts 10:41

---

is the continuation of the saving events initiated by Jesus; 'Jesus' has become identical with the salvation-event and is present in the act of the common meal."

[183] Lk 24:18–21; cf. the disciples' question in Acts 1:6.

[184] Cf. Lk 24:44–47.

[185] Cf. Acts 2:36.

[186] On this faith, see Betz, 'The Origin and Nature of Christian Faith according to the Emmaus Legend (Luke 24:13–32),' p. 38.

[187] Cf. above on Jesus' abstinence from eating at the final Passover meal with his disciples.

[188] Lk 24:30–31. Note the imperfect ἐπεδίδου. As Jesus begins to give the bread to the two, he is taken from their sight. Cf. Lk 22:17–18.

[189] Lk 24:31, 35.

[190] Cf. Lk 21:28.

[191] The translation of συναλιζόμενος is problematic, though it may imply table fellowship. See BDAG, s.v. συναλίζω.

is explicit. In Acts 10:41, the time which Jesus spent after his resurrection teaching the apostles about the kingdom of God (Acts 1:3) is characterized as a time of eating and drinking with Jesus. In anticipation of his enthronement,[192] Jesus now shares table fellowship with his apostles.[193] To these apostles is entrusted the proclamation of the kingdom of God[194]—and this proclamation will constitute the people of God upon whom the kingdom is bestowed.[195] What the apostles experienced directly in table fellowship with Jesus, Christians in the present experience through faith. For the author of Lk-Acts, the ritual meal thus constitutes the people of God and expresses the way in which the kingdom of God is experienced as a present reality in this world by the followers of Jesus.[196]

Paul's farewell and the coming of the kingdom

Table fellowship among Jesus' followers is a participation in Jesus' blood (Lk 22:20). In Paul's farewell speech, the author again refers to the blood of Jesus, which is now explicitly connected to the church.[197] The

---

[192] Acts 2:29–36; cf. Luke 22:30.

[193] Although Acts 10:41 does not specifically mention wine, it is almost certainly implied as part of the table fellowship shared with the apostles. There is an apologetic interest in this reference to eating and drinking. In Lk 24:41–43 Jesus eats to prove that he is flesh and blood, not a spirit. In other words, the existence of Jesus after his resurrection is understood in terms of Jewish apocalyptic expectations for the bodily resurrection of the dead. The author of Lk-Acts has connected the incident in Lk 24:36–43 with the Emmaus legend. After Cleopas and his companion return to Jerusalem, they report to the assembly of Jesus' disciples that Jesus is indeed alive and that they recognized him in the act of his breaking bread (Lk 24:35). While they are reporting this, Jesus appears to the gathering of his followers (Lk 24:36). This time, Jesus does not disappear, but actually partakes of food. Jesus is not a spirit, but is indeed alive from the dead. As he had done previously for Cleopas and his companion, Jesus goes on to explain the significance of his death and resurrection (Lk 24:44–49). For the author of Lk-Acts, the kingdom of God is not 'spiritual,' if this means incorporeal. To eat and drink again in the kingdom of God, Jesus must be flesh and blood, not spirit. (Cf. Lk 22:30—though the author of Lk-Acts never explains what this corporeal existence means in detail for the existence of the people of God after Jesus' Parousia.)

[194] Cf. Acts 1:6–8; 2:14–40; 3:17–26.

[195] Luke 22:29; cf. Acts 14:22–23; 20:25–32; 28:30–31; cf. Acts 1:6–8.

[196] Cf. Lk 17:20–21.

[197] Paul's words in Acts 20:28, τὴν ἐκκλησίαν τοῦ θεοῦ, ἥν περιεποιήσατο διὰ τοῦ αἵματος τοῦ ἰδίου, recall the words of Jesus in his farewell to the apostles in Lk 22:20: τοῦτο τὸ ποτήριον ἡ καινὴ διαθήκη ἐν τῷ αἵματί μου τὸ ὑπὲρ ὑμῶν ἐκχυννόμενον. The author probably intends Paul's words here as an allusion to the ritual meal instituted by Jesus in his farewell. The author of Lk-Acts has likely taken the reference to the blood of Jesus in Acts 20:28 from the tradition of the celebration of the meal in Christian

author has constructed his narrative of the history of the proclamation of the kingdom of God in such a way that Jewish national expectations (expressed in the apostles' question in Acts 1:6)[198] are replaced by the whole purpose of God proclaimed by Paul (Acts 20:27), whose proclamation constitutes the church of God obtained by the blood of Jesus. The author characterizes Paul's proclamation as preaching the kingdom of God (Acts 20:25). Preaching the kingdom is teaching about Jesus (Acts 28:31). This preaching of the word by Paul (Lk 1:2) as it is rejected by the Jews and received with joy by the Gentiles (Acts 13:48; 28:28) determines for the author the historical origin of Christianity over against Judaism, whereby Christians as those who receive by faith the salvation accomplished by God are the heirs of the kingdom of God.[199]

Jesus' final words to the apostles in Lk have thus been distanced from the present (in developmental terms) vis-à-vis Paul's farewell address. The Jewish national expectations, which shape Jesus' farewell address and the expectations of the apostles at the beginning of Acts, have been universalized in Paul's farewell speech. The readers' present is no longer determined by Jewish national expectations of the kingdom, but by the proclamation of salvation through repentance and faith in Jesus.[200] Paul's farewell speech explicitly establishes historical continuity between the Jewish past and the audience's Christian present while differentiating Christianity from Judaism.

Paul's farewell speech is not a defense of Paul. Lk 1:1–4 determines the author's interest in Paul. The author is not defending Paul, but narrating events associated with the proclamation of the word. The author's thoroughgoing historical differentiation of the Christian present from the Jewish past to which Jesus, the Twelve, and Paul himself belong as Jews is not motivated by an apologetic concerning Paul, but by the need to construct an accurate account of the development of the

---

communities familiar to him (see Conzelmann, *Acts of the Apostles*, on this verse). There is no particular connection to Paul's own theology. Conzelmann (*1 Corinthians*, p. 199) comments on the reference to the blood of Christ in Paul's discussion of the ritual meal in 1 Corinthians 11:25 (cf. 10:16): "The blood of Christ plays in Paul's own soteriology only a traditional role: the term appears only where he is quoting (Rom 3:24f), and in one further passage where this tradition is echoed (Rom 5:9)."

[198] Note that Lk 22:24–30 reinterprets what ruling over Israel in the kingdom might mean.
[199] Acts 20:32; cf. Acts 14:22–23.
[200] See Acts 28:28–31.

'events accomplished among us' (Lk 1:1) linking the Jewish past and the Christian present. This Jewish past is characterized as a time of anticipating the kingdom of God, which was particularly associated with the Jewish temple and hopes of national redemption.[201] The Christian present, however, is determined by the rejection of the proclamation of the kingdom of God by the Jews (and the consequent destruction of Jerusalem) and the reception of the message of salvation by the Gentiles. Paul's farewell speech establishes the link between this past and present and thus defines the emergence of Christianity. The following observations on this speech are important.

(1) Paul addresses the Ephesian elders in Acts 20:17–35 as the founder of the community at Ephesus. Indeed, Paul is portrayed by the author of Lk-Acts as a founder of Christian communities from Antioch to Rome, but the author's understanding of 'Pauline communities' emerges not from but in spite of his information about various local Christian centers. What will be demonstrated in the next chapter can only be asserted here in summary. There is little, if any, information available to the author about an actual Pauline community at Ephesus.[202] When Paul addresses his farewell to the Ephesian elders, he addresses a church belonging to a Christian unity from Jerusalem to Rome, but this Christian unity determined by the mission of Paul has been impressed upon, not derived from, the material available to the author.[203] The author has no demonstrable connection to an amorphous, living body of traditional stories about Paul circulating in Pauline communities, particularly at Ephesus. Such 'Pauline communities' and the author's knowledge of the traditions of these communities are the author's own historiographical construct (Lk 1:1–4). This construct gives a defining unity to the origin of Christianity in the Graeco-Roman world.

(2) Paul, as he addresses the Ephesian elders, stands between Jerusalem and Rome. He is about to embark on the final stage of his ministry by returning to Jerusalem for the last time.[204] He thus in his person expresses the unity of the Christian λόγοι (Lk 1:4) as the λόγος of salvation (Lk 1:2) has been proclaimed from Jerusalem to Rome. Decisive for this Christian unity are three points:

---

[201] See Lk 1:5–25, 30–33, 46–55; 2:25–38.
[202] Cf. Rev 2:1–7; this letter to Ephesus takes no notice of any Pauline basis for the community.
[203] The author of Acts has very little interest in local Christian communities as such. See note 140 above.
[204] Acts 20:22–24, 37–38; 21:12–14.

First, the author of Lk-Acts does not use the term 'Christianity' (χριστιανισμός). Instead, to designate what came to be labeled as 'Christianity' he prefers the term ὁδός ('the Way'), which he uses as a label for proper religious service to God according to the way of salvation.[205] The Way is also designated as a αἵρεσις in relation to other religious parties within Judaism.[206] As such, the author's terminology for the new movement does not establish a contrast between Judaism and Christianity, but between various religious parties with roots in Jewish culture and the sacred scriptures.[207] Nevertheless, although the author does not use the term Christianity, he twice uses the term Christian (χριστιανός): Acts 11:26 and 26:28. In both contexts, the term is connected with the ministry of Paul. The origin of the term is associated with Gentile converts at Antioch, for which church Paul and Barnabas provide leadership (Acts 11:26). The second use of the term, placed on the mouth of Agrippa, occurs in the context of Paul's defense of his conduct (as a Christian) over against Jewish accusations against him concerning the law and the temple, a defense that has led to his appeal to Caesar. The author apparently intends to explain the origin of the term 'Christian' in relation to the emergence of a distinct identity determined by the preaching of the word to the Gentiles associated with the ministry of Paul. At this level, the author introduces a contrast approximating later notions of 'Judaism' and 'Christianity': through the person of Paul, the author develops a contrast between 'the Jews' who do not believe the message about the manifestation of the kingdom of God in the preaching about Jesus (Acts 13:44–48; 18:6; and decisively, 28:23–31) versus the Christians who do believe and come to participate in the kingdom salvation. Christians are those who accept God's universalistic intentions for the kingdom in Jesus apart from Jewish culture and as such stand in contrast to the Jews who do not.

Second, the farewell speech of Paul foreshadows Paul's death at Rome, knowledge of which is assumed for the intended readers of

---

[205] For ὁδός used absolutely, see Acts 9:2; 19:9, 23; 22:4; 24:22; qualified as the way of salvation, the way of the Lord, or the way of God, see Acts 16:17; 18:25, 26; qualified as religious service to God, see Acts 24:14; cf. 26:5. On the distinctive use of this term in Acts, see Conzelmann, *The Theology of St. Luke*, p. 227; idem, *Acts of the Apostles*, p. 71; Michaelis, ὁδός, *TDNT* 5.88–90.

[206] The Sadducees, Acts 5:17; the Pharisees, Acts 15:5; 26:5. For the author, these parties are understood as religious associations within Judaism (Acts 26:5; cf. 24:14). Note, e.g., Paul's attempt to play off the various groups against one another in Acts 23:6–10.

[207] See especially Acts 24:14; 26:5.

Lk-Acts.[208] Paul's farewell and anticipated death mark for the author of Lk-Acts the decisive point of transition and historical continuity in the handing on of the traditions from past to present (Lk 1:2). Paul's ministry as summarized in his farewell speech thus gives closure to the definitionally foundational period of Christian history.[209] In Paul's summation of his ministry to the unified church at Ephesus, the author characterizes the preaching of Paul as the public, universal[210] proclamation of the kingdom of God (Acts 20:25). The Paul who has proclaimed this message of the kingdom to the believers at Ephesus is the Paul who is about to renounce his religious and political association with Judaism based on his Roman citizenship by appealing to Caesar as a result of the upcoming conflict at Jerusalem. In this appeal, Paul rejects the religious and political authority of the Jewish leaders over him and transfers his *patria* from Jerusalem to Rome.[211] The author suggests that Paul dies at Rome because of the Jews.[212] He dies, though, not as a Jew subject to Jewish law, but as a Roman subject to Roman law. Thus, in a sense, Christianity as a contrasting reality to Judaism has its defining beginning with Paul, particularly in his appeal to Caesar, inasmuch as the author's narrative of the origin of Christianity depends on two factors: the manifestation of the kingdom of God in the life of Jesus and the rejection of Jewish national expectations for the kingdom. In

---

[208] See especially Acts 9:16; 21:13. See also Katter ('Luke 22:14–38: A Farewell Address,' p. 125) on the context of imminent death as typical of farewell addresses. That the reader is assumed to know about the death of Paul at Rome is further evidence for an intended Christian audience for Lk-Acts.

[209] Unlike the death of apostles in the apocryphal acts, the death of Paul in itself has no intrinsic significance in Lk-Acts because the narrative unity of Lk-Acts is not derived from the life of Paul (or any other character). Rather the character Paul is important in terms of his mission: Paul's mission is expressive of Christian unity. Only Jesus' death (and ascension) takes on intrinsic significance as a necessary step in his enthronement as the precondition for the giving of the spirit (Acts 2:32–33; cf. Lk 24:49; Acts 1:8).

[210] From Ephesus, Paul preached to all Jews and Gentiles in Asia, Acts 19:10.

[211] Tajra (*The Trial of St. Paul. A Juridical Exegesis of the Second Half of the Acts of the Apostles*, p. 201) comments: "The Jewish authorities could only consider the appeal to Caesar not so much as directed *to* Rome but *against* Jerusalem. Such an appeal was the right of a Roman citizen, but it was hardly to be expected of a Pharisaic Jew. By rejecting the Sanhedrin's political and juridical authority over him and by invoking the Emperor's exclusive legal competence in the case, the apostle had consummated the break with official Judaism at least on the political and judicial levels." Although Tajra too easily blends historical reality with narrative representation in this conclusion to his study, his analysis captures the importance of Paul's appeal to Caesar for understanding the author's portrayal of Paul's relation to Judaism.

[212] See Acts 21:13; 25:9–12; 26:2, 30–32.

this sense, the author portrays Christianity as Paulinism. The mission of Paul defines the constitutive identity of Christians as separate from Judaism.

Third, in Paul's preaching of the kingdom of God, the true nature of religion is revealed, and the failure of the Jews to appropriate Paul's message is tied to the author's conception of false worship. Cult artifacts are at best a poor reflection of the divinity and at worst a manifestation of human self-interest at odds with God's intentions for humanity. Both pagan religion[213] and Jewish devotion to the temple[214] are characterized as mistaking human attempts to represent the deity for the deity itself. For the author, local cults are portrayed as controlled by a self-interest inappropriate for worship of the divinity.[215] Just as Paul's preaching stirs up the wrath of local participants in the Artemis cult at Ephesus, so Paul's presence at Jerusalem precipitates a Jewish riot in defense of the temple at Jerusalem. The author acknowledges that the Jewish temple belongs to a certain period of salvation history characterized by prayerful anticipation of the kingdom of God,[216] but the realization of the kingdom transcends the Jewish temple. According to Acts 22:17–21, it is while Paul is praying in the temple that Jesus appears to him to send him to the Gentiles, the same Paul who stood by as Stephen was stoned for attacking the temple.[217] The author portrays Paul's message of the kingdom at Lystra (Acts 14:8–18), at Athens (Acts 17:22–34), at Ephesus (Acts 19:23–40), and at Jerusalem (Acts 22:2–22)[218] as a proclamation of a true, universal religion freed from the misleading representations of God, whether maintained by local cults (including Jerusalem) or supported by popular magic (whether pagan or Jewish, Acts 19:13–20). In Paul's preaching of Jesus there is revealed the true, universal relationship between humanity and God.[219] Jesus himself, whose life and death are decisive for the manifestation of the

---

[213] Acts 14:8–18; 17:22–31; 19:23–40.

[214] Especially Acts 7:44–53.

[215] Whether pagan (Acts 19:23–40) or Jewish (Lk 19:45–48; Acts 6:8–14; 7:48–53). Authors could portray the self-interest of local cults quite negatively. See, e.g., Lucian, *Alexander the False Prophet*.

[216] Lk 1:10; 2:25–38; 18:9–14; 19:45–48. Likewise, pagan culture anticipates the Christian message: Acts 17:22–31.

[217] Acts 22:20; see Acts 6:8–8:1.

[218] Cf. Stephen's speech in Acts 7.

[219] See Acts 17:24–31; also Vielhauer ('On the "Paulinism" of Acts,' pp. 48–49), who commenting on the author's understanding of history states: "The absolute claim of the Jews to be the people of God was replaced by the idea of natural man's immediacy

kingdom in the giving of the spirit, is indeed a Jew according to Lk-Acts, but he is ultimately the son of Adam, the son of God (Lk 3:23–38). The Jews as a national collective fail to accept the nature of this kingdom, and ultimately God rejects them (Acts 28:23–28) and their temple (Lk 21:24; Acts 7:44–53). Christians as part of the church of God obtained by the blood of Jesus, whose leaders Paul addresses in his farewell, follow the Way of true religion that fulfills both Jewish and pagan culture. As such, Christians are heirs of the kingdom (Acts 20:32).

(3) The 'us' of Lk 1:1–2 is the audience implicitly addressed in Paul's farewell speech. In Lk 1:1–4, the author of Lk-Acts characterizes the relationship between the present (ἡμῖν, vv. 1 and 2[220]) and the events remembered in stories as a handing over from eyewitnesses. This transfer of tradition from 'them' to 'us' is achieved in Paul's farewell address to the Ephesian elders. Paul in his person (preaching from Jerusalem to Rome) embodies the unity of the past in such a way that his speech can bridge the gap between the Jewish past and the Christian present. The assurance offered to Theophilus with reference to stories (Lk 1:4)—that is, with reference to a fragmentation of the past—is realized in Paul's handing over to the care of the Ephesian elders a unified Christian past based on the public, unified, and comprehensive declaration of the kingdom of God, of teaching about Jesus,[221] within the Graeco-Roman world.[222]

(4) The farewell addresses of both Jesus and Paul establish a succession of leadership.[223] This succession of leadership is not, however, conceived in terms of a preservation of doctrine (as, for example, in terms of an office of teaching).[224] Instead, the succession of leadership established by Jesus and Paul is intended to protect the inheritance of Jesus' followers in the kingdom of God against hostile spiritual powers. Jesus confers on the Twelve the kingdom, in which they will act as judges

---

to God, and the significance of Judaism was relativized to that of a venerable *antiqua religio*."

[220] Fitzmyer (*The Gospel according to Luke I-IX*, 293–94) attempts to distinguish between the referents of 'us' in these verses.

[221] See Acts 28:31.

[222] Significantly, an eyewitness vouchsafes for the final stage of Paul's life, which will culminate in the movement of the word from Jerusalem to Rome. See chapter 4 under *Philippi* on the 'we' narrator in Acts.

[223] See, e.g., Katter, 'Luke 22:14–38: A Farewell Address,' pp. 204–16; Walton, *Leadership and Lifestyle*, e.g., pp. 84–86.

[224] Contrast, e.g., Talbert's identification of the genre of Lk-Acts as biography plus succession narrative in terms of philosophical schools (discussed above).

of the twelve tribes of Israel.²²⁵ This position of authority is in actuality, however, a position of service (Lk 22:24–27), especially in the face of trials (Lk 22:28). Peter himself is in danger of falling away, but Jesus intercedes that his faith may not fail, and Peter is in turn charged with strengthening his brothers – all of whom are in danger of being sifted like wheat by Satan (Lk 22:31–32). Jesus in his farewell address provides for the protection of his followers against hostile powers threatening their faith. Likewise, Paul charges the Ephesian elders with the task of protecting the flock of God from the dangers that threaten believers' allegiance to Jesus (Acts 20:28–32). From without and within, there will arise those who will seek to draw away disciples after themselves. The threat from λύκοι βαρεῖς and ἄνδρες λαλοῦντες διεστραμμένα is given no specific doctrinal content in Acts other than danger to faith in Jesus.²²⁶ In the face of such dangers, Paul commits the elders and by extension all Christians to the grace of God, just as Jesus interceded for the faith of Peter.²²⁷ The author of Lk-Acts has not treated succession as an entrustment of doctrine, but as a guardianship of inheritance of the kingdom of God.

In short, the narrative of the life of Jesus in Mk has been recast as one part of a sequence of events, events that bring to light true religion as the fulfillment of Jewish and pagan culture in the preaching by Paul of the kingdom of God.²²⁸ The life of Jesus as a Jew, associated

---

²²⁵ Lk 22:29–30. The imagery of the twelve tribes represents the people of God in national Jewish terms.

²²⁶ The only concrete examples of the exercise of leadership in the church to protect the flock from ravenous wolves come in the context of confrontations between the apostles or Paul with magicians who seek to undermine the proclamation of the kingdom. Simon's attempt to buy the gift of the spirit is rejected by Peter and John (Acts 8:18–24), and Paul denounces Elymas, who is seeking διαστρέψαι τὸν ἀνθύπατον ἀπὸ τῆς πίστεως (Acts 13:8) by διαστρέφων τὰς ὁδοὺς τοῦ κυρίου τὰς εὐθείας (Acts 13:10). Both Simon and Elymas are denounced as captives of evil (Acts 8:23; 13:10). The author of Lk-Acts also recounts the burning of magic books at Ephesus by the believers (Acts 19:17–20). For the author of Lk-Acts, Satan stands behind magic and is an ever-present, active threat to the faith of believers. See, e.g., Lk 22:31, in which Satan is identified as the threat to Peter's faith. In contrast to Peter, who is protected in order that he might restore his brothers, Judas is indeed sifted like wheat by Satan in order that the scripture might be fulfilled (Acts 1:15–20). In Lk 22:3, the author specifically attributes the betrayal of Judas to the influence of Satan (in contrast to Mk 14:10, but note Jn 13:27). Note also the actions of Ananias and Sapphira, whose actions are directly attributed to the activity of Satan (Acts 5:3).

²²⁷ Cf. Acts 14:21–23.

²²⁸ Acts 1:1–2 characterizes the content of Lk as what Jesus did and taught. This biographical genre identification is, however, immediately subverted by the qualification

with the national expectations of Israel, has been subordinated to an account of salvation history accomplished through divinely appointed individuals, among whom Jesus is the most important but not the end of salvation history.[229] Thus, John's life has been expanded, Jesus' childhood elaborated, and the unfolding of God's plans for the spread of the gospel from Jerusalem to Rome in the preaching of Peter and Paul recounted.[230] This historical perspective implicitly subordinates the local community (as, for example, addressed by Paul at Ephesus) to a broader conception of the place of Christians in the world. For the author of Lk-Acts, Christians are defined not on the basis of the life and words of Jesus alone (which in themselves belong to a qualified Jewish past defined within the framework of Jewish expectations), but by the proclamation of the kingdom of God from Jerusalem to Rome[231]—a proclamation freed from Jewish particularism.[232]

Because what Jesus did and said (Acts 1:1) is in itself inadequate for the author of Lk-Acts to define the identity of Christians,[233] certainty in relation to fragmented stories of the past (Lk 1:4) has become an acute problem. The author of Lk-Acts thus understands the relation of the λόγος (Lk 1:2) to the λόγοι (Lk 1:4) historiographically.[234] The author

---

'began': the life of Jesus has become one set of events linked to subsequent events. Rather than Lk-Acts as biography plus succession narrative or Gospel plus Acts of the Apostles, Lk-Akts narrates beginning events and subsequent events (see Lk 1:1). The implications of Acts 1:1–2 for this subordination of the life of Jesus to an account of the origin of Christianity are anticipated when, unlike Mk and Graeco-Roman biographies, which tend to mention the name of the protagonist at the beginning or immediately after the preface, the author of Lk-Acts delays the mention of Jesus until after recounting the events associated with John's promised birth.

[229] The reference to what Jesus began to do and say in Acts 1:1 does not imply that Acts is about what he continues to do, but rather that Jesus' life, while decisive, is still only part of a broader movement (cf. Conzelmann, *Acts of the Apostles*, p. 3).

[230] The tendency to conceive of history in terms of legendary figures is typical of both Jewish and Graeco-Roman historiography. The history of Israel preserved in the Septuagint is largely an account of individuals leading God's people to (or in some cases, away from) God. The histories of the Greeks and Romans are likewise organized in terms of the deeds of important individuals. See Fornara, *The Nature of History in Ancient Greece and Rome*, pp. 91–98; cf. p. 63; Dihle, *A History of Greek Literature From Homer to the Hellenistic Period*, p. 221. Cf. note 114 above. The author of Lk-Acts needed to construct the characters of Peter and Paul to give Christians a history.

[231] See especially Acts 28:31.

[232] See Schwartz, 'The End of the Line: Paul in the Canonical Book of Acts,' especially pp. 22–24.

[233] Compare Acts 1:11 ("Why are you standing looking up into the sky?") with Mk 16:7.

[234] Talbert's emphasis on the biographical character of Lk-Acts subordinates Acts

gives Christians a history. In so doing, he does not write for the Christians of a specific local community or as a mouthpiece for one Christian faction (Pauline or otherwise) against another. Instead, he writes for Christians whom he envisions as belonging to a decisive movement of God in world history (Greek, Roman, and Jewish) – a movement the author claims is capable of historiographical verification.[235] This vision boldly relativized the life of Jesus in terms of the proclamation of the gospel in the Graeco-Roman world.[236]

These observations on Paul's farewell discourse correlated with the dialogue between author and reader (patron) in Lk 1:1–4 and Acts 1:1–2 suggest that the portrayal of Paul in Lk-Acts has been determined by the author's literary and historiographical intentions to convert fragmented Christian stories into a history of the origin of Christianity for Christians as participants in God's purposes in world history embracing Graeco-Roman culture (geographically, from Jerusalem to Rome). Paul's narrative character supplies literary and historical unity to the development of a Christian identity apart from Judaism and connects Christians to biblical history and the Graeco-Roman world in all its diversity. Thus, Paul is portrayed as a Roman citizen, an orator, an eminent Pharisee, a called instrument of God's purposes for salvation: in short, an idealized participant in the fulfillment of biblical history as conceived by the author of Lk-Acts, an idealized character bridging Jewish and Graeco-Roman society.[237] Lk-Acts' 'Paulinism' is a lit-

---

to the life of Jesus, when in fact the author's work subordinates the life of Jesus to the narrative of Acts. This historicizing of the life of Jesus in Lk-Acts creates not a succession narrative guaranteeing true Christianity against heresy (e.g., gnosticism), but a connection of Christians to salvation history expressed in terms of Hellenistic culture.

[235] See Acts 26:26.

[236] The narrative pattern set by Mk is adopted for Jesus' place in this history, but the importance of the narration of Jesus' life has been reconceptualized by the author of Lk-Acts. In contrast, see chapter 2 above on the reception of Lk-Acts in early Christianity, a reception marked by the subordination of the narrative of Acts to a certain construction of the Gospel. There is, for example, no sense of positive historical development in the historical reconstruction offered by Irenaeus. The Acts of the Apostles is used to demonstrate that all the apostles at all times proclaimed the Gospel, which itself exists as an abstraction from the four canonical gospels. For Irenaeus, the full measure of Christian truth was present from the beginning, from which heresy is a willful departure. The narrative of the 'Acts of the Apostles' is thus subordinated to a fourfold gospel canon read as a deposit of a certain construction of ecclesiastical truth.

[237] Similarly, Hellenistic-Jewish history provided heroes of the past with whom the people of the present could identify in the intellectual context of Hellenistic culture. See John J. Collins, *Between Athens and Jerusalem: Jewish Identity in the Hellenistic Diaspora*, p. 51.

erary construct that has been imposed on, not derived from, the λόγοι (Lk 1:4) available to the author.[238] The importance of the character of Paul in the author's portrayal of the development of Christianity out of Judaism from Jerusalem to Rome should be understood in terms of the author's historiographical intentions toward his sources. Lk-Acts' 'Paulinism' is not a reflection of some form of Pauline Christianity to be construed as one of various competing factions within Christianity or as part of a Pauline trajectory in early Christianity of which the author is a representative or for which the author is an apologist.

The character of Paul in Lk-Acts is a necessary literary construct to achieve the author's purposes to bring order to stories about the past in such a way as to connect the past of Jesus, the apostles, and Paul to the Christian's present in the Graeco-Roman world. However, once the narrative unity of Lk-Acts was reinterpreted by Irenaeus and his successors and the 'Acts of the Apostles' was placed alongside the Pauline letters in the Christian canon, the literary 'Paulinism' of Lk-Acts became the basis for both the Irenaean as well as various modern reconstructions of the place of Paul in early Christian communities, communities defined over against other forms of Christianity (or heresy).[239] In other words, the role of Paul in the Acts of the Apostles has become evidence for the existence of some form of 'Pauline Christianity,' and the author's connection to this 'Pauline Christianity' in one way or another has been taken virtually for granted. There remains, therefore, the need to assess accurately the relation of the author's literary 'Paulinism' to the 'Paulinism' of his sources, an assessment to which the following chapter will turn.

---

[238] The next chapter will defend this claim in relation to the author's use of traditional material to construct his narrative about Paul.

[239] The unity imposed on early Christianity by the author of Lk-Acts was obviously useful for the Irenaean construction of Christian history, once the interpretative context for Lk-Acts was shifted to inner-Christian apologetics in an attempt to define true Christianity over against heresy. This shift in interpretive context for the narrative of Acts to inner-Christian apologetics has influenced modern scholarship on Acts as well. Since F. C. Baur's historical-critical reconstruction of the relation of the narrative of Acts to Paulinism (see chapter 1 above), the author's attempt to give unity to Christianity in the preaching of Paul from Jerusalem to Rome has been read as a window through which to view early Christian factionalism. The author's literary undertaking to constitute Christianity as a unity through the character of Paul has been misread in modern scholarship as revealing a form of Pauline Christianity over against other forms of early Christianity.

CHAPTER 4

THE PAUL OF ACTS AND PAULINE COMMUNITIES IN EARLY CHRISTIANITY

The account of Paul's mission in Acts, particularly when read alongside the corpus of Pauline letters preserved in the canon,[1] tends to obscure the context for the literary Paulinism of Acts in early Christianity. Whether in the Irenaean construction of the 'Acts of the Apostles' and the 'Pauline' Luke or in modern critical reconstructions of Pauline movements, communities, and traditions, the portrayal of Paul in Acts has repeatedly been taken to presuppose the importance of Paul and his legacy in the early Christian communities of Asia Minor, Macedonia, and Achaea known to the author. The power of the assumption that the portrayal of Paul in Acts can be correlated with Pauline movements, communities, and/or traditions in early Christianity is evident in the common ground shared by the critical options that have been laid out in this century for the interpretation of the Paul of Acts. Constant in the various attempts to sort out redaction, tradition, and historical value in Acts' portrayal of Paul is a presupposed reservoir of Pauline material available to the author. This Pauline material available to the author is usually defined in terms of traditions from the Pauline mission territories,[2] a Pauline letter collection,[3] and/or personal association with Paul himself.[4] The content of this reservoir of information about Paul, how-

---

[1] This perspective on Acts and the Pauline letters is first clearly evident in Irenaeus. See chapter 2 above for the reception of Acts in early Christianity.

[2] Haenchen, *The Acts of the Apostles*, p. 86. See also Bauer, *Orthodoxy and Heresy in Earliest Christianity*, pp. 82–83; Conzelmann, *Acts of the Apostles*, pp. xxxix-xl; Lüdemann, *Early Christianity according to the Traditions in Acts*, p. 8.

[3] See, e.g., Lindemann, *Paulus im ältesten Christentum. Das Bild des Apostels und die Rezeption der paulinischen Theologie in der frühchristlichen Literatur bis Marcion*, pp. 163–70. Contrast Lüdemann, *Early Christianity according to the Traditions in Acts*, pp. 7–8.

[4] Near the turn of the century, Harnack (*The Acts of the Apostles*, p. 162) commented: "If St. Luke the physician is the author of the Acts, the question of sources is simply and speedily settled for the whole second half of the book. So far as a considerable portion of this second half is concerned, he has written as an eye-witness, and for the rest he depends upon the report of eye-witnesses who were his fellow workers." See also Dibelius, *Studies in the Acts of the Apostles*, pp. 104–5.

ever, is too often determined by prior commitments to theories of the development of early Christianity and reconstructions of the place of Paul in this development.[5] Because it has proved impossible to recover well-defined sources for the narrative of Acts, such prior commitments tend to guide the distinction among redaction, tradition, and history in the portrayal of Paul on an episode-by-episode basis.[6] On this basis, no clear understanding of the author's connection to Paulinism in early Christianity can be gained as long as the author's portrayal of Paul is taken from the outset to be a redactional (or compositional)[7] construct that can be related to the (supposed) Pauline traditions available to the author. This shared Paulinism (however the relationship is defined) between the author of Lk-Acts and his sources (whether written or oral,

---

[5] For example, Haenchen (*The Acts of the Apostles*, p. 86) comments: "When, years after Paul had run his course, Luke set about the task of describing the era of primitive Christianity, various possibilities of collecting the required material lay open to him. He could himself, for example, look up the most important Pauline communities—say Philippi, Corinth, Ephesus, Antioch. He might even visit Jerusalem. But it was also possible for him to ask other Christians travelling to these places to glean for him whatever was still known of the old times.... Lastly, he could have written to the congregations in question and asked them for information." Cf. Jervell (*The Unknown Paul*, p. 69): "Luke's problem was the incessant, ever-growing crop of sayings, rumors, gossip, apologetic, polemic, veneration, admiration, declaration of aversion, etc., from Paul's foes and friends, and from Paul himself.... Luke had too much material on the disputed missionary Paul." For Jervell's assessment of Luke's sources, see *The Theology of the Acts of the Apostles*, pp. 1–10.

[6] Lüdemann (*Early Christianity according to the Traditions in Acts*, e.g. pp. 10–11) is confident that he can not only untangle tradition and redaction, but also assess the historical value of details in the narrative. He proposes a 'tradition hypothesis' that presupposes the importance of Paul's legacy in the areas of his mission. He confidently asserts: "The names of Paul's colleagues were, of course, part of the store of knowledge in the Pauline communities..."

[7] Jervell (*The Unknown Paul*, pp. 68–69) prefers to speak in terms of a skillful authorial composition rather than the distinction between redaction and tradition. The problem of sorting out traditions, redaction, and composition in the author's portrayal of Paul is not, however, that the author has so carefully constructed his narrative that redaction and traditions have become one. Rather, attempts to distinguish tradition and redaction have been burdened by misleading assumptions about Pauline traditions available to the author (an assumption Jervell shares with those whom he criticizes; see especially *The Theology of the Acts of the Apostles*, p. 6).

There are in fact several instances in the author's narrative about Paul in which the author's redaction of source material can be detected by the seams in the narrative (see below under *Ephesus* and *Corinth*). At other points, though, the author's narrative about Paul is probably better understood not as a redaction of sources but a composition based on little or no information. As a result, both redaction and composition are useful terms in describing the author's construction of his narrative about Paul.

reliable or legendary) needs to be demonstrated from the text of Acts, not assumed from a prior reconstruction of early Christianity.

In these prior reconstructions of early Christianity, three issues are important for evaluating the nature of the 'Pauline' sources of information about Paul available to the author. Specific details related to these issues will be taken up below in the text and notes, but some general observations need to be brought to the forefront.

First, the author's knowledge of a collection of Pauline letters (and thus of some form of Pauline Christianity) is often taken for granted, and the later Lk-Acts is dated, the more compelling this assumption becomes for many.[8] This supposed knowledge of the Pauline letters by the author is an assumption because arguments for the author's direct use of one or more of the letters remain unconvincing.[9] This assumption is directly tied to reconstructions of 'Pauline' Christianity of which the author of Lk-Acts is taken to be a representative. Knox has put the matter this way:

> I agree with Enslin ['"Luke" and Paul,' *Journal of American Oriental Society* LVIII (1938), 81ff.] that it is all but incredible that such a man as Luke, writing in any one of the later decades of the first century about Paul and his career, should have been "totally unaware that this hero of his had ever written letters" and quite as hard to believe that he would have found it impossible, or even difficult, to get access to these letters if he had wanted to. Paul had been too central and too controversial a figure in his own time to have been forgotten so soon. Too many churches owed their existence to him for his name not to have been held in reverence in many areas and his work remembered.[10]

---

[8] See, e.g., Lüdemann, *Early Christianity according to the Traditions in Acts*, p. 7: "The assumption that Luke knew letters of Paul is a well-founded hypothesis, which becomes the more compelling, the later Luke-Acts is to be dated." Lüdemann concurs with Knox, 'Acts and the Pauline Letter Corpus,' p. 282–83: "One can hardly reflect at all on what Luke's situation would have been as he began to write Acts without deciding that he must have known letters of Paul."

[9] Lüdemann, *Early Christianity according to the Traditions of Acts*, pp. 7–8; Knox, 'Acts and the Pauline Letter Corpus,' pp. 281–82. Cf. Walton, *Leadership and Lifestyle*, pp. 203–12. Contrast, e.g., Blasi, *Making Charisma*, pp. 39–74. Supposed parallels between the narrative of Acts and passages in various Pauline letters remain unconvincing because they require one to believe that the author of Acts perused one or more Pauline letters for a few details of Paul's mission yet passed over a multitude of other details and utterly failed to convey Paul's interpretation of these details. The parallels of names and places, apart from any distinctive Pauline interpretation of events, do not suggest literary dependence and require little more than a travel diary preserving a bare minimum of information about Paul's mission. See also chapter 2, note 169.

[10] 'Acts and the Pauline Letter Corpus,' p. 283. Cf. Lüdemann, *Early Christianity according to the Traditions in Acts*, p. 7: "If Luke belonged to the third Christian generation,

In other words, the centrality of Paul in this reconstructed history of Christianity would have made the letters available to an author for whom Paul was a hero. However, the centrality of Paul (and his letters) for the history of early Christianity is a reconstruction in which the narrative of Acts has played a crucial role.[11] Acts cannot be evidence for reconstructing the centrality of Paul in the history of early Christianity prior to the composition of the literary Paulinism of Lk-Acts while at the same time this centrality of Paul is evidence for what the author of Acts knew about Paul in constructing his literary Paulinism. The circularity of this reconstruction of the author's knowledge of Pauline letters and Pauline Christianity is self-reinforcing and has become a fixed point of departure for the investigation of the author's portrayal of Paul in relation to an assumed form of 'Pauline' Christianity represented by the letters.[12] This assumption needs to be set aside to assess accurately what actual relation of the author to 'Pauline' Christianity (whether represented by the letters or not) can be demonstrated from the narrative of Acts itself.

Second, the model for 'traditions'[13] about Paul to which the author is often thought to have had access is implicitly that of followers of Jesus telling stories about Jesus. Traditions about Paul on this model imply Pauline Christians telling stories about Paul; if the author tells stories about Paul, he must have had contact with these Pauline Christians. On such a model, any information the author has about Paul can easily be converted into a 'tradition' implying some form of 'Pauline'

---

in view of the fact that he understands himself to be a pupil of Paul or – to put it more cautiously – belongs within the circle of Pauline tradition (otherwise I cannot explain to myself the detailed portrait of Paul), his knowledge of the existence of Pauline letters is (almost) certain…" Knox ('Acts and the Pauline Letter Corpus,' pp. 283–86) suggests that the author's nonuse of known letters of Paul was due to their association with pre-Marcionite or Marcionite Christians.

[11] See chapter 2 above.

[12] Whether a collection of Pauline letters known to the author would necessarily imply a form of 'Pauline' Christianity also known to the author (as if the collection of Ignatian letters in circulation in the second century necessarily implies 'Ignatian' Christianity as a social reality) is a matter beyond the scope of this study. It seems possible, though, that 'Pauline' Christianity in connection with a collection of Paul's letters did not come into existence until Marcion. In other words, once one moves beyond Paul and those closely connected to Paul in the composition of the deutero-Pauline letters, 'Pauline' Christianity is perhaps entirely a phenomenon of the second century. The author of Lk-Acts, Marcion, and Irenaeus are important individuals in the second-century construction of various forms of 'Pauline' Christianity.

[13] See note 5 above.

community.[14] This method of creating a 'Pauline' Christianity known to the author also becomes quite circular and almost inescapably self-reinforcing. The author certainly has some accurate information about Paul. Information about Paul, however, does not in itself constitute 'traditions' about Paul. The author's literary Paulinism has too easily been mistaken for a social reality characterizing his sources. Even on a cursory reading of the account of Paul's mission in Acts 16–20, the narrative does not read very much like the collection of stories about Jesus that form the basis for the mission of Jesus in Lk 4:1–19:27. The comparative scarcity of episodes in Acts that may be traditional stories about Paul suggests that the author was *not* in contact with Pauline communities telling (lots of) stories about Paul. Instead, as the analysis below will show, 'traditional' stories about Paul actually appear not to have been readily available to the author.

Third, the author is often thought to have been a companion of Paul. If such were the case, this association would account for the source of some of the author's information about Paul[15] and might in fact characterize the author as a 'Pauline' Christian. However, such a canonical interpretation of the biography of the author of the 'Acts of the Apostles' is not only a late, apologetic construction of the author's relationship to Paul,[16] but is unsupported by a careful analysis of the way the author constructs his narrative about Paul. The identification of the 'we' narrator in Acts 16–28 with the author himself fails to appreciate the lack of narrative coherence between the (author's) literary Paulinism and the details (one detail of which is the 'we' narrator) associated with each city. This point will be developed in the sections below on each of the major cities of Paul's mission. The 'I' of Lk 1:1–4 is not the 'we' of Acts.[17]

---

[14] See especially below on *Corinth* for a discussion of Lüdemann's appeal to Pauline traditions.

[15] See note 4 above.

[16] See chapter 2 above.

[17] See the discussion below under *Philippi* (especially note 194) in relation to the discussion in chapters 2 and 3 above of the 'I' of Lk 1:1–4 (see especially chapter 3, note 56). Lüdemann's method of arguing against the author of Lk-Acts as a companion of Paul is inadequate (*Early Christianity according to the Traditions in Acts*, p. 5): "Convincing arguments that Luke was not a companion of Paul may only be derived from such historical statements as betray a total lack of personal acquaintance with Paul on the part of the author of Acts." Limits can hardly be set on the extent to which an individual might intentionally or unintentionally distort the 'facts' about an acquaintance so as to appear to "betray a total lack of personal acquaintance with" that person. (Put another way, even if the author had been a companion of Paul, this connection to Paul would

What follows is an attempt to delineate the author's redactional and compositional methodology for constructing his narrative about Paul so that the author's literary Paulinism[18] can be differentiated from the Paulinism of his sources. Two questions are important. (1) What residue of information about Paul can be demonstrated in the narrative of Acts once the author's redactional and compositional procedures have been identified? (2) Does this information come from some form of Pauline Christianity? On the basis of the answers to these questions, the author's relation to Pauline Christianity (as a label for movements, traditions, and communities in early Christianity associated with Paul) can be assessed.

In Acts, Paul is the central dramatic character of the narrative from chapter 16 to the end.[19] This second half of the narrative of Acts describes Paul's mission to Asia Minor, Macedonia, Achaea, and finally Rome. Paul's return to Jerusalem in Acts 21:17 brings to a close the distinctly Pauline mission in Acts 16–20 and initiates his legal struggle with the Jewish authorities at Jerusalem, the result of which is Paul's transfer to Rome and proclamation of the gospel at the center of the empire.

The importance of Paul in the narrative of Acts from chapter 16 onwards is anticipated by the account of his call (Acts 9:1–31; cf. 8:1–3) and mission with Barnabas (13:1–14:28; cf. 9:26–30; 11:19–29; 15:12). This introduction to Paul is incorporated into what is predominantly a narrative of the mission of the Twelve, especially Peter, in the first half of Acts. The first half of Acts ends with the Jerusalem council, at which the gospel to the Gentiles proclaimed by Peter (Acts 10:1–11:18; cf. 15:7–11) and Paul (with Barnabas, Acts 13–14; cf. 15:12) receives the approval

---

not in any way resolve the question of the reliability of the narrative.) The matter is best put to rest by a careful reading of Lk 1:1–4 in relation to the 'we' narrator of Acts: the author does not claim to be an eyewitness of any of the events he is reporting in Lk-Acts.

[18] See chapter 3 above.

[19] Acts 16–28 is marked out as a narrative unit for several reasons: (1) It is united by the voice of the narrator, the 'we' strand of narrative (see Acts 16:10; 20:5; 28:16). (2) Paul is the principal, and in fact, sole focus of the material. The leading characters of Acts 1–15 virtually disappear except for a brief appearance of James in Acts 21. In this section, the character of Paul is present in almost every episode. (Those episodes in which Paul does not appear are, therefore, of particular interest for understanding the author's construction of the Pauline mission from his sources. See below under *Ephesus* [concerning Acts 18:24–28 and Acts 19:17–20] and Thessalonica [Acts 17:5–9].) (3) Acts 16–20 functions as the introduction to the judicial drama of chapters 21–28.

of the Jerusalem leadership. Paul's return to Antioch with the Jerusalem decree marks the transition from the mission under the direction of the Twelve based in Jerusalem to the mission of Paul based in Antioch.[20]

The acceptance of the Gentile mission by the leaders of the community at Jerusalem in Acts 15 contrasts with the rejection of the Gentile mission by the Jewish authorities at Jerusalem when Paul returns to Jerusalem for a final time in Acts 21. In this confrontation between Paul and the Jews, the character of Paul—whose call is narrated as a conversion that thwarts the extension of hostile Jewish authority over followers of Jesus at Damascus;[21] whose mission with Barnabas is closely connected to the emergence of the name 'Christian' at Antioch;[22] whose preaching in Asia Minor, Macedonia, and Achaea is marked by opposition from and rejection of unbelieving Jews;[23] and whose appeal to Caesar revokes the religious and political authority of Jerusalem and brings Paul to Rome[24]—this Paul defines the emergence of Christianity and distinguishes Judaism from Christianity.[25] His mission and confrontation with Judaism constitute the author's portrayal of Christianity as Paulinism. The Pauline mission that gives content to this emergence of Christianity will be examined in what follows to understand the author's compositional and redactional method for portraying Christianity as Paulinism.

Ephesus

In the narrative of Paul's mission in Acts, the author recounts more episodes related to Ephesus (Acts 18:19–20:1) than any other 'Pauline' city in Acts,[26] and it is the Ephesian elders whom Paul addresses in his farewell speech as representatives of a church whose unity is determined by the mission of Paul. In contrast to this Pauline unity, however, there is a surprising diversity of characters, groups, and incidents portrayed at Ephesus—a diversity only loosely connected to Paul. There

---

[20] Paul's travels are narrated in such a way as to unite these two important centers of Christianity for the narrative of Acts. See below under *Ephesus* (concerning Acts 18:18–23).

[21] Acts 9:1–2; cf. 8:1.

[22] Acts 11:25–29, anticipating chapters 13 and 14.

[23] Acts 13:45–48; 17:5, 13; 18:6; 19:9; cf. 28:23–28.

[24] Acts 25:10–12; 26:32.

[25] See chapter 3 under *Paul's farewell and the coming of the kingdom*.

[26] The cities of Jerusalem and Antioch are important in the narrative of Acts, but Paul is not portrayed as the founder of the community of believers in either city.

are, in fact, three distinct groups in the author's narrative of Paul's mission to Ephesus: the ἀδελφοί who commend Apollos to Achaea, with whom Priscilla and Aquila are associated (18:24–28); the μαθηταί associated with John (19:1–7); and μαθηταί of Paul (19:8–20:1).[27] The Pauline unity that emerges in the author's narrative of this diversity at Ephesus provides the clearest indication of the author's redactional and compositional method in portraying Pauline communities.

The author's narrative of the Pauline mission to Ephesus is unusual in that there are two separate accounts of what (in the author's portrayal) typically marks the beginning of Paul's mission in a city. Paul's preaching in the Jewish synagogue is recounted on two separate occasions: when Paul first arrives in the city in 18:19–21 and then when he returns to the city in 19:8. In no other city does the author recount two separate 'beginnings' of the Pauline mission in the Jewish synagogue. Instead, Paul's subsequent visits to the other cities of Asia Minor, Macedonia, and Achaea all presuppose the foundation of the Christian community based on Paul's first visit.[28] The events characteristic of such foundations of Christian communities elsewhere—preaching in the Jewish synagogue, rejection of the message by unbelieving Jews, and subsequent turn to the Gentiles[29]—correspond to the events of the second beginning of Paul's mission in Ephesus, Acts 19:8–10. This narrative of the founding of the 'Pauline' community in Acts 19:8–10 takes no notice of the previously narrated events concerning Ephesus, Acts 18:19–19:7. Priscilla, Aquila, and Apollos play no role in the narrative of the Pauline mission in 19:8–20:1, nor do the disciples of John. As a result, the relationship of the ἀδελφοί associated with Priscilla, Aquila, and Apollos in 18:27 and the μαθηταί with John in 19:1–7 to the μαθηταί of Paul in 19:9, 19:30, and 20:1 is unclear.[30] Acts 19:8–10 appears to be

---

[27] These disciples are specifically mentioned in Acts 19:9, 19:30, and 20:1. The individuals in 19:18 at a narrative level belong to this group, but 19:18–20 is probably not a Pauline tradition. See discussion below in this section.

[28] Cf. Acts 20:1–4, where Paul revisits the communities he has founded in 16:11–18:17.

[29] Acts 18:5–8; cf. 13:44–48; 17:1–5; 28:23–31.

[30] At a narrative level, the disciples in 19:9 (as well as 19:30 and 20:1) presumably include the individuals in the preceding episodes (18:19–20; 18:26–27; 19:1). This intended unity at the level of the narrative is, however, very superficial and hardly covers the lack of connection between the episodes in the author's information about Ephesus. For example, even at a narrative level, the disciples of John in 19:1–7 have no connection with a synagogue, unlike the Pauline group in 19:9 and the group connected to Apollos in 18:26–27.

a fresh start for Christianity in Ephesus, and some explanation of the author's unusual narrative of Paul's mission in Ephesus is required.

Acts 18:24–28, the incident involving Apollos at Ephesus, is one of very few episodes in Acts 16–28 in which Paul does not play a role and is the only example in Acts of someone apart from Paul preaching in a synagogue.[31] The basis for this episode in the author's sources is difficult to reconstruct due to the author's attempt to fit it into his schema of the Pauline mission. In the narrative of Acts, Paul and Apollos never meet, and there is no interaction between Paul and Priscilla and Aquila at Ephesus that would suggest the nature of their mutual relationship in this city.[32] The information on which Acts 18:24–28 is based suggests a community of disciples of Jesus existing in Ephesus independent of a Pauline mission in the city—a community with which Apollos, Priscilla, and Aquila were associated. To superimpose the character of Paul over this apparent (non-Pauline) diversity in the author's sources pertaining to the origin of Christianity at Ephesus, the author has narrated two distinct beginnings of Paul's mission at Ephesus. The travel information in 18:18–23, which connects the arrival of Priscilla and Aquila at Ephesus with the arrival of Paul, establishes Paul as present even in his absence in 18:24–28. Paul is the first to proclaim the gospel to the Jews in the city (Acts 18:19), not Apollos (Acts 18:26) nor Priscilla and Aquila (Acts 18:19). Priscilla and Aquila are thus portrayed as acting as Paul's lieutenants in correcting the inadequacy of the preaching of Apollos, who himself then (by implication) becomes part of the Pauline mission and is sent off to Corinth (where Paul has already established the Christian community).

There are good reasons to think this notice of Paul's travels in 18:18–23 is, insofar as it concerns Paul, entirely a composition of the author independent of any sources he may have had.[33] The narration of Paul's departure from the ἀδελφοί at Corinth contains two details: (1) Priscilla and Aquila accompany Paul from Corinth, and (2) Paul shaves his head in Cenchreae because of a previously made vow. The author's purpose in mentioning these details becomes clear only in relation to Paul's destination, Syria, and his intermediate stop, Ephesus. The

---

[31] οὗτος [Ἀπολλῶς] τε ἤρξατο παρρησιάζεσθαι ἐν τῇ συναγωγῇ (Acts 18:26).

[32] See, however, Acts 18:2–3 (discussed below in this chapter under *Corinth*).

[33] Contrast, e.g., Haenchen, *The Acts of the Apostles*, pp. 87–88; Conzelmann, *Acts of the Apostles*, pp. 155–56; Lüdemann, *Early Christianity according to the Traditions in Acts*, pp. 204–7. Whether or not the author had any information about a journey of Priscilla and Aquila from Corinth to Ephesus cannot be determined.

phrase κειράμενος ἐν Κεγχρεαῖς τὴν κεφαλήν, εἶχεν γὰρ εὐχήν in Acts 18:18 is difficult to interpret in any precise manner.[34] Nevertheless, the participial phrase should be construed with Paul, not Aquila;[35] the vagueness of its precise cultic significance corresponds to the general vagueness of Paul's travels in 18:18–23. Paul's arrival in Jerusalem is marked only by a participial phrase (ἀναβὰς ... κατέβη).[36] The only detail supplied that might explain the reason for this journey is Paul's vow. The vow, in some general sense understood by the author, requires Paul's journey to Syria. There is no reason to suppose that the author intends anything more by the vow than that it necessitates Paul's return to Jerusalem.[37] This vow and consequent need to go to Jerusalem explain why Paul cannot stay in Ephesus and thus why Paul is absent in Acts 18:24–28.

In contrast to the general lack of details concerning Paul's vow and consequent journey in 18:18–23, the notice concerning his stop in Ephesus gains prominence. Paul drops off Priscilla and Aquila in Ephesus and himself enters the synagogue, reasons with the Jews, and promises to return. This notice serves no other purpose than to bring the proclamation of the gospel in Ephesus into the Pauline orbit. With this brief account of Paul's first arrival in Ephesus, the author indicates how the rest of his narrative about Ephesus should be read—that is, in light of the mission of Paul. This compositional framework for the Christian mission to Ephesus—established by the notice of Paul's preaching in the synagogue at Ephesus in 18:18–23,[38] which is cut short by the necessity of his journey to Syria—is supplied by the author to subordinate Priscilla and Aquila (who arrive with Paul) and the preaching of Apollos (as corrected by Priscilla and Aquila) to the Pauline mission.[39] There is no reason to suppose that the vague notice about Paul's vow and con-

---

[34] See the commentaries. Note the frequent attempts to specify the exact ritual procedures intended by this brief and rather cryptic notice.

[35] The author has no reason to relate such a detail about Aquila.

[36] That ἀναβὰς ... κατέβη in Acts 18:22 implies a visit to Jerusalem, see, e.g., Conzelmann, *Acts of the Apostles*, p. 156.

[37] Cf. Acts 21:23–24; Josephus *Jewish War* 2.313. Speculation about the author's understanding of the precise cultic requirements of such a vow are beside the point.

[38] For this compositional motif, see Acts 17:2–3; 17:10–11; 18:4–5.

[39] In contrast, Lüdemann (*Early Christianity according to the Traditions in Acts*, p. 206) comments: "... it seems likely that here Luke has used a list of stations from the tradition which included the journey to Jerusalem." To Lüdemann, the redactional significance of the journey in Acts 18:18–23 is not clear, and so he has recourse to the traditions the author has about Paul's mission areas.

sequent need to go to Jerusalem are anything more than narrative constructs to explain the only precise detail in the travel notice, Paul's brief stop at Ephesus—a detail necessitated by the author's Pauline schema for the origin of Christianity at Ephesus.

Although the author has superimposed his schema of the Pauline mission on the activities of Priscilla, Aquila, and Apollos at Ephesus, he has not entirely covered the essentially non-Pauline elements in the episode. In the information available to the author, Apollos is apparently a missionary proclaiming some form of spiritual renewal associated with Jesus,[40] independently of Paul,[41] perhaps under the patronage of Priscilla and Aquila.[42] That he could preach accurately the things of Jesus yet know only the baptism of John[43] is an interpretation of the information about Apollos motivated by the author's attempt to establish a salvation-historical genealogy of the groups at Ephesus in relation to Paul. The description of Apollos in 18:25, ἐδίδασκεν ἀκριβῶς τὰ περὶ τοῦ Ἰησοῦ ἐπιστάμενος μόνον τὸ βάπτισμα Ἰωάννου, should be compared to the description of Paul in Acts 28:31, διδάσκων τὰ περὶ τοῦ κυρίου Ἰησοῦ Χριστοῦ. Apollos is presented as teaching about Jesus based on his knowledge of the baptism of John—that is, apparently, some approximation of the message of John reported in Luke 3:16.[44]

---

[40] ζέων τῷ πνεύματι probably comes from the author's sources. See Käsemann, 'The Disciples of John the Baptist in Ephesus,' in *Essays on New Testament Themes*, pp. 136–48. ζέων occurs only here in Acts. Whether it comes from the language of Christian paraenesis (Rom 12:11; cf. Conzelmann, *Acts of the Apostles*, p. 158) or from some form of Christian enthusiasm (Lüdemann, *Early Christianity according to the Traditions in Acts*, p. 208), the language and conception are different from the author's description of the spirit elsewhere. See, e.g., Acts 6:5 (cf. 6:10): ... Στέφανον ἄνδρα πλήρης πίστεως καὶ πνεύματος ἁγίου. Possession by the spirit in Lk-Acts, with the associated charismatic manifestations, is a mark of belonging to the kingdom of God inaugurated with Jesus' enthronement and giving of the spirit (Acts 2:33; 11:15–17). The description of Apollos as ζέων τῷ πνεύματι would, of course, have recommended Apollos to the author as a Christian preacher of this salvation history associated with John and Jesus; whether the author recognized his reinterpretation of the description cannot be determined.

In 1 Corinthians 1–4, Paul associates Apollos with divisions in the Corinthian community that appear to involve claims about spiritual wisdom. See especially 2:1–3:23. This association may give some hint of the historical situation behind the information available to the author about Apollos.

[41] For their relationship from Paul's perspective, see especially 1 Cor 16:12; cf. 1 Cor 1:12; 3:4–6, 22; 4:6.

[42] Cf. Paul's ambiguous relation to Priscilla and Aquila at Corinth, discussed below under *Corinth*.

[43] A problem that has often been recognized. See, e.g., Lüdemann, *Early Christianity according to the Traditions in Acts*, p. 208.

[44] Cf. Acts 1:5; 11:16.

This message is accurate as far as it goes,[45] but needs further elaboration in terms of the unfolding of salvation history based on Jesus' ascension and giving of the Christian spirit (Acts 2:33). The following episode, Acts 19:1–7, conveys what in the author's construction is lacking in knowledge based only on the baptism of John. In the author's understanding of the origin of Christianity, the knowledge about Jesus based on John's baptism is a preliminary stage on the way to full knowledge of the risen and ascended lord Jesus Christ, who has poured out the Christian spirit. For the author, this is the message proclaimed by Paul, about which Apollos is instructed by Priscilla and Aquila (themselves acting as Paul's representatives at Ephesus in view of his absence). There is, however, in contrast to Paul's baptism of the disciples in the following episode, Acts 19:1–7, no notice that Apollos was baptized into the Christian spirit after being instructed by Priscilla and Aquila—an omission that creates a tension between the description of Apollos as ζέων τῷ πνεύματι yet ἐπιστάμενος μόνον τὸ βάπτισμα Ἰωάννου.

The information the author had about Apollos apparently associated him with a Jesus movement or mission closely connected to the synagogue.[46] Apollos's missionary pattern—the note about the preaching of Apollos in the synagogue in 18:26—is usually taken to be redactional according to the pattern attributed by the author to Paul.[47] Another possibility, however, is that the missionary pattern of this Jewish movement associated with Jesus and the synagogue, of which Apollos was a part, served as the model for the author's pattern of the Pauline mission in Acts.[48] In other words, the portrayal of the Pauline mission at Ephesus in Acts 19:8–40 (as well as at other cities) has been made to conform with the information the author had about the origin of Jesus movements at Ephesus (and perhaps elsewhere) in connection with the synagogue.[49] The plausibility of this suggestion will become

---

[45] For the author, the proclamation of John marks a decisive transition in the manifestation of the kingdom of God (Lk 16:16).

[46] Lüdemann (*Early Christianity according to the Traditions in Acts*, pp. 208–9) sees evidence of the founding of pre-Pauline Christianity in Ephesus in this passage. That Apollos founded Christian communities seems likely from 1 Corinthians, in which Paul implies that at least some individuals perceived Apollos as a founder figure. See, e.g., 1 Cor 1:12; 3:1–23.

[47] See, e.g., Lüdemann, *Early Christianity according to the Traditions in Acts*, p. 208. Compare Acts 18:26, οὗτος τε ἤρξατο παρρησιάζεσθαι ἐν τῇ συναγωγῇ, with 19:8, εἰσελθὼν δὲ εἰς τὴν συναγωγὴν ἐπαρρησιάζετο. See also 18:19.

[48] In contrast, see Paul's delineation of mission fields in Galatians 2:1–10.

[49] The author's intention to conform the mission of Paul to the origin of Christianity

more clear as further evidence to indicate the social context for the author's sources about Christianity at Ephesus is presented below.

Paul's comments in 1 Cor 16:19 and Rom 16:3–5[50] suggest that Priscilla and Aquila were wealthy patrons of a local house church at Ephesus and were active in supporting the Christian mission. In their capacity as patrons, they aided Paul,[51] but there is no need to presume that they were 'Pauline' Christians[52] nor that they would not have been active in aiding other missionaries.[53] The author's note about the departure of Priscilla and Aquila from Rome because of the expulsion of Jews by Claudius (Acts 18:2–3) suggests that they were active in a Jesus movement at Rome.[54] If so, they would likely have continued to

---

in connection with local synagogues would not likely have been suggested by 'Pauline' sources. See Gal 2:1–10.

[50] If Romans 16 is taken as a letter fragment originally sent to Ephesus.

[51] See also 2 Tim 4:19.

[52] τοὺς συνεργούς μου ἐν Χριστῷ Ἰησοῦ (Rom 16:3) does not necessarily imply that Priscilla and Aquila were Paulinists. Paul also describes Apollos as συνεργός (1 Cor 3:9). See BDAG, s.v. In light of the apparent difficulties at Ephesus perhaps indicated by Rom 16:17–20, Paul's invoking the support of a major patron of the Christian mission at Ephesus appears to be an attempt to gain support for his position at Ephesus. In 1 Cor 16:19, Paul sends greetings from Priscilla and Aquila at Ephesus to Corinth because they are major patrons of the Christian mission. (The inference that the greeting from Priscilla and Aquila in 1 Cor 16:19 is based on their prior residence at Corinth depends on the narrative of Acts!) It would have been to the apologetic advantage of Paul to invoke such support, both in 1 Cor 16:19 (in relation to the difficulties at Corinth with Apollos, whose mission they may have been supporting) and in Rom 16:3–5 (in relation to the difficulties suggested by Rom 16:17–20).

[53] Whether or not the association of Apollos with Priscilla and Aquila in Acts 18:24–28 is the author's compositional construction is difficult to determine. See, e.g., Lüdemann, *Early Christianity according to the Traditions in Acts*, pp. 208–9. The author could easily have conflated information about the house church of Priscilla and Aquila with information about Apollos connected to Ephesus. The somewhat harsh transitions between the scenes in the episode—Apollos preaching in the synagogue, Apollos being corrected by Priscilla and Aquila (a redactional construct), and the Christians commending Apollos to Achaea (with no mention of the synagogue or Priscilla and Aquila) could suggest the author's piecing together of unrelated bits of information. On the other hand, 18:24–28 is similar to 18:2–3. In both episodes, Priscilla and Aquila appear as patrons of a Christian missionary (Paul, Apollos). The seams in the author's narrative are probably the result of his attempt to impose his schema of the Pauline mission on Priscilla and Aquila, who in his sources are probably patrons independent of both Paul and Apollos.

[54] Suetonius (*Claudius* 25) reports *Judaeos impulsore Chresto assidue tumultantes Roma expulit*. The name χριστός has probably been confused with χρηστός, so that Suetonius is reporting an action taken by Claudius against Jews associated with a Jesus movement at Rome. See Haenchen, *The Acts of the Apostles*, p. 65. Priscilla and Aquila were presumably among those targeted by the action of Claudius against the disturbances associated with this Jesus movement.

support this movement at Ephesus, independently of Paul. The lack of clarity in the connection of these individuals to Paul's mission at both Corinth[55] and Ephesus[56] in the narrative of Acts suggests that the author's information about Priscilla and Aquila did not subordinate them to the Pauline mission. Indeed, the author is unable to suppress entirely their independence from the Pauline mission as he finds it in his sources, especially those behind Acts 18:24–28. For the author, superimposing the narrative construct of Paul's travels in Acts 18:18–23 over the non-Pauline information about a Jesus movement in Ephesus in Acts 18:24–28 is sufficient to bring order to the lack of order in his sources about Christianity at Ephesus.[57]

The episode involving the disciples associated with John the Baptist in 19:1–7 introduces another group at Ephesus.[58] This group is not, at least in the narrative of Acts, explicitly connected with the synagogue. Paul, however, has now reappeared in Ephesus and participates in the story. The overlay of the author's portrayal of Paul on this episode makes it difficult to determine the nature of the sources available to the author. In the context of the narrative of Acts, the author has connected the disciples in Acts 19:1–7 with Apollos in terms of John the Baptist, but this connection is a compositional construct of the author. The author does not actually introduce the persons discussed in 19:1–7 as disciples of John the Baptist. They are simply identified as μαθηταί (19:1). This vagueness perhaps suggests that even the subsequent connection of these disciples to John the Baptist, as in the case of Apollos, is redactional. In this case, the author has used the figure of John the Baptist to categorize individuals and groups originally having no con-

---

[55] See below on *Corinth*. Haenchen (*The Acts of the Apostles*, p. 533, n. 4) comments on the relationship of Paul to Aquila and Priscilla at Corinth: "It is probable that Aquila and Priscilla had a house church in Corinth (corresponding to that in 1 Cor 16:19). On the other hand, they had not begun a mission." This attempt to harmonize the narrative of Acts with an underlying historical reality raises more questions than it answers (note Haenchen's comments on p. 538, discussed below) and only serves to indicate the difficulties of the narrative in Acts.

[56] Their joint arrival in Ephesus in Acts 18:18–19 is the author's construction of their relationship to Paul. See discussion above in this section. Speculations concerning the basis for 18:18–19 in information the author has about their actual travels with Paul are misguided.

[57] Cf. the author's stated intentions in Lk 1:1–4.

[58] Acts 19:7 is probably redactional and does not indicate the actual size of the group. See, e.g., Lüdemann, *Early Christianity according to the Traditions in Acts*, p. 210. The small size of the group minimizes its importance.

nection at all to John.[59] Whether in fact the author's information about these disciples was even actually localized at Ephesus cannot be determined.[60] In any case, the overlay of Paul's proclamation,[61] baptism,[62] and the reception of the spirit through the laying on of Paul's hands[63] is characteristic of the author's composition. There is no residue of a Pauline tradition as a source for the author's story in 19:1–7.

These disciples associated by the author with John the Baptist in 19:1–7 would probably have been Jews. The narrative of Acts 18:24–19:7 thus appears to preserve information about pneumatic and perhaps baptist movements[64] in the Jewish communities at Ephesus.[65] Paul's missionary persona in Acts has been overlaid[66] on what the author portrays as deficient manifestations of the Christian message, construed in terms of salvation history. The author has no concept of competing or diverse forms of 'Christianity.'[67] Instead, the author has reconceptualized diversity in early Jewish movements associated with Jesus and perhaps John as stages (albeit sometimes overlapping) in the proclamation of the kingdom of God from John to Paul.[68] The author has failed, however, to

---

[59] On the other hand, the prologue to the Fourth Gospel and the accounts of John in the synoptic gospels (see, e.g., Mk 1:7–8; 2:18) suggest followers of John and Jesus polemically interacting with one another within Judaism of the first century. If the disciples in Acts 19:1–7 were actually followers of John the Baptist, the narrative of Acts does not explain how these followers of John got to Ephesus. Perhaps the author intends that they were Jews residing in Ephesus who had become familiar with the preaching of John the Baptist, perhaps on a trip to Jerusalem. Whether or not the author knew these followers of John to be a distinct movement cannot be discerned. Cf. Lk 7:18–35.

[60] See, e.g., Conzelmann, *Acts of the Apostles*, p. 159. A decision one way or the other cannot be made with any certainty. Nevertheless, the author relates more about Ephesus than any other center of the Pauline mission, and all of it very tenuously connected with Paul. Does the author have a special connection to Ephesus or to information about Ephesus?

[61] Acts 19:4; cf. 13:24–25; also Luke 3:1–18; Acts 1:5; 11:16.

[62] Baptism εἰς τὸ ὄνομα τοῦ κυρίου Ἰησοῦ (Acts 19:5) is characteristic of the narrative of Acts.

[63] Acts 19:6; cf. 8:17–19.

[64] There is no reason to suppose that the later Christian connection between baptism and the reception of the spirit implies an original connection between such movements.

[65] The diversity of viewpoints within Judaism at Ephesus was probably as great as that in Palestine. This diversity would most likely have created a great deal of diversity among the followers of Jesus within these Jewish communities at Ephesus and elsewhere in the Diaspora.

[66] Acts 18:19–20; 19:1.

[67] For the author, diversity exists within Judaism. See esp. Acts 23:1–10.

[68] Cf. Lk 1:1–4, especially 1:4 in relation to 1:5.

suppress the fact that the information in his sources about Apollos, Priscilla, and Aquila does not entirely fit his schema for the origin of Christianity portrayed in Paul's mission.

When Paul begins (again) his preaching in the synagogue at Ephesus (19:8), no further notice is taken of the individuals and groups in Acts 18:24–19:7. The Pauline disciples of 19:9, 19:30, and 20:1 have presumably absorbed them. These Pauline disciples, however, are difficult to locate in the author's sources about Christianity at Ephesus. Although Acts 19:8–10 describes the origin of this Pauline community, this origin is determined by the narrative themes of Acts hung on a few pieces of information about Paul's presence in the city. Whether or not the typical note of the location of Paul's mission at Ephesus after his characteristic split with the synagogue (19:9, the lecture hall of Tyrannus)[69] or the length of time of the Pauline mission in the city (19:10, two years)[70] reflects information available to the author about the historical mission of Paul in the city,[71] this information is not embedded in any traditional story of the founding of a Pauline community at Ephesus.[72] The notice of disciples accompanying Paul from the synagogue to the school of Tyrannus (19:9) implies the foundation of a 'Pauline' community (these disciples are associated with Paul in 19:30 and 20:1), but this 'foundation' is determined by the author's schema of the Pauline mission.[73] As

---

[69] Cf. Philippi (16:15, 40) and Corinth (18:3, 7).

[70] Cf. Corinth (18:11) and Rome (28:30).

[71] Cf. 1 Cor 16:8–9; Rom 16:3–5.

[72] See below under *Corinth* on the use of the word 'tradition' in relation to information about Paul in Acts. The lack of connection of the details in 19:8–10 to Priscilla and Aquila suggests that the information about Paul at Ephesus available to the author is not connected to the information about the founding of a Christian community at Ephesus that the author has preserved in 18:24–28. Such information about Paul, characteristic of most of the Pauline details in Acts 16–20 (including Acts 20:4–6, where Paul is connected with certain individuals in the various cities of his mission), is consistent with some form of travel diary. See below under *Philippi* on the 'we' narrator of Acts.

[73] This pattern is summarized in Paul's farewell speech, in which Paul characterizes himself as (1) δουλεύων τῷ κυρίῳ μετὰ ... πειρασμῶν τῶν συμβάντων μοι ἐν ταῖς ἐπιβουλαῖς τῶν Ἰουδαίων (20:19) and (2) διαμαρτυρόμενος Ἰουδαίοις τε καὶ Ἕλλησιν τὴν εἰς θεὸν μετάνοιαν καὶ πίστιν εἰς τὸν κύριον ἡμῶν Ἰησοῦν (20:21). Acts 19:8–10 conveys little about a distinctly Pauline community in the city beyond a brief notice of his presence. That Paul's mission had its starting place in the Jewish synagogue of the various cities of his mission has often been recognized as problematic and unhistorical. Paul's understanding of the agreement of the Jerusalem council in Galatians 2:1–10, as well as the composition of his communities (see especially Rom 15:26–28), suggests that Paul's communities were largely Gentile, and his problems seem to have stemmed from his attempt to relate these communities to other Jewish followers of Jesus (see especially Paul's concerns in Galatians and Romans), followers of Jesus probably associated with

such, these 'Pauline' disciples are a narrative construct reflecting the successful preaching of the word of God by Paul in Asia (19:10). Once the author's compositional schema is removed, however, the Pauline details in 19:8–10 suggest no traditions that presuppose a specifically Pauline community at Ephesus known to the author.[74]

The specific content (otherwise lacking) related to the founding of the community by Paul portrayed in Acts 19:8–10 is to be supplied from the rest of the narrative of Acts. The content of Paul's message in the synagogue, which leads to his split with the Jews of the synagogue, is suggested by examples the author has supplied on other occasions, especially Acts 13:13–41. The content of Paul's reasoning in the hall of Tyrannus (presumably with Gentiles) is probably suggested by Acts 14:8–18 and Acts 17:16–31. Paul's relationship to the Christian community in the preaching of the gospel is supplied in his farewell address, Acts 20:17–35.[75] None of these speeches is particularly Pauline,[76] but in the narrative of Acts, they give substance to the mission of Paul that is otherwise lacking in terms of specifically Pauline stories available to the author. For the author of Lk-Acts, Paul founds communities based on the same message that characterized Peter's proclamation to the Jews on the day of Pentecost—that is, the author's understanding of salvation history and the origin of Christianity.[77] The author of Lk-Acts, in a manner typical of Hellenistic historiography, has used speeches to supply the necessary interpretive framework for his narrative, and these speeches subordinate any lack of coherence in the details to the author's larger interpretive picture.

The notice of Paul's mission in 19:8–10 is immediately followed by a summary of Paul's miraculous deeds (19:11–12) serving to preface the two episodes in 19:13–20. This summary is intended by the author to superimpose the character of Paul on these episodes. Yet, apart

---

the local synagogues. At Ephesus the author seems to have had material available about followers of Jesus associated with the synagogue and to have overlaid his schema of the Pauline mission on it.

[74] On the correlation of communities and traditions, see below under *Corinth*.

[75] See below under *Paul's Farewell*.

[76] See, e.g., Vielhauer, 'On the "Paulinism" of Acts,' pp. 34–43. For a dissenting view, see Walton, *Leadership and Lifestyle*, e.g., pp. 212–13. On Walton, see my review scheduled for publication in the January 2002 issue of the *Journal of Religion*.

[77] Note, e.g., how Paul's speech in Acts 13:16–41 locates John the Baptist in the author's portrayal of the history of salvation; the author's construction of the history of salvation is the basis for the author's portrayal of the Jewish groups at Ephesus in Acts 18:24–19:7.

from what look to be secondary intrusions of the name of Paul in the story of the Jewish exorcists in 19:13–16,[78] neither episode is distinctly Pauline. Acts 19:13–16 is a story involving the magical use of the name Jesus, reminiscent of the very similar episode in Luke 9:49–50 // Mark 9:38–40. The episode appears to reflect a controversy between different (Jewish) groups invoking the name of Jesus to cast out demons.[79] Unlike Jesus' response in Luke 9:49–50, the author puts a Pauline spin to the moral of the story in Acts 19:13–16: only those belonging to the Pauline mission have the authority to perform miracles in the name of Jesus (and Paul). Paul's name is thus given the quasi-magical status of the name of Jesus, and the use of this name is restricted, unlike the inclusiveness of the Markan episode (and the parallel in Lk). This story of the rival exorcists using Jesus' (and Paul's) name magnifies Paul's missionary persona as a preacher of the name of Jesus.[80]

The following episode of the burning of the magical books (19:18–20), linked by the author to the story of the Jewish exorcists, does not even mention Paul. The author, of course, intends to imply that the Pauline mission produced these results.[81] At a narrative level, πολλοὶ τῶν πεπιστευκότων (19:18) belong to the disciples of Paul, but there is no compelling reason to assume that this story had a connection to Paul in the author's sources. The lack of a 'Pauline' basis for the author's information about Ephesus is here evident in another episode that does not even mention Paul.[82]

The details involving the Pauline mission summarized in 19:21–22 are similar in character to the notes about the Pauline mission in 19:9–10.[83] Whether this information is historical, traditional, or redac-

---

[78] ὁρκίζω ὑμᾶς τὸν Ἰησοῦν ὃν Παῦλος κηρύσσει (19:13); τὸν Ἰησοῦν γινώσκω καὶ τὸν Παῦλον ἐπίσταμαι (19:15). The italicized clauses look like redactional additions to an episode that originally was about Jesus. The probability of this conclusion is increased in relation to the author's procedure in composing the rest of the episode at Ephesus. For what appears to be a similar procedure in relation to his sources, see also the incidental description of Paul as an apostle in Acts 14:4, 14 (see below under *Paul's Mission with Barnabas*).

[79] The social dynamic of 'us' against 'them' is evident in Mk 9:38–40 // Lk 9:49–50, as well as in Acts 19:13–16.

[80] The author's connection of the story to Paul is consistent with the author's portrayal of Paul and the apostles as miracle workers.

[81] See 19:11–12, 21.

[82] Cf. Acts 18:24–28, discussed above in this section.

[83] Cf. 20:4.

tional,⁸⁴ it contributes little to any knowledge of a Pauline community at Ephesus. Instead, the author reports the travel plans to create the impression of a Pauline mission, including several associates,⁸⁵ unifying Christianity in Asia Minor, Macedonia, and Achaea.⁸⁶ The dramatic discourse reporting Paul's mission goal, μετὰ τὸ γενέσθαι με ἐκεῖ δεῖ με καὶ Ῥώμην ἰδεῖν (19:21), is the author's composition, integrating the travel notes into the author's narrative structure of Acts.⁸⁷

The last event of the Pauline mission in Ephesus is the controversy with artisans associated with the temple of Artemis (Acts 19:23–40). The importance of the temple of Artemis at Ephesus was well known in antiquity.⁸⁸ This temple was a religious, social, and economic center for Ephesus, and as the largest Greek temple in antiquity it was an important representation of Greek cultic religion. The author of Acts narrates a controversy between this center of Greek cultic life and the message preached by Paul. However, the role of Paul in this controversy exists entirely at the level of redaction. This Pauline role consists of a summary of the mission of Paul put into the mouth of Demetrius (19:25–27) and an explanation of why Paul is not really involved (19:28–31) in the ensuing disturbance.⁸⁹ The author has created an impression of how important Paul really was in inciting the uproar, though he is

---

⁸⁴ As Lüdemann (*Early Christianity according to the Traditions in Acts*, pp. 212–15) tries to sort out.

⁸⁵ See especially 20:4–6. On this list of Paul's associates, see Betz, *2 Corinthians 8 and 9*, pp. 50–52. To the extent that the author has information about Paul's return to Jerusalem with a collection and accompanied by certain individuals, he has received this apart from any distinctly 'Pauline' stories connected to 'Pauline' churches in these cities.

⁸⁶ Cf. Acts 19:10.

⁸⁷ Against Lindemann (*Paulus im ältesten Christentum. Das Bild des Apostels und die Rezeption der paulinischen Theologie in der frühchristlichen Literatur bis Marcion*, p. 166), this statement is not derived from Rom 15:22–28. The geographical statements are not in agreement. In Romans, Spain is Paul's goal, whereas in Acts, Rome is the endpoint of Paul's mission. Further, the author's portrayal of the historical circumstances surrounding the collection Paul brought to Jerusalem argues against the author's knowledge of Rom 15:22–28. See below under *Rome* on Acts 24:17. Finally, δεῖ με (Acts 19:21) is characteristic of the author's compositional style in relating a divine imperative; the author is perhaps suggesting the irony that Paul must go to Rome not of his own free will, but as a prisoner in accordance with the plan of God (see Acts 20:22–23).

⁸⁸ See Oster, 'Ephesus' *ABD* II.542–49; idem, 'Ephesus as a Religious Center under the Principate, I. Paganism before Constantine,' *ANRW* II 18.3.1661–1728.

⁸⁹ Cf. Acts 18:18–23, discussed above, in which the author explains Paul's absence from the narrative in Acts 18:24–28.

absent as the events actually unfold.[90] Paul is exhorted to keep away from the disturbance even by some of the officials of the province, who are his friends (19:31)![91] His absence notwithstanding, his image has been enhanced.

Despite the mention of Gaius and Aristarchus in 19:29,[92] the controversy does not really even seem to involve (Gentile) Christians, but rather Jews and pagans. Verse 33a, ἐκ δὲ τοῦ ὄχλου συνεβίβασαν Ἀλέξανδρον, προβαλόντων αὐτὸν τῶν Ἰουδαίων, is unintelligible.[93] The meaning and subject of συνεβίβασαν have been lost in the author's overlay of the character of Paul (verses 25–32) on a non-Pauline story (verses 33–40). For no reason given in the narrative, it is the Jews (whose involvement in a conflict between Paul and Demetrius is left unexplained) who push Alexander to the front of the rioting crowds (προβαλόντων αὐτὸν τῶν Ἰουδαίων),[94] and it is when the crowds recognize he is a Jew (not a Christian) that they riot.[95] There is no reason to suppose, apart from the author's redaction, that this is a tradition about a controversy between Christians and pagans, much less Pauline Chris-

---

[90] The reference to the Pauline disciples in 19:30 belongs to the redactional level of the episode.

[91] Cf. Paul's relationship to officials elsewhere (e.g., Acts 13:7, 12; 25:13–26:32; 28:7). Cf. also Lentz (*Luke's Portrait of Paul*, e.g., pp. 168–71) on the status with which Paul is portrayed in Acts.

[92] Their presence in this episode is probably redactional. For the author's information about these individuals, see Acts 20:4 and 27:2. The author has simplified the geographical notice in 20:4 so that Gaius and Aristarchus are both described as Macedonians in 19:29.

[93] This lack of intelligibility was felt by later scribes, as the variants for συνεβίβασαν indicate. Conzelmann (*Acts of the Apostles*, p. 166) comments: "What was Alexander supposed to do? As a trusted representative of the Jews, was he to explain that they had nothing to do with this matter? Did Luke no longer understand his source here?" Haenchen (*The Acts of the Apostles*, p. 575) attempts to elaborate on the narrative in Acts: "The position Luke has in mind appears to be roughly as follows: the crowd makes no distinction between Jews and Christians. The Jews then feel themselves threatened, and send Alexander forward. He is now informed about the real situation by some of the crowd, who know the facts, and on this basis wants to make a defense for the Jews. But he is not even allowed to speak!" Why the author would have meant this, yet failed so utterly to make it clear, is difficult to understand. Instead, the author seems to have overlaid the missionary persona of Paul on a non-Pauline story in a way that destroys the coherence of the story. (Cf. the comments below on the Gallio episode and Acts 18:17.) This lack of a Pauline basis for the story corresponds to the general lack of an underlying Pauline coherence to the information used by the author to recount the origin of Christianity at Ephesus.

[94] The assumption that the Jews are also the subjects of συνεβίβασαν is unwarranted grammatically.

[95] ἐπιγνόντες δὲ ὅτι Ἰουδαῖός ἐστιν (19:34).

tians (or Paul) and pagans. The most likely social context for this story (whether or not historical) is the Jewish community of Ephesus, not a Pauline (Gentile) community.⁹⁶ The story reflects tensions between Jewish and Greek cultic practices. The author, however, has redacted this episode to set the message of Jesus proclaimed by Paul over against the religious and economic interests of a Greek cult. This foreshadows the conflict between the message of Paul and the interests of the Jerusalem cult.⁹⁷ The author intends to differentiate Christianity as proclaimed by Paul from cultic allegiance to idols and temples (whether pagan or Jewish). In anticipation of the narrative events soon to take place in Jerusalem, the author has taken what looks like a Jewish story of conflict at Ephesus and inserted Paul as the chief provocateur.⁹⁸

The lack of an underlying Pauline social context for the stories used by the author to construct the narrative of Paul's mission to Ephesus is glossed over by the author's portrayal of Paul's relationship to the believers in the city in 20:1 and 20:17.⁹⁹ Before leaving the city in 20:1, Paul sends for the disciples in the city,¹⁰⁰ and on his way to Jerusalem he summons the elders of the community in Acts

---

⁹⁶ Whether the Jewish community may in fact have included followers of Jesus in the synagogue cannot be determined. The author's descriptive categories make it impossible to reconstruct with precision the diversity of Christianity and Judaism at Ephesus in the author's sources. Cf. Acts 18:2–3 and 18:12–17, on which see below under *Corinth*.

⁹⁷ See Acts 21:28. Cf. also Stephen's rejection of the temple (Acts 7:48; cf. 6:12–14), with which Paul is connected (Acts 8:1; 22:20).

⁹⁸ Lüdemann (*Early Christianity according to the Traditions in Acts*, pp. 218–20) comes to a different assessment of Acts 19:23–40. He suggests this episode is largely the result of the author's own literary composition. Against this, however, is the difficult syntax of 19:33, which is hard to explain if the author is largely composing this narrative from scratch. Cf. Conzelmann, *Acts of the Apostles*, pp. 164–65. There is, however, little reason to suppose that 1 Cor 15:32 and 2 Cor 1:8–10 reveal the real events behind Acts 19:23–40. Conzelmann's suggestion that "the real events have been toned down" is an understatement. If Paul's personal confrontation with death at Ephesus related in 1 Cor 15:32 and 2 Cor 1:8–10 reflects the 'real events' behind Acts 19:23–40, the author has not toned them down, but completely changed them. In Acts 19:23–40 Paul is absent at the moment of danger.

⁹⁹ The use of loose temporal connections in the Ephesus account (19:21, 23; cf. 18:12) to string together otherwise unconnected episodes portrayed as Pauline is similar to the author's compositional style elsewhere. See, e.g., Lk 7:11. See also Lk 5:29 // Mk 2:15 for the author's willingness to introduce specific connections into his source material.

¹⁰⁰ For the compositional character of this statement, see especially 16:40; also 17:10, 14; 18:18. Acts 18:11 probably refers to Paul's missionary efforts (see Acts 28:31), not his teaching in a 'Pauline' community; ἐν αὐτοῖς (18:11) refers to the inhabitants of the city of Corinth (ἐν τῇ πόλει ταύτῃ, 18:10). See also 17:17 and 19:9–10.

20:17. Acts 20:1 and 20:17 imply a single community of believers at Ephesus that is unified around Paul. Such a community is not evident in the author's sources.[101] The author's historiographic intention to impose order on the origins of Christianity[102] has determined the relationship of Paul to the author's largely non-Pauline sources for Ephesus.[103] The Pauline Christianity at Ephesus portrayed in Acts is a narrative construct of the author, hung on the barest information about Paul's presence in the city. The author has no Pauline stories that can be correlated with a social context defined as Pauline Christianity at Ephesus.

The author's account of Paul's missionary journeys is fundamental for creating the impression of a Pauline order uniting the non-Pauline sources used by the author. Not only does Paul's journey to Syria in 18:18–23 explain his absence from Ephesus in 18:24–28,[104] but this return to Jerusalem and Antioch reinforces his position at the center of Christianity in relation to the complexity of the situation at Ephesus. Having touched base with the centers of the Christian movement at Jerusalem and Antioch, Paul returns to Ephesus and confronts the 'John the Baptist' problem introduced in the story about Apollos—a problem portrayed as lack of knowledge about the events 'accomplished among us'[105]—and the Christian spirit is given (19:1–7). With this apparent diversity at Ephesus resolved, the author then portrays Paul as proceeding to preach the gospel to all Jews and Greeks in Asia. This preaching decisively triumphs over magic[106] and threatens the business of Demetrius and the silversmiths associated with Artemis and her temple. With these incidents, the author's use of Paul's persona to exemplify

---

[101] Every mention of disciples associated with Paul (19:9, 30; 20:1) belongs to the compositional layer of the narrative of Acts.

[102] See Lk 1:4. See also chapter 3 above.

[103] Lüdemann (*Early Christianity according to the Traditions in Acts*, p. 220) comments: "The historical problem of Luke's account of Paul's activity in Ephesus therefore amounts to this: 'Luke gives the longest time to this period of Paul's activity and has the least ancient material for it' (Schille 1983, 392)." In contrast to the author's comparative wealth of information about Ephesus, the lack of distinctly Pauline missionary episodes associated with the city indicates that the author himself has no connections to a Pauline community in the city. Indeed, if Romans 16 is a letter fragment originally addressed to Ephesus, Paul himself attests the presence of non-Pauline forms of Christianity at Ephesus. See Rom 16:17–20. Cf. Rev 2:1–7.

[104] See discussion above in this section.

[105] Lk 1:1; Acts 19:2–4.

[106] Cf. Acts 13:4–12; also 8:4–25.

Christianity has gone beyond any information available to the author about Paul's historical mission.[107] Finally, after traveling through Macedonia and Greece, Paul again returns to address the elders of the Ephesian community at Miletus (20:17–35) and emphasizes the unity of the community[108] based on his proclamation of the kingdom of God, but warns of threats in the future, after his departure. This warning, however, is not directed toward any particular heresy,[109] but rather emphasizes the past unity of the community based on the character of Paul.[110] Such a 'Pauline community' and the author's knowledge of the traditions of this community are the author's own historiographical construct to present an ordered account of the events that have taken place 'among us' (Lk 1:1–4).

---

[107] The lack of historical individuality to the persona of Paul in Acts is evident in the portrayal of Paul as an orator throughout the narrative. In this portrayal of Paul as a powerful speaker, Paul's character as a distinct historical individual (see, e.g., 2 Cor 10:10) is transcended so that Paul's persona becomes the dramatic correlate of the author's vision of Christianity. The author places several speeches into the mouth of Paul: at Pisidian Antioch (a recitation of 'salvation history,' Acts 13:16–41), at Lystra (against pagan religion, Acts 14:8–18), at Athens (concerning Hellenistic philosophy, Acts 17:22–31), at Miletus (Paul's farewell, Acts 20:17–35), and at Jerusalem and Caesarea (Paul's apologetic orations, Acts 22–26). Such speeches are neither unique to the character of Paul (compare, e.g., Paul's first speech, Acts 13:16–41, with Jesus' speech in Lk 4:16–30, Peter's speech in Acts 2, and Stephen's speech in Acts 7) nor distinctly Pauline. Instead, as was typical of Hellenistic historiography, these speeches provide commentary on the history narrated. Paul, as a mouthpiece for the author's interpretation of his narrative, has lost his historical individuality.

[108] That the author of Acts has very little interest in local Christian communities as such has already been noted. (The lack of a developed ecclesiology in Acts has been observed often.) The author's correlation of Paul with communities serves the larger purpose of connecting Paul to in the spread of the proclamation of the kingdom of God from Jerusalem to Rome. This spread is narrated as a series of political and religious confrontations between the Jews and Jesus' witnesses (Acts 1:8; cf. Lk 21:12–13), among whom Paul is specially chosen (Acts 9:15; 16:6–10; 18:9–10; 22:15; 23:11; 26:16, 22).

[109] There is a complete lack of polemic against any specific heresy in Acts, whether associated with Paul or anyone else. The author's characterizations of Paul's preaching and teaching contain no specific content intended to refute any particular Christian heresy. See especially Acts 20:30 as part of Paul's farewell address; cf. the summary statement in Acts 28:31. See chapter 3 under *Paul's farewell and the coming of the kingdom*.

[110] For Paul's actual place in the Christian communities at Ephesus around the time of the writing of Acts, see, e.g., the comments of Bauer (*Orthodoxy and Heresy in Earliest Christianity*, pp. 82–83). Bauer suggests the eclipse of Paul at Ephesus. If Romans 16 is a letter to Ephesus, Rom 16:17–20 suggests divisions in the community at Ephesus already in the time of Paul. (See also 1 Cor 16:9; Rev 2:1–7.)

Paul's Farewell

The Pauline mission in Acts 16–20 reaches its climax in the farewell discourse of Paul in Acts 20:17–35 directed toward the Ephesian elders. With this address to the Ephesian elders, Paul summarizes his mission in Ephesus and by implication in the other cities in which he has founded Christian communities.[111] This farewell speech, foreshadowing Paul's death,[112] connects the unified Christian movement to the character of Paul as he returns to Jerusalem to begin the final act in his mission to the Gentiles that will take him to Rome.

There is, however, little connection between the audience of Paul's farewell speech[113] and the incidents the author reports from his sources concerning the Christian mission to Ephesus in chapters 18 and 19—or, for that matter, concerning the Christian mission to Philippi, Thessalonica, or Corinth. Only the notice in Acts 14:23 that Paul and Barnabas appointed elders[114] as part of the early mission from Antioch prepares the reader for the summoning of the elders of Ephesus in Acts 20:17. Nothing in what can be inferred about the author's sources for Acts 18:18–20:1 suggests that Paul appointed elders for a Christian community at Ephesus. The actual relationship between these Ephesian elders and the various individuals and groups portrayed in the account of the Christian mission at Ephesus in Acts 18 and 19[115] is left unspecified. These elders are an authorial construct to provide an appropriate audience for Paul's farewell speech—a literary device superimposing a 'Pauline' order on the information the author has about Ephesus.[116]

---

[111] For example, in his farewell speech, Paul claims to have labored with his hands at Ephesus to supply his needs (20:34–35), but the author only reports Paul having labored at Corinth. Paul refers to the plots of the Jews (20:19, cf. 19:9) at Ephesus, but in the narrative of Paul's mission these plots are more fully developed at Corinth (18:12–17) and Thessalonica-Beroea (17:1–15). Paul's farewell address summarizes the Pauline mission of chapters 16–20.

[112] The genre of farewell speech often implies the death of the character. See Katter, 'Luke 22:14–38: A Farewell Address,' p. 125. See also Acts 20:38; cf. 20:22–24, 29–32; 21:7–14. See discussion below under *Rome* on the idea of suffering associated with the tradition of Paul's call (Acts 9:16).

[113] Acts 20:17, πέμψας εἰς Ἔφεσον μετεκαλέσατο τοὺς πρεσβυτέρους τῆς ἐκκλησίας.

[114] On χειροτονήσαντες, see BDAG, s.v. χειροτονέω.

[115] Apollos; Priscilla and Aquila; Paul; the group of ἀδελφοί associated with Apollos, Priscilla and Aquila (18:27); the μαθηταί of John the Baptist (19:1–7); and the μαθηταί associated with Paul (19:9, 30; 20:1). See above under *Ephesus* on these groups.

[116] This Pauline order imposed on the community at Ephesus is expressed clearly in 20:17–21.

In Paul's farewell to these elders, he emphasizes his teaching role in the Christian community (20:20, 31). The only notice of Paul actually exhorting believers at Ephesus comes in the brief note in 20:1, marking the end of his stay in Ephesus.[117] Just like the elders of the church in 20:17, so the disciples forming the church mentioned in 20:1 (over which these elders watch) are a redactional construct, uniting the Christian community at Ephesus (as elsewhere) to Paul prior to his departure.[118] The note in 20:1 is of particular importance because the author follows it with a general summary of Paul's final passage through Macedonia and Achaea, where Paul exhorts the communities he has previously founded in these areas.[119] Without actually having related any specific episodes, the author has created the impression of Paul's teaching relationship to these communities in anticipation of the farewell discourse.[120]

The only episode of Paul actually teaching believers, apart from the author's transitional statements like 20:1, is found immediately preceding the farewell discourse, at Troas (20:7–12). Of the founding of the ('Pauline'?) Christian community at Troas, the author tells nothing.[121] Instead, the author tacitly assumes that any community in the area of the Pauline mission was established by Paul, and thus the ritual meal and teaching by Paul at Troas are entirely appropriate as a paradig-

---

[117] Cf. 16:40. Paul's activities at the school of Tyrannus are directed toward proclaiming the word of God to all the inhabitants of Asia (19:9–10), not exhorting the community of disciples that have joined him from the synagogue.

[118] On the unclear relation of these Pauline μαθηταί in 20:1 to the μαθηταί at Ephesus in 19:1 and the ἀδελφοί in 18:27, see above under *Ephesus*.

[119] Compare παρακαλέσας αὐτοὺς λόγῳ πολλῷ in 20:2 (cf. 20:1) with οὐκ ἐπαυσάμην μετὰ δακρύων νουθετῶν ἕνα ἕκαστον in 20:31 (cf. 20:20).

[120] Paul can summon such communities (20:1, μεταπεμψάμενος) just as he sends for the leaders of these communities (20:17, μετεκαλέσατο). Such groups are idealized constructs serving the author's narrative intentions.

[121] See 16:8–11. The author hurries Paul on to Macedonia, suggesting a lack of information about the Christian community in this area. Cf. Conzelmann, *Acts of the Apostles*, p. 126. Although the author does not relate any information about the founding of the Christian community at Troas, Paul receives his vision to go to Macedonia while staying at Troas (during which time, by implication, he established a Christian community). Apart from the fact of Paul's visit to Troas, the account in Acts has little connection to the information in 2 Cor 2:12–13, evidence for Paul's historical mission to Troas. There is no reason to presuppose a literary dependence of Acts 16:8–11 on 2 Cor 2:12–13. Note also that the summary in Acts 20:1–3 of Paul's travels before returning to Jerusalem has not been influenced by 2 Cor 1:15–2:4. The author does not seem to have made any attempt to cull travel information from 2 Corinthians as the basis for his narrative in Acts.

matic presentation of Paul's relationship to the Christian communities in the cities of his mission, otherwise indicated by brief transitional comments. The ritual meal cements the relationship between Paul and the communities he has founded. Whether or not the story concerning the raising of Eutychus (over which the author has superimposed the ritual meal with Paul) was connected with Paul at Troas in the author's source for this story cannot be determined.[122] The lack of information about the founding of a community at Troas would suggest that the role of Paul in this story is the author's construct—the ritual meal with Paul having been composed to create a parallel with Jesus' final meal with the disciples recounted in Luke 22:7–38. That only here, at the end of Paul's mission just before his confrontation with the Jews at Jerusalem, does the author portray Paul's relationship to a community in terms of a meal and teaching suggests this schematic parallel with the last days of Jesus. The ritual meal, however, is not the setting for Paul's farewell discourse because the community of disciples as heirs of the kingdom (the proper setting for the ritual meal) is no longer identical to the leadership of the community (whom Paul charges in his farewell speech with the task of safeguarding Jesus' followers).[123]

In short, the social context of elders, disciples, and local communities the author portrays as the basis for Paul's farewell discourse is a compositional construct,[124] unifying Christianity around the missionary per-

---

[122] The author has narrated the story in the first person plural of his 'we' narrator. On this narrator, see below under *Philippi*. In a manner similar to events at Philippi (16:11–40) and on Paul's voyage to Rome (27:1–28:16), the author appears to have elaborated a sparse record of Paul's travels with suitable stories for narrative effect. On the origin of the story, see Dibelius, *Studies in the Acts of the Apostles*, pp. 17–18. Lüdemann's conclusions (*Early Christianity according to the Traditions in Acts*, pp. 222–24), largely following Dibelius, are plausible. An anecdote has been transferred to Paul by the author. This transference of non-Pauline traditions and anecdotes to Paul is consistent with the author's method of composition of the Pauline mission throughout the narrative of Acts. See *Acts of Paul* 11.1 for a similar story. Pervo ('A Hard Act to Follow: The *Acts of Paul* and the Canonical Acts,' pp. 10–12) argues that the story concerning Patroclus in the *Acts of Paul* is dependent on the story of Eutychus in Acts; his argument for such dependence, however, assumes a relative position between the narrative of Acts and the *Acts of Paul* that gives a prominence to the narrative of Acts in the second century that cannot be demonstrated. See chapter 2 under *Acts and the Apocryphal Acts in the Second Century*.

[123] Compare Lk 22:29 with Acts 14:22 and 20:32; Lk 22:30–32 with Acts 20:28–31. See also chapter 3 under *Paul's Farewell Speech and the Literary Paulinism of Lk-Acts*.

[124] The list of Paul's traveling companions in 20:4–6, who link Paul to certain areas of his mission, is similar to other notes about companions of Paul. These companions are part of the fragmentary information about Paul the author has, on which the author

sona of Paul.¹²⁵ This unity extends beyond Ephesus to include the entirety of Paul's mission in Asia Minor, Macedonia, and Achaea (20:1–3).

Corinth

In the narrative of Acts, early Christianity at Corinth (18:1–17) shares a number of connections with Ephesus. Priscilla and Aquila (who later accompany Paul to Ephesus) are said to be at Corinth when Paul arrives (18:1–3), and Apollos is later sent to Corinth from Ephesus by the believers at Ephesus (18:27). The actual details of the Pauline mission at Corinth, though, are much fewer than those at Ephesus. There are roughly two narrative units, both including a note about an ἀρχισυνάγωγος, though the individuals so identified are different.¹²⁶ The vision in 18:9–11 is transitional, ending one episode and anticipating the second episode.

Acts 18:1–8 schematically summarizes the Pauline mission at Corinth, giving the typical information about his turn from the Jews in the synagogue to the Gentiles,¹²⁷ notices of the first converts,¹²⁸ places of residence,¹²⁹ and length of stay.¹³⁰ Of note, however, is the lack of clear logical connection between the details in 18:2–3 and the rest of the section.¹³¹ The separate notices of Paul's place of lodging are, for

---

hangs his portrayal of Paul and Pauline communities. See below, e.g., on Acts 18:5–8. On Paul's collection for Jerusalem, see below under *Rome*.

¹²⁵ Typical of Hellenistic historiography, in which speeches are literary constructs intended to interpret the narrative and display the rhetorical skills of the author, Paul's farewell speech in Acts imposes an interpretive unity on the mission of Paul. See note 107 above on Paul as an orator.

¹²⁶ An ἀρχισυνάγωγος is in Lk-Acts an important official in the synagogue, who presides over the meeting (Lk 13:14; Acts 13:15; cf. 13:42). There may be more than one present at a time (Acts 13:15). Although the word is usually translated as 'leader of the synagogue' (see BDAG, s.v.), Rajak and Noy ('ARCHISYNAGOGOI: Office, Title and Social Status in the Graeco-Jewish Synagogue,' pp. 75–93) have argued that this meaning reflects a literary (Christian) representation of the function of ἀρχισυνάγωγοι, a portrayal that misrepresents their actual social position vis-à-vis a Jewish synagogue. Such individuals were actually, according to Rajak and Noy, important patrons honored with this title. If such were the case, Lk-Acts represents the social structure of the synagogue as a (Gentile) Christian outsider, not someone familiar with the actual workings of a synagogue. See especially their comments on pp. 78–79.

¹²⁷ See Acts 13:46 and 28:25–28.
¹²⁸ See Philippi (16:14–15) and Athens (17:34).
¹²⁹ See Philippi (16:15, 40).
¹³⁰ See Ephesus (19:10) and Rome (28:30).
¹³¹ The often supplied historical harmonization that Silas and Timothy brought a

example, unrelated to one another.¹³² After the announcement of Paul's arrival in Corinth in 18:1, before what marks the typical beginning of Paul's mission in a city in verse 4, the author has inserted a brief note in verses 2–3 concerning Paul's residence with Priscilla and Aquila on the basis of a common trade.¹³³ Priscilla and Aquila play no role in Paul's mission, however. No further notice is taken of them once Paul begins his preaching in verses 4 and 5, in which verses the arrival of Silas and Timothy is narrated.¹³⁴ Paul takes up residence with Titius Justus after the characteristic break with the Jews in the synagogue. Only the note in 18:18 that Priscilla and Aquila accompanied Paul from Corinth to Ephesus suggests they were involved somehow in the Pauline mission; the nature of this involvement is left unclear in the narrative.

The information conveyed by Acts 18:2–3, which interrupts the expected connection between 18:1 and 18:4, does not fit well with the author's intention to portray a Pauline origin for Christianity at Corinth. The author identifies Aquila as a Jew (18:2) and a σκηνοποιός (18:3),¹³⁵ but avoids any suggestion that he and his wife are Christians. There

---

collection to support Paul, so that he moved from the house of Priscilla and Aquila to the house of Justus, depends on information not supplied by the narrative. Such a harmonization does not explain the narrative in Acts.

¹³² Haenchen, *The Acts of the Apostles*, pp. 537–41, is too confident in the narrative coherence of this section in his reconstruction of the author's handling of his source material and his account of Paul's mission at Corinth that underlies this narrative.

¹³³ On the tortured syntax of verses 2–3, see Lüdemann, *Early Christianity according to the Traditions in Acts*, p. 198.

¹³⁴ Paul had left Silas and Timothy in Beroea according to Acts 17:14–15. The translation of συνείχετο in v. 5 to imply that the arrival of Timothy and Silas marks a transition in Paul's mission (cf. BDAG, s.v. συνέχω) is an unwarranted harmonization of vv. 2–3 with vv. 4–8. There is no suggestion in the narrative of Acts that Timothy and Silas brought a gift that allowed Paul to cease his manual labor with Priscilla and Aquila and devote himself 'full time' to the preaching of the word. Instead, the imperfects διελέγετο, ἔπειθεν, and συνείχετο of vv. 4–5 are intended to convey that Paul did not wait for Silas and Timothy to begin his mission at Corinth, but was already occupied with preaching the word when they arrived. Verse 4 resumes v. 1 with no notice of the circumstances of vv. 2–3. See the pattern of Paul's arrival at Thessalonica (17:1–2) and Beroea (17:10). Note also Acts 19:1–8. Between Paul's second arrival in Ephesus (19:1) and the beginning of his mission (19:8), the author has inserted the story of Paul's encounter with disciples of John the Baptist. Just as no further notice of this encounter is taken once Paul's mission in the synagogue at Ephesus begins, so at Corinth no further notice is taken of Paul's association with Priscilla and Aquila once his mission at Corinth begins. In both cases, the author has minimized diversity among early followers of Jesus in the city prior to the beginning of Paul's mission in the synagogue.

¹³⁵ See BDAG, s.v., for the difficulty in determining the precise meaning of this word.

can be no Christian mission at Corinth prior to Paul's arrival.[136] Since, however, no account of their conversion to Christianity is given, the impression that Priscilla and Aquila are not associated with a Jesus movement in Acts 18:2–3 makes little sense in light of 18:18–28. The awkwardness of the author's portrayal of Priscilla and Aquila as Jews at Corinth (18:2–3) and (Pauline) Christians at Ephesus (18:18–28), who now teach more accurately the way of God,[137] suggests the author has pressed information in his sources into his narrative schema of the Pauline mission.[138] As in the case of the episode involving Apollos, Priscilla, and Aquila at Ephesus (18:24–28), the author's lack of any categories for diversity *within* early Christianity has created problems for

---

[136] Haenchen, *The Acts of the Apostles*, p. 533, n. 4, suggests that they had not begun a mission in Corinth before Paul arrived. See note 55 above. This attempt at historical harmonization is unwarranted given the paucity of reliable information that the author has concerning their activities in Corinth. The fact that in the narrative of Acts Priscilla and Aquila accompany Paul to Ephesus and later send Apollos to Corinth from Ephesus only makes the author's narrative of the origin of Christianity at Corinth more difficult to sort out. In the narrative of Acts, 18:24–28 connects Priscilla and Aquila to the Christian community in Ephesus but no such connection exists to the community at Corinth, where they are only linked to Paul in terms of a common trade.

[137] Apollos is described in a similar fashion as Priscilla and Aquila. Both are characterized as Jews (18:2, 24) apparently receptive to the message of Jesus. Upon being instructed in the way of God more accurately (explicitly in the case of Apollos; implicitly in the case of Priscilla and Aquila), they become powerful teachers of the word of God. Priscilla and Aquila accompany Paul to Ephesus where they teach Apollos; Apollos is sent back to Corinth to encourage the disciples there.

[138] The information in 18:2–3 may actually belong to Ephesus. The evidence of Paul's letters locates Priscilla and Aquila in Ephesus, where Paul apparently received support from them (Rom 16:3–5; 1 Cor 16:19). Paul claims to have founded the community at Corinth, but makes no mention of the role of Priscilla and Aquila at Corinth. According to Paul, the household of Stephanas was the ἀπαρχὴ τῆς Ἀχαΐας (1 Cor 16:15), and there is no indication in his letters that he claims to have 'converted' Priscilla and Aquila.

The author of Acts actually suggests that Paul labored at Ephesus (Acts 20:34). This establishes a literary link between 18:2–3 (the only example of Paul actually laboring in connection with his mission) and Ephesus and may indicate that the information in 18:2–3 came to the author associated with Ephesus. Since the notice in 18:18–23 of the journey of Priscilla and Aquila from Corinth to Ephesus is the author's composition (see above under *Ephesus*), it cannot be taken as evidence that the author has information about such a journey. Instead, the journey from Corinth to Ephesus (required in the narrative to get Priscilla and Aquila from Corinth to Ephesus) allows them to be characterized as Paulinists without any actual details of their participation in a Pauline mission ever being recounted. For the author's willingness to rearrange information in his sources, see the transposition of Jesus' activities at Nazareth as reported in Mk 6:1–6 to the beginning of his ministry in Galilee in Luke 4:16–30 (note the difficulty thus created by Lk 4:23).

his historical account of the relationship between Paul and Priscilla and Aquila at Corinth.[139] What is confusing in details, however, is clear in narrative intention: Paul is the founder of Christianity at both Corinth and Ephesus—not Priscilla and Aquila or a mission associated with their patronage.

One detail in 18:1–8 is confirmed by Paul's own account of his mission to Corinth.[140] The notice of the conversion and baptism of Crispus (Acts 18:8) is corroborated by the mention of Crispus as one of those whom Paul baptized at Corinth (1 Cor 1:14). This connection, however, between Paul's actual mission in Corinth and the mission as portrayed in Acts exists purely at the level of the name. The name is merely a peg on which the author hangs his own portrayal of the Pauline mission.[141] The narrative of Acts identifies Crispus as the synagogue leader, which connects Paul's mission in the city to the synagogue according to the author's understanding of the origin of (Pauline) Christian communities in the various cities of the East.[142] Furthermore, Crispus is not singled out as one of the *few* Paul baptized at Corinth (1 Cor 1:14), but becomes representative of *all* those among the Corinthians who believed in Paul's message and were baptized (presumably by Paul, Acts 18:8). This assimilation of Crispus to the author's schema of the Pauline mission suggests no dependence on information from 1 Corinthians. The name has, apparently, come to the author apart from any context in a distinctly Pauline story recalling the historical Pauline mission. The Christian community that emerges from the synagogue in 18:4–8 is a compositional construct of the author of Lk-Acts.[143] This construct is not likely the Pauline community of Paul's historical mission.[144] Thus,

---

[139] The author portrays only a straightforward, linear development from synagogue Jews to early Christian communities in the various cities of Paul's mission. For the author, there is only one 'Christian' community in each city of Paul's mission, and Paul is its founder.

[140] For the note about Paul's association with Justus, compare 17:6 and 19:9. See below under *Thessalonica and Beroea*.

[141] The name could have come from what was little more than an entry in a diary or a note on an itinerary ('Paul came to the city, stayed with..., converted and baptized..., and left after...').

[142] On Paul's association with the leaders of synagogues, see Acts 13:15, in which Paul is connected with the leaders of the synagogue at Pisidian Antioch to establish the occasion for his speech in 13:16–41 (a speech that leads to his break with the Jews of the city [13:44–52]). On Paul's association with the synagogue, see notes 49 and 73 above.

[143] See 18:18.

[144] Nevertheless, that there was a Christian mission associated with synagogues in the cities of the East is not at all implausible. Gal 2:1–10 suggests such a mission to the

the identification of Crispus in Acts 18:8, a piece of information that connects to Paul's historical mission as reported in 1 Corinthians, does not in fact presuppose a 'Pauline' community known to the author as the basis for the narrative in Acts 18:1–8.

Any lack of coherence in the details of Acts 18:1–8 is diminished by the divine stamp placed on Paul's mission to Corinth in 18:9–11. The vision in 18:9–11 is typical of the author's compositional style. In Acts, visions accompany important turning points in the spread of the gospel.[145] The vision in 18:9–11 impresses Paul's image as the missionary to the Gentiles upon the Christian community at Corinth in 18:1–8 and, with its promise of protection, anticipates the following incident before Gallio. This incident involving Gallio, in comparison with the somewhat disjointed details in 18:1–8, is the only extended dramatic episode associated with Paul's mission at Corinth.

The Gallio episode (18:12–17) has had an importance in determining the chronology of the historical Pauline mission far beyond what the passage warrants.[146] The role Paul plays in the story as it stands in Acts has been shaped by the author's schema of the Pauline mission and confrontation with unbelieving Jews,[147] anticipating the judicial conflict to ensue at Jerusalem. This redactional shaping of Paul's role in the episode is generally assumed to be grounded in a tradition linking Paul and Gallio and a conflict in Corinth.[148] Acts 18:17 undermines this assumption. (1) The identification of the πάντες in verse 17 is problematic; (2) the mention of Sosthenes as the leader of the synagogue and

---

Jews and does not imply any geographical division that would have restricted in what cities such a mission could be carried out. In fact, the factionalism at Corinth associated with Paul, Cephas, and Apollos may have had some of its roots in the tensions created by a mission to the Jews alongside Paul's own mission to the Gentiles in the city. As the agreement in Gal 2:1–10 did not forestall the problems at Antioch suggested by Gal 2:11–14, so too Paul ran into problems at Corinth. On Paul's relation to Jews at Corinth, see especially 1 Cor 9:19–23 and 10:32–33.

[145] For Paul, see Acts 9:1–19; 16:9–10; 22:6–11, 17–21; 26:12–19; 27:21–26. Cf. Peter's vision in Acts 10:1–33 and 11:1–18, authorizing him to go to the Gentiles. The transitional character of the vision in 18:9–11, unifying the Pauline community at Corinth in 18:1–11 and promising divine protection for Paul in the upcoming trial before Gallio, indicates that the vision is a compositional construction.

[146] See, e.g., the exchange between Murphy-O'Connor ('Paul and Gallio,' pp. 315–17) and Slingerland ('Acts 18:1–18, the Gallio Inscription, and Absolute Pauline Chronology,' pp. 439–49) for the terms of the debate.

[147] 18:12b–15 is redactional. Cf. 19:25–27, the words of Demetrius inciting the incident involving the temple of Artemis at Ephesus.

[148] See, e.g., Lüdemann, *Early Christianity according to the Traditions in Acts*, p. 199.

recipient of a beating is unmotivated.[149] As the episode stands, πάντες in verse 17 refers to the αὐτούς of verse 16, who are the Jews addressed by Gallio in verses 14–15. This identification of πάντες suggests that the Jews, having been thwarted by Gallio, turned against a follower of Paul and beat him to vent their wrath against Paul.[150] Paul himself is mysteriously unavailable for the beating.[151] This somewhat unsatisfactory and unmotivated substitution of Sosthenes for Paul has led some to identify the πάντες of verse 17 not with the αὐτούς of verse 16 but with an otherwise unidentified pagan crowd. These pagans turn against the Jewish delegation, led by Sosthenes,[152] and mete out a just punishment upon the Jews for their wrongful accusations against Paul.[153] There are, however, no crowds in this narrative, and the conflict involves Jews and Paul, not pagans and Jews, at least as the narrative stands in Acts. Sosthenes is not identified as the leader of the anti-Pauline Jewish delegation, and why anti-Jewish pagan crowds would turn against him and not Paul is unclear.

The lack of intelligible connection between verse 17 and verses 12–16 has probably been created by the insertion of Paul into a conflict that

---

[149] The narrative difficulty between verses 16 and 17 recalls the similar problem in the Artemis episode, Acts 19:33.

[150] Presumably the Jews would be beating a Christian, though no other hint of Sosthenes' identity as a Christian is given in the narrative other than a possible connection to the conversion of Crispus, another leader of the synagogue, in 18:8. (Or, have the Jews turned against one of their own, perhaps the leader of the Jews who failed in his lawsuit against Paul?) If the narrative of Acts intends Sosthenes to be a Christian, this may be the Sosthenes of 1 Cor 1:1. See, e.g., Betz and Mitchell, 'Corinthians, First Epistle to the,' *ABD* 1.1140. However, there is no indication in the narrative of Acts that Sosthenes is a traveling companion of Paul, nor for that matter even a (Pauline) Christian in the author's sources since there is reason to believe Paul's role in the episode is redactional. See Haenchen, *The Acts of the Apostles*, p. 536, n. 5. The difficulty with this episode is that the author has no categories for expressing diversity in early Christianity. His solution of superimposing Paul over diverse stories (cf. Lk 1:4) leaves noticeable seams in his narrative.

[151] Cf. Paul's absence in the Artemis episode at Ephesus, discussed above under *Ephesus*. Lüdemann (*Early Christianity according to the Traditions in Acts*, p. 199) suggests a contradiction between the dismissal from the judgment seat in v. 16 and the beating before the judgment seat in v. 17.

[152] The historical harmonization that Sosthenes has replaced Crispus (because Crispus became a Christian) is not intended by the narrative of Acts; for the author of Acts, a synagogue can have more than one ἀρχισυνάγωγος (see Acts 13:15).

[153] See, e.g., Haenchen, *The Acts of the Apostles*, pp. 536–37. On this interpretation of the narrative of Acts, Sosthenes is not a Christian, and thus should not be identified with the Sosthenes of 1 Cor 1:1. See note 150 above.

had nothing to do with him in the author's sources.¹⁵⁴ If the controversy was originally one between Jews (or Jewish Christians?)¹⁵⁵ and pagans, perhaps of the sort that led to the expulsion of Jews like Priscilla and Aquila from Rome, the refusal of the governor to intervene on behalf of the Jews and the attack on a Jewish synagogue and its leader (Sosthenes?) become plausible.¹⁵⁶ That this episode had anything to do with Paul rests entirely on the assumption that the author is motivated by a specifically Pauline tradition to connect this event with Paul in the narrative of Acts. This assumption is unnecessary and unwarranted in light of the material examined above concerning Ephesus. If Paul were actually part of the tradition behind Acts 18:12–17, the disjunction between 18:12–16 and 18:17 would not be so severe.¹⁵⁷ As with the

---

[154] See above under *Ephesus* on the author's composition of the Artemis controversy. Haenchen's summary comments (*The Acts of the Apostles*, p. 541) on the Gallio episode are worth noting for their attempt to provide a historical harmonization of the episode in Acts with an actual event in the mission of Paul: "But that Gallio rejected a Jewish complaint and that afterwards the anti-Jewish crowd beat the Jewish speaker without interference from Gallio, may very well have been an event which remained in the memory of the Christian community. On the other hand, it is difficult to conceive on what grounds Gallio rejected the complaint, other than those stated by Luke, namely that the issue belonged to the internal affairs of the contending parties. So although we may not regard the text as an exact reproduction of events, we can view the report as a whole with confidence." Against this reconstruction, there is no anti-Jewish crowd in the narrative, Sosthenes is not identified as the speaker for the Jewish accusers, and it is difficult to understand why a dispute among Jews led to the beating of one party (but not the other) by an anti-Jewish crowd, which would presumably have been as hostile to Paul as to Sosthenes. (Cf. Acts 16:19–24; 17:5–9.) The problem is that Haenchen, along with most commentators, creates a harmonized narrative that relates only loosely to the details of the text, a harmonized narrative determined to maintain Paul as an integral character in the historical tradition behind the story. The difficulties in the narrative become explicable once it is recognized that the connection between Paul and the information about a conflict (between Jews and pagans) before Gallio exists at a redactional level.

[155] The author's own categories for describing diversity in the early history of Christian communities obscure the context that may have been suggested by his source.

[156] See the controversies involving Jews and non-Jews reported by Josephus in Egypt (*Jewish War* 2.487) and Syria (e.g., *Jewish War* 2.266–70.). Another possibility, however, is that Sosthenes is a Jewish-Christian and this story stems from a controversy between the synagogue and a Jewish-Christian community. For such a community in the sources used by the author of Acts, see Acts 18:24–28. A controversy between an old cult and a new cult was a typical theme of foundation legends. If 18:12–17 preserves remnants of such a foundation legend, then the missionary persona of Paul in Acts has perhaps been overlaid on a story associated with the origin of a Jewish-Christian community at Corinth.

[157] Cf. Acts 19:33, which exhibits the same disjunction between Paul and the underlying story. On Acts 19:33, see above under *Ephesus*.

Artemis conflict at Ephesus, there is in the Gallio episode at Corinth no residual information about Paul once the author's redactional portrayal has been subtracted.

The results of this analysis of the episodes at Corinth are thus consistent with the portrayal of Paul's mission at Ephesus. The Pauline community at Corinth in Acts is a reflection of the literary Paulinism of the narrative of Acts, not of an underlying social context definable as a Pauline community preserving Pauline traditions available to the author. The author has reworked a controversy involving Jews and Gallio into an episode that gives substance to the portrayal of Paul's mission to Corinth. This episode portrays Paul defending himself before Roman officials against Jewish hostility, anticipating the drama at Jerusalem that will send Paul to Rome.

The account of Paul's mission at Corinth—particularly to the extent that the identification of Crispus and perhaps Sosthenes suggests information available to the author about an actual Pauline community at Corinth—raises the problem of speaking of 'Pauline traditions' in terms of the information about Paul in Acts to a much greater extent than did the narrative about Paul at Ephesus. The account of Paul's stay in Corinth is mined by Lüdemann, for example, to yield the following scraps of 'traditional' information about Paul out of which the narrative is composed:[158] Paul's journey to Corinth, Paul's manual work with Aquila and Priscilla, the arrival of Silas and Timothy from Macedonia, Paul's teaching in the house of Titius Justus, the conversion of Crispus, the note of 'eighteen months,' the note about a trial before Gallio, the name of Sosthenes. Lüdemann, however, does not address the problem of the transmission of such traditions.[159] The word 'tradition' implies a social context in the handing down of information. As such, 'traditions' about Paul imply (Pauline) communities as the social presupposition for the handing down of such stories.[160] Any information derived from either a written source that the author recovered after years of neglect or from personal reminiscences uncovered by the author

---

[158] *Early Christianity according to the Traditions in Acts*, pp. 198–204; his analysis is typical of his method employed elsewhere, and though his specific conclusions distinguishing tradition and redaction are his own, his assumptions in the use of the word 'tradition' are broadly shared by interpreters of Acts.

[159] Cf. Haenchen's solution (*The Acts of the Apostles*, p. 86): "[The author] could himself look up the most important Pauline communities." (See note 5 above.) This claim depends on the improbable assumption that the author knows Pauline communities.

[160] See Lüdemann, *Early Christianity according to the Traditions in Acts*, p. 8.

would not accurately be described as 'traditional information' about Paul preserved over the years by a Pauline community.[161] Such information would not presuppose any community underlying its preservation. Using the label 'Pauline traditions' to describe information about Paul in Acts begs the question of the social correlate of these traditions. Lüdemann's use of the word *tradition* to denote written sources, oral tradition, and general information[162] is so vague as to be almost useless in sorting out the problem of the author's sources about Paul.[163] His tendency to confuse specificity with historical or traditional information— a tendency that produces arbitrary distinctions between redaction, tradition, and history in his analysis—arises from his loose use of the word tradition that obscures the nature of the author's sources about Paul.[164] As a result, Lüdemann never persuasively addresses the problem of the relation between the redactional portrayal of Paul in Acts and the Paul of the traditions that he uncovers. Consequently, he moves much too easily from details in the narrative of Acts to traditional and then historical information about Paul.[165] The handling of material concerning Corinth and Ephesus by the author of Lk-Acts indicates a lack of any coherent Pauline social context determining the transmission of information the author has about these communities. Scraps of information the author has about the Pauline mission should not be confused with 'Pauline traditions.' What is remarkable about the portrayal of Paul in Acts, evident in the description of Paul's mission at both Corinth and Ephesus, is the information the author has about Paul apart from any coherent Pauline narrative context in the author's sources.[166]

---

[161] Whether the scraps of information about Paul in Acts are better understood as deriving from orally transmitted memories or from written sources cannot be determined in every case, but the 'we' narrator seems to presuppose a written source for some of the information about Paul. See below under *Philippi*.

[162] See, e.g., Lüdemann, *Early Christianity according to the Traditions in Acts*, p. 9.

[163] Such vagueness has allowed interpreters of Acts to assume without demonstration Pauline traditions behind Acts.

[164] Expansively multiplying such traditions does not solve the problem, against Jervell, *The Unknown Paul*, p. 69.

[165] Only the unexamined assumption of 'Pauline traditions' available to the author lends an appearance of plausibility to such an analysis. See his comments, *Early Christianity according to the Traditions in Acts*, p. 9. See also Lüdemann's and Conzelmann's conclusions about the historical basis of the travel narrative in Acts 18:18–23 (see note 33 above).

[166] See also below under *Philippi* on the 'we' narrator of Acts.

Thessalonica and Beroea

The connected narrative of Paul's mission to Thessalonica and Beroea in Acts 17:1–15 develops the motif of Jewish opposition to the Pauline mission,[167] foreshadowing the conflicts at Corinth and at Jerusalem. The narrative of Paul's mission to Thessalonica divides into two sections, 17:1–4 and 17:5–9. The first section consists of the author's typical portrayal of Paul's mission to the synagogue that fits neither Paul's summary of his mission to Thessalonica in 1 Thessalonians[168] nor Paul's report of the Jerusalem agreement in Galatians 2.[169] Instead, 17:1–4 corresponds to the author's pattern for Paul's mission at Corinth (18:4–8) and Ephesus (19:8–10) in relation to the local synagogue. This proclamation of the gospel in the synagogue by Paul serves to introduce what is the only substantive episode at Thessalonica, 17:5–9.

Acts 17:5–9 recounts yet another episode in which Paul is noteworthy for his absence. As with the Gallio episode at Corinth and the Artemis episode at Ephesus, the author claims Paul is the reason for the dispute in 17:5–9, but it is Jason (in this case) who bears the brunt of the conflict. Paul and Silas are only indirectly mentioned; the αὐτούς of verses 5 and 6 connects at a narrative level back to the author's summary of the mission of Paul and Silas in 17:1–4. The accounts of Paul's mission to Thessalonica and Corinth are quite similar: both entail a schematic portrayal of the Pauline mission followed by a judicial controversy whose only connection to Paul is determined by the author's compositional intentions.[170] The opposition of the Jews to the preaching of Paul (17:5—ζηλώσαντες δὲ οἱ Ἰουδαῖοι...) is a narrative theme of Acts and also connects the episode in 17:5–9 back to the mission of Paul and Silas in 17:1–4. οἱ ἀδελφοί in 17:10 suggests a Pauline community based on 17:1–4 and signals the author's intention to identify the group associated with Jason in 17:6 (Ἰάσονα καί τινας ἀδελφούς) as Pauline.

---

[167] See Acts 13:13–14:28 and 16:1–3.

[168] See 1 Thess 1:5, 9. The description of believers as having turned from idols to serve the living God in 1 Thess 1:9 does not fit with a mission to the synagogue.

[169] That the Pauline mission began with preaching to Jews in the synagogue would certainly violate Paul's understanding of the agreement in Galatians 2:1–10. (See especially Acts 17:11!)

[170] Yet, it is a commonplace to supplement the information of the Pauline letters with information from Acts to reconstruct the foundation of Pauline communities. For example, despite the paucity of details in Acts apart from the compositional schema of Paul's mission, the account in Acts of the Pauline mission at Thessalonica is often used to supplement the information in 1 Thessalonians. See, e.g., Haenchen, *The Acts of the Apostles*, pp. 505–14.

Nevertheless, the remaining details of this controversy do not suggest a story shaped by a Pauline community at Thessalonica (or elsewhere). The notice of converts in 17:4 (similarly repeated in 17:12) should not too readily be taken as information available to the author about Paul's mission in Thessalonica.[171] The narrative in 17:1–15 is of the type of narrative found in the apocryphal acts—the preaching of the gospel by an apostle, the conversion of women, often prominent in the community, and the anger of the men of the community against the apostle. Any apostle and any city could be placed into this pattern.[172] The author has superimposed the theme of opposition between Paul (and Pauline Christians) and Jews on a story pattern that presupposes no particular relation to Paul.[173] What information the author had in his sources for Christianity at Thessalonica associated with Jason cannot be determined.

The incidents at Beroea are dependent on the author's portrayal of the situation at Thessalonica and are intended to underscore the unreasonable, perverse opposition of 'the Jews' at Thessalonica to Paul's mission.[174] The note of the Beroeans searching the scriptures recalls Luke 24:27 and 24:44–47 and clarifies the source of Jewish opposition to the Pauline mission as a lack of understanding of the Jewish scriptures. This lack of understanding culminates in Paul's rejection of the unbelieving Jews at Rome.[175] The conversion of prominent women at Beroea (17:12) mirrors the similar conversions at Thessalonica (17:4). Of the actual founding of the Christian community at Beroea, Acts preserves little.[176] Nevertheless, the travel dispositions in 17:14–15, which correspond to those in 18:5 and 19:21–22, serve to reinforce the impression of a unified Pauline mission determining the origin of Christianity at Thessalonica and Beroea.[177]

---

[171] Against, e.g., Lüdemann, *Early Christianity according to the Traditions in Acts*, pp. 187–88.

[172] See, e.g., *Acts of Paul* 3.7–21 (concerning Thecla); *Acts of Peter* 34–41.

[173] Acts 17:5 accomplishes this narrative construct.

[174] 17:13; cf. 17:5.

[175] 28:25–28; cf. 13:16–48.

[176] The information in 20:4 concerning Paul's traveling companions from Beroea and Thessalonica may have motivated the author's expansion of Paul's mission to Thessalonica to include Beroea despite his lack of information associated with Beroea.

[177] Whether or not the author is dependent on information from a source at this point, there is no reason to suppose that this source is the basis for the 'Pauline' episodes in 17:2–13. Concerning the travel notes in Acts 17:14–15, Paul makes no mention of Beroea in his letters, and 1 Thess 3:1–2 implies Timothy accompanied Paul to Athens. In contrast, the author of Lk-Acts narrates Paul's departure, alone, from Beroea to

Philippi

The portrayal of the Pauline mission at Philippi has a large degree of dramatic unity around Paul and is noteworthy for its lack of Paul's typical confrontation with the Jews of the local synagogue. Paul's mission at Philippi begins with the conversion of Lydia at a Jewish place of prayer.[178] Paul then finds lodging with Lydia. On a subsequent visit to the place of prayer,[179] Paul casts out a spirit, an action that causes an uproar and leads to Paul's imprisonment. Upon the resolution of this conflict, Paul exhorts the (Pauline) Christian community at Philippi and takes leave from Lydia's house for another city.

The seams in the narrative, however, suggest the author's redaction.[180] Acts 16:16 is probably a redactional connection of the casting out of the spirit to the location of the previous episode. Although the narrator is initially present in 16:16–17, he or she drops out of the story and does not reappear until 20:4–5. Acts 16:25–40 is a compositional expansion of a brief note about Paul's imprisonment preserved in 16:22–24.[181] This expansion has three distinct elements, unrelated to one another but important in the author's narration of the Pauline mission. (1) Acts 16:25–34 recounts events of which no notice is taken when 16:24 is resumed in 16:35.[182] This miraculous prison conversion establishes a parallel between the prison experiences of Paul and Peter,[183]

Athens. The author has little if any information about Athens, either. The list of Pauline converts in 17:34 is typically compositional; cf. similar notices of a Pauline community in 16:40; 17:6, 14; 18:18; 20:1. Whether the author derived the names from information associated with Athens cannot be determined. The speech of Paul at Athens and its setting are the author's composition. See, e.g., Vielhauer, 'On the "Paulinism" of Acts,' pp. 34–37.

[178] Although the term used could refer to a synagogue, the note that only women were present suggests otherwise. The lack of any reference to Paul's mission to a synagogue according to the schema of Acts perhaps indicates dependence on information about Paul at this point, perhaps associated with the conversion of Lydia.

[179] 16:16; cf. 16:13.

[180] See, e.g., Conzelmann, *Acts of the Apostles*, p. 131.

[181] Whether or not this notice of Paul's imprisonment was connected in the author's sources to the story of the slave girl in 16:16–21 cannot be determined.

[182] See, e.g., Conzelmann, *Acts of the Apostles*, p. 133.

[183] Cf. Acts 12:1–19. There is no need to postulate a legend specifically attached to Paul behind 16:25–34 (any more than there is one behind the account of the shipwreck in chapter 27 or the events of Paul's stay on Malta in chapter 28; see discussion below under *Rome*). The conversion story of the jailer is typical of the author's conversion accounts, culminating in the baptism of the converts and summarized in terms of the message: believe in the Lord. See especially Acts 2:38, 44; also 26:27–29. For a different assessment, see Conzelmann, *Acts of the Apostles*, p. 132, commenting on 16:23–24.

though matters turn out much better for Paul's jailer than for Peter's.[184] (2) Acts 16:35–39 resumes 16:24 with themes important for the portrayal of Paul in Acts, specifically Paul's claim to be a Roman citizen[185] and the respectful response of the authorities to Paul. Attempts to create a historical explanation for Paul's delayed announcement of his citizenship at Philippi[186] are a misreading of a seam in the narrative created by the author's overlay of his portrayal of Paul on the brief note of Paul's imprisonment in 16:22–24. (3) The connection back to Lydia (Paul's first convert at Philippi, 16:11–15) and Paul's departure from the Christian community in Acts 16:40 establish a Pauline community at Philippi, typical of the author's portrayal of a united Pauline community in a city prior to his departure.[187] Little content, however, has been given to this community in the actual narrative of Paul's mission at Philippi.

The Pauline community at Philippi in 16:40 is a compositional construct of the author based on the conversion of Lydia. There is no strong reason to doubt that the conversion of Lydia, who then provides lodging for Paul, and the note about Paul's imprisonment in 16:24 are both connected to Paul in the information available to the author.[188] Rather than a Pauline community behind this Pauline information in Acts 16, however, the author appears to be dependent on a first-person narrative source connected to Philippi.[189] This narrator is first introduced in 16:10 in connection with the mission to Macedonia, participates in Paul's mission through 16:17, but then does not reappear again until 20:5, when Paul is leaving Philippi for Jerusalem, accompanied by converts from his mission to Macedonia, Achaea, and Asia.[190] The

---

[184] Compare Acts 12:19 with 16:27–34.

[185] See 22:25–29. The entire drama of Paul's trial in chapters 22–26 turns on Paul's Roman citizenship. See especially 25:10–11. See below under *Rome*.

[186] Contrast 16:22–24 with 22:22–29.

[187] See comments above on 20:1.

[188] Whether the exorcism story as it is elaborated in 16:16–24 was also connected to Paul in the author's sources is more difficult to determine. The first person narrator disappears after v. 17; furthermore, the author has elsewhere elaborated the first person narrative with stories whose connection to Paul is doubtful. See, e.g., Acts 28:1–10, discussed below under *Rome*.

[189] See especially 16:11–17. Note, however, that after 16:17, this narrator disappears from the author's narrative of events associated with Paul's imprisonment.

[190] The names of the traveling companions of Paul in 20:4, who appear to connect Paul to his historical mission in the various regions mentioned, are probably derived from this source, which is likely a written document that would not presuppose a Pauline social context for the author's knowledge of these names.

narrator returns with Paul to Jerusalem[191] and eventually accompanies Paul to Rome.[192] Only at Philippi and in Paul's final return to Jerusalem is this narrator actually associated with events of the Pauline mission.[193] The lack of specificity concerning Paul's movements prior to his arrival in Macedonia (16:6–8) and the beginning of the 'we' narration coinciding with Paul's journey to and from Philippi suggest that the author has a source associated with Philippi and Paul's final return to Jerusalem (20:4–5).[194] This written source provides the barest of connections to the

---

[191] See Acts 20:5–8; 20:13–16; 21:1–18.

[192] 27:2–28:16.

[193] See 16:16–17. In 20:8 (at Troas), 20:15 and 21:1 (which bracket Paul's farewell to the Ephesian elders), and 21:18 (at Jerusalem), the narrator accompanies Paul on his return to Jerusalem, but beyond notice of his or her presence does not participate in the episodes at Troas, Miletus, and Jerusalem. Likewise, at Philippi, the narrator is present in 16:16–17, but then disappears as events unfold. The narrator appears to have only a tangential connection to the actual events supposedly taking place in his or her presence.

[194] On the intractable problem of the 'we' passages of Acts, see, e.g., Praeder, 'The Problem of First Person Narration in Acts,' pp. 193–218. Although a definitive solution is elusive, the voice of the 'we' narrator is not adequately explained with reference to the author himself, either in terms of his actual participation in the Pauline mission (see discussion in chapter 2 under *Traditions of Authorship and Titles*) or in terms of a literary convention (e.g., in relation to Jewish literature as argued by Wehnert, *Die Wir-Passagen der Apostelgeschichte. Ein lukanisches Stilmittel aus jüdischer Tradition*, e.g., p. 202; or in relation to the travails expected of a Hellenistic historian enduring dangers from the sea as argued by Plümacher, 'Luke. Luke as Historian,' *ABD* IV.398). See Porter, 'The "We" Passages,' pp. 546–61. There does not appear to be a compelling explanation for the sudden appearances and unexplained disappearances of the narrator in terms of the narrator as a literary device. It is, e.g., an overstatement to say, as does Plümacher, that "it is only in conjunction with maritime travel that the 'we' references occur." Note, e.g., Acts 16:16–17; 21:18. That the first person singular of the author in Lk 1:3 and Acts 1:1 is intended to be read as the same voice as the first person plural of the narrator who appears in certain sections in Acts (the position taken by, e.g., Cadbury, '"We" and "I" Passages in Luke-Acts,' pp. 128–32) is unlikely. In the preface to Lk, the author characterizes himself as an investigator into reports from eyewitnesses, not an eyewitness himself. The author thus separates himself from the reliable (eyewitness) conveyers of these traditions. He does not claim to have participated in the events of his narrative. Paul and his companions belong with those who hand on the preaching of the word (Lk 1:2; Acts 1:8) from the past to the present (Acts 20:17–38). The narrator of Acts, an eyewitness of Paul's activities, belongs to this past from which the author has distanced himself.

Instead, the close association of the first-person narrator with Philippi and Paul's final journey to and from Jerusalem suggests that the author has preserved the voice of a source, but has broken up the unity of the source to construct the author's picture of the Pauline mission in Acts 16–20. Such a source provides a plausible explanation for acquisition of the information the author has about Paul in chapters 16–28. The author of Lk-Acts perhaps preserved the voice of this source to increase the credibility of his

mission of the historical Paul in Philippi and his return to Jerusalem, on which the author has hung his own reconstruction of Pauline communities in Asia Minor, Macedonia, and Achaea. Such a written source detailing travel stops and Pauline associates presupposes no Pauline community or social context for its preservation and eventual use by the author of Lk-Acts.[195]

The beginning and ending of Paul's mission in chapters 16–20 form a ring composition that defines the intention of these chapters. The beginning of the distinctly Pauline mission in chapter 16 is marked by the problem of Jewish customs (the circumcision of Timothy, διὰ τοὺς Ἰουδαίους τοὺς ὄντας ἐν τοῖς τόποις ἐκείνοις, 16:1–3). This notice anticipates the legal controversy at Philippi over Jewish customs (16:20–21), a controversy that leads to Paul's identification with Rome as a Roman citizen over against these customs (16:37). Paul's arrival in Jerusalem at the end of his mission to Macedonia, Achaea, and Asia Minor is likewise marked by the problem of Jewish customs (21:20–29), which leads to Paul's identification with Rome as a Roman citizen over against these customs (22:22–29; 25:10–11).[196] The narrative of the Pauline mission in chapters 16–20, beginning with Paul's mission to Philippi, defines the missionary persona of Paul in anticipation of the judicial struggle over Jewish customs between Paul and the Jews at Jerusalem that serves to differentiate Christianity and Judaism for the author and his readers.[197]

---

account (cf. Lk 1:2). If this source was little more than a few brief notes of people and places, there is no reason to suppose it would have left a stylistic impact on the language of Acts beyond the inclusion of the 'we' itself. Contrast the comments of Witherington, *The Acts of the Apostles*, p. 53.

[195] Lucian (*How to Write History* 16) compares certain poorly written histories to travel diaries: "Another of them has compiled a bare record of events and set it down on paper, completely prosaic and ordinary, such as a soldier or artisan or pedlar following the army might have put together as a diary of daily events." (Translation by K. Kilburn, *Lucian* VI [LCL].)

[196] The historicity of Paul's Roman citizenship cannot be resolved given the evidence available. It should be observed, however, that the portrayal of Paul's Roman citizenship in Acts is determined by the author's intention to separate Christianity from Judaism based on Paul's appeal to Caesar. The status ascribed to Paul in Acts as a citizen of Tarsus, a citizen of Rome, and a Pharisee suggests an improbable combination of allegiances in terms of the social realities of the first century. See Lentz, *Luke's Portrait of Paul*, pp. 23–61. On Paul's status suggested by the granting of his appeal by Festus, see also Garnsey, *Social Status and Legal Privilege in the Roman Empire*, p. 76.

[197] See below under *Rome*.

Despite the importance of the character of Paul for defining Christianity for the author, the Pauline mission in Acts 16–20 is remarkably devoid of information and stories connecting Paul to any social context identifiable as Pauline Christianity at the important centers of Christianity in Asia Minor, Macedonia, and Achaea. Paul's relation to the Christian community or communities at Philippi, Thessalonica, Corinth, and Ephesus exists in the narrative largely as a compositional construct imposed by the author on non-Pauline information associated with these cities. If the question of the actual historical existence of Pauline communities at these various centers of early Christianity is left aside as a problem created for interpreting Acts by the shape of the canon, the narrative of Acts suggests the author has little or no knowledge from his sources about Pauline Christianity as a social phenomenon in these cities.[198]

The author, in fact, seems to be aware that his sources do not deliver an obvious Pauline order of events, and that he, as a historian, imposes that order.[199] His categories for development, however, are not entirely adequate for the task of explaining the relationship between his present and the past preserved in his sources. The wide historical gap between what the author portrays as Christianity of his own day and the source materials he was able to scrape together has been bridged by his portrayal of Paul's mission.[200] Working backwards from his conception of Christianity, he conceives of an opposition of Jews versus the proclamation of the gospel (especially by Paul), which for him defines the emergence of the Christianity in the Graeco-Roman world of his own day. Lacking historiographical categories to describe the diversity of early Christian movements in his sources—he uses no

---

[198] Although the Pauline letter collection gives the impression of Pauline communities throughout Asia Minor, Macedonia, and Achaea, the problems that Paul had in Galatia and at Corinth should caution against too quickly assuming that a majority of believers in these centers would have defined themselves as Pauline. Nevertheless, the supposed social phenomenon of 'Pauline Christianity' has been the object of detailed investigation. See, e.g., Meeks, *The First Urban Christians*, pp. 7–8; M. MacDonald, *The Pauline Churches*, pp. 31–84

[199] See Lk 1:3–4.

[200] The author's claim to have narrated the development of Christianity in terms of the standards for truth of Graeco-Roman historiography is intended to establish a place for Christians in Graeco-Roman culture (see chapter 3 under *The Prefaces of Lk-Acts*). As a result, the author's redaction of his sources provides little information about his experience of inner-Christian diversity or conflict of his own day. In this, he contrasts markedly with the Irenaean construction of the history of true Christianity over against heresy. Note, e.g., the vagueness of Acts 20:29–30 on specifically Christian heresies.

category adequate to relate Priscilla, Aquila, Apollos, and the various other individuals mentioned in connection with Ephesus, Corinth, and the other cities of Paul's mission—he superimposes his overarching framework for the development of Christianity on the lack of order he finds in his sources.[201] However, his developmental superstructure of John the Baptist, Jesus, the Twelve Apostles, and Paul has not been carried back into the individual episodes of Paul's mission without leaving certain cracks in place.[202]

These observations on the author's portrayal of Christianity in Asia Minor, Macedonia, and Achaea clarify one aspect of the portrayal of Paul in Acts that has been difficult to interpret. According to Paul's account of the Jerusalem council in Galatians 2, Paul understood himself to be entrusted with a mission to the Gentiles that existed alongside a Jewish mission.[203] The author of Acts, though aware of the story of the call of Paul to go to the Gentiles,[204] knows nothing of a (Pauline) division between Jewish and Gentile missions.[205] As a result, the author has overlaid the missionary persona of Paul on essentially non-Pauline and largely Jewish (-Christian) stories. The missionary pattern in Acts of Jews (synagogue) first then Gentiles reflects the author's Jewish (-Christian) sources overlaid with the idea of the Gentile Pauline mission.[206] This overlay is the author's explanation of how a movement

---

[201] See Lk 1:3-4.

[202] The author's imposition of a 'Pauline order' in the second half of Acts is preceded by the imposition of an apostolic order in the first part of Acts. See, e.g., the smoothing over of the differences in Acts 6:1-7 concerning the relationship of those Jews speaking Greek and those speaking Aramaic, a dispute over which the Twelve preside. Note how the author superimposes the apostles on the early Christian mission from Jerusalem to Antioch (Peter and John at Samaria [Acts 8:14-25]; Peter at Caesarea [Acts 10]). See Haenchen, *The Acts of the Apostles*, p. 341. The Lukan order of John, Jesus, the Twelve, and Paul provides the framework for integrating his sources into an account of the emergence of Christianity (cf. Lk 1:1-4).

[203] Paul's delineation of mission fields in Gal 2:1-10 seems to be corroborated by the apparent composition of his churches and missionary style suggested by his letters. See note 206 below.

[204] Acts 9:15; see also 22:21. See below under *Rome*.

[205] Note, e.g., that Peter is marked in Acts as the apostle to the Gentiles (Acts 10:1-11:18; cf. esp. 15:7). Note also the conflict between those Jews speaking Greek and those speaking Aramaic in Acts 6:1-7, a conflict which the author portrays as a minor disturbance interrupting the mission of the Twelve. This disturbance explains the origin and function of certain officials in the early community, but does not threaten what the author narrates as the fundamental unity of the movement.

[206] Because Paul's actual mission was oriented primarily towards the Gentiles (Gal 2:1-10; Rom 15:22-29; cf. the characterization of his converts in 1 Thess 1:9), his intention to return to Jerusalem with the Gentile collection (Rom 15:25-32) was an

that began as largely Jewish, and in fact remained 'Jewish' even in his sources about communities from Antioch to Rome, became a Gentile movement.[207] The effect of this compositional method is to create a tension between (1) the author's non-Pauline sources for Christianity in Asia Minor, Macedonia, and Achaea and (2) the author's portrayal of the origin of Christianity in terms of the mission of Paul, whose mission culminates in the pronouncement of Acts 28:25–28.[208] The problems in his narrative of Paul's mission created by his attempt to superimpose the missionary persona of Paul on a movement that in his sources lacks any (Pauline) narrative coherence are evident in the details of the narrative. Nevertheless, the canonical juxtaposition of Acts with the Pauline letters has established a self-reinforcing way of reading Paul's role in early Christianity that makes the portrayal of Paul in Acts seem almost self-evidently related to some form of 'Pauline' Christianity known to the author.

The author's portrayal of the Pauline mission serves the author's intention to define Christianity in terms of the judicial confrontation between Paul (as the divinely appointed missionary to both Jews and Gentiles, an appointment that leads to his death as a Christian[209]) and Judaism carried out in chapters 21–28—a confrontation leading to

---

attempt to express a unity between Jewish and Gentile believers (a unity that was not always apparent – see Gal 2:11–14). In Romans (written to a non-Pauline church) Paul explains this unity in terms of salvation history (Rom 15:27; cf. Rom 1:14–16; 2:9–10; 3:1–9; 9–11). Paul certainly had dealings with Jews (1 Cor 9:20; 2 Cor 11:24) and dealt with the problems of Jew-Gentile relations in his letters (1 Cor 1:22–24; 10:32; 12:13), but it is unlikely that he reenacted what for him is a pattern of salvation history as a mission strategy (particularly in relation to synagogues) in each city he entered. There is little evidence (beyond the narrative of Acts!) that Paul's churches had their origins in the local synagogue.

For the missionary pattern of Jew first, then Gentile as a history of missions, see Mt 10:5–42; 28:19–20.

[207] Jervell (*The Unknown Paul*, e.g. pp. 13–25; cf. *The Theology of the Acts of the Apostles*, pp. 11, 123–27) has attempted to pay attention to the Jewish perspective of much of Acts, though his conclusions that Paul belongs to this Jewish-Christian social context confuse the author's intentions with information from his sources (cf. Jervell, *The Unknown Paul*, pp. 26–51).

[208] See chapter 3 under *Paul's Farewell Speech and the Literary Paulinism of Lk-Acts*.

[209] The author of Acts interprets Paul's (foreshadowed) death as suffering for the name of Jesus in connection with his status as an appointed witness for Jesus (Acts 9:15–16; 20:22–24; 21:10–14). Cf. Col 1:24; *Ep. Ap.* 31, on which see below under *Rome*. Note also that Stephen's death in Acts is closely connected to his status as a witness for Jesus (τὸ αἷμα Στεφάνου τοῦ μάρτυρός σου—Acts 22:20). The tradition of Paul's death at Rome was an important factor in the development of his reputation in early Christianity.

Paul's arrest, appeal, and proclamation of the gospel at Rome. Before the Paulinism of this confrontation is examined, however, the account of Paul's mission with Barnabas needs to be considered.

Paul's Mission with Barnabas

Although the mission in Acts 13–14 is not presented as distinctly Pauline, a few comments should be made concerning the author's overlay of Paul on this mission associated with Antioch.[210] Chapters 13 and 14 describe the travels of Paul with Barnabas.[211] Their association ends with Paul's departure from Antioch without Barnabas due to a dispute over John Mark (15:36–41), after which Paul's connection to Antioch is maintained by the author's portrayal of Antioch as a base of operations for Paul's mission in Asia Minor, Macedonia, and Achaea.[212]

The mission from Antioch begins with the setting apart of Barnabas and Paul by the community at Antioch for the work appointed by the holy spirit (13:1–3). The mission consists of four episodes—at Paphos, Pisidian Antioch, Iconium, and Lystra. These episodes are united by a summary in Acts 14:21–28 that brings Paul and Barnabas back to Antioch.

The distinctive activities of Paul on Cyprus (Acts 13:4–12) consist of a brief word in confrontation with a magician in the court of Sergius Paulus, in connection with whom Saul's Roman name Paul is noted (13:9). The key themes of this confrontation—positive portrayal of the Roman authority (13:7), confrontation with a magician,[213] and the presence of Paul before high officials—are all narrative themes of Acts.[214] That the author created Paul's role in this story in analogy to Acts 8 cannot be ruled out.[215] Although a place for Paul in this episode in the

---

[210] Paul's own account of events at Antioch (Gal 2:11–14) gives little reason to suppose that the community of believers in this city was 'Pauline.' There is, therefore, some warrant for doubting any particular 'Paulinism' in the sources the author has associated with Antioch.

[211] For the narrative connection of Paul and Barnabas, see especially 9:27 and 11:25. On Paul's conversion, see below under *Rome*.

[212] See Acts 18:22–23.

[213] Compare Acts 13:10 with 8:23.

[214] Cf. especially 28:7–10 for another similar encounter on an island. See below under *Rome*.

[215] Paul's confrontation with the sorcerer Bar-Jesus parallels Peter's confrontation with Simon; Paul's speech at Pisidian Antioch parallels Peter's speech on Pentecost; Paul's healing of the lame man at Lystra parallels Peter's healing of the lame man

information available to the author cannot be ruled out, neither can it be demonstrated. The shift in the narrative from the use of the name Saul to the name Paul in this episode about Sergius Paulus suggests that the author intends to emphasize the Roman character of Paul's name.[216]

The actions of Paul in the subsequent episode in Pisidian Antioch (Acts 13:13–52) are probably entirely supplied by the author. The speech at the beginning of the mission in this locality parallels Jesus' speech in Lk 4:14–30 and Peter's speech in Acts 2, corresponding very closely in content to the latter. The link with Peter's speech in Acts 2 and Jesus' speech in Lk 4 connects Paul's mission to the life of Jesus and the apostolic office of Peter in the unfolding of salvation history. The account of the decisive turn from Jews to Gentiles associated with the synagogue is a narrative theme of Acts and traces the roots of Paul's final pronouncement at Rome (28:28) to the earliest days of the Christian mission from Antioch (13:46)[217] – and in fact to the earliest days of Jesus' mission.

The material in chapter 14 associated with Iconium and Lystra indicates the non-Pauline character of the information used by the author associated with Antioch. In 14:1–7 Paul and Barnabas are not mentioned. Instead, the episode is connected to 'apostles' (14:4). These apostles are again mentioned in Acts 14:14, where Paul and Barnabas are explicitly identified. This identification, however, is probably secondary.[218] Although Acts 14:4 and 14:14 identify Paul and Barnabas as 'apostles,' the author of Acts does not elsewhere consider Paul (or Barnabas) to be an apostle. In the narrative of Acts, Paul does not meet the criteria for an apostle set out in Acts 1:15–26. Acts 14:4 and 14:14 probably preserve residues from a source used by the author.[219] The stories

---

outside the temple (Acts 3). The portrayal of Paul in Acts 13–14 appears to establish a rather precise parallel between Peter and Paul, anticipating the transition in the narrative from a focus on Peter to a focus on Paul.

[216] The *Epistula Apostolorum* explains the name Paul as a translation of Saul. (On the relation of the *Epistula Apostolorum* to Acts, see below under *Rome*.) The author of Lk-Acts goes further, however, to emphasize the distinctly Roman character of the name. This emphasis conforms to the author's pro-Roman attitude and identification of Paul as a Roman citizen.

[217] Cf. 18:6; also above under *Ephesus*.

[218] οἱ ἀπόστολοι *Βαρναβᾶς καὶ Παῦλος*; the italicized words appear to be redactional. See above under *Ephesus* on Acts 19:13–16.

[219] The failure of the author to redact his sources carefully to make them consistent with his narrative themes has already been observed above in the Gallio and Artemis

associated with Iconium and Lystra used by the author were likely not about Paul and Barnabas, but about apostles (whoever they may have been) and perhaps the hostility that their mission provoked in these cities.[220] The speech of Paul, which contains themes similar to Acts 17:22–31, and the dramatic expansion based on the legend about Zeus and Hermes are probably the author's composition, intended to portray Paul's confrontation with pagan religion.[221] The miracle story as it stands in Acts 14:8–18 has been modeled after the similar healing by Peter in Acts 3, although it may have been associated with certain apostles (whoever they were) in the author's sources. Despite the lack of distinctly Pauline information evident in the author's sources, the author has given Paul prominence over Barnabas, as at Pisidian Antioch.

The final episode of the first half of Acts is the Jerusalem council. The author apparently has knowledge of certain details of the Jerusalem council associated with Paul.[222] Nevertheless, Paul plays little role in the actual council as narrated in Acts 15.[223] Instead Peter and James are given prominence to establish a unity between the Jerusalem church and the Gentile mission. The narrative in Acts portrays the Jerusalem council as a separation of the Way from the Pharisees (Acts 15:5)—that is, one more step on the road from Jerusalem to Rome. Whether or not the so-called apostolic decree was actually associated with the Jerusalem council in the author's sources cannot be determined.[224] In any case, Paul's dissemination of the decree in Acts 15:22–31 and 16:4 is probably redactional.[225] The account of the council in Acts is determined by the compositional intentions of the author to portray the Gentile mission as an evolutionary continuation of the Jewish mission (rather than as a distinct mission field, which is the perspective of Paul in Galatians). This evolutionary connection between the Jewish and Gentile mission is the pattern on which the author bases Paul's own mission in Acts 16–28. Neither the author's account of the

---

episodes, as well as in his portrayal of the relationship of Paul to Priscilla, Aquila, and Apollos.

[220] On this hostility, compare Lk 9:1–5 and 10:1–16.

[221] In these two speeches, Paul confronts pagan religiosity, both popular and philosophical.

[222] Compare Acts 15:1–29 with Galatians 2:1–10.

[223] Acts 15:12 appears to be a compositional link to the previously narrated mission of Paul and Barnabas. Contrast Gal 2:1–10.

[224] Paul's account in Galatians 2:1–10 does not mention it.

[225] Cf. Gal 2:10.

Jerusalem council nor the information out of which he has constructed his account suggests the influence of traditions preserved by a Pauline community.

Rome

The climax of the narrative of Acts is the founding of the Christian community at Rome based on the preaching of Paul and the decisive rejection of unbelieving Jews (28:17–31). Acts 28:15 preserves information from the author's sources about a community at Rome prior to Paul's arrival.[226] The 'we' narrator that the author has used to establish the framework for his account of Paul's return to Jerusalem from Philippi[227] and subsequent journey to Rome[228] disappears with Paul's arrival in Rome (28:14–16), an arrival marked by a friendly greeting by certain ἀδελφοί at Rome and a note about his lodging.[229] What follows in Acts 28:17–31 creates the impression that Paul is the first to proclaim the Christian gospel at Rome. Acts 28:21–22 implies a neutral position for the Jewish community at Rome concerning the Christian αἵρεσις based on second-hand knowledge from elsewhere. This portrayal of the state of affairs at Rome is not consistent with the information from the author's sources,[230] but instead allows Paul to be the first to proclaim

---

[226] Such a non-Pauline origin for Christianity at Rome is corroborated by Paul's letter to Rome.

[227] Acts 20:4–6; cf. 21:17–18; see above under *Philippi*.

[228] Acts 27:2; note that Aristarchus is mentioned in 20:4.

[229] The information preserved in Acts 18:2–3 suggests the presence of followers of Jesus at Rome prior to Paul's arrival. See above under *Corinth*. The time reference in 28:30 may be derived from the author's source. Nevertheless, the use of the 'we' narrator for the framework of the narrative in 20:4–28:16 in no way implies that the particular episodes connected with this journey are derived from this source. Each must be judged on its own merits.

[230] Acts 28:21–22 makes little sense in relation to 28:15. Although a Christian community already exists at Rome (28:15), Paul is the first to bring the message of this 'party' to the Jewish leaders at Rome, who until his arrival only have second-hand knowledge of this party. If the expulsion of Priscilla and Aquila from Rome (18:2–3) is connected to disturbances in the Jewish community at Rome involving Jewish-Christians (though the author himself may not have known this), then the neutral attitude of the Jewish leaders in 28:21–22 to the Christian sect is both historically unlikely and also unlikely to have been part of any story associated with Paul's arrival in Rome available to the author. In Acts 28:17–28 the author has not carefully reconstructed the historical circumstances of Paul's connection to Jewish and Christian communities at Rome (which the author might have deduced from the information he reports in 28:14–15, as well as 18:2–3), but rather has impressed the missionary persona of Paul upon the spread of the gospel to Rome.

the Christian message to the Jews at Rome.[231] For the author, Paul's missionary persona defines the emergence of Christianity at Rome, the endpoint of the spread of the proclamation of the kingdom of God into the Graeco-Roman world.[232]

The preceding narrative of Paul's journey from Caesarea to Rome enhances Paul's image as an agent of God divinely ordained to proclaim the gospel at Rome.[233] Though Paul is a prisoner, his companions accord him remarkable status.[234] The account of the shipwreck, which has its conclusion in 28:4-6, places a divine seal on his innocence.[235] The subsequent miracles on Malta (28:7-10) conclude with the compositional theme of Paul receiving honor not only from the leading local official, but in this case also from all the inhabitants of the island.[236] There is no residual information about Paul below the compositional

---

[231] Cf. the author's portrayal of the Christian mission at Corinth and Ephesus, discussed above.

[232] ἕως ἐσχάτου τῆς γῆς in Acts 1:8 is not a precise geographical designation, but is a reference to lands beyond Israel, that is, a reference to the Gentiles. The spread of the word ἕως ἐσχάτου τῆς γῆς is taken by the author of Lk-Acts to be a fulfillment of Isa 49:6, which is quoted by Paul in Acts 13:47 with reference to the offer of salvation to the Gentiles. See Haenchen, *The Acts of the Apostles*, p. 143, n. 9. When Paul announces at Rome to the unbelieving Jews that the message of salvation has been sent to the Gentiles, the author's understanding of the spread of the message of salvation from Jews to Samaritans to Gentiles in Acts 1:8 has been accomplished. Note that Paul is the only character in Acts physically to visit all the major centers of Christianity in Acts. Paul is portrayed as specially chosen by God to be a witness to Jews and Gentiles. Compare Acts 1:8 with 9:15; 22:15; 23:11; 26:16, 22-23; cf. Lk 21:12-13.

[233] See especially Acts 27:24.

[234] See, e.g., Acts 27:42-44.

[235] See, e.g., the account by Josephus of his shipwreck on his voyage to Rome, which Josephus presents as a sign of God's favor upon him (κατὰ θεοῦ πρόνοιαν, *Life* 15). Josephus (*Life* 13-16) claims to have overcome the dangers of the sea, surviving a shipwreck, on a journey to Rome in service to his people. Shipwrecks, of course, were not uncommon, and the dangers of the sea were well-known, both as actual events and literary motifs. Paul himself claims to have been shipwrecked three times (see 2 Cor 11:25). Shipwrecks played an important role in Hellenistic novels, and Lucian (see, e.g., *How to Write History* 4, 29) comments on the dangers of the sea that the historian in search of information is expected to brave. On Lucian and accounts of sea voyages, see Betz, *Lukian von Samosata und das Neue Testament*, pp. 171-74; see also note 194 above on Plümacher's understanding of the voice of the 'we' narrator. In the case of the account of the shipwreck in Acts, the author suggests a role played by Paul in relation to the centurion and sailors on board that corresponds more to the author's portrayal of Paul's relation to political authorities (see especially Acts 16:35-39; 21:37-40) than anything likely to have actually happened or to have been preserved in sources available to the author.

[236] See Haenchen (*The Acts of the Apostles*, p. 716) on the image of Paul conveyed by the author as Paul nears Rome.

level of the narrative that suggests that either the shipwreck or the events on Malta were connected to Paul in information available to the author.[237] For this journey to Rome, there is no need to suppose any information associated with Paul other than a brief notice indicating little more than Paul's arrival at Rome.[238] The narrative of Paul's journey to Rome and foundational proclamation of Christianity at Rome is an authorial *tour de force* in the portrayal of Paul as the defining figure of Christianity conceived as a unified movement from Jerusalem to Rome.

The account of Paul as a political and religious prisoner at Jerusalem and Caesarea (Acts 21–26), of which Paul's journey to Rome (chapters 27 and 28) forms the conclusion, suggests the historiographical intentions of the author's portrayal of Paul. The narrative in Acts 21–26 incorporates two important pieces of information connected to the historical Paul. The drama at Jerusalem and Caesarea turns on a charge against Paul of rejecting the Jewish law (21:21, 28). The author associates this charge with Paul's return to Jerusalem to present alms to his people.[239] These two pieces of information can be correlated with statements Paul himself makes concerning his return to Jerusalem bearing an offering,[240] probably for poor Jewish-Christians at Jerusalem,[241] to reconcile his Gentile mission to the Jewish-Christian community at Jerusalem headed by James.[242] This offering to the saints in Jerusalem was intended, according to Paul, to refute the erroneous conclusions his Jewish-Christian opponents were drawing about his law-free gospel to the Gentiles.[243] Information about this collection (interpreted by the author as alms for the Jewish people) and the associated charge proba-

---

[237] There is no evidence apart from Acts of a Pauline community having ever existed on Malta. In the absence of such a community, a Pauline social context for these stories cannot be demonstrated. The dramatic events of chapters 27–28 suggest not the voice of an eyewitness, but the voice of the author. See Lentz (*Luke's Portrait of Paul*, pp. 139–70) on the social implications of the author's portrayal of Paul's transfer to Rome, as well as the historical probabilities surrounding Paul's actual transfer to Rome.

[238] The tension between 28:15 and 28:21–22 suggests the use of some source for Paul's journey to Rome. See above under *Philippi* on the 'we' narrator.

[239] Acts 24:17. Cf. 21:24.

[240] See Rom 15:25–32.

[241] Rom 15:26; see Gal 2:10.

[242] See Gal 2:1–14.

[243] This concern occupies the defense of his gospel in Romans, which concludes with his intention to go to Jerusalem to reconcile his Gentile mission to the church at Jerusalem (Rom 15:22–33).

bly came to the author through the source the author had about Paul's return to Jerusalem.²⁴⁴

This information about Paul is incorporated into the narrative of Acts not to defend Paul's role in the Gentile mission to other Christians, but rather to portray Paul as a representative of Christianity over against Judaism.²⁴⁵ The charge against Paul that he rejected the law was in fact characteristic of Paul's conflict with other followers of Jesus in Antioch, Asia Minor and Rome about his role in the Gentile mission.²⁴⁶ A suggestion of this context for the conflict is preserved in the words the author puts into the mouth of James,²⁴⁷ but the charge has become for the author of Acts defined by the dispute between Paul and unbelieving Jews narrated in Acts 16–20.²⁴⁸ According to the author, unnamed informants²⁴⁹ who are slandering Paul have created the tension between believing Jews at Jerusalem and Paul.²⁵⁰ These informants are not other believers, but are the unbelieving Jews from the areas of Paul's mission (Acts 21:27). Moreover, the slander is not about a law-free gospel to Gentiles²⁵¹ but about Jewish observance of national customs.²⁵² These Jews charge Paul with teaching other Jews to violate Jewish national customs. These Jews from the Diaspora thus align themselves with the unbelieving opposition to Paul and his mission at Jerusalem.²⁵³

The author has viewed this charge through the eyes of a Graeco-Roman historian relating the customs of foreigners to his audience, not through the eyes of any form of 'Pauline Christianity' defining or defending itself against other forms of Christianity. In Acts 24:17 Paul claims to have returned to Jerusalem after many years for the purpose

---

²⁴⁴ This source is likely the first-person account of Paul's return to Jerusalem from Philippi.
²⁴⁵ See also chapter 3 under *Paul's Farewell Speech and the Literary Paulinism of Lk-Acts*.
²⁴⁶ See, e.g., Rom 3:8.
²⁴⁷ Acts 21:17–25, esp. v. 21.
²⁴⁸ Compare Rom 15:31a with 15:31b. For the author of Lk-Acts, only Paul's dispute with unbelieving Jews is of interest. The author has conveyed little of the historical specificity connected to Paul's return to Jerusalem with the collection, but has rather interpreted the issues associated with this return in terms of his understanding of the origin of Christianity over against Judaism.
²⁴⁹ κατηχήθησαν, 21:21.
²⁵⁰ The author makes it clear in 21:26 that these charges were false and that there were no grounds for any conflict between Paul and other Jewish believers.
²⁵¹ Contrast Paul's portrayal of the dispute in Gal 2:1–10.
²⁵² Acts 21:21; cf. 21:28; 28:17. Paul's actions in 21:26 are interpreted in this light.
²⁵³ Compare 21:27–29 with 22:22; 23:1–5, 12; 24:1–9.

of presenting alms and offerings to his nation.²⁵⁴ Paul's collection for Jerusalem is for the author an example of his general piety toward his people and the temple,²⁵⁵ the issue about which he is being falsely charged. What was historically primarily a conflict among followers of Jesus concerning the mission to the Gentiles—a conflict that Paul tried to resolve with the Gentile collection for the saints in Jerusalem—has become for the author of Lk-Acts a dispute between Christianity and Judaism involving loyalty to national customs. For the author of Acts, this understanding of the conflict motivates the dynamics of the trial of Paul²⁵⁶ leading to his anticipated death at Rome, events which in the narrative of Acts separate Christianity from Judaism.²⁵⁷ Whether or not the author understood the historical context of this charge from his source, there is no need to suppose that the author has taken over this charge against Paul from any traditions of 'Paulinism' or 'anti-Paulinism' (as inner-Christian polemic) known to him.²⁵⁸

---

²⁵⁴ The future participle ποιήσων indicates this purpose. Acts 20:16 suggests Paul's desire to reach Jerusalem by Pentecost, but this does not indicate the purpose of his return. This reference to Paul's bringing alms to his people should probably be taken as the author's interpretation of information he has about Paul's actual collection for the Jewish Christians in Jerusalem, a collection that occupied his attention in the letters and motivated his return to Jerusalem (Rom 15:25–32). Knox (*Chapters in a Life of Paul*, pp. 43–52, esp. p. 51) has argued that the schema of Paul's visits to Jerusalem in Acts suggests that the author has portrayed Paul's offering as having been made in Acts 11:27–30, not in his final visit. Paul's connection with the events in 11:27–30 does indeed pose difficulties in terms of the visits to Jerusalem Paul recounts in Galatians 1 and 2. Perhaps the author has in fact composed this visit in analogy with Paul's final trip to bring offerings to his nation. Nevertheless, it is too much to say that Acts 11:27–30 *is* the offering visit. In Acts 24:17 the author narrates Paul's explicit intention to return to Jerusalem to present gifts. The author has not given this offering the symbolic significance that it had for Paul in terms of Christian unity, but instead reports Paul's intention to bring gifts in the context of his defense against the charges of the unbelieving Jews. The author has not, however, omitted an offering from the story of Paul's final visit to Jerusalem.

²⁵⁵ For the author of Lk-Acts, almsgiving is characteristic of general piety. See, e.g., Cornelius (Acts 10:2) and Tabitha (Acts 9:36). The giving of alms is connected with the temple in Acts 3:2–5.

²⁵⁶ The drama of Paul's legal confrontations dominates the portrayal of Paul in Acts. Chapters 21–28 balance chapters 9, 13–14, and 16–20 (the missionary travels of Paul), but the content of the latter is dramatically constructed to foreshadow events at Jerusalem and Caesarea. Acts 13–14 sets up the Jerusalem council and the events of chapter 21 leading to the arrest of Paul; Acts 16–20 introduces Paul's Roman citizenship and confrontation with Jews before Roman political authorities.

²⁵⁷ See chapter 3 under *Paul's Farewell Speech and the Literary Paulinism of Lk-Acts*.

²⁵⁸ In contrast, see the anti-Paulinism of the Pseudo-Clementines, an anti-Paulinism

The author of Lk-Acts treats the Jewish law as part of the ancestral customs of the nation[259] and as such to be respected but not universalized.[260] In Acts 25:1–12 Paul is portrayed by the author as respecting the customs of the Jews,[261] not as a Jew but as a Roman: he claims to belong not under the jurisdiction of a Jewish court, but of a Roman court.[262] Paul's appeal to Caesar, by rejecting Jewish authority over him, relativizes his proclaimed allegiance to the religious customs of his people.[263] The author's (historiographical) interest in the law of the Jews as a body of national customs[264] is evident in the association of the charge against Paul concerning the law with the temple, the political and religious center of Judaism.[265] Though the charge against Paul is initially presented in terms of the law (21:21), the focus is immediately shifted to the temple.[266] According to the author of Acts, Paul demonstrates his obedience to the law by entering the temple (21:22–26), and his subsequent orations focus on his relation to the temple.[267] The Jewish law

---

that reflects an inner-Christian controversy. See Strecker, *Das Judenchristentum in den Pseudoklementinen*, pp. 187–96.

[259] See especially 28:17. Such national customs were of interest to Hellenistic historians. See, e.g., Josephus *Jewish War* 1.25. See also Balch, '"...you teach all the Jews...to forsake Moses, telling them not to...observe the customs" (Acts 21:21; cf. 6:14),' pp. 369–83.

[260] See especially Acts 26:3; also 15:1, 19–21; 22:3; 25:8. See also Vielhauer, 'On the "Paulinism" of Acts,' pp. 37–38.

[261] This respect extends to the presentation of alms to the nation, 24:17.

[262] The result of Paul's trial is the transfer of his *patria* from Jerusalem to Rome. See Tajra, *The Trial of St. Paul. A Juridical Exegesis of the Second Half of the Acts of the Apostles*, esp. p. 201. The political and religious jurisdiction of the Jews and their law over Christians (who belong under the political authority of Rome) is denied. The kingdom of God (Acts 1:6; 20:25; 28:30–31) is not a Jewish political and/or religious reality.

[263] See, e.g., Acts 25:8; 26:4–23.

[264] The apostolic decree is noteworthy in this regard. The author interprets it as the respect Gentile Christians are to accord to Jewish customs (cf. Acts 15:21). The four prohibitions from the Jewish law enjoined upon the Gentiles are specifically those that the Jewish law applied to foreigners living among the Israelites. See Haenchen, *The Acts of the Apostles*, pp. 469–70. The Jewish law as a whole belongs to the national customs (ἔθη—see, e.g., Acts 6:14; 26:3; 28:17; cf. 16:21; 18:15) of the Jews. The author has separated the kingdom of God and the fulfillment of scripture from the political and religious identity of Judaism.

[265] Compare Acts 21:21 with 21:28; cf. 24:6.

[266] This shift indicates how the charge has become divorced from the original context of Paul's ministry.

[267] See, e.g., Acts 21:27–29 and 22:17–21; 24:6 and 24:12–21; 26:19–23. Paul in Acts implies that the charge against him of bringing Gentiles into the temple, while in fact untrue, is founded on a wrong understanding of God's intentions toward the Gentiles. Cf. Stephen's attitude toward the temple (Acts 6:11–14; 7:47–53). Paul specifically alludes

belongs to the constellation of Jewish religious customs centered on the temple, customs that the author (as a Hellenistic historian) respects but separates from Christianity and the message of the kingdom of God.[268] The proclamation of this message from Jerusalem to Rome, defining the emergence of Christianity, is the legacy of Paul according to Lk-Acts.[269]

Paul's conversion is the linchpin of this portrayal of the legacy of Paul according to Lk-Acts.[270] An account of Paul's conversion is repeated three times in Acts,[271] and Paul's commission to bear Jesus' name before Gentiles, their kings, and the people of Israel[272] defines the scope of Paul's mission in Acts[273] and is fundamental to his defense against the

---

to Stephen (Acts 22:20) in his defense at Jerusalem. This defense consists of a claim that he received a vision while piously praying *in the temple* to go to the Gentiles (Acts 22:17–21).

[268] See, e.g., Stephen's speech in Acts 7, especially 7:48–53 (cf. 17:22–31). Note that the theme of Paul's confrontation with false or inadequate images of God runs through Acts (see also Acts 14:8–18; 19:23–40). It is not coincidental that in the narrative of Acts the conflict immediately preceding the Jews' wrath about Paul's supposed defiling of their temple is the wrath of certain artisans at Ephesus concerning Artemis and her temple.

[269] This proclamation brings the narrative of Acts to an end. Paul's solemn pronouncement in Acts 28:25–28, culminating in the declaration γνωστὸν οὖν ἔστω ὑμῖν ὅτι τοῖς ἔθνεσιν ἀπεστάλη τοῦτο τὸ σωτήριον τοῦ θεοῦ· αὐτοὶ καὶ ἀκούσονται (a declaration foreshadowed in Acts 13:46; 18:6; 19:9) signals the resolution of Paul's confrontation with unbelieving Jews and thus the end of the narrative. The author's intentions expressed in Lk 1:1–4, Acts 1:1–2, and Acts 1:8 (on the phrase ἕως ἐσχάτου τῆς γῆς, see note 232 above) have been realized in the message proclaimed by Paul in Acts 28:17–31. There is nothing missing in the ending of Acts, nor anything more to say.

[270] The portrayal of Paul's encounter with Jesus as a conversion reflects the author's conceptual differentiation between Christians and Judaism. For the author, Paul has fundamentally changed his allegiance on the road to Damascus. He goes to Damascus to exercise the religious and political authority of Jerusalem over followers of Jesus connected with the synagogues in Damascus. (On the historical difficulties with this portrayal, see, e.g., Conzelmann, *Acts of the Apostles*, p. 71.) It is against just such an extension of the authority of Judaism over followers of Jesus that as a Christian Paul appeals to Caesar (Acts 25:10–11). As a sign of his conversion, he humbly receives baptism (Acts 9:18; cf. 22:16). On the meaning of baptism for the author of Lk-Acts, see especially Acts 2:37–47; 8:36, 38; 16:31–34. On Paul's conversion as a change of allegiance from one social group to another, see Segal, *Paul the Convert. The Apostolate and Apostasy of Paul the Pharisee*, pp. 17, 72–114.

[271] Acts 9:1–19; 22:1–21; 26:9–18. See Löning, *Die Saulustradition in der Apostelgeschichte*, appendix 1 for a synopsis of the three passages. See Lüdemann (*Early Christianity according to the Traditions in Acts*, pp. 106–116) for a recent summary of the issues in reconstructing sources for these passages.

[272] Acts 9:15; cf. 22:14–15; 26:17–18.

[273] Cf. Acts 1:8. Paul's commission by Jesus corresponds to that commission given to

charges of unbelieving Jews in Acts 22–26.[274] In Acts, Paul's encounter with Jesus on the road to Damascus constitutes Paul's persona as missionary to Jew and Gentile. Unlike most of the other stories about Paul in Acts, there is evidence for an actual tradition of Paul's call in early Christianity—a tradition that has a specific context.

The *Epistula Apostolorum* preserves an account of Paul's vision of Jesus that defines his commission to preach to the Gentiles.[275] Common in the narratives of the *Epistula Apostolorum* and Acts is the association of Saul's vision of Jesus with the persecution of believers at Damascus. Both accounts predict Paul's suffering (as a reference to his death)[276] and identify Paul as a chosen instrument. However, differences in the narrative framework for these details indicate the literary independence of the two texts. In terms of the overall relation of Acts to the *Epistula Apostolorum*, the list of apostles in *Ep. Ap.* 2 does not agree with the list in Acts 1:13 (cf. 1:26). The prediction of the imprisonment of one of the apostles in *Ep. Ap.* 15, though similar to, has not been influenced by the narrative order of Acts 12:3–19. More specifically concerning Paul, in the *Epistula Apostolorum* the apostles (not Ananias) remove Paul's blindness. Furthermore, in Acts, Paul is going from Jerusalem to Damascus when he receives the vision; in the *Epistula Apostolorum* Paul is going from Cilicia to Damascus. In general, neither account preserves anything distinctive of the other's composition.[277]

The *Acts of Paul* also preserves an account of Paul's conversion.[278] In this version of the story, Judas guides Paul into the Christian commu-

---

the Twelve and in fact determines the unity of the proclamation of the gospel from Jerusalem to Rome.

[274] Paul recounts his commission by Jesus before the people of Israel (Acts 22) and before King Agrippa (Acts 26).

[275] See *Ep. Ap.* 31 and 33. On the place of Paul and the Gentile mission in the *Epistula Apostolorum*, see Hornschuh, *Studien zur Epistula Apostolorum*, pp. 84–91.

[276] On Acts 9:16, cf. 20:22–24; 21:10–14. Paul's farewell implies his death (Acts 20:25, 37–38).

[277] See Barrett, *A Critical and Exegetical Commentary on the Acts of the Apostles*, 1.38–40, for a comparison of the *Epistula Apostolorum* with Acts. The readiness with which the *Epistula Apostolorum* is taken to presuppose Acts is based on a wrong assessment of the importance of Acts before the end of the second century. Cf., e.g., Hengel, 'The Titles of the Gospels and the Gospel of Mark,' p.72. Since Acts can be dated as late as about 130 and the *Epistula Apostolorum* can be dated as early as 120, there is no obvious reason why the direction of influence should be assumed to go from Acts to the *Epistula Apostolorum*. When the accounts are judged apart from the bias of the priority of Acts, no direction of dependence can be determined.

[278] See Schneemelcher, *New Testament Apocrypha*, rev. ed. (1992), 2.264.

nity.²⁷⁹ Other than this shared character with the version of the story in Acts 9 (though in a quite different role) and the connection to Damascus shared by all three versions of the story, the details in the version in the *Acts of Paul* appear to be independent of the versions in Acts and the *Epistula Apostolorum*.²⁸⁰ Common to all three narratives, however, is the point of the conversion: Paul's integration into the company of the apostles.²⁸¹

Neither the story as preserved in the *Epistula Apostolorum*, nor in the *Acts of Paul*, nor in Acts suggests a social context of Pauline Christianity. Instead, the context of the story of Paul's conversion appears to have been the integration of the memory of Paul into 'non-Pauline' forms of Christianity. In all three, the story of Paul's conversion at Damascus is the basis for Paul's acceptance by the apostles.²⁸² This story probably has its roots in the life of Paul, and Paul himself suggests the non-Pauline context of the story:

> I was unknown by face to the churches of Judea which are in Christ. They were only hearing that the one persecuting us formerly now proclaims the faith that formerly he was attempting to destroy.²⁸³

The *Epistula Apostolorum*, the *Acts of Paul*, and Acts apparently elaborate with different details a common tradition of how Paul was remembered by non-Pauline communities.²⁸⁴

The elaboration of what was probably already during his own lifetime a tradition of Paul's conversion from persecutor to proclaimer took place in the context of the status that his death at Rome as a Christian

---

²⁷⁹ Cf. Acts 9:11; also the role of Ananias in Acts 9:10–19.

²⁸⁰ On the independence of the version in the *Acts of Paul* from that in Acts 9, see Rordorf, 'Paul's Conversion in the Canonical Acts and in the *Acts of Paul*,' pp. 137–43. For a different assessment, see Bauckham, 'The *Acts of Paul*: Replacement of Acts or Sequel to Acts?' pp. 159–67. The form of the story in the *Acts of Paul* has probably been influenced by Gal 1:15–16. See Rordorf, 'Paul's Conversion in the Canonical Acts and in the *Acts of Paul*,' p. 143.

²⁸¹ Judas in the *Acts of Paul* is probably the apostle Judas Thomas. See Rordorf, 'Paul's Conversion in the Canonical Acts and in the *Acts of Paul*,' p. 142.

²⁸² The basis for Paul's acceptance by Cephas in Gal 1:18 is unclear, probably because Paul intends to avoid any implication that his call required validation by the apostles at Jerusalem.

²⁸³ Gal 1:22–23.

²⁸⁴ On the connection of Acts 9:1–22 with Gal 1:23, cf. e.g. Löning, *Die Saulustradition in der Apostelgeschichte*, pp. 48–53; Burchard, *Der dreizehnte Zeuge*, pp. 126–28; the caution of Lüdemann (*Early Christianity according to the Traditions in Acts*, p. 113) in avoiding a too precise reconstruction of the history of the tradition at this point is well taken.

brought to him as a preeminent missionary to the Gentiles.[285] Both the *Epistula Apostolorum* and Acts portray suffering (as a reference to death) as the consequence of Paul's vision of Jesus. The close connection of Paul's image as a missionary and as one who died for Jesus at Rome is evident in the status Paul has for Clement of Rome. For Clement, Paul is, alongside Peter, preeminent as one who endured suffering even to death to proclaim the gospel—though the Christian communities at Rome were not Pauline.[286]

> But let us pass from ancient examples to those who contended for the faith in our own time. It was due to jealousy and envy[287] that the greatest and most righteous pillars (of the Church) were persecuted and contended to the death. Let us set before our eyes the good apostles. There was Peter, who because of unrighteous jealousy endured not just one or two but many hardships, and having thus borne his witness, went to the place of glory he deserved. Because of jealousy and strife, Paul showed how to win the prize of patient endurance: seven times he was in bonds, he was banished, he was stoned, he became a messenger (of the gospel) in both east and west, and earned well-merited fame for his faith; for he taught righteousness to the whole world, having traveled to the limits of the west; and when he had borne his witness before the rulers, he departed from the world an outstanding example of patient endurance.[288]

Clement's portrayal of Paul, alongside that portrayal in Acts and the *Epistula Apostolorum*, suggests that the tradition of Paul's call or conversion, his universal mission, and his death at Rome as a Christian became the basis for his emergence as an apostle of such status as to be placed alongside Peter and the Twelve in early forms of Christianity not determined by Paulinism.[289]

---

[285] This status associated with his death is evident in the deutero-Pauline letters. For perhaps the earliest example of this, see Col 1:24. See Betz, 'Paul's "Second Presence" in Colossians,' esp. p. 513.

[286] Rom 15:22–24 suggests that the Jesus movement had made its way to Rome years before Paul arrived. On Paul's memory in non-Pauline communities, note also Ignatius, who remembers Paul as preacher and as one who died for Jesus at Rome, though Antioch was not a specifically Pauline community (see especially Gal 2:11–14; cf. Acts 11:20–21). See note 289 below.

[287] Clement is citing the example of Peter and Paul to combat the discord which has arisen at Corinth. Clement describes the root problem of this discord as envious persecution of the righteous.

[288] *1 Clem* 5. Cited according to the translation by Robert M. Grant and Holt H. Graham (*The Apostolic Fathers. A New Translation and Commentary*). This passage is independent of the narrative of Acts. The tradition of Paul's death at Rome has been elaborated by Clement as an example of patient endurance.

[289] On the influence of Paul's death on the elaboration of Paul's image in the deutero-

For the author of Lk-Acts, the story of Paul's conversion is interpreted to designate Paul as God's chosen instrument[290] to define the emergence of Christianity over against Judaism. Paul belongs with John, Jesus, and the Twelve as the endpoint of the history of the early proclamation of the kingdom of God in the Graeco-Roman world. This is the legacy of Paul according to Lk-Acts. Pauline traditions, movements, or communities do not determine this legacy in early Christianity. Instead, this legacy is a literary construct created to serve the author's intention to narrate an ordered account of the events that have recently taken place concerning the preaching of the Christian message.[291] However, with the emergence of Acts as an authoritative text alongside the Irenaean collection of gospels and Pauline letters at the end of the second century, the legacy of Paul according to Lk-Acts was granted an importance for the reconstruction of Paul's place in early Christianity far beyond what is warranted by the author's actual information about Paul.

Pauline letters, see note 285 above. Cf. also Ignatius, whose Paulinism consists largely of a desire to follow Paul's steps to death at Rome as a Christian. For Ignatius, Paul shares with Peter the status of one who died at Rome for the sake of the gospel. See Ign. *Rom.* 4 and Ign. *Eph.* 12.

[290] σκεῦος ἐκλογῆς epitomizes Paul's life and death for Jesus. See *Ep. Ap.* 31.
[291] See Lk 1:1–4; Acts 26:26.

CHAPTER 5

LK-ACTS AND THE CONSTRUCTION OF CHRISTIAN ORIGINS IN THE SECOND CENTURY

The prominence of Paul in the New Testament—in which the Jesus of the four gospels stands alongside the Paul of the Acts of the Apostles and the collection of Pauline letters—has exerted an enormous influence on the construction of Christian origins. As a result of the shape of the New Testament, Jesus and Paul (by default) have become the two central figures for reconstructing the beginning of Christianity. In the traditional construction of Christian origins—what is basically a recitation of the story presupposed by the shape of the New Testament canon read in terms of the narrative of the Acts of the Apostles—Jesus announced the Gospel, and this Gospel was spread throughout the Roman world by Paul and the other apostles.[1] This proclamation of the Gospel, preserved in the sacred texts of the New Testament, was then defended against heresy by the church fathers.[2] In the revision of this picture undertaken since the Enlightenment, the harmonious agreement of canon and history has been taken apart, but the framework has largely remained in place. Critical reconstructions of Christian origins have tended to posit the alternative of Jesus (in one way or another reconstructed from the canonical gospels)[3] or Paul (reconstructed in one way or another from the Pauline letter collection and the Acts of the Apostles)[4] as the individual in whom the essence of the new religion is to be found. Ironically, this choice between Jesus and Paul, no matter how critically the actual New Testament documents

---

[1] See especially *Adv. haer.* 3.1.1, cited below and discussed in detail in chapter 2.
[2] This construction of Christian origins forms the framework for Eusebius's history of the church.
[3] On the role the hypothetical document Q (reconstructed from pieces of the New Testament gospels) has played in the reconstruction of the religion of Jesus and his followers, see, e.g., Mack, *A Myth of Innocence*, pp. 53–55; idem, *Who Wrote the New Testament? The Making of the Christian Myth*, pp. 47–53; idem, *The Lost Gospel. The Book of Q and Christian Origins*, e.g., pp. 106–7. Crossan (*The Historical Jesus*, e.g., pp. 383–94) has given prominence to non-canonical sources to recontstruct the religion of Jesus, but see the response of Allison (*Jesus of Nazareth*, pp. 1–33).
[4] See, e.g., chapter 1 above on F. C. Baur.

are treated, is determined by the construction of early Christianity presupposed by the shape of the New Testament canon.

There is reason to question the adequacy of this critical reshuffling of Jesus and Paul, tied as it is to the shape of the New Testament, for understanding Christian beginnings. The New Testament is not a reservoir of materials preserving in some form or another the essence of Christianity from which its beginnings can be discovered.[5] Instead, the New Testament itself, in which Paul is prominent, is already a construction of Christian origins that emerged out of competing second-century attempts to define a normative apostolic tradition on the basis of which Christianity could be defended against perceived heresy. This second-century dispute about Christian origins that determined the shape of the New Testament canon involved Christian intellectuals and Christian leaders attempting to arbitrate authentic Christian doctrine, practice, and history itself. The outlines of this second-century dispute about the origin of Christianity—a dispute in which Lk-Acts became the Gospel of Luke and the Acts of the Apostles—need to be highlighted if the study of Christian beginnings is to be brought into proper relationship to the texts and characters of the New Testament, particularly that of Paul.

How the Gospel according to Matthew, the Gospel according to Mark, the Gospel according to Luke, and the Gospel according to John came to define the Gospel of Jesus alongside a collection of Pauline letters in the second century is a process whose development is too often mapped by presupposing the end in the beginning. The anachronistic assumption that Lk is a gospel and Acts is a narrative that presupposes the importance of a collection of Pauline letters mistakes the construction of the origin of Christianity proposed by Irenaeus for the situation in which the author of Lk-Acts wrote.[6] The shape of the Christian New Testament is a reconfiguration of the relationship of literary texts on

---

[5] That the New Testament is presumed to contain, in one way or another, the essence of Christian origins is evident in the way Christian history is often reconstructed. Early Christian history, whether understood in terms of the expansion of Christianity in the Roman Empire or the development of Christian theology, is often construed as a religious phenomenon whose connection to the New Testament needs to be explained in terms of evolutionary development. In the Eusebian model, this development is either positive (orthodox) or negative (heretical).

[6] For example, Jervell (*The Theology of the Acts of the Apostles*, esp. pp. 1–10) begins his study of the theology of the Acts of the Apostles with the anachronistic statement: "Luke had already written a Gospel..." (See also his comments on pp. 116–17.) See chapter 2 above under *Traditions of Authorship and Titles*.

the basis of specific theories of Christian origins, a debate about origins whose background lies in the diversity of first-century Judaism. For reasons that can no longer be recovered with any certainty, an unknown author sometime around 70 C.E. wrote what has come to be known as the Gospel according to Mark. The author wrote anonymously and gave no clear indication of the literary precursors to this work, but simply introduced this work with the heading ἀρχὴ τοῦ εὐαγγελίου Ἰησοῦ Χριστοῦ υἱοῦ θεοῦ—'the beginning of the gospel of Jesus Christ, son of God.' Whatever the author's intentions in constructing this account of 'beginnings,' the text was not immediately received as a 'gospel'—certainly not the Gospel according to Mark—nor was it recognized at first as an entirely satisfactory basis for interpreting the religious significance of Jesus. Instead, although much of its content was more or less accepted, its narrative conception of Jesus was judged to be inadequate.

Some years later, the author of the text now known as the Gospel according to Matthew undertook a major revision of the text of Mk. This author introduced this work as βίβλος γενέσεως Ἰησοῦ Χριστοῦ υἱοῦ Δαυὶδ υἱοῦ Ἀβραάμ—'the book of the origin of Jesus Christ, son of David, son of Abraham.' Whereas the narrative of Mk begins with the baptism of the adult Jesus (an event which according to the text of Mk constitutes Jesus as the son of God and differentiates Jesus from John the Baptist), the text of Mt begins by tracing the genealogy of Jesus from the Jewish patriarch Abraham and recounts his miraculous birth by the divine spirit to Mary and Joseph. This beginning suggests that the author of Mt intended to give a more satisfactory account of the life of Jesus and thus of the identity of the followers of Jesus. Also written anonymously, the text of Mt characterizes neither itself nor its literary precursors as 'gospels.'

For neither the text of Mt nor the text of Mk does the authority of the text depend on the identity of its author. Rather, their authority is two-fold. First, they preserve the oral proclamation of the gospel by Jesus. According to the text of Mk, the 'gospel of Jesus Christ' in Mk 1:1 is in fact that gospel proclaimed by Jesus in Galilee (Mk 1:14).[7] Second, the point of departure for each in narrating the life of Jesus is the Jewish scriptures.[8] Jesus' relation to first-century Judaism determines the identity of the followers of Jesus presupposed by both texts. For the

---

[7] Cf. Mt 28:16–20.
[8] Note Mk 1:2 – καθὼς γέγραπται ἐν τῷ Ἠσαΐᾳ τῷ προφήτῃ ('just as it is written in Isaiah the prophet'); cf. Mt 1:1–17; also, e.g., 1:22; 2:17.

author of Mk, the end of this age is expected in connection with the imminent return of Jesus and the destruction of the Jewish temple by the Romans. Although the connection between the past of Jesus and the present of the church has become more problematic for the author of Mt (there are, for example, the two commissions of the apostles in Mt), the author of Mt has not abandoned the life of Jesus (determined as it is by Judaism) as a means for defining the religion of his followers.[9] Neither the text of Mk nor the text of Mt identifies itself as Christian, though both are concerned with beginnings associated with Jesus the Messiah.

The first twenty chapters of the text that has come to be known as the Gospel according to John, like the texts of Mk and Mt, were written anonymously and also recount a life of Jesus determined by Judaism as a means for defining the religion of his followers. Jn probably presupposes knowledge of Mk on the part of at least some of its readers.[10] To a much greater extent than Mt, however, Jn appears to have revised the 'beginning of the gospel of Jesus Christ, son of God' in Mk 1:1. Whereas Mk had defined beginnings in terms of the gospel of Jesus Christ proclaimed in Galilee, Jn conceptualized beginnings in terms of the pre-existent Logos—ἐν ἀρχῇ ἦν ὁ λόγος ('in the beginning was the word'). Sometime after the composition of the main body of the text (chapters 1–20), a subsequent editor or editors expanded the work with chapter 21. This chapter ends with an explicit appeal to the identity of the

---

[9] On the understanding of the connection between Jesus and the church in the text of Mt, see Betz, 'The Sermon on the Mount in Matthew's Interpretation,' pp. 279–89. In the abrupt ending of Mk, the fear provoked by Jesus' absence stands alongside the expectation of seeing Jesus in Galilee and the imminent expectation of the return of Jesus associated with the destruction of the temple by the Romans (see chapter 3 under *Jesus' apocalyptic discourse and the coming of the kingdom*). Such an ending is possible only as long as the absence of Jesus is not perceived to disrupt the connection between the life of Jesus and the life of the believer. The two mission charges in Mt, one to the Jews (Mt 10:5–6) and one to the Gentiles (Mt 28:19), suggest that already the connection between the life of Jesus and the life of his followers was beginning to lose the immediacy it had for the author of Mk.

Although Paul on the whole took little notice of stories about the life of Jesus (though he does apparently refer to the sayings of Jesus now and then; see, e.g., 1 Cor 7:10; 1 Thess 4:15), his proclamation of the religious significance of Jesus as the resurrected Christ also included the expectation of the imminent return of Jesus. As a result, the continuing absence of Jesus was a problem for some of those who believed Paul's message. See, e.g., 1 Thess. 4:13–5:11. On Paul's attempt to define the religion he proclaimed, see Betz, 'Christianity as Religion: Paul's Attempt at Definition in Romans,' pp. 210–34.

[10] See Bauckham, 'John for Readers of Mark,' pp. 147–71.

author as the basis for the authority of the text. Because the text was written by the beloved disciple, according to Jn 21:24, it is true. This expansion suggests the problem of authority that would come to be attached to written texts about Jesus. This problem of authority would have a significant impact on the direction in which beginnings associated with Jesus the Messiah would be reconstructed by later Christians.

Both Mk and Mt were written anonymously. Sometime early in the second century, however, Christians supplied these texts with the names of authors, and details about the composition of the narratives were added. In this Christian hagiography, the apostles began to emerge as defining figures of distinctly Christian origins belonging to a past whose historical contours were no longer clearly seen. The Christian author Papias, writing sometime before about 130,[11] reports that Mark, identified as a follower of the apostle Peter, wrote the text of Mk. The apostle Matthew wrote the text of Mt. According to Papias:[12]

> Mark, having become Peter's translator, wrote accurately, though not in order, the things either said or done by the Lord, as many things as he remembered. For he neither heard the Lord nor followed him, but later, as I said, followed Peter. Peter was accustomed to teach using *chreiai* [or: as the need arose], but did not as it were produce an ordered arrangement of the sayings of the Lord, so that Mark in no way erred by so having written some as he remembered...[13]

> Matthew arranged the sayings in the Hebrew language, and each translated them as he was able.[14]

---

[11] The date of Papias's writing has been traditionally put around 130, but a date early in the second century has been suggested. See, e.g., Gundry, *Mark*, pp.1027–29, who argues for a date of 101–108. Against such an early date, however, there is no reason to be confident that Eusebius is well informed about the precise chronological relationship of Papias to Clement of Rome, Ignatius, and Polycarp. Moreover, even if Eusebius is right in associating Papias with Clement of Rome and Ignatius (*Hist. eccl.* 3.36.1–2; cf. 3.39.1), there is no need to conclude that Papias necessarily wrote his work on the sayings of the Lord prior to the death of either individual or even during the reign of Trajan. A date between 101–108 suggests a precision that is not possible on the basis of the evidence available.

[12] The following comments on Papias summarize the discussion of Papias in chapter 2 above under *Traditions of Authorship and Titles*.

[13] Μάρκος μὲν ἑρμηνευτὴς Πέτρου γενόμενος, ὅσα ἐμνημόνευσεν, ἀκριβῶς ἔγραψεν, οὐ μέντοι τάξει, τὰ ὑπὸ τοῦ κυρίου ἢ λεχθέντα ἢ πραχθέντα. οὔτε γὰρ ἤκουσεν τοῦ κυρίου οὔτε παρηκολούθησεν αὐτῷ, ὕστερον δέ, ὡς ἔφην, Πέτρῳ· ὃς πρὸς τὰς χρείας ἐποιεῖτο τὰς διδασκαλίας, ἀλλ' οὐχ ὥσπερ σύνταξιν τῶν κυριακῶν ποιούμενος λογίων, ὥστε οὐδὲν ἥμαρτεν Μάρκος οὕτως ἔνια γράψας ὡς ἀπεμνημόνευσεν. See Eusebius, *Hist. eccl.* 3.39.15–16 (cited according to the edition by Kirsopp Lake, LCL).

[14] Ματθαῖος μὲν οὖν Ἑβραΐδι διαλέκτῳ τὰ λόγια συνετάξατο, ἡρμήνευσεν δ' αὐτὰ ὡς

Thus both texts preserve apostolic preaching, but not without defect. Mark relied on the preaching of Peter so that his account of the life of Jesus lacks order (τάξις), though it is accurate (ἀκριβῶς) according to Papias. Because Matthew wrote either in Hebrew (Aramaic) or in terms of the style of Jewish discourse (either sense is possible for Ἑβραΐδι διαλέκτῳ), there is a certain difficulty attached to the interpretation or translation of the text. These comments about the texts of Mk and Mt by Papias suggest the reason for the literary undertaking of Papias himself. Papias composed his own collection and interpretation of the sayings of Jesus to supplement these texts. According to Papias, he collected sayings of Jesus from the remembrances of those who had heard the other apostles. Thus, Papias conceived oral and written traditions about Jesus as circulating under the authority of the apostles, not just Jesus. 'Jesus said' is now qualified by 'according to this apostle, Jesus said.' Neither the text of Mk nor the text of Mt was itself concerned with claiming an apostolic seal of authenticity upon their respective accounts of the life of Jesus.[15] Papias's comments give an indication of the direction the search for Christian origins would take in the second century: the creation of apostolic authority. The apostles begin to emerge in the second century as normative figures around whom definitions of Christianity begin to coalesce.[16] For Papias, however, the texts of Mt and Mk are not yet authoritative gospels, and Pauline traditions have not been conceded a status equal to those of Jesus in understanding Christian religion.

Papias's criticisms of the texts of Mk and Mt are relatively subdued. A thorough critique of these early attempts to recount the life of Jesus as the basis of the religion of his followers was undertaken by the author of the two-volume work that has come to be known as the Gospel of Luke and the Acts of the Apostles. This two-volume work was probably completed sometime before about 130.[17] Unlike the anonymous authors

---

ἦν δυνατὸς ἕκαστος. See Eusebius, *Hist. eccl.* 3.39.15–16 (cited according to the edition by Kirsopp Lake, LCL).

[15] Mt 16:18, however, represents an advance in this direction over Mk.

[16] What has come to be known as the Gospel according to John underwent a similar expansion in terms of authority. Chapter 21 identifies chapters 1–20 with apostolic authority by rehabilitating Peter and identifying the author of the work as the beloved disciple, who may already have been identified with the apostle John.

[17] Conceptually, Lk-Acts belongs after Mk and Mt, but before Marcion (whom Tertullian places in Rome around 144; see *Adversus Marcionem* 1.19; Harnack, *Marcion. Das Evangelium vom fremden Gott*, pp. 19*-20*; see also idem, *Marcion. The Gospel of the Alien God*, pp. 15–20). In Lk-Acts, Paul is remembered for his mission and death; he

of Mk, Mt, and Jn 1–20, the author of Lk-Acts takes his starting point in Graeco-Roman culture, not Judaism. In the Christian New Testament, these two volumes are separated in terms of title, perceived genre, and relative place. The Acts of the Apostles does not follow the Gospel of Luke in the received grouping of New Testament texts, but instead comes after the fourfold gospel collection (in which the Gospel according to Luke is placed third) and immediately before the Pauline letters (to which it serves as an introduction). Nevertheless, these two volumes were originally written as two parts of one narrative of Christian origins.[18] The author introduces the first volume of this work with a concise preface consisting of one long, well-balanced, periodic sentence in Greek defining his intentions:

> Inasmuch as many have attempted to compile a narrative about the events that have been accomplished among us, just as those who from the beginning were eyewitnesses and became servants of the word handed down to us, it seemed good for me also, most excellent Theophilus, since I have investigated from the beginning all things, to write for you accurately, in an orderly manner a narrative, in order that you might know the truth of the stories about which you have been informed.[19]

At the beginning of his second volume, there is a short secondary preface indicating the continuation of a single work:

> I wrote the first volume, Theophilus, about all that Jesus began to do and teach...[20]

In the author's prefaces to his two-volume work, he provides a carefully defined conceptualization of the problem of constructing Christian origins.

---

is not important as a figure in inner-Christian polemics. Lk-Acts thus stands between Clement of Rome and Ignatius, on the one hand, and Marcion on the other. The date usually given for Papias's comments, sometime in the second century before 130, is the most likely for Lk-Acts as well. That the author of Lk-Acts makes no use of the Pauline letters does not imply that Lk-Acts was written before collections of Pauline letters began to emerge in early Christianity. Instead, Lk-Acts provides evidence that such collections were not as important for defining 'Pauline' Christianity as has often been thought.

[18] See chapter 3 under *The Prefaces of Lk-Acts*.

[19] Ἐπειδήπερ πολλοὶ ἐπεχείρησαν ἀνατάξασθαι διήγησιν περὶ τῶν πεπληροφορημένων ἐν ἡμῖν πραγμάτων, καθὼς παρέδοσαν ἡμῖν οἱ ἀπ' ἀρχῆς αὐτόπται καὶ ὑπηρέται γενόμενοι τοῦ λόγου, ἔδοξε κἀμοὶ παρηκολουθηκότι ἄνωθεν πᾶσιν ἀκριβῶς καθεξῆς σοι γράψαι, κράτιστε Θεόφιλε, ἵνα ἐπιγνῷς περὶ ὧν κατηχήθης λόγων τὴν ἀσφάλειαν.

[20] Τὸν μὲν πρῶτον λόγον ἐποιησάμην περὶ πάντων, ὦ Θεόφιλε, ὧν ἤρξατο ὁ Ἰησοῦς ποιεῖν τε καὶ διδάσκειν..

The fundamental problem, according to this early Christian author, is that no one has yet succeeded in compiling a narrative to bring order, and thus historical reliability as that would be understood in Graeco-Roman culture, to the stories about the events associated with Jesus and his early followers.[21] Typical of such prefaces, the author of the two-volume work Lk-Acts takes note of previous literary efforts (πολλοὶ ἐπεχείρησαν—'many have attempted'), but suggests he will do a better job. Among the previous narratives about events associated with Jesus that the author finds inadequate, the author implicitly includes the narrative of Mk, a major source for his own work. The author had no intention for his work to sit beside other narratives about Jesus as one among equals.

He specifically lists his qualifications to do a better job. He claims to have investigated all things from the beginning (παρηκολουθηκότι ἄνωθεν) so that he can write an accurate (ἀκριβῶς), ordered (καθεξῆς) account. Moreover, he claims that eyewitness accounts (αὐτόπται) are the basis for his narrative. These eyewitnesses have handed on a reliable tradition about the events associated with Jesus. These eyewitnesses include, according to the author, none other than the apostles, who were with Jesus from the beginning.[22]

The author of Lk-Acts does not understand his own work or that of his predecessors as 'gospels' (in this he belongs to the same conceptual world as Papias), but instead as narratives about events (πράγματα) of the recent past. The precise events with which the author is concerned are characterized as 'accomplished' or 'fulfilled.' As his narrative unfolds, he offers a view of history as moving according to a recognizable divine plan from a Christian perspective. Moreover, the author is not an anonymous conveyer of tradition. He speaks in the first person and writes self-consciously as a Christian, not a Jew.[23]

The claim to have investigated carefully events of the recent past based on eyewitness accounts is a commonplace among Hellenistic historians offering an apology for the accuracy of their work (often against what is claimed to be the inferior efforts of others). Such an apology, of course, was often more rhetorical than substantial. Nevertheless, by

---

[21] What follows summarizes the discussion in chapter 3 above.

[22] See Acts 1:21–22.

[23] On the shift from first person to third person narrative after the prefaces, see chapter 3, note 43.

adopting this rhetorical stance toward his narrative, the author of Lk-Acts has identified the nature of his authority to narrate the truth about Christian origins: he claims to be a historian in terms understandable within the context of Hellenistic literature of the time. He claims to have adopted the standards for historical truth that would have been acknowledged by his close contemporaries for a narrative about the past.[24] The Jewish historian Josephus characterized his account of the Jewish War in such terms in hopes of increasing the credibility of his work for a Graeco-Roman audience. The Hellenistic satirist Lucian gives some indications of the expectations of such an audience. Writing sometime before the end of the Parthian war of 162–165, Lucian turned his literary wit against the frivolous accounts of the war that were being passed off as serious histories. In his brief essay entitled *How to Write History*, Lucian (drawing on the historiographic tradition begun especially by Thucydides) summarized the requirements of a reliable history.

> [47] [The historian] should not bring together the events themselves haphazardly, but by inquiring about them diligently and at great personal expense. It is best if he is present and observes the events, but if not, he should pay attention to those who give the less biased account and whom one would infer least likely to take away from or add to what happened as a favor or out of hatred. Then let the historian be both discerning and skilled in putting together what is more likely to have taken place.

> [51] Above all, let him furnish a mind like a mirror: clear, glistening, accurately focused. Whatever the appearances of the actions he receives, let him also display them without distortion, discoloration, or misrepresentation. For what is to be said [by the historian] is not as some write for orators, but is so in reality and will speak for itself, for it has happened already. It only needs to be put in order and recounted.

Of course, Lucian is talking about events of war; such events were the object of the investigation of the Jewish historian Josephus, but not the investigation of the author of Lk-Acts. The events that the author of Lk-Acts has chosen to investigate hardly constitute the object of inquiry of a typical political or military history. His intentions in claiming the

---

[24] In this he stands in contrast to Papias, who identifies himself in terms compatible with understanding Jesus as the founder of a philosophical school. Papias prefers oral tradition to that which is written in books and characterizes Peter's teachings in terms of *chreiai*. Papias's five-volume work explaining the sayings of Jesus should probably be understood as an attempt to elaborate Jesus' teachings as though he were a founder of a philosophical school.

standards for historical truth acknowledged in the context of Hellenistic culture lie elsewhere.

These intentions are evident in the structure of his two-volume work. The author has subordinated the life of Jesus to an account of the spread of the proclamation of the gospel from Jerusalem to Rome. The text of Mk ends with an angel at Jesus' tomb sending a message for the disciples to meet Jesus in Galilee, presumably in anticipation (for the reader of the text) of Jesus' imminent return. In contrast, the text of Acts begins with two angels asking the disciples why, after Jesus' ascension from the Mount of Olives near Jerusalem, they remain staring into the sky. According to the narrative of Lk-Acts, the story is not yet at an end, for the proclamation of the gospel by his followers will define the beginning of Christianity. This gospel is carried forth primarily in the preaching of Peter and Paul, but the origin of the term 'Christian' is associated, according to the author, with Paul. The author portrays the mission of Paul as central to the history of early Christianity, a Paul whose confrontation with unbelieving Jews comes to define Christianity as a distinct religion over against Judaism. No earlier texts about Jesus had taken much notice of Paul, nor had they required anything more than an account of the life of Jesus to define discipleship.

In the narrative of Acts, Paul's status as the figure in whom Christian religion is defined is not based on the importance of the Pauline letters for the author. The narrative of Acts was not originally intended to serve as an introduction to the Pauline letters, despite the impression created by the shape of the New Testament canon. The Pauline letters play little or no role in the author's portrayal of Paul. The emergence of the Pauline letters as a basis on which to define Christian religion is a later development. The Paul of Acts is not a preacher of normative Christian doctrine (doctrine preserved in texts, an impression created by the New Testament canon), but someone who preaches a religion that is suitable for establishing a place for Christians in the Greek East under the imperial domination of Rome. Speaking in Athens, the symbolic center of Greek philosophy and culture, the Paul of Acts claims Hellenistic culture as the presupposition for Christianity.[25]

The author of Lk-Acts intends to present to Theophilus, the individual addressed in his preface and presumably his literary patron,

---

[25] Acts 17:22–31; see Vielhauer, 'On the "Paulinism" of Acts,' p. 37.

an account of the origin of Christianity that separates Christianity from Judaism and establishes Christianity as a respectable religion in the Graeco-Roman world. Paul himself has become not only a Greek philosopher but also a Roman citizen in the author's account of the origin of Christianity. In the narrative of Acts, Paul's appeal to Caesar marks the decisive break between Christianity and Judaism.[26] With this appeal, Paul renounces the political and religious authority of Judaism and defines the *patria* of Christians in relationship to Rome.[27] Notwithstanding the actual historical improbability of this portrayal of Paul, the author of Lk-Acts has constructed his account of Christian origins in such a way that the religion associated with following Jesus is no longer determined by an immediate encounter with the words of Jesus (whether preserved in a written text like Mk or oral stories about Jesus, both associated as they are with Judaism) but by an understanding of the Christian's place in the history and culture of the Graeco-Roman world. This place is determined by the author's portrayal of the character of Paul. This construction of Paul's role in Christian origins seems to have been carried out not as a polemic against other Christian groups, but in relation to the failure of previous accounts of the life of Jesus to provide an adequate conception of Christianity in the context of Graeco-Roman culture.

The author of Lk-Acts ends his narrative about the early history of Christianity, 'the events that have been accomplished among us' (Lk 1:1), with Paul preaching the message of Jesus at Rome 'unhindered.'[28] Paul stands under Roman protection proclaiming the word of the

---

[26] Acts 25:9–12. The strained relations between Jews and Rome in the first and second century—evidenced by the first Jewish revolt (which led to the destruction of the temple, an event of which notice is taken in the narrative of Lk-Acts; see Lk 21:20), by the revolt of the Jews in the Diaspora under Trajan, and by the second Jewish revolt in Palestine under Hadrian—suggest a plausible context for the author's portrayal of Paul's (and thus Christians') allegiance to Rome (see especially Acts 25:10–11). On the Jewish revolts under Trajan and Hadrian, see Schürer, *The History of the Jewish People in the Age of Jesus Christ (175 B. C. - A. D. 135)*, revised English edition, 1.529–57. For possible links of the revolt in the Diaspora under Trajan to messianic expectations among the Jews, see Fuks, 'Aspects of the Jewish Revolt in A. D. 115–117,' pp. 103–4; see also Hengel, '"Messianische Hoffnung und politischer "Radikalismus" in der "jüdisch-hellenistischen Diaspora,"' pp. 668–83. The revolt under Trajan was noteworthy for its violence. See Cassius Dio *Roman History* 68.32.1–2; Eusebius *Hist. eccl.* 4.2; Fuks, 'Aspects of the Jewish Revolt in A. D. 115–117,' pp. 102–3.

[27] Contrast Mt 23:2–3: "The scribes and the Pharisees sit in the chair of Moses; therefore all that they tell you, do and observe."

[28] ἀκωλύτως.

kingdom of God. Christianity has been given a distinct history over against Judaism, the kingdom of God has been placed in the context of the Roman Empire, and the narrative ends. Christian existence has been defined in relation to the mission of Paul in the Roman Empire, not the life of Jesus associated as it was with Palestine and Jerusalem. There is no need for a third volume.

For the author of Lk-Acts, the apostles and Paul are not transparent conveyers of the gospel as proclaimed by Jesus, but are themselves decisive figures in the history of the proclamation of the kingdom of God—a proclamation that leads from the Judaism of Jesus to the Christianity of Paul. Though the author of Lk-Acts shared with other second-century writers an interest in the role of the apostles in the origin of Christianity, his particular solution was distinctive in the second century. In contrast to those who would come after him, his construction of Christian origins in relation to Paul and the apostles was not yet an apologetic history of texts, certainly not texts in a canon. On the other hand, his appeal to the standards for historiography of Hellenistic culture to understand Christianity in relation to Judaism set him apart from his predecessors. To be sure, later second-century authors carried on the apologetic defense of Christianity in the context of Hellenistic culture. However, their arguments for Christianity were cast in terms of the ancient history of culture posed as an alternative between the two great givers of culture, Homer and Moses.[29] In this apologetic defense of Christianity, the historical problem of the (recent) relationship of Christianity to Judaism was glossed over as Christian apologists claimed the Jewish scriptures as the basis for the antiquity of Christianity. Attempts to define specifically Christian origins in relation to Judaism and the Jewish scriptures became a matter of inner-Christian polemics in which particular constructions of Christian origins were correlated with collections of authoritative texts. In this inner-Christian dispute about the origin of Christianity, the two-volume narrative of Lk-Acts in fact played a decisive role; it did not, however, do so on its own terms, but as it served the needs of later Christians. The two volumes were separated and emerged as the Gospel according to Luke and the Acts of the Apostles.

Sometime around 140, the Christian Marcion proposed a theological standard for reconstructing Christian origins based on a collection

---

[29] See Droge, *Homer or Moses?*, e.g., pp. 9–11.

of Pauline letters.[30] Marcion deduced from the Pauline letters of his collection that the God of the Jews was not the same as the God of the Christians. Prior to Marcion, there is evidence for the circulation of some of the Pauline letters, but there is nothing that suggests these letters shared a status equal to traditions about Jesus.[31] According to Marcion, however, Paul alone preached the true Gospel proclaimed by Jesus. In a manner not unlike Luther of the Protestant reformation, Marcion identified the struggle he saw in Paul's letters between Paul and the Judaizers (the archetypal corrupters of the Gospel) with opponents of his own time and concluded that the gospel preached by Paul had been falsified in the church. Marcion identified the other apostles as the villains in this falsification, and the root cause of the falsification was the corruption of the Christian Gospel with Judaism.[32] To recover the true Gospel preached by Jesus and Paul, Marcion rejected the Jewish scriptures and in their place edited a collection of Pauline letters and a single account of the life of Jesus to free Christianity from the influence of Judaism, which for him was the religion of a lesser God.[33]

Marcion took the decisive step of correlating a history of Christianity with a collection of texts. In so doing, he identified a single written text as an authoritative gospel.[34] Although his gospel was in fact an edited form of the first volume of Lk-Acts, Marcion did not ascribe this gospel

---

[30] Marcion was not the first to make a collection of Pauline letters. On the basis of a careful study of the Marcionite text of the Pauline letters as attested by later church fathers, Clabeaux (*A Lost Edition of the Letters of Paul*; see especially his statement of the problem, pp. 1–6) has suggested that Marcion's collection of Pauline letters was in fact based on a previously existing collection of Pauline letters. In contrast to previously existing collections of Pauline letters, Marcion's significance lies in his reconstruction of Christian origins based specifically on a collection of Pauline letters used as evidence for 'Pauline' Christianity.

[31] Polycarp, e.g., is often cited as evidence for the status of the Pauline letters prior to Marcion. Polycarp, however, collected not only Pauline letters, but also the letters of Ignatius. Ignatius and Clement of Rome both wrote letters claiming authority by virtue of their position in the church. For both, Paul is cited as a preeminent example because of his death at Rome (see chapter 4 under *Rome*), but there is no reason to suppose that either accorded a special scriptural authority to the writings of Paul. Just as Marcion's designation of a single text as an authoritative gospel is an innovation, so too is the status he accorded the Pauline letters alongside the words of Jesus. See von Campenhausen, *The Formation of the Christian Bible*, p. 153.

[32] See Tertullian *Adversus Marcionem* 1.21; Harnack, *Marcion. The Gospel of the Alien God*, p. 91.

[33] According to Marcion, Paul received the true gospel by revelation. See Irenaeus *Adv. haer.* 3.13.1; cf. Gal 1:15–16; 2 Cor 12:1–5; von Campenhausen, *The Formation of the Christian Bible*, pp. 154–55; Harnack, *Marcion. The Gospel of the Alien God*, pp. 27, 91–92.

[34] See chapter 2 under *Traditions of Authorship and Titles*.

to anyone, nor did he take any notice of the narrative of Acts. Instead, Marcion joined this gospel to a collection of Pauline letters as normative written texts, over against the Jewish scriptures and the Jewish falsification of the Gospel in the church. Marcion thus made it clear, as had the author of Lk-Acts in his own way, that texts about Jesus could not stand alone, but required a normative interpretation of apostolic tradition. For Marcion, the Pauline letters provided this interpretation.

Marcion's specific construction of Christian origins, though it gained many followers and persisted for centuries, faced several problems. First, it was based on a theological postulation of a fundamental difference between the God of the Jews and the God of the Christians, or the God of the Jewish scriptures and the God of the Christian Gospel. The importance of the Jewish scriptures for many second-century Christians could not so easily be set aside. For example, without the Jewish scriptures, Christianity had no lineage and was subject to the accusation of being a 'new' religion, something to be avoided if respect was to be gained in Hellenistic culture. Second, other texts similar to Marcion's gospel (that is, the text of Mk and the text of Mt, not to mention the text of Jn) were associated with apostles other than Paul, and many Christians were not ready to jettison Peter, John, and the rest of the apostles in favor of Paul, nor the gospels attributed to Mark and Matthew in favor of Marcion's single gospel. For many, Marcion's collection of scripture could not be a suitable basis on which to define Christianity. Third, his construction of Christian origins was a challenge to the authority of other Christian leaders.

An important intellectual response to Marcion's canon and reconstruction of Christian origins came from Irenaeus, writing about 185 from Lyons.[35] In a five-volume work, Irenaeus set out to expose and refute what he identified as knowledge falsely so-called; the work has come to be known as *Against Heresies*, and in traditional understandings of early Christianity, it has often been considered a comprehensive 'Christian' refutation of the so-called 'Gnostics.' Instead, however, it is a systematic construction of a normative Christian history to establish one form of late second-century Christianity as the true church founded on the deposit of truth left by all the apostles. This deposit was preserved in a specific collection of texts. After refuting the logic of those whom he labels heretics in volumes one and two, Irenaeus turned

---

[35] See chapter 2 under *Irenaeus*.

to the task of defining a normative apostolic tradition in book three on the basis of which he could refute the heretics' claims to be the ones preserving apostolic truth. Against Marcion, Irenaeus interpreted apostolic tradition not through the Pauline letters, but through the narrative of the second volume of Lk-Acts construed as the 'Acts of the Apostles.' Irenaeus's construction of a normative Christian history took the form of a defense of all the apostles, certain written texts attributed to them, and the bishops supposedly appointed by them and their successors. These formed a unified standard of truth against which all heresy could be intellectually driven from the church. To construct his genealogy of apostolic truth and the true preaching of the Gospel, he reconfigured the pieces of tradition that were available to him from earlier generations of Christians, filled in what was missing, and constructed a suitable account of the origin of Christianity. In this undertaking, the second volume of Lk-Acts, obscure prior to the writing of Irenaeus, became crucial. The Acts of the Apostles emerged as the decisive text for what became the construction of Christian origins preserved in the shape of the New Testament.

Marcion claimed that all the apostles but Paul had falsified the Gospel. Yet Marcion identified the Gospel of Paul with an edited form of the first volume of Lk-Acts. Marcion was not the only opponent of Irenaeus who acknowledged the value of the first volume of Lk-Acts for stories about Jesus. Whether these heretics were favorably disposed toward Paul (Valentinians) or not (certain Jewish-Christian groups who opposed Paul), this use of stories from the text of Lk provided the basis for Irenaeus to refute theories of Christian origins that set Paul over against the other apostles. Irenaeus rescued the second volume of Lk-Acts from obscurity and argued that this text, having been written by the same author who wrote a reliable gospel, demonstrated that all the apostles preached the same doctrine. Irenaeus called this text the Acts of the Apostles, a title that makes little sense in terms of the narrative of Lk-Acts. The designation, however, perfectly suited Irenaeus's apologetic against heresies. The Acts of the Apostles provided what he considered to be an irrefutable demonstration of apostolic unity in the proclamation of the Gospel. What for the author of Lk-Acts had been the second volume of a description of the historical development of Christianity out of Judaism in the context of Hellenistic culture became for Irenaeus the basis for a static construction of Christian origins based on the unity of all the apostles in the proclamation of the Gospel delivered to them by Jesus.

Specifically, the Acts of the Apostles proved two things for Irenaeus. First, since all the apostles agreed in preaching the same doctrine, all the gospels written by the apostles (or their followers) had to be in fundamental agreement. Irenaeus thus formulated the idea that the four written gospels are a normative deposit of apostolic truth on the basis of which the true Gospel could be derived. Each supplies important parts of this true Gospel. For Irenaeus, the first volume of Lk-Acts, the Gospel according to Luke in relation to the texts of Mt, Mk, and Jn, is now just one among four equals. Irenaeus supplemented his 'historical' argument for the four gospels based on the narrative of the Acts of the Apostles with the first theological argument for the normative perfection of a fourfold canon of gospels. Just as, according to Irenaeus, there are four corners of the world and the divine cherubim are four-faced, so there must be four gospels: no more, no less. Plurality and unity exist in the fourfold canon of gospels in relation to the divine perfection of the created order.[36]

Second, the Acts of the Apostles proves that Paul was in agreement with the other apostles and therefore that the Pauline letters belong alongside (and are to be interpreted in the context of) a plurality of gospels written by the other apostles. Thus the Irenaean construction of Christian origins is mirrored in the canon of four gospels from the apostles, alongside a collection of Pauline letters, held together by the Acts of the Apostles in what has become the New Testament. This construction of Christian origins was the basis for the authority of bishops who could trace their lineage to these apostles.

Irenaeus's collection of four gospels, the Acts of the Apostles, and the Pauline letters lacked one important piece of historical information. Whereas the gospels according to Mark, Matthew, and John were firmly connected to specific apostles in traditions known to Irenaeus, the texts of Lk and Acts lacked this connection. Prior to Irenaeus, the text of Lk appears to have been only loosely connected to the apostles based on the author's claim in his preface to be dependent on eyewitnesses. Its use by groups hostile to Paul suggests it was not connected to a follower of Paul. Consequently, Irenaeus not only supplied the title for the second volume of Lk-Acts, he produced a biography for the author of the Gospel according to Luke and the Acts of the Apostles. The Luke who wrote the Gospel and the Acts of the Apostles was none other than

---

[36] *Adv. haer.* 3.11.8–9.

Luke the companion of Paul, mentioned in some of the Pauline letters. This identification established the reliability of Irenaeus's construction of Christian origins.

At the beginning of book three of *Against Heresies*, Irenaeus gives his construction of Christian origins in terms of individuals and texts:[37]

> Matthew also brought forth a written gospel among the Hebrews in their own language, while Peter and Paul were proclaiming the gospel at Rome and laying the foundation of the church. After their departure, Mark, the disciple and interpreter of Peter, himself also handed down to us in writing what was proclaimed by Peter. Luke also, the companion of Paul, set down in a book the gospel preached by him. Afterwards, John, the disciple of the Lord, who also reclined on his breast, himself also published the gospel while he was staying at Ephesus in Asia.[38]

In this passage, Irenaeus fills out the information he received from Papias about Mt and Mk, adds information he has received about John, and fits Luke into the apostolic history in relation to Paul. He provides a geographical and a chronological explanation for the origin of the four gospels based on the preaching of the apostles. Most importantly, he connects Peter and Paul at Rome and thus parallels Luke as the companion of Paul with Mark as the companion of Peter. The lack of traditional information about the author of the Gospel of Luke and the Acts of the Apostles is evident in the paucity of information Irenaeus actually relates about Luke, particularly in relation to what he recounts about Mt, Mk, and Jn. He supplies this Luke with a biography derived from those Pauline letters that associate a certain Luke with Paul. This 'Pauline' Luke conveniently supports the image of Paul constructed by Irenaeus against Marcion. The supposed connection of the author of the Acts of the Apostles to Paul has caused a great deal of mischief in attempts to reconstruct Christian origins since Irenaeus. The correlation of the Acts of the Apostles with a 'Pauline' Luke has given the legacy of Paul as portrayed in

---

[37] What follows summarizes the discussion of this passage in chapter 2 above under *Traditions of Authorship and Titles*.

[38] [3.1.1] Ὁ μὲν δὴ Ματθαῖος ἐν τοῖς Ἑβραίοις τῇ ἰδίᾳ αὐτῶν διαλέκτῳ καὶ γραφὴν ἐξήνεγκεν εὐαγγελίου, τοῦ Πέτρου καὶ τοῦ Παύλου ἐν Ῥώμῃ εὐαγγελιζομένων καὶ θεμελιούντων τὴν ἐκκλησίαν. Μετὰ δὲ τὴν τούτων ἔξοδον, Μάρκος, ὁ μαθητὴς καὶ ἑρμηνευτὴς Πέτρου, καὶ αὐτὸς τὰ ὑπὸ Πέτρου κηρυσσόμενα ἐγγράφως ἡμῖν παραδέδωκεν. Καὶ Λουκᾶς δέ, ὁ ἀκόλουθος Παύλου, τὸ ὑπ' ἐκείνου κηρυσσόμενον εὐαγγέλιον ἐν βίβλῳ κατέθετο. Ἔπειτα Ἰωάννης, ὁ μαθητὴς τοῦ Κυρίου, ὁ καὶ ἐπὶ τὸ στῆθος αὐτοῦ ἀναπεσών, καὶ αὐτὸς ἐξέδωκεν τὸ εὐαγγέλιον, ἐν Ἐφέσῳ τῆς Ἀσίας διατρίβων. Cited according to the edition by Rousseau and Doutreleau, *Irénée de Lyon. Contre les hérésies* (Sources Chrétiennes).

Lk-Acts an importance in reconstructions of Christian origins that is unwarranted.

The New Testament canon of four gospels, the Acts of the Apostles, and certain Pauline letters preserves a narrow selection of early Christian texts that emerged on the basis of competing attempts to construct Christian origins in terms of Jesus and Paul. The idea that a history of early Christianity can be correlated with a specific collection of texts has its origin in second-century apologetics. The New Testament itself represents a polemical construction of Christian origins proposed at the end of the second century to bring order to a diversity of religious movements associated with Jesus. This construction of Christian origins, supported by a particular reading of the Acts of the Apostles, eventually led to the suppression of competing accounts of Jesus and the apostles and established the importance of a certain image of Jesus and Paul for understanding the origins of Christianity—in fact for the definition of Christianity itself.

The Irenaean presuppositions about Christian origins and the nature of the New Testament texts have been undermined by critical scholarship since the Enlightenment. Nevertheless, the New Testament construed either as canon or accidental collection has continued to provide the basic building blocks for the search for Christian origins and the definition of Christianity. The essentialistic notion of 'Christianity' that underpinned the apologetic construction of Christian origins in the second century continues to influence the search for Christian origins and the investigation of early Christian traditions today. To define Christian origins in terms of the choice between Jesus and/or Paul; or to define Christian origins in terms of the correlation of texts with specific genealogical constructions of orthodoxy, heresy, or trajectories; to define Christian origins in terms of the search for the originating essence of Christianity in heroic individuals and primitive beginnings is to accept uncritically the categories established by second-century Christian polemics. The importance of Paul for Christian origins is an intellectual construct of the author of Lk-Acts and Marcion, whose quite different understandings of the place of Paul in the origin of Christianity were synthesized in the Irenaean construction of Christian origins mirrored in the Christian New Testament. The preservation in the New Testament of these constructions of Christian origins centered on Paul has obscured the limits of the modern category of 'Pauline Christianity' as descriptive of historical developments in early Christianity associated with Jesus and Paul.

BIBLIOGRAPHY

Aland, Kurt, and Aland, Barbara. *The Text of the New Testament. An Introduction to the Critical Editions and to the Theory and Practice of Modern Textual Criticism*. 2nd edition, revised and enlarged. Translated by Erroll F. Rhodes. Grand Rapids: Eerdmans; Leiden: Brill, 1989.

Aland, Kurt, ed. *Synopsis Quattuor Evangeliorum*. Stuttgart: Deutsche Bibelgesellschaft, 1976.

Alexander, Loveday. 'Luke's Preface in the Context of Greek Preface-Writing.' *Novum Testamentum* 28 (1986):48–74.

———. 'The Preface to Acts and the Historians.' In *History, Literature, and Society in the Book of Acts*, pp. 73–103. Edited by Ben Witherington, III. Cambridge: Cambridge University Press, 1996.

———. *The Preface to Luke's Gospel. Literary Convention and Social Context in Luke 1:1–4 and Acts 1:1*. SNTSMS 78. Cambridge: Cambridge University Press, 1993.

Allison, Dale C. *Jesus of Nazareth. Millenarian Prophet*. Minneapolis: Fortress Press, 1998.

Anderson, Graham. *Ancient Fiction. The Novel in the Graeco-Roman World*. London and Sydney: Croom Helm; Totowa, New Jersey: Barnes & Noble Books, 1984.

———. *Lucian. Theme and Variation in the Second Sophistic*. Mnemosyne Supp. 41. Lugduni Batavorum: Brill, 1976.

Ante-Nicene Fathers, The. Translations of the Writings of the Fathers down to A.D. 325. Volume 1. *The Apostolic Fathers.—Justin Martyr.—Irenaeus*. Edited by Alexander Roberts and James Donaldson; revised and chronologically arranged by A. C. Coxe; American reprint of Edinburgh edition. Grand Rapids: Eerdmans, 1950.

Aune, David. *The New Testament and Its Literary Environment*. Library of Early Christian Literature 8. Philadelphia: Fortress Press, 1987.

———. 'The Problem of the Genre of the Gospels: A Critique of C. H. Talbert's *What is a Gospel?*' In *Gospel Perspectives. Studies of History and Tradition in the Four Gospels*. 2.9–60. Edited by R. T. France and David Wenham. Sheffield: JSOT Press, 1981.

———, editor. *Graeco-Roman Literature and the New Testament. Selected Forms and Genres*. SBLSBS 21. Atlanta: Scholars Press, 1988.

Avenarius, Gert. *Lukians Schrift zur Geschichtsschreibung*. Meisenheim/Glan: Hain, 1956.

Baird, William. *History of New Testament Research. Volume One: From Deism to Tübingen*. Minneapolis: Fortress Press, 1992.

Balch, David L. 'Acts as Hellenistic Historiography.' In *Society of Biblical Literature 1985 Seminar Papers*, pp. 429–32. Edited by Kent Harold Richards. Atlanta: Scholars Press, 1985.

———. '"...you teach all the Jews...to forsake Moses, telling them not to...observe the customs" (Acts 21:21; cf. 6:14).' In *Society of Biblical Literature 1993 Seminar Papers*, pp. 369–83. Edited by Eugene H. Lovering, Jr. Atlanta: Scholars Press, 1993.

Barr, David L., and Wentling, Judith L. 'The Conventions of Classical Biography and the Genre of Luke-Acts.' In *Luke-Acts: New Perspectives from the Society of Biblical Literature Seminar*, pp. 63–88. Edited by Charles H. Talbert. New York: Crossroad, 1984.

Barrett, C. K. *A Critical and Exegetical Commentary on the Acts of the Apostles*. Volume 1: Preliminary Introduction and Commentary on Acts I-XIV. International Critical Commentary. Edinburgh: T&T Clark, 1994.

———. *The Gospel according to St. John. An Introduction with Commentary and Notes on the Greek Text*. 2nd edition. Philadelphia: Westminster Press, 1978.
———. 'How History Should Be Written.' In *History, Literature, and Society in the Book of Acts*, pp. 33–57. Edited by Ben Witherington, III. Cambridge: Cambridge University Press, 1996.
———. *Luke the Historian in Recent Study*. A. S. Peake Memorial Lecture No. 6. London: Epworth Press, 1961.
———. 'The Third Gospel as a Preface to Acts? Some Reflections.' In *The Four Gospels. 1992. Festschrift Frans Neirynck*, 2.1451–66. Edited by F. Van Segbroeck, C. M. Tuckett, G. Van Belle, and J. Verheyden. BETL 100. Leuven: Leuven University Press, 1992.
Barton, Stephen C. 'Can We Identify the Gospel Audiences?' In *The Gospels for All Christians*, pp. 173–94. Edited by Richard Bauckham. Grand Rapids: Eerdmans, 1998.
Bauckham, Richard. 'The *Acts of Paul* as a Sequel to Acts.' In *The Book of Acts in Its Ancient Literary Setting*, pp. 105–52. The Book of Acts in Its First Century Setting, vol. 1. Edited by Bruce W. Winter and Andrew D. Clarke. Grand Rapids: Eerdmans; Carlisle: Paternoster Press, 1993.
———. 'The *Acts of Paul*: Replacement of Acts or Sequel to Acts?' In *The Apocryphal Acts of the Apostles in Intertextual Perspectives*. Edited by Robert F. Stoops, Jr. *Semeia* 80 (1997):159–68.
———. 'For Whom Were Gospels Written?' In *The Gospels for All Christians*, pp. 9–48. Edited by Richard Bauckham. Grand Rapids: Eerdmans, 1998.
———. 'John For Readers of Mark.' In *The Gospels for All Christians*, pp. 147–72. Edited by Richard Bauckham. Grand Rapids: Eerdmans, 1998.
———, editor. *The Book of Acts in Its Palestinian Setting*. The Book of Acts in Its First Century Setting, vol. 4. Grand Rapids: Eerdmans; Carlisle: Paternoster Press, 1995.
———, editor. *The Gospels for All Christians*. Grand Rapids: Eerdmans, 1998.
Bauer, Walter. *Orthodoxy and Heresy in Earliest Christianity*. Translated by a team from the Philadelphia Seminar on Christian Origins and edited by Robert A Kraft and Gerhard Krodel. Philadelphia: Fortress Press, 1971. German: *Rechtgläubigkeit und Ketzerei im ältesten Christentum*. BHT 10. Tübingen: J. C. B. Mohr (Paul Siebeck), 1934[1], 1964[2].
Baur, F. C. 'Die Christuspartei in der korinthischen Gemeinde, der Gegensatz des petrinischen und paulinischen Christentums in der ältesten Kirche, der Apostel Petrus in Rom.' *Tübinger Zeitschrift für Theologie* 4 (1831):61–206. Reprinted in *Ferdinand Christian Baur, Ausgewählte Werke in Einzelausgaben*. Volume 1. Edited by K. Scholder. Stuttgart: Frommann, 1963.
———. *Paul, the Apostle of Jesus Christ. His life and work, his epistles, and his doctrine. A contribution to a critical history of primitive Christianity*. 2 volumes. Translated from the second German edition edited by Eduard Zeller. Revised by A. Menzies. London: Williams and Norgate, 1876. German: *Paulus, der Apostel Jesu Christi. Sein Leben und Wirken, seine Briefe und seine Lehre. Ein Beitrag zu einer kritischen Geschichte des Urchristenthums*. 2nd edition. Edited by Eduard Zeller. Leipzig: Fues, 1866.
Becker, Jürgen. *Paul: Apostle to the Gentiles*. Translated by O. C. Dean, Jr. Louisville: Westminster/John Knox Press, 1993. German: *Paulus: Der Apostel der Völker*. Tübingen: J. C. B. Mohr (Paul Siebeck), 1989.
Berger, Klaus. 'Hellenistische Gattungen im Neuen Testament.' *ANRW* (1984) II.25.2.1031–1432.
Betz, Hans Dieter. 'Christianity as Religion: Paul's Attempt at Definition in Romans.' In *Paulinische Studien. Gesammelte Aufsätze III*, pp. 206–39. Tübingen: J. C. B. Mohr (Paul Siebeck), 1994.
———. 'Jesus as Divine Man.' In *Synoptische Studien. Gesammelte Aufsätze II*, pp. 18–34. Tübingen: J. C. B. Mohr (Paul Siebeck), 1992.

———. *Lukian von Samosata und das Neue Testament. Religionsgeschichtliche und paränetische Parallelen. Ein Beitrag zum Corpus Hellenisticum Novi Testamenti.* Texte und Untersuchungen zur Geschichte der altchristlichen Literatur 76 (= 5. Reihe, Bd. 21). Berlin: Akademie-Verlag, 1961.

———. 'The Origin and Nature of Christian Faith according to the Emmaus Legend (Luke 24:13–32).' *Interpretation* 23 (1969):32–46. German: 'Ursprung und Wessen christlichen Glaubens nach der Emmauslegende (Lk. 24:13–32).' In *Synoptische Studien. Gesammelte Aufsätze II*, pp. 35–49. Tübingen: J. C. B. Mohr (Paul Siebeck), 1992.

———. 'Paul's Ideas about the Origins of Christianity.' In *Paulinische Studien. Gesammelte Aufsätze III*, pp. 272–88. Tübingen: J. C. B. Mohr (Paul Siebeck), 1994.

———. 'Paul's "Second Presence" in Colossians.' In *Texts and Contexts. Biblical Texts in Their Textual and Situational Contexts. Essays in Honor of Lars Hartman*, pp. 507–18. Edited by Tord Fornberg and David Hellholm; assisted by Christer D. Hellholm. Oslo: Scandinavian University Press, 1995.

———. *2 Corinthians 8 and 9. A Commentary on Two Administrative Letters of the Apostle Paul.* Hermeneia. Philadelphia: Fortress Press, 1985.

———. 'The Sermon on the Mount in Matthew's Interpretation.' In *Synoptische Studien. Gesammelte Aufsätze II*, pp. 270–90. Tübingen: J. C. B. Mohr (Paul Siebeck), 1992.

Betz, Hans Dieter, and Mitchell, Margaret M. 'Corinthians, First Epistle to the,' *ABD* 1.1140.

Black, C. Clifton. *Mark: Images of an Apostolic Interpreter.* Studies on personalities of the New Testament. Columbia, S.C.: University of South Carolina Press, 1994.

———. 'The Presentation of John Mark in the Acts of the Apostles.' *Perspectives in Religious Studies* 20/3 (1993):235–54.

Blasi, Anthony J. *Making Charisma. The Social Construction of Paul's Public Image.* New Brunswick and London: Transaction Publishers, 1991.

Boismard, M.-É., and Lamouille, A. *Les Actes des deux Apôtres.* 3 volumes. Études Bibliques 12, 13, 14. Paris: J. Gabalda, 1990.

Borgen, Peder. 'From Paul to Luke. Observations toward clarification of the theology of Luke-Acts.' *Catholic Biblical Quarterly* 31 (1969):168–82.

Bovon, François. *Das Evangelium nach Lukas.* EKKNT III/1. Zürich: Benziger; Neukirchen-Vluyn: Neukirchener, 1989.

———. *Luke the Theologian. Thirty-three years of research (1950–1983).* Translated by Ken McKinney. Allison Park, Pa.: Pickwick Publications, 1987.

———. 'The Synoptic Gospels and the Noncanonical Acts of the Apostles.' *Harvard Theological Review* 81 (1988):19–36.

Bovon, François, and Junod, Eric. 'Reading the Apocryphal Acts of the Apostles.' In *The Apocryphal Acts of the Apostles.* Edited by Dennis Ronald MacDonald. *Semeia* 38 (1986):161–71.

Bowie, Ewen Lyall. 'Apollonius of Tyana: Tradition and Reality.' *ANRW* (1978) II.16.2.1652–99.

Brawley, Robert L. *Luke-Acts and the Jews: Conflict, Apology, and Conciliation.* SBLMS 33. Atlanta: Scholars Press, 1987.

———. 'Paul in Acts: Lucan Apology and Conciliation.' In *Luke-Acts: New Perspectives from the Society of Biblical Literature Seminar*, pp. 129–47. Edited by Charles H. Talbert. New York: Crossroad, 1984.

Brown, Peter. *The Body and Society. Men, Women and Sexual Renunciation in Early Christianity.* New York: Columbia University Press, 1988.

Bruce, F. F. 'The Acts of the Apostles: Historical Record or Theological Reconstruction?' *ANRW* (1985) II.25.3.2569–2603.

Bultmann, Rudolf. *The History of the Synoptic Tradition.* Translated by John Marsh.

Revised, second edition. New York: Harper & Row, 1968. German: *Die Geschichte der synoptischen Tradition*. 2nd edition. Göttingen: Vandenhoeck & Ruprecht, 1931.

Burchard, Christoph. *Der dreizehnte Zeuge. Traditions- und kompositionsgeschichtliche Untersuchungen zu Lukas' Darstellung der Frühzeit des Paulus*. FRLANT 103. Göttingen: Vandenhoeck & Ruprecht, 1970.

———. 'Paulus in der Apostelgeschichte.' *Theologische Literaturzeitung* 100 (1975):881–95.

Burridge, Richard A. *What Are the Gospels? A Comparison with Graeco-Roman Biography*. SNTSMS 70. Cambridge: Cambridge University Press, 1992.

Cadbury, Henry J. *The Book of Acts in History*. London: Adam and Charles Black, 1955.

———. 'Commentary on the Preface of Luke.' In *The Beginnings of Christianity*. Part I: The Acts of the Apostles. Volume 2: Prolegomena 2. Criticism. Appendix C, pp. 489–510. Edited by F. J. Foakes Jackson and Kirsopp Lake. London: Macmillan, 1922.

———. *The Making of Luke-Acts*. New York: The Macmillan Company, 1927.

———. '"We" and "I" Passages in Luke-Acts.' *New Testament Studies* 3 (1957):128–32.

Callan, Terrance. 'The Preface of Luke-Acts and Historiography.' *New Testament Studies* 31 (1985):576–81.

Cameron, Averil. *Christianity and the Rhetoric of Empire. The Development of Christian Discourse*. Sather Classical Lectures 55. Berkeley: University of California Press, 1991.

Campbell, Thomas H. 'Paul's "Missionary Journeys" as Reflected in His Letters.' *Journal of Biblical Literature* 74 (1955):80–87.

Campenhausen, Hans von. *The Formation of the Christian Bible*. Translated by J. A. Baker. Philadelphia: Fortress Press, 1972. German: *Die Entstehung der christlichen Bibel*. Tübingen: J. C. B. Mohr (Paul Siebeck), 1968.

Cancik, Hubert. 'Die Gattung Evangelium. Markus im Rahmen der antiken Historiographie.' In *Markus-Philologie. Historische, literargeschichtliche und stilistische Untersuchungen zum zweiten Evangelium*, pp. 85–113. Edited by Hubert Cancik. WUNT 33. Tübingen: J. C. B. Mohr (Paul Siebeck), 1984.

———. 'The History of Culture, Religion, and Institutions in Ancient Historiography: Philological Observations Concerning Luke's History.' *Journal of Biblical Literature* 116 (1997):673–95.

Cassidy, Richard J. *Society and Politics in the Acts of the Apostles*. Maryknoll, New York: Orbis Books, 1987.

Clabeaux, John J. *A Lost Edition of the Letters of Paul. A Reassessment of the Text of the Pauline Corpus Attested by Marcion*. CBQMS 21. Washington, D. C.: The Catholic Biblical Association of America, 1989.

Collingwood, R. G. *The Idea of History*. Oxford: Clarendon Press, 1946; revised edition 1993.

Collins, Adela Yarbro. *Is Mark's Gospel a Life of Jesus? The Question of Genre*. The Père Marquette Lecture in Theology 1990. Milwaukee: Marquette University Press, 1990. Reprinted in *The Beginnings of the Gospel. Probings of Mark in Context*, pp. 1–38. Minneapolis: Fortress Press, 1992.

Collins, John J. *Between Athens and Jerusalem: Jewish Identity in the Hellenistic Diaspora*. New York: Crossroad, 1983.

Conzelmann, Hans. *Acts of the Apostles A Commentary on the Acts of the Apostles*. Hermeneia. Translated by James Limburg, A. Thomas Kraabel, and Donald H. Juel; edited by Eldon Jay Epp with Christopher A. Matthews. Philadelphia: Fortress Press, 1987. German: *Die Apostelgeschichte*. 2nd edition. Tübingen: J. C. B. Mohr (Paul Siebeck), 1972.

———. *1 Corinthians. A Commentary on the First Epistle to the Corinthians*. Translated by James W. Leitch. Hermeneia. Philadelphia: Fortress Press, 1975. German: *Der erste Brief an die Korinther*. Göttingen: Vandenhoeck & Ruprecht, 1969.

———. *History of Primitive Christianity*. Translated by John E. Steely. Nashville: Abingdon

Press, 1973. German: *Geschichte des Urchristentums*. GNT 5. Göttingen: Vandenhoeck & Ruprecht, 1969.

———. 'Luke's Place in the Development of Early Christianity.' In *Studies in Luke-Acts*, pp. 298–316. Edited by Leander E. Keck and J. Louis Martyn. London: SPCK, 1968.

———. *The Theology of St. Luke*. Translated by Geoffrey Buswell. Philadelphia: Fortress Press, 1961. German: *Die Mitte der Zeit*. Tübingen: J. C. B. Mohr (Paul Siebeck), 1953¹, 1957².

Crossan, John Dominic. *The Historical Jesus. The Life of a Mediterranean Jewish Peasant*. San Francisco: HarperSanFrancisco, 1991.

Dawsey, J. M. 'The Literary Unity of Luke-Acts: Questions of Style—A Task for Literary Critics.' *New Testament Studies* 35 (1989):48–66.

Delebecque, Édouard. *Les deux Actes des Apôtres*. Études Bibliques 6. Paris: J. Gabalda, 1986.

Desjardins, Michel. 'Bauer and Beyond: On Recent Scholarly Discussions of Αἵρεσις in the Early Christian Era.' *The Second Century* 8 (1991):65–82.

Dibelius, Martin. *A Fresh Approach to the New Testament and Early Christian Literature*. The International Library of Christian Knowledge. New York: Charles Scribner's Sons, 1936.

———. *Studies in the Acts of the Apostles*. Translated by Mary Ling. New York: Charles Scribner's Sons, 1956. German: *Aufsätze zur Apostelgeschichte*. Edited by Heinrich Greeven. Göttingen: Vandenhoeck & Ruprecht, 1951.

Dihle, Albrecht. *A History of Greek Literature From Homer to the Hellenistic Period*. Translated by Clare Krojzl. London and New York: Routledge, 1994.

Dillon, Richard J. 'Previewing Luke's Project from his Prologue (Luke 1:1–4).' *Catholic Biblical Quarterly* 43 (1981):205–27.

Dormeyer, Detlev. *Evangelium als literarische und theologische Gattung*. ErFor 263. Darmstadt: Wissenschaftliche Buchgesellschaft, 1989.

———. 'Die Kompositionsmetapher "Evangelium Jesu Christi, des Sohnes Gottes" Mk 1.1. Ihre theologische und literarische Aufgabe in der Jesus-Biographie des Markus.' *New Testament Studies* 33 (1987):452–68.

Droge, Arthur J. *Homer or Moses? Early Christian Interpretations of the History of Culture*. HUT 26. Tübingen: J. C. B. Mohr (Paul Siebeck), 1989.

———. 'Josephus between Greeks and Barbarians.' In *Josephus' Contra Apionem. Studies in its Character and Context with a Latin Concordance to the Portion Missing in Greek*, pp. 115–42. Edited by Louis H. Feldman and John R. Levison. Leiden: Brill, 1996.

Dupont, Jacques. *Études sur les Actes des Apôtres*. Lectio Divina 45. Paris: Cerf, 1967.

———. *Nouvelles études sur les Actes des Apôtres*. Lectio Divina 118. Paris: Cerf, 1984.

Edwards, Douglas R. 'Acts of the Apostles and Chariton's Chaereas and Callirhoe: A Literary and Sociohistorical Study.' Ph.D. dissertation. Boston University, 1987.

———. 'Acts of the Apostles and the Graeco-Roman World: Narrative Communication in Social Context.' In *Society of Biblical Literature 1989 Seminar Papers*, pp. 362–77. Edited by David J. Lull. Atlanta: Scholars Press, 1989.

Enslin, Morton S. '"Luke" and Paul.' *Journal of the American Oriental Society* 58 (1938):81–91.

Epp, Eldon J. 'The Ascension in the Textual Tradition of Luke-Acts.' In *New Testament Textual Criticism. Its Significance for Exegesis. Essays in Honor of Bruce M. Metzger*, pp. 131–45. Edited by Eldon J. Epp and Gordon D. Fee. Oxford: Clarendon Press, 1981.

———. *The Theological Tendency of Codex Bezae Cantabrigiensis in Acts*. Cambridge: Cambridge University Press, 1966.

Esler, Philip Francis. *Community and Gospel in Luke-Acts. The Social and Political Motivations of Lucan Theology*. SNTSMS 57. Cambridge: Cambridge University Press, 1987.

Evans, Ernest. *Tertullian's Homily on Baptism*. London: SPCK, 1964.

Fitzmyer, Joseph A. *The Gospel According to Luke (I-IX)*. AB 28. Garden City: Doubleday, 1981.
———. *The Gospel According to Luke (X-XXIV)*. AB 28A. Garden City: Doubleday, 1985.
Fornara, Charles William. *The Nature of History in Ancient Greece and Rome*. EIDOS. Studies in Classical Kinds. Berkeley: University of California Press, 1983.
Fuks, Alexander. 'Aspects of the Jewish Revolt in A. D. 115–117.' *Journal of Roman Studies* 51 (1961):98–104.
Fusco, Vittorio. '"Point of View" and "Implicit Reader" in Two Eschatological Texts (Lk 19,11–28; Acts 1,6–8).' In *The Four Gospels. 1992. Festschrift Frans Neirynck*, 2.1677–1696. Edited by F. Van Segbroeck, C. M. Tuckett, G. Van Belle, and J. Verheyden. BETL 100. Leuven: Leuven University Press, 1992.
Garnsey, Peter. *Social Status and Legal Privilege in the Roman Empire*. Oxford: Clarendon Press, 1970.
Gasque, W. Ward. *A History of the Interpretation of the Acts of the Apostles*. Peabody, Mass.: Hendrickson, 1989.
Gerhart, Mary. *Genre Choices, Gender Questions*. Oklahoma project for discourse and theory 9. Norman: University of Oklahoma Press, 1992.
Gill, David W. J., and Gempf, Conrad, editors. *The Book of Acts in Its Graeco-Roman Setting*. The Book of Acts in Its First Century Setting, vol. 2. Grand Rapids: Eerdmans; Carlisle: The Paternoster Press, 1994.
Goodspeed, Edgar J. 'Some Greek Notes. I. Was Theophilus Luke's Publisher?' *Journal of Biblical Literature* 73 (1954):84
Goulder, Michael D. 'Is Q a Juggernaut?' *Journal of Biblical Literature* 115 (1996):667–81.
———. *Luke: A New Paradigm*. JSNTSup 20. Sheffield: Sheffield Academic Press, 1989.
Grant, Robert M. 'The Bible of Theophilus of Antioch.' *Journal of Biblical Literature* 66 (1947):173–96; reprinted in *Christian Beginnings: Apocalypse to History*, chapter XX. London: Variorum Reprints, 1983.
Grant, Robert M., and Graham, Holt H. *The Apostolic Fathers. A New Translation and Commentary. Volume 2: First and Second Clement*. New York: Thomas Nelson & Sons, 1965.
Grässer, Erich. 'Acta-Forschung seit 1960.' *Theologische Rundschau* 41 (1976):141–94; 42 (1977):1–68.
Gundry, Robert H. 'ΕΥΑΓΓΕΛΙΟΝ: How Soon a Book?' *Journal of Biblical Literature* 115 (1996):321–25
———. *Mark. A Commentary on His Apology for the Cross*. Grand Rapids: Eerdmans, 1993.
Haenchen, Ernst. *The Acts of the Apostles. A Commentary*. Translated by Bernard Noble and Gerald Shinn, under the supervision of Hugh Anderson, and with the translation revised and brought up to date by R. McL. Wilson from the 14th German edition (Göttingen: Vandenhoeck & Ruprecht, 1965). Philadelphia: Westminster Press, 1971.
———. 'The Book of Acts as Source Material for the History of Early Christianity.' In *Studies in Luke-Acts*, pp. 258–78. Edited by Leander E. Keck and J. Louis Martyn. London: SPCK, 1968.
Hägg, Tomas. *The Novel in Antiquity*. Berkeley: University of California Press, 1983.
Hahneman, Geoffrey Mark. *The Muratorian Fragment and the Development of the Canon*. Oxford Theological Monographs. Oxford: Clarendon Press, 1992.
Halliwell, Stephen. *Aristotle. Poetics*. LCL. Cambridge, Mass.: Harvard University Press, 1995.
Harnack, Adolf von. *The Acts of the Apostles. New Testament Studies III*. Translated by J. R. Wilkinson. Crown Theological Library 27. New York: G. P. Putnam's Sons; London: Williams and Norgate, 1909. German: *Die Apostelgeschichte*. Beiträge zur Einleitung in das Neue Testament III. Leipzig: J. C. Hinrichs, 1908.

———. *The Date of the Acts and of the Synoptic Gospels. New Testament Studies IV.* Translated by J. R. Wilkinson. Crown Theological Library 33. New York: G. P. Putnam's Son; London: Williams & Norgate, 1911. German: *Neue Untersuchungen zur Apostelgeschichte und zur Abfassungszeit der synoptischen Evangelien.* Beiträge zur Einleitung in das Neue Testament IV. Leipzig: J. C. Hinrichs, 1911.

———. *Marcion: The Gospel of the Alien God.* Translated by John E. Steely and Lyle D. Bierma. Durham, N.C.: The Labyrinth Press, 1990. German: *Marcion. Das Evangelium vom fremden Gott. Eine Monographie zur Geschichte der Grundlegung der katholischen Kirche. Neue Studien zu Marcion.* Darmstadt: Wissenschaftliche Buchgesellschaft, 1985 (reprint of 1924 edition).

———. *The Origin of the New Testament and the Most Important Consequences of the New Creation.* Translated by J. R. Wilkinson. New York: Macmillan, 1925.

Harris, William V. *Ancient Literacy.* Cambridge, Mass.: Harvard University Press, 1989.

Hemer, Colin J. *The Book of Acts in the Setting of Hellenistic History.* WUNT 49. Edited by Conrad H. Gempf. Tübingen: J. C. B. Mohr (Paul Siebeck), 1989; Winona Lake, Indiana: Eisenbrauns, 1990.

Hengel, Martin. *Acts and the History of Earliest Christianity.* Translated by John Bowden. Philadelphia: Fortress Press, 1980. German: *Zur urchristlichen Geschichtsschreibung.* Stuttgart: Calwer Verlag, 1979.

———. *Between Jesus and Paul. Studies in the Earliest History of Christianity.* Translated by John Bowden. London: SCM Press, 1983.

———. *Die johanneische Frage. Ein Lösungsversuch.* WUNT 67. Tübingen: J. C. B. Mohr (Paul Siebeck), 1993.

———. *The Johannine Question.* Translated by John Bowden. London: SCM Press; Philadelphia: Trinity Press International, 1989.

———. 'Messianische Hoffnung und politischer "Radikalismus" in der "jüdisch-hellenistischen Diaspora."' In *Apocalypticism in the Mediterranean World and the Near East. Proceedings of the International Colloquium on Apocalypticism. Uppsala, August 12–17, 1979,* pp. 655–86. Edited by David Hellholm. Tübingen: J.C.B. Mohr (Paul Siebeck), 1983[1], 1989[2].

———. 'The Pre-Christian Paul.' In *The Jews among Pagans and Christians in the Roman Empire,* pp. 29–52. Edited by Judith Lieu, John North, and Tessa Rajak. London and New York: Routledge, 1992.

———. 'The Titles of the Gospels and the Gospel of Mark.' In *Studies in the Gospel of Mark,* pp. 64–84. Translated by John Bowden. Philadelphia: Fortress Press, 1985. German: *Die Evangelienüberschriften.* Heidelberg: Carl Winter, 1984.

Hills, Julian V. 'The *Acts of Paul* and the Legacy of the Lukan Acts.' In *The Apocryphal Acts of the Apostles in Intertextual Perspectives.* Edited by Robert F. Stoops, Jr. *Semeia* 80 (1997):145–58.

Hirsch, E. D., Jr. *Validity in Interpretation.* New Haven and London: Yale University Press, 1967.

Homeyer, H. *Lukian. Wie man Geschichte schreiben soll. Griechisch und Deutsch.* München: Wilhelm Fink Verlag, 1965.

Hornschuh, Manfred. *Studien zur Epistula Apostolorum.* Patristische Texte und Studien 5. Berlin: De Gruyter, 1965.

Jervell, Jacob. *The Theology of the Acts of the Apostles.* New Testament Theology. Cambridge: University Press, 1996.

———. *The Unknown Paul. Essays on Luke-Acts and Early Christian History.* Minneapolis: Augsburg Publishing House, 1984.

Johnson, Luke Timothy. *The Acts of the Apostles.* Sacra Pagina Series, volume 5. Collegeville, Minnesota: The Liturgical Press, 1992.

———. *The Literary Function of Possessions in Luke-Acts.* SBLDS 39. Missoula, Montana: Scholars Press, 1977.

———. 'On Finding the Lukan Community.' In *Society of Biblical Literature 1979 Seminar Papers*, pp. 87–100. Edited by Paul J. Achtemeier. Missoula, Montana: Scholars Press, 1979.

Jones, F. Stanley. 'An Ancient Jewish Christian Rejoinder to Luke's Acts of the Apostles: Pseudo-Clementine *Recognitions* 1.27–71.' In *The Apocryphal Acts of the Apostles in Intertextual Perspectives*. Edited by Robert F. Stoops, Jr. *Semeia* 80 (1997):185–206.

———. *An Ancient Jewish Christian Source on the History of Christianity. Pseudo-Clementine Recognitions 1.27–71*. Texts and Translations 37. Christian Apocrypha Series 2. Atlanta: Scholars Press, 1995.

Josephus. Translated by H. St. J. Thackeray, Ralph Marcus, Allen Wikgren, and Louis H. Feldman. 9 volumes. LCL. Cambridge: Harvard University Press; London: William Heinemann, 1926–1964.

Kaestli, Jean-Daniel. *L'eschatologie dans l'oeuvre de Luc. Ses caractéristiques et sa place dans le développement du christianisme primitif*. Nouvelle série théologique 22. Genève: Labor et Fides, 1969.

———. 'Les principales orientations de la recherche sur les Actes apocryphes des apôtres.' In *Les Actes apocryphes des apôtres: christianisme et monde païen*, pp. 49–67. Publications de la Faculte de théologie de l'Université de Genève, 4. Genève: Labor et Fides, 1981.

Käsemann, Ernst. 'The Disciples of John the Baptist in Ephesus.' In *Essays on New Testament Themes*, pp. 136–48. Translated by W. J. Montague. SBT 41. Naperville, Ill.: Aec R. Allenson, 1964.

———. 'Ephesians and Acts.' In *Studies in Luke-Acts*, pp. 288–97. Edited by Leander E. Keck and J. Louis Martyn. London: SPCK, 1968.

Katter, Calvin K. 'Luke 22:14–38: A Farewell Address.' Ph.D dissertation. University of Chicago, 1993.

Kent, Thomas L. 'The Classification of Genres.' *Genre* 16 (1983):1–20.

Knox, John. 'Acts and the Pauline Letter Corpus.' In *Studies in Luke-Acts*, pp. 279–87. Edited by Leander E. Keck and J. Louis Martyn. London: SPCK, 1968.

———. *Chapters in a Life of Paul*. Revised edition. Macon, Georgia: Mercer University Press, 1987.

———. *Marcion and the New Testament. An Essay in the Early History of the Canon*. Chicago: University of Chicago Press, 1942; reprint ed., with a new preface by the author, New York: AMS Press, 1980.

Koester, Helmut. *Ancient Christian Gospels: Their History and Development*. London: SCM Press; Philadelphia: Trinity Press International, 1990.

———. *Introduction to the New Testament. Volume 2. History and Literature of Early Christianity*. New York and Berlin: Walter De Gruyter, 1982. German: *Einführung in das Neue Testament*. Berlin: Walter De Gruyter, 1980.

Koskenniemi, Erkki. *Apollonios von Tyana in der neutestamentlichen Exegese: Forschungsbericht und Weiterführung der Diskussion*. WUNT 2.61. Tübingen: J. C. B. Mohr (Paul Siebeck), 1994.

Kümmel, Werner Georg. 'Die älteste Form des Apostoldekrets.' In *Heilsgeschehen und Geschichte. Gesammelte Aufsätze 1933–1964*, pp. 278–88. Edited by Erich Grässer, Otto Merk, and Adolf Fritz. Marburger Theologische Studien 3. Marburg: N. G. Elwert Verlag, 1965.

———. *The New Testament: The History of the Investigation of Its Problems*. Translated by S. McLean Gilmour and Howard C. Kee. Nashville: Abingdon Press, 1972. German: *Das Neue Testament: Geschichte der Erforschung seiner Probleme*. 2nd edition. Freiburg/München: Verlag Karl Alber, 1970.

Lake, Kirsopp. *Eusebius. The Ecclesiastical History*. LCL. Cambridge, Mass.: Harvard University Press; London: William Heinemann, 1926.

Lake, Kirsopp, and Cadbury, Henry. *The Beginnings of Christianity*. Part I: The Acts of the Apostles. Volume 4: English Translation and Commentary; volume 5: Additional Notes to the Commentary. Edited by F. J. Foakes Jackson and Kirsopp Lake. London: Macmillan, 1933.

Lauenstein, Ursula von. *Der griechische Alexanderroman. Rezension Γ. Buch I*. Beiträge zur klassischen Philologie 4. Meisenheim am Glan: Hain, 1962.

Lentz, John C., Jr. *Luke's Portrait of Paul*. SNTSMS 77. Cambridge: Cambridge University Press, 1993.

Levinskaya, Irina. *The Book of Acts in Its Diaspora Setting*. The Book of Acts in Its First Century Setting, volume 5. Grand Rapids: Eerdmans; Carlisle: Paternoster Press, 1996.

Lindemann, Andreas. *Paulus im ältesten Christentum. Das Bild des Apostels und die Rezeption der paulinischen Theologie in der frühchristlichen Literatur bis Marcion*. BHT 58. Tübingen: J. C. B. Mohr (Paul Siebeck), 1979.

Löning, Karl. *Die Saulustradition in der Apostelgeschichte*. Neutestamentliche Abhandlungen 9. Münster: Verlag Aschendorff, 1973.

Lucian. Translated by A. M. Harmon, K. Kilburn, and M. D. Macleod. 8 volumes. LCL. Cambridge, Mass.: Harvard University Press; London: William Heinemann, 1913–1967.

Lüdemann, Gerd. *Early Christianity according to the Traditions in Acts. A Commentary*. Translated by John Bowden. Minneapolis: Fortress Press, 1989. German: *Das frühe Christentum nach den Traditionen der Apostelgeschichte. Ein Kommentar*. Göttingen: Vandenhoeck & Ruprecht, 1987.

———. *Opposition to Paul in Jewish Christianity*. Translated by M. Eugene Boring. Minneapolis: Fortress Press, 1989.

———. *Paul. Apostle to the Gentiles. Studies in Chronology*. Translated by E. Stanley Jones. Philadelphia: Fortress Press, 1984.

Luz, Ulrich. *Matthew 1–7. A Commentary*. Translated by Wilhelm C. Linss. Minneapolis: Augsburg, 1989. German: *Das Evangelium nach Matthäus. 1. Teilband. Mt 1–7*. EKKNT 1/1. Zurich: Benziger; Neukirchen-Vluyn: Neukirchener, 1985.

McCoy, W. J. 'In the Shadow of Thucydides.' In *History, Literature, and Society in the Book of Acts*, pp. 3–32. Edited by Ben Witherington, III. Cambridge: Cambridge University Press, 1996.

MacDonald, Dennis Ronald. 'Apocryphal and Canonical Narratives about Paul.' In *Paul and the Legacies of Paul*, pp. 55–70. Edited by William S. Babcock. Dallas: Southern Methodist University Press, 1990.

———. *The Legend and the Apostle. The Battle for Paul in Story and Canon*. Philadelphia: Westminster, 1983.

———. 'Which Came First? Intertextual Relationships Among the Apocryphal Acts of the Apostles.' In *The Apocryphal Acts of the Apostles in Intertextual Perspectives*. Edited by Robert F. Stoops, Jr. *Semeia* 80 (1997):11–42.

McDonald, Lee Martin. 'Anti-Marcionite (Gospel) Prologues.' *ABD* I.262–63.

MacDonald, Margaret Y. *The Pauline Churches. A Socio-Historical Study of Institutionalization in the Pauline and Deutero-Pauline Writings*. SNTSMS 60. Cambridge: Cambridge University Press, 1988.

McGiffert, A. C. 'The Historical Criticism of Acts in Germany.' In *The Beginnings of Christianity*. Part I: The Acts of the Apostles. Volume 2: Prolegomena 2. Criticism, pp. 363–95. Edited by F. J. Foakes Jackson and Kirsopp Lake. London: Macmillan, 1922.

Mack, Burton L. *The Lost Gospel. The Book of Q and Christian Origins*. San Francisco: HarperSanFrancisco, 1993.

———. *A Myth of Innocence. Mark and Christian Origins*. Philadelphia: Fortress Press, 1988.

———. *Who Wrote the New Testament? The Making of the Christian Myth*. San Francisco: HarperSanFrancisco, 1995.
Macleod, Matthew D. *Luciani opera*. Volume 3. Scriptorum Classicorum Bibliotheca Oxoniensis. Oxford: Oxford University Press, 1980.
———. 'Lucian's Relationship to Arrian.' *Philologus* 131 (1987):257–64.
Maddox, Robert. *The Purpose of Luke-Acts*. FRLANT 126. Göttingen: Vandenhoeck & Ruprecht, 1982.
Marguerat, Daniel. 'The *Acts of Paul* and the Canonical Acts: A Phenomenon of Rereading.' Translated by Ken McKinney. In *The Apocryphal Acts of the Apostles in Intertextual Perspectives*. Edited by Robert F. Stoops, Jr. *Semeia* 80 (1997):169–84.
Mason, Steve. *Josephus and the New Testament*. Peabody, Mass.: Hendrickson, 1992.
Maurer, Christian. πρᾶξις. *TDNT* 6.642–44.
Meeks, Wayne A. *The First Urban Christians. The Social World of the Apostle Paul*. New Haven and London: Yale University Press, 1983.
Metzger, Bruce M. *A Textual Commentary on the Greek New Testament. A Companion Volume to the United Bible Societies' Greek New Testament (third edition)*. Corrected edition. London and New York: United Bible Societies, 1975.
Michaelis, Wilhelm. ὁδός. *TDNT* 5.42–96.
Michel, Hans-Joachim. *Die Abschiedsrede des Paulus an die Kirche Apg 20, 17–38. Motivgeschichte und theolgische Bedeutung*. SANT 35. München: Kösel-Verlag, 1973.
Moessner, David P. 'And Once Again, What Sort of "Essence?": A Response to Charles Talbert.' In *Genre, Narrativity, and Theology*. Edited by Mary Gerhart and James G. Williams. *Semeia* 43 (1988):75–84.
———. 'The Meaning of ΚΑΘΕΞΗΣ in the Lukan Prologue as a Key to the Distinctive Contribution of Luke's Narrative among the "Many."' In *The Four Gospels. 1992. Festschrift Frans Neirynck*, 2.1513–28. Edited by F. Van Segbroeck, C. M. Tuckett, G. Van Belle, and J. Verheyden. BETL 100. Leuven: Leuven University Press, 1992.
Momigliano, Arnaldo. *The Development of Greek Biography. Four Lectures*. Cambridge, Mass.: Harvard University Press, 1971.
———. 'The Historians of the Classical World and Their Audiences: Some Suggestions.' *The American Scholar* 47 (1978):193–204.
Moscato, Mary. 'Current Theories Regarding the Audience of Luke-Acts.' *Currents in Theology and Mission* 3 (1976):355–61.
Murphy-O'Connor, Jerome. 'Paul and Gallio.' *Journal of Biblical Literature* 112 (1993):315–17.
Neyrey, Jerome H., editor. *The Social World of Luke-Acts. Models for Interpretation*. Peabody, Mass.: Hendrickson Publishers, 1991.
Nock, Arthur Darby. 'The Book of Acts.' In *Arthur Darby Nock. Essays on Religion and the Ancient World*, 2.821–32. Edited by Zeph Stewart. Cambridge, Mass.: Harvard University Press, 1972. Originally published as a review of Martin Dibelius, *Aufsätze zur Apostelgeschichte*, in *Gnomen* 25 (1953):497–506.
O'Connor, D. J. 'On Resemblance.' *Proceedings of the Aristotelian Society* 46 (1945–1946):47–76.
Ó Fearghail, Fearghus. *The Introduction to Luke-Acts: A Study of the Role of Lk 1,1–4,44 in the Composition of Luke's Two-Volume Work*. Analecta Biblica 126. Roma: Editrice Pontificio Istituto Biblico, 1991.
O'Neill, J. C. *The Theology of Acts in Its Historical Setting*. 2nd edition revised and supplemented. London: SPCK, 1970.
Oster, Richard E. 'Ephesus.' *ABD* II.542–49.
———. 'Ephesus as a Religious Center under the Principate, I. Paganism before Constantine.' *ANRW* (1990) II.18.3.1661–1728.
Overbeck, F. 'Zur Einleitung in die Apostelgeschichte.' In W. M. L. de Wette, *Kurze*

Erklärung der Apostelgeschichte., pp. XIX-LXXI. 4th edition edited by Franz Overbeck. Leipzig: Hirzel, 1870.
Parker, D. C. *Codex Bezae. An Early Christian Manuscript and Its Text*. Cambridge: Cambridge University Press, 1992.
Parsons, Mikeal C. *The Departure of Jesus in Luke-Acts. The Ascension Narratives in Context.* JSNTSup 21. Sheffield: JSOT Press, 1987.
Parsons, Mikeal C., and Pervo, Richard I. *Rethinking the Unity of Luke-Acts*. Minneapolis: Fortress Press, 1993.
Parsons, Mikeal C., and Tyson, Joseph B., editors. *Cadbury, Knox, and Talbert. American Contributions to the Study of Acts*. Atlanta: Scholars Press, 1992.
Perkins, Judith B. 'This World or Another? The Intertextuality of the Greek Romances, the Apocryphal Acts and Apuleius' *Metamorphoses*.' In *The Apocryphal Acts of the Apostles in Intertextual Perspectives*. Edited by Robert F. Stoops, Jr. Semeia 80 (1997):247–60.
Pervo, Richard I. 'Egging on the Chickens: A Cowardly Response to Dennis MacDonald and Then Some.' In *The Apocryphal Acts of the Apostles in Intertextual Perspectives*. Edited by Robert F. Stoops, Jr. Semeia 80 (1997):43–52.
———. 'A Hard Act to Follow: The *Acts of Paul* and the Canonical Acts.' *The Journal of Higher Criticism* 2/2 (1995):3–32.
———. 'Must Luke and Acts Belong to the Same Genre?' In *Society of Biblical Literature 1989 Seminar Papers*, pp. 309–16. Edited by David J. Lull. Atlanta: Scholars Press, 1989.
———. *Profit with Delight: The Literary Genre of the Acts of the Apostles*. Philadelphia: Fortress Press, 1987.
Pesch, Rudolf. *Die Apostelgeschichte*. EKKNT V/1, V/2. Zürich: Benziger; Neukirchen-Vluyn: Neukirchener, 1986.
Plümacher, Eckhard. 'Acta-Forschung 1974–1982.' *Theologische Rundschau* 49 (1984):138–53.
———. 'Die Apostelgeschichte als historische Monographie.' In *Les Actes des Apôtres: Traditions, rédaction, théologie*, pp. 457–66. Edited by Jacob Kremer. BETL 48. Gembloux: J. Duculot; Leuven: University Press, 1979.
———. 'Lukas als griechischer Historiker.' PWSup 14:235–64.
———. *Lukas als hellenistischer Schriftsteller. Studien zur Apostelgeschichte*. SUNT 9. Göttingen: Vandenhoeck & Ruprecht, 1972.
———. 'Luke. Luke as Historian.' *ABD* IV.398.
Porter, Stanley E. 'The "We" Passages.' In *The Book of Acts in Its Graeco-Roman Setting*, pp. 545–74. Edited by David W. J. Gill and Conrad Gempf. The Book of Acts in Its First Century Setting, vol. 2. Grand Rapids: Eerdmans; Carlisle: Paternoster Press, 1994.
Powell, Mark Allan. *What Are They Saying About Acts?* New York and Mahwah, New Jersey: Paulist Press, 1991.
Praeder, Susan Marie. 'Luke-Acts and the Ancient Novel.' In *Society of Biblical Literature 1981 Seminar Papers*, pp. 269–92. Edited by Kent Harold Richards. Chico, Ca.: Scholars Press, 1981.
———. 'The Problem of First Person Narration in Acts.' *Novum Testamentum* 39 (1987):193–218.
Rajak, Tessa, and Noy, David. 'ARCHISYNAGOGOI: Office, Title and Social Status in the Graeco-Jewish Synagogue.' *Journal of Roman Studies* 83 (1993):75–93.
Rapske, Brian. *The Book of Acts and Paul in Roman Custody*. The Book of Acts in Its First Century Setting, volume 3. Grand Rapids: Eerdmans; Carlisle: Paternoster Press, 1994.
Rawson, Elizabeth. *Intellectual Life in the Late Roman Republic*. Baltimore: Johns Hopkins University Press, 1985.

Reasoner, Mark. 'The Theme of Acts: Institutional History or Divine Necessity in History?' *Journal of Biblical Literature* 118 (1999):635–59.

Regner, Friedemann. *"Paulus und Jesus" im 19. Jahrhundert. Beiträge zur Geschichte des Themas "Paulus und Jesus" in der neutestamentlichen Theologie.* Studien zur Theologie und Geistesgeschichte des neunzehnten Jahrhunderts 30. Göttingen: Vandenhoeck & Ruprecht, 1977.

Robbins, Vernon K. 'Prefaces in Greco-Roman Biography and Luke-Acts.' In *Society of Biblical Literature 1978 Seminar Papers*, 2.193–207. Edited by Paul J. Achtemeier. Missoula, Montana: Printing Department, University of Montana, 1978.

——. 'The Social Location of the Implied Author of Luke-Acts.' In *The Social World of Luke-Acts. Models For Interpretation*, pp. 305–32. Edited by Jerome H. Neyrey. Peabody, Mass.: Hendrickson, 1991.

Robinson, James M. *The Problem of History in Mark*. Studies in Biblical Theology 21. Naperville, Illinois: Alec R. Allenson, 1957.

Robinson, James M., and Koester, Helmut. *Trajectories through Early Christianity*. Philadelphia: Fortress Press, 1971.

Ropes, James Hardy. *The Beginnings of Christianity*. Part I: The Acts of the Apostles. Volume 3: The Text of Acts. Edited by F. J. Foakes Jackson and Kirsopp Lake. London: Macmillan, 1926.

Rordorf, Willy. 'Paul's Conversion in the Canonical Acts and in the *Acts of Paul*.' Translated by Peter W. Dunn. In *The Apocryphal Acts of the Apostles in Intertextual Perspectives*. Edited by Robert F. Stoops, Jr. *Semeia* 80 (1997):137–44.

Rousseau, Adelin, and Doutreleau, Louis. *Irénée de Lyon. Contre les hérésies. Livre III.* 2 volumes. Sources Chrétiennes. Paris: Les Éditions du Cerf, 1974.

Sacks, Kenneth. 'Rhetoric and Speeches in Hellenistic Historiography.' *Athenaeum* 64 (1986):383–95.

Sanders, Jack T. *The Jews in Luke-Acts*. Philadelphia: Fortress Press, 1987.

——. 'The Salvation of the Jews in Luke-Acts.' In *Luke-Acts: New Perspectives from the Society of Biblical Literature Seminar*, pp. 104–28. Edited by Charles H. Talbert. New York: Crossroad, 1984.

Schmidt, Daryl. 'The Historiography of Acts: Deuteronomistic or Hellenistic?' In *Society of Biblical Literature 1985 Seminar Papers*, pp. 417–27. Edited by Kent Harold Richards. Atlanta: Scholars Press, 1985.

Schmithals, Walter. 'Die Bedeutung der Evangelien in der Theologiegeschichte bis zur Kanonbildung.' In *The Four Gospels. 1992. Festschrift Frans Neirynck*, 1.129–58. Edited by F. Van Segbroeck, C. M. Tuckett, G. Van Belle, and J. Verheyden. BETL 100. Leuven: Leuven University Press, 1992.

Schmitt, Wolfgang Oskar. 'Bemerkungen zu Lukians Schrift *Wie man Geschichte schreiben muß*.' *Klio* 66 (1984):443–55.

Schneemelcher, Wilhelm. 'The Acts of Paul.' In *New Testament Apocrypha*. Revised edition edited by Wilhelm Schneemelcher (1992), 2.213–270.

——. 'The Acts of Peter.' In *New Testament Apocrypha*. Revised edition edited by Wilhelm Schneemelcher (1992), 2.275.

——. 'Gospels. Non-Biblical Material about Jesus. Introduction.' In *New Testament Apocrypha*. Revised edition edited by Wilhelm Schneemelcher (1991), 1.77–87.

——, editor. *New Testament Apocrypha*. 2 volumes. Revised edition. Translation edited by R. McL. Wilson. Cambridge: James Clark; Louisville: Westminster/John Knox Press, 1991, 1992.

Schneider, Gerhard. *Die Apostelgeschichte*. HTKNT V/1, V/2. Freiburg, Basel, Wien: Herder, 1980, 1982.

——. *Lukas, Theologe der Heilsgeschichte: Aufsätze zum lukanischen Doppelwerk*. Bonner biblische Beiträge 59. Königstein/Ts.-Bonn: P. Hanstein, 1985.

Schoeps, Hans-Joachim. *Jewish Christianity. Factional Disputes in the Early Church.* Translated by Douglas R. A. Hare. Philadelphia: Fortress Press, 1969.

Schürer, Emil. *The History of the Jewish People in the Age of Jesus Christ (175 B. C. – A. D. 135).* A new English version revised and edited by Geza Vermes and Fergus Millar. Volume 1. Edinburgh: T. & T. Clark, 1973.

Schürmann, Heinz. 'Das Testament des Paulus für die Kirche: Apg 20,18–35.' In *Unio Christianorum: Festschrift für Erzbischof Dr. Lorenz Jaeger zum 70. Geburtstag am 23. September 1962.* Edited by Othmar Schilling and Heinrich Zimmermann. Paderborn: Bonifacius-Druckerei, 1962.

Schüssler Fiorenza, Elisabeth. 'Miracles, Mission, and Apologetics: An Introduction.' In *Aspects of Religious Propaganda in Judaism and Early Christianity*, pp. 1–25. University of Notre Dame Center for the Study of Judaism and Christianity in Antiquity 2. Edited by Elisabeth Schüssler Fiorenza. Notre Dame: University of Notre Dame Press, 1976.

Schwartz, Daniel R. 'The End of the Line: Paul in the Canonical Book of Acts.' In *Paul and the Legacies of Paul*, pp. 1–24. Edited by William S. Babcock. Dallas: Southern Methodist University Press, 1990.

Segal, Alan F. *Paul the Convert. The Apostolate and Apostasy of Paul the Pharisee.* New Haven and London: Yale University Press, 1990.

Slingerland, Dixon. 'Acts 18:1–18, the Gallio Inscription, and Absolute Pauline Chronology.' *Journal of Biblical Literature* 110 (1991):439–49.

Smith, D. Moody. 'John and the Synoptics and the Question of the Gospel Genre.' In *The Four Gospels. 1992. Festschrift Frans Neirynck*, 3.1783–97. Edited by F. Van Segbroeck, C. M. Tuckett, G. Van Belle, and J. Verheyden. BETL 100. Leuven: Leuven University Press, 1992.

Smith, Jonathan Z. *Drudgery Divine. On the Comparison of Early Christianities and the Religions of Late Antiquity.* Jordan Lectures in Comparative Religion, 14; Chicago Studies in the History of Judaism. Chicago: University of Chicago Press, 1990.

———. 'Fences and Neighbors: Some Contours of Early Judaism.' In *Imagining Religion. From Babylon to Jonestown*, pp. 1–18. Chicago Studies in the History of Judaism. Chicago: University of Chicago Press, 1982.

———. 'Good News is No News: Aretalogy and Gospel.' In *Map is not Territory*, pp. 190–207. Leiden: Brill, 1978.

Spencer, F. Scott. *The Portrait of Philip in Acts. A Study of Roles and Relations.* JSNTSup 67. Sheffield: JSOT Press, 1992.

Stegemann, Wolfgang. *Zwischen Synagoge und Obrigkeit. Zur historischen Situation der lukanischen Christen.* FRLANT 152. Göttingen: Vandenhoeck & Ruprecht, 1991.

Sterling, Gregory E. *Historiography and Self-Definition. Josephos, Luke-Acts and Apologetic Historiography.* Supplements to Novum Testamentum 64. Leiden: Brill, 1992.

Stolle, Volker. *Der Zeuge als Angeklagter. Untersuchungen zum Paulusbild des Lukas.* BWANT 102. Stuttgart: Verlag W. Kohlhammer, 1973.

Stoneman, Richard. *The Greek Alexander Romance.* Translated with an Introduction and Notes. Penguin Classics. London: Penguin Books, 1991.

Stoops, Robert F., Jr. 'The *Acts of Peter* in Intertextual Context.' In *The Apocryphal Acts of the Apostles in Intertextual Perspectives.* Edited by Robert F. Stoops, Jr. *Semeia* 80 (1997):57–86.

———, editor. *The Apocryphal Acts of the Apostles in Intertextual Perspectives. Semeia* 80. Atlanta: Scholars Press, 1997.

Stowers, Stanley K. 'Comment: What Does *Unpauline* Mean?' In *Paul and the Legacies of Paul*, pp. 70–77. Edited by William S. Babcock. Dallas: Southern Methodist University Press, 1990.

Strange, W. A. *The Problem of the Text of Acts*. Cambridge: Cambridge University Press, 1992.
Strecker, Georg. *Das Judenchristentum in den Pseudoklementinen*. 2nd edition. Texte und Untersuchungen zur Geschichte der altchristlichen Literatur 70. Berlin: Akademie-Verlag, 1981.
Sundberg, Albert C., Jr. 'Canon Muratori: A Fourth-Century List.' *Harvard Theological Review* 66 (1971):1–41.
Tajra, H. W. *The Trial of St. Paul. A Juridical Exegesis of the Second Half of the Acts of the Apostles*. WUNT 2.35. Tübingen: J. C. B. Mohr (Paul Siebeck), 1989.
Talbert, Charles H. 'The Acts of the Apostles: Monograph or *Bios*?' In *History, Literature, and Society in the Book of Acts*, pp. 58–72. Edited by Ben Witherington, III. Cambridge: Cambridge University Press, 1996.
——. *Literary Patterns, Theological Themes and the Genre of Luke-Acts*. SBLMS 20. Missoula, Montana: Scholars Press, 1974.
——. 'Once Again: Gospel Genre.' In *Genre, Narrativity, and Theology*. Edited by Mary Gerhart and James G. Williams. *Semeia* 43 (1988):53–73.
——. *Reading Acts. A Literary and Theological Commentary on the Acts of the Apostles*. Reading the New Testament. New York: Crossroad Publishing Company, 1977
——. *What is a Gospel? The Genre of the Canonical Gospels*. Philadelphia: Fortress Press, 1977.
——, editor. *Luke-Acts. New Perspectives from the Society of Biblical Literature Seminar*. New York: Crossroad, 1984.
Tannehill, Robert C. *The Narrative Unity of Luke-Acts: A Literary Interpretation*. 2 volumes. Foundations and Facets. Philadelphia: Fortress Press, 1986; Minneapolis: Fortress Press, 1990.
Thomas, Christine M. 'Canon and Antitype: The Relationship Between the *Acts of Peter* and the New Testament.' In *The Apocryphal Acts of the Apostles in Intertextual Perspectives*. Edited by Robert F. Stoops, Jr. *Semeia* 80 (1997):185–206.
Thornton, Claus-Jürgen. *Der Zeuge des Zeugen. Lukas als Historiker der Paulusreisen*. WUNT 56. Tübingen: J. C. B. Mohr (Paul Siebeck), 1991.
Trocmé, Étienne. *Le "Livre des Actes" et l'histoire*. Études d'Histoire et de Philosophie Religieuses 45. Paris: Presses Universitaires de France, 1957.
Tyson, Joseph B. *Images of Judaism in Luke-Acts*. Columbia: University of South Carolina Press, 1992.
——. 'The Jewish Public in Luke-Acts.' *New Testament Studies* 30 (1984):574–83.
——, editor. *Luke-Acts and the Jewish People. Eight Critical Perspectives*. Minneapolis: Augsburg Publishing House, 1988.
Valantasis, Richard. 'The Nuptial Chamber Revisited: The *Acts of Thomas* and Cultural Intertextuality.' In *The Apocryphal Acts of the Apostles in Intertextual Perspectives*. Edited by Robert F. Stoops, Jr. *Semeia* 80 (1997):261–76
Van Unnik, Willem Cornelis. 'Die Apostelgeschichte und die Häresien.' *Zeitschrift für die neutestamentliche Wissenschaft* 58 (1967):240–46.
——. 'Luke's Second Book and the Rules of Hellenistic Historiography.' In *Les Actes des Apôtres: Traditions, rédaction, théologie*, pp. 37–60. Edited by Jacob Kremer. BETL 48. Gembloux: J. Duculot; Leuven: University Press, 1979.
Vielhauer, Philipp. *Geschichte der urchristlichen Literatur. Einleitung in das Neue Testament, die Apokryphen und die Apostolischen Väter*. De Gruyter Lehrbuch. Berlin and New York: Walter de Gruyter, 1975.
——. 'On the "Paulinism" of Acts.' In *Studies in Luke-Acts*. Edited by Leander E. Keck and J. Louis Martyn. London: SPCK, 1968.
Votaw, Clyde Weber. 'The Gospels and Contemporary Biographies.' *American Journal of Theology* 19 (1915):45–73, 217–49. Reprint: *The Gospels and Contemporary Biographies in the Greco-Roman World*. Facet Books. Biblical Series 27. Philadelphia: Fortress Press, 1970.

Walasky, Paul W. *'And so we came to Rome': The Political Perspective of St. Luke*. SNTSMS 49. Cambridge: Cambridge University Press, 1983.
Walton, Steve. *Leadership and Lifestyle. The Portrait of Paul in the Miletus Speech and 1 Thessalonians*. SNTSMS 108. Cambridge: Cambridge University Press, 2000.
Walzer, Richard. *Galen on Jews and Christians*. Oxford classical and philological monographs. London: Oxford University Press, 1949.
Wehnert, Jürgen. *Die Wir-Passagen der Apostelgeschichte. Ein lukanisches Stilmittel aus jüdischer Tradition*. GTA 40. Göttingen: Vandenhoeck & Ruprecht, 1989.
Wikenhauser, Alfred. *Die Apostelgeschichte und ihr Geschichtswert*. Neutestamentliche Abhandlungen VIII/3–5. Münster: Aschendorff, 1921.
——. *New Testament Introduction*. Translated by Joseph Cunningham. New York: Herder and Herder, 1958.
Wilken, Robert L. *The Christians as the Romans Saw Them*. New Haven: Yale University Press, 1984.
Williamson, G. A. *Eusebius. The History of the Church*. Penguin Classics. London: Penguin Books, 1965.
Wills, Lawrence M. 'The Depiction of the Jews in Acts.' *Journal of Biblical Literature* 110 (1991):631–54.
Winter, Bruce W., and Clarke, Andrew D., editors. *The Book of Acts in Its Ancient Literary Setting*. The Book of Acts in Its First Century Setting, volume 1. Grand Rapids: Eerdmans; Carlisle: Paternoster Press, 1993.
Wiseman, T. P. 'Practice and Theory in Roman Historiography.' *History* 66 (1981):375–93.
Wisse, Frederik. 'The Use of Early Christian Literature as Evidence for Inner Diversity and Conflict.' In *Nag Hammadi, Gnosticism, and Early Christianity*, pp. 177–91. Edited by Charles W. Hedrick and Robert Hodgson, Jr. Peabody, Mass.: Hendrickson, 1986.
Witherington, Ben, III. *The Acts of the Apostles. A Socio-Rhetorical Commentary*. Grand Rapids: Eerdmans; Carlisle: Paternoster Press, 1998.
——, editor. *History, Literature, and Society in the Book of Acts*. Cambridge: Cambridge University Press, 1996.
Wrege, Hans-Theo. *Die Gestalt des Evangeliums: Aufbau und Struktur der Synoptiker sowie der Apostelgeschichte*. BBET 11. Frankfurt am Main: Lang, 1978.

INDEX OF ANCIENT LITERATURE

A. Hebrew Bible/Old Testament
B. Other Jewish Literature
C. New Testament
D. Other Christian Literature
E. Graeco-Roman Literature

A. HEBREW BIBLE/OLD TESTAMENT

Chronicles (Septuagint)
- 12:15   41
- 13:22   41
- 28:26   41

Isaiah
- 49:6   153

Jeremiah
- 31:31–34   92

Joel
- 2:28–32   90

B. OTHER JEWISH LITERATURE

Josephus
  Against Apion
- 1.1   71–72, 74
- 1.44–56   71
- 1.46   70
- 1.53   72, 77
- 1.53–54   71
- 1.53–55   77
- 1.53–56   70
- 1.55   70
- 2.1   74

  Antiquities
- 1.2   72
- 1.4   72
- 1.8–9   74
- 14.68   41
- 18.11–25   80

  Jewish War
- Preface   70, 74
- 1.1   71
- 1.1–3   70–71
- 1.1–4   72
- 1.1–6   72
- 1.2   69
- 1.13–16   71
- 1.14–18   71–72
- 1.15   72
- 1.16   72, 77
- 1.17–18   71, 77
- 1.17–38   70
- 1.18   70-71, 78
- 1.25   157
- 1.30   72
- 2.119   80
- 2.266–70   137
- 2.313   114
- 2.487   137

  Life
- 3   76
- 10–12   80
- 13–16   153
- 15   153
- 113   80
- 336–67   72, 74–75
- 361–67   74
- 430   74

Letter of Aristeas
- 1–8   74

C. NEW TESTAMENT

Matthew		1:1–4	4, 20, 29–30, 39, 60–
1:1	32		61, 65–66, 69–72, 78,
1:1–17	165		81, 95–96, 100, 103,
1:22	165		109–110, 118–119,
2:17	165		127, 147, 162
10:5–6	166	1:2	23, 30, 32–33, 39,
10:5–42	148		55, 60, 70, 74, 76–77,
10:37–39	53		79–80, 83–84, 89,
16:18	59, 168		95–96, 98, 102,
16:18–19	32		144–145
18:15–18	32	1:3	9, 59, 73, 79–80, 84,
18:15–20	59		144
19:28	92	1:3–4	146–147
23:2–3	173	1:4	70, 77, 79, 81, 83, 96,
27:52–53	89		100, 102, 104, 119,
28:16–20	59, 165		126
28:19	166	1:5	77, 81, 119
28:19–20	148	1:5–25	83, 96
		1:10	99
Mark		1:11–38	82
1:1	30, 42, 59, 79, 165–166	1:16–17	78
		1:26–38	83
1:1–2	32, 74	1:30–33	96
1:2	79, 165	1:32	78, 90
1:7–8	119	1:33	88
1:14	165	1:46–55	96
2:15	125	2:1–2	74, 80
2:18	119	2:14	17
6:1–6	133	2:25–38	78, 83, 90, 96, 99
9:38–40	122	3:1	74, 80
13	85	3:1–18	119
13:8	85	3:2	83
13:9–13	85–86	3:15–17	90
13:10	85	3:15–18	83
13:14	85	3:16	115
13:24	86	3:23–38	83, 100
13:37	85	4	150
14:10	101	4:1–19:27	109
14:22	90	4:14–30	150
14:25	91	4:16–28	79
16:8	87	4:16–30	127, 133
16:9–20	12	4:23	133
		5:29	125
Luke		6:20–22	52
1:1	30, 32, 34, 55, 59, 60–61, 69, 70–72, 74–76, 78, 80, 84–85, 96, 102, 126	7:11	125
		7:18–35	119
		9:1–5	151
		9:49–50	122
1:1–2	100	10:1–16	150

INDEX OF ANCIENT LITERATURE

13:14	131	24:25–27	93
13:28–30	92	24:26	93
16:16	78, 83, 85, 89–90, 116	24:27	141
		24:30	93
17:20–21	94	24:30–31	93
17:21	92	24:31	93
18:9–14	99	24:35	93–94
19:41–48	86	24:36	94
19:45–48	99	24:36–43	94
21	85	24:41–43	94
21:5–36	86	24:44	32, 69, 82
21:12	85	24:44–47	81–82, 89, 93, 141
21:12–13	127, 153	24:44–48	83
21:12–19	24, 85–86	24:44–49	77, 88, 94
21:12–20	87	24:46	83
21:15	86	24:47	88
21:20	86, 173	24:49	17, 24
21:20–24	85–86	24:52	24
21:24	87, 100		
21:25	87	**John**	
21:25–28	87	1–20	169
21:28	93	1:14	32
21:29–36	87	3:11	32, 59
22:3	101	13:27	101
22:7–38	130	20:19–23	59
22:14–18	91	21:24	32, 167
22:14–38	85, 88		
22:15	91–92	**Acts**	
22:16	91–92	1–15	110
22:16–20	92	1:1	33, 42, 59, 60, 72–73, 76, 84, 102
22:17	91–92	1:1–2	29–30, 60–61, 101, 103, 158
22:17–18	93	1:3	84, 88, 94
22:17–20	92	1:3–5	90
22:18	91	1:4	93
22:19	90	1:5	90, 115, 119
22:19–20	91–92	1:6	88–89, 90, 93, 95, 157
22:20	94	1:6–8	94
22:24–27	92, 101	1:7–8	90
22:24–30	95	1:8	17, 84, 88, 98, 127, 144, 153–154, 158
22:28	101	1:11	88, 102
22:28–30	92	1:13	159
22:29	94, 130	1:15–20	101
22:29–30	101	1:15–26	81, 83
22:30	92, 94	1:21–22	84, 170
22:30–32	130	1:21–25	42
22:31	101	1:26	82, 159
22:31–32	102	2	127, 150
24	12	2–3	86
24:13–15	92		
24:18–21	93		
24:20	93–94		
24:22–23	93		

2:14–36	63	8:14–25	147
2:14–40	94	8:17–19	119
2:16–21	90	8:18–24	101
2:22	91	8:23	101, 149
2:22–36	82, 87	8:36	158
2:23	86	8:38	48, 158
2:23–24	83–84	9	156
2:23–33	98	9:1–2	111
2:29–36	94	9:1–19	82, 135, 158
2:30–36	90	9:1–22	160
2:32	91	9:1–31	110
2:33	115–116	9:2	97
2:36	91, 93	9:10–19	160
2:37–47	158	9:11	160
2:38	90, 142	9:15	60, 83–84, 89, 127, 147, 153, 158
2:38–40	89		
2:39	88	9:15–16	148
2:42	92	9:16	98, 128, 159
2:44	142	9:18	48, 158
3	150	9:22	86
3:2–5	156	9:26–30	110
3:12–26	88	9:27	149
3:17–26	87, 90, 94	9:36	156
3:19–21	89	10:1–33	135
3:19–26	88	10:1–48	82
3:25–26	86	10:1–11:18	87, 110, 147
4:7–22	86	10:2	156
4:32	89	10:9–29	89
5:3	101	10:41	91, 93–94
5:17	97	10:47	90
5:29	27	11:1–18	81, 89, 135
6:1–5	84	11:2–3	89
6:1–6	81	11:15–17	115
6:1–7	147	11:16	115, 119
6:5	115	11:17	89
6:8–10	86	11:19–29	110
6:8–14	99	11:20–21	161
6:8–8:1	99	11:25	149
6:10	115	11:25–26	89
6:11–14	157	11:25–29	111
6:12–14	125	11:26	97
6:14	157	11:27–30	82, 156
7	84, 99, 127, 158	11:28	80
7:2–53	63	12:1–19	142
7:44–53	99–100	12:3–19	159
7:47–53	157	12:19	143
7:48	125	13–14	110–111, 149–150, 156
7:48–53	86, 99, 158	13:1–3	82, 149
8	149	13:1–14:28	110
8:1	111, 125	13:4–12	126, 149
8:1–3	110	13:7	124, 149
8:4–25	126	13:9	149

13:10	101, 149	16–28	109–110, 113, 144
13:12	124	16:1–3	140, 145
13:13	34	16:6–8	144
13:13–41	121	16:6–10	127
13:13–42	79	16:8–11	129
13:13–52	150	16:9–10	82, 135
13:13–14:28	140	16:10	110, 143
13:15	131, 134	16:10–17	35
13:16–41	63, 127, 121	16:11–15	143
13:16–48	141	16:11–17	143
13:24–25	119	16:11–40	130
13:38–39	89	16:13	142
13:42	131	16:14–15	131
13:44–48	97, 112	16:15	120, 131
13:44–52	134	16:16	142
13:45–48	111	16:16–17	142, 144
13:46	131, 150, 158	16:16–21	142
13:46–48	87	16:16–24	143
13:47	153	16:17	97, 143
13:47–48	82	16:19–24	137
13:48	95	16:20–21	145
14	150	16:21	157
14:1–28	149	16:22–24	143
14:4	43, 84, 122	16:22–44	142–143
14:8–18	99, 121, 127, 158	16:23–24	142
14:14	43, 84, 122	16:24	142–143
14:15–17	83	16:25–34	142
14:21–23	84, 101	16:25–40	142
14:22	87, 89, 130	16:27–34	143
14:22–23	94–95	16:31–34	158
14:23	128	16:35	142, 153
15	84, 111	16:35–39	143
15:1	157	16:37	145
15:1–5	89	16:40	120, 125, 129, 131, 142–143
15:1–29	151		
15:1–35	81	17:1–2	132
15:5	97	17:1–4	140
15:7–11	110	17:1–5	112, 140
15:12	110, 151	17:1–15	128, 141
15:13–18	87	17:2–3	114
15:13–21	63	17:2–13	141
15:16–18	90	17:4	141
15:17	147	17:5	111, 140–141
15:19–21	157	17:5–9	110, 137, 140
15:20	27	17:6	134, 140, 142
15:21	157	17:10	125, 132, 140
15:29	27	17:10–11	114
15:36–40	34	17:11	140
15:36–41	81, 149	17:12	141
16	143, 145	17:13	111, 141
16–20	109–110, 128, 144–146, 155–156	17:14	125, 142
		17:14–15	132, 141

202   INDEX OF ANCIENT LITERATURE

17:16–31	121		120, 122–123, 126, 133, 137
17:17	125		
17:22–31	56, 99, 127, 158, 172	18:24–19:7	119–121
17:22–34	99	18:25	70, 97, 115
17:24–31	83, 99	18:26	97, 113, 116
17:31	83, 87–88, 90–91	18:26–27	112
17:34	131, 142	18:27	128–129, 131
18	38	19:1	112, 118–119, 129, 132
18–19	128	19:1–7	90, 112, 116, 118–119, 126, 128
18:1	132		
18:1–3	131		
18:1–8	131, 134–135	19:1–8	132
18:1–11	135	19:2–4	126
18:1–17	131	19:4	119
18:2	132–133	19:5	119
18:2–3	113, 117, 125, 131–133, 152	19:6	119
		19:7	118
18:3	120, 132	19:8	112, 116, 120, 132
18:4	132	19:8–10	112, 120–121, 140
18:4–5	114, 132	19:8–40	116
18:4–8	134, 140	19:8–20:1	112
18:5	141	19:9	97, 111–112, 120, 126, 128, 134, 158
18:5–8	112, 131		
18:6	87, 97, 111, 150, 158	19:9–10	122, 125, 129
18:7	120	19:10	84, 98, 120–121, 123, 131
18:8	131, 134–136		
18:9–10	82, 127	19:11–12	121, 122
18:9–11	131, 135	19:13	122
18:10	125	19:13–16	122, 150
18:11	120, 125	19:13–20	99, 121
18:12	125	19:15	122
18:12–16	136–137	19:17–20	101, 110
18:12–17	125, 127, 135, 137	19:18	112, 122
18:12b–15	135	19:18–20	112, 122
18:14–15	136	19:21	122–123, 125
18:15	157	19:21–22	122, 141
18:16	136	19:23	97, 125
18:17	124, 135–137	19:23–40	99, 123, 125, 158
18:18	114, 125, 132, 134, 142	19:25–27	123, 135
18:18–19	118	19:25–32	124
18:18–23	111, 113–114, 118, 123, 126, 133, 139	19:28–31	123
		19:29	124
18:18–28	133	19:30	112, 120, 124, 126, 128
18:18–20:1	128		
18:19	113, 116	19:31	124
18:19–20	112, 119	19:33	125, 136–137
18:19–21	112	19:33a	124
18:19–19:7	112	19:33–40	124
18:19–20:1	111	19:34	124
18:22–23	149	20:1	112, 120, 125–126, 128–129, 142–143
18:24	133		
18:24–28	110, 112–114, 117–118,	20:1–3	129, 131

20:1–4	112	21:17	110
20:2	129	21:17–18	152
20:4	122, 143, 152	21:17–25	155
20:4–5	142, 144	21:18	144
20:4–6	120, 152	21:18–26	81
20:4–28:16	152	21:21	70, 154–155, 157
20:5	110, 143	21:27–29	155, 157
20:5–8	144	21:22–26	157
20:5–21:18	35	21:23–24	114
20:7–12	129	21:24	70, 154
20:8	144	21:26	155
20:13–16	144	21:28	125, 154–155, 157
20:16	156	21:37–40	153
20:17	84, 125–126, 128–129	22	159
		22–26	143, 159
20:17–21	128	22:1–21	158
20:17–35	19, 84, 96, 121, 127–128	22:2–22	99
		22:3	157
20:17–38	60, 144	22:4	97
20:19	128	22:6–11	135
20:20	129	22:14–15	158
20:20–21	84	22:15	127, 153
20:21	83–84, 88, 120	22:16	158
20:22–24	96, 128, 148, 159	22:17–21	82, 99, 135, 157–158
20:24	83		
20:25	83, 88, 95, 98, 157, 159	22:20	99, 125, 148, 158
		22:21	147
20:25–27	89	22:22	155
20:25–32	94	22:22–29	143, 145
20:27	82–84, 95	22:25–29	143
20:28	84, 91, 94	23:1–5	155
20:28–31	130	23:1–10	119
20:28–32	101	23:6–10	97
20:29–30	146	23:11	127, 153
20:29–32	72, 128	23:12	155
20:30	127	24:1–9	155
20:31	129	24:6	157
20:32	83, 87, 95, 100, 130	24:12–21	157
		24:14	97
20:34	133	24:17	123, 154–156
20:34–35	128	24:22	97
20:37–38	96, 159	24:24–25	83
20:38	128	25:1–12	157
21	110–111	25:8	157
21–26	154	25:9–12	98, 173
21–28	110, 148, 156	25:10–11	143, 145, 158, 173
21:1–18	144		
21:7–14	128	25:10–12	111
21:10–14	82, 148, 159	25:13–26:32	124
22:12–13	153	26	159
21:12–14	97	26:2	86, 98
21:13	55–56, 98	26:3	157

203

26:4–23	157	28:30–31	81, 83–84, 87, 94, 157
26:5	97	28:31	86, 88, 95, 100, 102, 115, 125, 127
26:6	77, 89		
26:6–7	88		
26:6–8	88		
26:9–11	86	Romans	
26:9–18	158	1:14–16	148
26:12–19	135	2:9–10	148
26:16	127, 153	3:1–9	148
26:17–18	158	3:8	155
26:19–23	157	3:24f	95
26:22	127	5:9	95
26:22–23	153	9–11	148
26:24	49	12:11	115
26:25–29	72, 76, 80	15:22–24	161
26:26	80, 103, 162	15:22–29	123, 147
26:27	77	15:22–33	154
26:27–28	89	15:25–32	147, 154, 156
26:27–29	142	15:26	154
26:28	97	15:26–28	120
26:28–29	89	15:27	148
26:30–32	98	15:31a	155
26:32	111	15:31b	155
27–28	154	16	117, 127
27:1–28:16	35, 130	16:3	117
27:2	152	16:3–5	117, 120, 133
27:2–28:16	144	16:14	38
27:21–26	135	16:17–20	117, 126–127
27:23–25	82		
27:24	153	1 Corinthians	
27:42–44	153	1	38
28	142	1–4	115
28:4–6	153	1:1	136
28:7	124	1:12	115–116
28:7–10	149, 153	1:14	134
28:14–15	152	1:22–24	148
28:14–16	152	2:1–3:23	115
28:15	152, 154	3:1–23	116
28:15–31	49	3:4–6	115
28:16	110	3:9	117
28:17	155, 157–158	3:22	115
28:17–28	152	4:6	115
28:17–31	152	7:1	55
28:21	49	7:10	166
28:21–22	152, 154	9:19–23	135
28:23–28	82, 100, 111	9:20	148
28:23–31	86–88, 97, 112	10:16	95
28:25–28	86, 69, 131, 141, 148, 158	10:32	148
28:28	86, 95, 150	10:32–33	135
28:28–31	95	11:25	95
28:30	120, 131	12:13	148
		14:34–35	45, 48

15:32	125		2:11–14	135, 148–149, 161
16:8–9	120		3:26–28	48
16:9	127			
16:12	115	Philippians		
16:15	133		4:22	76
16:19	117–118, 133			
		Colossians		
2 Corinthians			1:24	148, 161
1:5–2:4	129		4:10	34
1:8–10	125		4:14	35
2:12–13	129			
10:10	127	1 Thessalonians		
11:24	148		1:5	140
11:25	153		1:9	140, 147
12:1–5	175		3:1–2	141
			4:13–5:11	166
Galatians			4:15	166
1–2	156			
1:15–16	160, 175	2 Timothy		
1:18	160		4:11	35
1:23	160		4:19	117
1:22–23	160			
2	140, 147	Philemon		
2:1–10	116–117, 120, 134, 140, 147, 151, 155		23	35
2:1–14	154	Revelation		
2:10	151, 154		2:1–7	96, 126–127

D. OTHER CHRISTIAN LITERATURE

Acts of Paul			Clement of Alexandria, *Stromata*	
3.5–6	52, 56		5.82.4	40
3.7–21	141			
3.7–40	53		Chrysostom, *Homilies on Acts*	
3.21	54		1	49
11	54			
11.1	130		*Epistula Apostolorum* (*Ep. Ap.*)	
			2	159
Acts of Peter			15	159
1–8	18		31	148, 159, 162
34–41	54, 141		33	159
36–39	56			
37–39	53		Eusebius, *Historia ecclesiastica* (*Hist. eccl.*)	
			2.15	15
Augustine, *Homilies on John*			2.23	15
6.18	49		3.3	46, 55
			3.4.6	37, 39
1 Clement (*1 Clem.*)			3.15	38
5	18, 161		3.25	14, 46, 49, 55
44	14		3.36.1–2	167

3.39	31	3.11.7–8	29
3.39.1	38, 167	3.11.7–9	21
3.39.1–7	33	3.11.8	13–15, 21
3.39.2–17	32	3.11.8–9	16, 178
3.39.11–12	21	3.11.9	14–15, 21
3.39.15	32	3.11.9–3.14.3	17
3.39.15–16	31, 167–168	3.12	17
4.2	173	3.12.9	17
5.1	54	3.12.14	25
5.1–2	27	3.13	16
5.2.5	27	3.13–15	15
5.4–5	11	3.13.1	175
5.7	12	3.13.3	29, 42
5.8.2–4	17, 31	3.14	13
5.20.4–8	20	3.14.1	36–37, 39, 49
5.23–24	19	3.14.1–3.15.1	35
5.24	27	3.14.2	22–23
5.24.7	27	3.14.3	14, 20, 22
6.12	15	3.14.4	21–22
6.14	40	3.14.4–3.15.1	15
		3.15	14
		3.15.1	21–22, 38, 42, 57
		3.25	47
		4.6.2	16
		5.33.4	38
		6.12.2	46

Ignatius
  Ephesians (Ign. *Eph.*)
    12   14, 162

  Romans (Ign. *Rom.*)
    4   18, 162
    9   18

Irenaeus *Adversus haereses* (*Adv. haer.*)
  1.23   15
  1.3.2   23
  3   15
  3.Preface   12
  3.1   13
  3.1.1   13, 16–17, 18, 21, 24,
                  31, 35, 37, 35, 163,
                  179
  3.1.2   13
  3.2–4   13, 16
  3.2.1–3.5.1   17
  3.2.2   13–14, 17–18
  3.3   13
  3.3–4   18
  3.3.1   13, 17–18
  3.3.2–3   18
  3.3.3   20
  3.3.4   20
  3.4.1   17
  3.5.1   17, 20, 31
  3.10.1   39
  3.11.7   13–14, 17, 21, 23

Justin
  1 Apology (*1 Apol.*)
    1.26   15
    50.12   24
    66.3   14, 75, 79
    67.3–4   14, 75, 79

  2 Apology (*2 Apol.*)
    2   55

Origen
  Commentary on John
    6:36   38
  Commentary on Romans
    10:31   38

Polycarp *Philippians* (*Phil.*)
  3.2   14
  13   14

Pseudo-Clementine *Recognitions*
  1.27–71   24, 27, 56

Tertullian
  Adversus Marcionem
    1.19   168
    1.21   175
  De baptismo
    17   45, 55
    18   46

  De oratione
    16   47
  De pudicitia
    10   47

Theophilus *Ad Autolycum*
    2.34   27

E. GRAECO-ROMAN LITERATURE

Aristotle *Poetics*
    9   81–82

Cassius Dio *Roman History*
    68.32.1–2   173

Diodorus Siculus
    3.1.1   40–41

Lucian
  Alexander the False Prophet
    1   41
  How to Write History
    2   73
    4   153
    5   73
    7–13   72
    16   145
    29   153
    42   72
    47   70, 171
    51   72, 171
    55   78
    62   72

Philostratus *Life of Apollonius*
    1.2   75

Pliny *Letters*
    10.96.3   54

Polybius *Histories*
    1.1.1–1.2.8   70
    1.4   70
    1.4.3   72

Suetonius *Claudius*
    25   117

Tacitus *Annals*
    15.44   54

Thucydides *The Peloponnesian War*
    1.1   70
    1.22   72
    5.26   69

SUPPLEMENTS TO NOVUM TESTAMENTUM

ISSN 0167-9732

2. Strobel, A. *Untersuchungen zum eschatologischen Verzögerungsproblem auf Grund der spätjüdische-urchristlichen Geschichte von Habakuk 2,2 ff.* 1961. ISBN 90 04 01582 5
16. Pfitzner, V.C. *Paul and the Agon Motif.* 1967. ISBN 90 04 01596 5
27. Mussies, G. *The Morphology of Koine Greek As Used in the Apocalypse of St. John.* A Study in Bilingualism. 1971. ISBN 90 04 02656 8
28. Aune, D.E. *The Cultic Setting of Realized Eschatology in Early Christianity.* 1972. ISBN 90 04 03341 6
29. Unnik, W.C. van. *Sparsa Collecta.* The Collected Essays of W.C. van Unnik Part 1. Evangelia, Paulina, Acta. 1973. ISBN 90 04 03660 1
31. Unnik, W.C. van. *Sparsa Collecta.* The Collected Essays of W.C. van Unnik Part 3. Patristica, Gnostica, Liturgica. 1983. ISBN 90 04 06262 9
34. Hagner, D.A. *The Use of the Old and New Testaments in Clement of Rome.* 1973. ISBN 90 04 03636 9
37. Reiling, J. *Hermas and Christian Prophecy.* A Study of The Eleventh Mandate. 1973. ISBN 90 04 03771 3
43. Clavier, H. *Les variétés de la pensée biblique et le problème de son unité.* Esquisse d'une théologie de la Bible sur les textes originaux et dans leur contexte historique. 1976. ISBN 90 04 04465 5
47. Baarda, T., A.F.J. Klijn & W.C. van Unnik (eds.) *Miscellanea Neotestamentica.* I. Studia ad Novum Testamentum Praesertim Pertinentia a Sociis Sodalicii Batavi c.n. Studiosorum Novi Testamenti Conventus Anno MCMLXXVI Quintum Lustrum Feliciter Complentis Suscepta. 1978. ISBN 90 04 05685 8
48. Baarda, T., A.F.J. Klijn & W.C. van Unnik (eds.) *Miscellanea Neotestamentica.* II. 1978. ISBN 90 04 05686 6
50. Bousset, D.W. *Religionsgeschichtliche Studien.* Aufsätze zur Religionsgeschichte des hellenistischen Zeitalters. Hrsg. von A.F. Verheule. 1979. ISBN 90 04 05845 1
52. Garland, D.E. *The Intention of Matthew 23.* 1979. ISBN 90 04 05912 1
53. Moxnes, H. *Theology in Conflict.* Studies in Paul's Understanding of God in Romans. 1980. ISBN 90 04 06140 1
56. Skarsaune, O. *The Proof From Prophecy.* A Study in Justin Martyr's Proof-Text Tradition: Text-type, Provenance, Theological Profile. 1987. ISBN 90 04 07468 6
59. Wilkins, M.J. *The Concept of Disciple in Matthew's Gospel, as Reflected in the Use of the Term 'Mathetes'.* 1988. ISBN 90 04 08689 7
64. Sterling, G.E. *Historiography and Self-Definition.* Josephos, Luke-Acts and Apologetic Historiography. 1992. ISBN 90 04 09501 2
65. Botha, J.E. *Jesus and the Samaritan Woman.* A Speech Act Reading of John 4:1-42. 1991. ISBN 90 04 09505 5
66. Kuck, D.W. *Judgment and Community Conflict.* Paul's Use of Apologetic Judgment Language in 1 Corinthians 3:5-4:5. 1992. ISBN 90 04 09510 1
67. Schneider, G. *Jesusüberlieferung und Christologie.* Neutestamentliche Aufsätze 1970-1990. 1992. ISBN 90 04 09555 1
68. Seifrid, M.A. *Justification by Faith.* The Origin and Development of a Central Pauline Theme. 1992. ISBN 90 04 09521 7

69. Newman, C.C. *Paul's Glory-Christology*. Tradition and Rhetoric. 1992. ISBN 90 04 09463 6
70. Ireland, D.J. *Stewardship and the Kingdom of God*. An Historical, Exegetical, and Contextual Study of the Parable of the Unjust Steward in Luke 16: 1-13. 1992. ISBN 90 04 09600 0
71. Elliott, J.K. *The Language and Style of the Gospel of Mark*. An Edition of C.H. Turner's "Notes on Marcan Usage" together with other comparable studies. 1993. ISBN 90 04 09767 8
72. Chilton, B. *A Feast of Meanings*. Eucharistic Theologies from Jesus through Johannine Circles. 1994. ISBN 90 04 09949 2
73. Guthrie, G.H. *The Structure of Hebrews*. A Text-Linguistic Analysis. 1994. ISBN 90 04 09866 6
74. Bormann, L., K. Del Tredici & A. Standhartinger (eds.) *Religious Propaganda and Missionary Competition in the New Testament World*. Essays Honoring Dieter Georgi.1994. ISBN 90 04 10049 0
75. Piper, R.A. (ed.) *The Gospel Behind the Gospels*. Current Studies on Q. 1995. ISBN 90 04 09737 6
76. Pedersen, S. (ed.) *New Directions in Biblical Theology*. Papers of the Aarhus Conference, 16-19 September 1992. 1994. ISBN 90 04 10120 9
77. Jefford, C.N. (ed.) *The Didache in Context*. Essays on Its Text, History and Transmission. 1995. ISBN 90 04 10045 8
78. Bormann, L. *Philippi – Stadt und Christengemeinde zur Zeit des Paulus*. 1995. ISBN 90 04 10232 9
79. Peterlin, D. *Paul's Letter to the Philippians in the Light of Disunity in the Church*. 1995. ISBN 90 04 10305 8
80. Jones, I.H. *The Matthean Parables*. A Literary and Historical Commentary. 1995. ISBN 90 04 10181 0
81. Glad, C.E. *Paul and Philodemus*. Adaptability in Epicurean and Early Christian Psychagogy. 1995 ISBN 90 04 10067 9
82. Fitzgerald, J.T. (ed.) *Friendship, Flattery, and Frankness of Speech*. Studies on Friendship in the New Testament World. 1996. ISBN 90 04 10454 2
83. Tilborg, S. van. *Reading John in Ephesus*. 1996. 90 04 10530 1
84. Holleman, J. *Resurrection and Parousia*. A Traditio-Historical Study of Paul's Eschatology in 1 Corinthians 15. 1996. ISBN 90 04 10597 2
85. Moritz, T. *A Profound Mystery*. The Use of the Old Testament in Ephesians. 1996. ISBN 90 04 10556 5
86. Borgen, P. *Philo of Alexandria - An Exegete for His Time*.1997. ISBN 90 04 10388 0
87. Zwiep, A.W. *The Ascension of the Messiah in Lukan Christology*. 1997. ISBN 90 04 10897 1
88. Wilson, W.T. *The Hope of Glory*. Education and Exhortation in the Epistle to the Colossians. 1997. ISBN 90 04 10937 4
89. Peterson, W.L., J.S. Vos & H.J. de Jonge (eds.). *Sayings of Jesus: Canonical and Non-Canonical*. Essays in Honour of Tjitze Baarda. 1997. ISBN 90 04 10380 5
90. Malherbe, A.J., F.W. Norris & J.W. Thompson (eds.). *The Early Church in Its Context*. Essays in Honor of Everett Ferguson. 1998. ISBN 90 04 10832 7
91. Kirk, A. *The Composition of the Sayings Source*. Genre, Synchrony, and Wisdom Redaction in Q. 1998. ISBN 90 04 11085 2
92. Vorster, W.S. *Speaking of Jesus*. Essays on Biblical Language, Gospel Narrative and the Historical Jesus. Edited by J. E. Botha. 1999. ISBN 90 04 10779 7
93. Bauckham, R. *The Fate of Dead*. Studies on the Jewish and Christian Apocalypses. 1998. ISBN 90 04 11203 0

94. Standhartinger, A. *Studien zur Entstehungsgeschichte und Intention des Kolosserbriefs.* ISBN 90 04 11286 3 *(In preparation)*
95. Oegema, G.S. *Für Israel und die Völker.* Studien zum alttestamentlich-jüdischen Hintergrund der paulinischen Theologie. 1999. ISBN 90 04 11297 9
96. Albl, M.C. *"And Scripture Cannot Be Broken".* The Form and Function of the Early Christian *Testimonia* Collections. 1999. ISBN 90 04 11417 3
97. Ellis, E.E. *Christ and the Future in New Testament History.* 1999. ISBN 90 04 11533 1
98. Chilton, B. & C.A. Evans, (eds.) *James the Just and Christian Origins.* 1999. ISBN 90 04 11550 1
99. Horrell, D.G. & C.M. Tuckett (eds.) *Christology, Controversy and Community.* New Testament Essays in Honour of David R. Catchpole. 2000. ISBN 90 04 11679 6
100. Jackson-McCabe, M.A. *Logos and Law in the Letter of James.* The Law of Nature, the Law of Moses and the Law of Freedom. 2001. ISBN 90 04 11994 9
101. Wagner, J.R. *Herald of the Good News.* Isaiah and Paul "In Concert" in the Letter to the Romans 2001. ISBN 90 04 11691 5
102. Cousland, J.R.C. *The Crowds in the Gospel of Matthew.* 2002. ISBN 90 04 12177 3
103. Dunderberg, I., C. Tuckett and K. Syreeni. *Fair Play: Diversity and Conflicts.* Essays in Honour of Heikki Räisänen. 2002. ISBN 90 04 12359 8
104. Mount, C. *Pauline Christianity.* Luke-Acts and the Legacy of Paul. 2002. ISBN 90 04 12472 1